Twenty-first Edition

Rugg's

Recommendations

on the

Colleges

*Compiled and Edited by the College Staff of
Rugg's Recommendations*

by Frederick E. Rugg

Rugg's Recommendations • Fallbrook, California

Copyright © 2004
Frederick E. Rugg

All rights reserved

Copies of this book may be ordered from:
Rugg's Recommendations
P.O. Box 417
Fallbrook, CA 92088
760-728-4558 or 760-728-4467

Price: $23.95

ISBN 1-883062-53-5
LC# 89-062896

Prior Editions: ©1980, 1982, 1984, 1986, 1988, 1989, 1990, 1991,1992, 1993, 1994,
1995, 1996, 1997, 1998, 1999, 2000, 2001, 2002, 2003, 2004
by Rugg's Recommendations

Notice of Copyright

To
Barbara, Betsie, and Sue

TABLE OF CONTENTS

SOME NOTES FROM THE AUTHOR

WHY THIS BOOK?

As a secondary school college counselor, I heard the following question from a student or parent almost daily: "Can you please give us a list of quality colleges where one can major in psychology (or engineering or business or whatever)?"

For many years I pulled out the college handbooks and came up with a list of hundreds of colleges for each category and spent too much time with the student sifting through the multitude of schools, trying to narrow down the huge list.

I thought about a way out of this dilemma for a long time. People from Harvard would find an easy solution. They might tell the parents and student not to worry about a college major—just go to a fine liberal arts college (like Harvard) and everything will fall into place. After all, it's not the major and professors that count, it's the wonderful student body that makes a great college great. Right?

Well...over the years, I had trouble convincing parents of the merits of that argument. I guess they realize that all good universities are not good in every field.

Today, there's just so much pressure on young people to line up their careers and pick their occupations in life early. Career education seems to start in kindergarten these days. I've noticed that many parents pick right up on it and give Johnny the business if he hasn't chosen his career by the sophomore year of high school or earlier. No matter what I told Johnny and his parents, they still wanted a list of "the quality colleges with a good psychology (or whatever) department."

This book lists the quality departments at quality colleges and it will make the school counselor's job easier. For example, a public school counselor can use it constantly in January when juniors (and sometimes sophomores) line up outside his/her office, asking for a list of colleges to "go with" their PSAT scores. Probably a prep school counselor, a junior and community college transfer counselor, or a librarian might even find more use of this guide for college majors. Since this book is for the aid of the counselor, it is, then, also a guide for students and their parents in the college admissions process.

WHY THESE 1000 COLLEGES?

From our experience in the college admissions process, we have chosen 1000 quality four-year colleges (out of over 2000 that offer bachelor degrees) to study. We began with the 275 colleges that have survived the careful screening process involved in the granting of a Phi Beta Kappa chapter. The Phi Beta Kappa schools are listed in Appendix A. These colleges received chapters for superior undergraduate performance in the liberal arts and sciences.

To this list were added 725 colleges—schools that our staff felt are as good (or better) as several of the Phi Beta Kappa colleges or have excellent specialized programs. We should also note that, in general, the more well-respected the college, the more departments and majors were included. Berkeley is listed under 32 departments while some others only under one. The typical school in the study was noted with 8.0 departments. A departmental page averages 138 recommended colleges.

HOW IT'S DONE

Over the years, college students have been surveyed - the number well into five figures. If you want a straight answer, the young folks seldom waver. We also receive monthly evaluations from secondary school counselors around the country. Some colleges submit to us departments at their schools that they consider "hidden gems". They also send us departments they consider their "strongholds". Weekly, a variety of college personnel lobby for a certain program at their university. Also, almost every week we get "tipped off" on a great department at a college at workshops I present around the U.S.A. on the college admissions process. Almost every year since 1977 I've added 300 departments to my list. This year the number is over 1000.

What can eliminate a department or stop its consideration? No balance. For example, too many professors from the same alma mater in a department, or too many professors in a department graduating from that very college. If the average college in America gives out 10% of it's degrees in, say, the field of Psychology, and the department in question is at a 5% level, this sets up a "red flag", too.

HOW DO YOU USE THIS BOOK?

If you know what you want to major in at college—great!—just look it up. In most cases, you will find each departmental section organized into three groups of colleges:

Group I—Most Selective Colleges

Colleges here are among the 100 most selective colleges in America. They accept very few students with high school averages below 80 (top prep schools can, of course, lower this figure significantly) and College Board scores below (recentered)1200 (SAT-1 combined) and 27 (on the American College Test).

Group II—Very Selective Colleges

Many of the students at these colleges have "B" averages (80-90), and College Board scores between 1100 and 1200 (SAT-1 total) and ACTs between 24 and 26.

Group III—Selective Colleges

Although these colleges are, in general, easier to get into than Group I and II colleges, please keep in mind that they are, in our opinion at least, among the top 1000 colleges in the country. Many students at these colleges have College Board scores just under 1100 (SAT-1 total), or just under 24 on the ACTs.

Now that we have an idea of the group breakdown, a student may need help deciding from which group(s) to select his/her colleges. The guidance counselor can help here—having knowledge of colleges and a student's grade point average, class rank, board scores, etc. Most students will want to start with a group of 8 to 10 colleges from the departmental major page. This "major page" is a starting point. Schools can be added to the student's list by his/her counselor—from the counselor's own knowledge of the student, and knowledge of other colleges that might "fit" the student. Schools can be eliminated from a student's list after reviewing the college catalogs (see Appendix F—The Get Going Form), checking out undesirable features (city vs. rural setting, etc.), visiting the colleges, and other personal preferences. If the student does *not* have a major in mind, he or she should go to a typical liberal arts (e.g., English or Math) page to get started. I've also included a letter code system for the college's enrollment figure. The enrollment letter appears beside each college name with the following code:

XL = Extra Large Enrollment (over 20,000 students)
L = Large Enrollment (from 8,000 to 20,000 students)
M = Medium Enrollment (from 3,000 to 8,000 students)
R = Moderate Enrollment (from 1,000 to 3,000 students)
S = Small Enrollment (under 1,000 students)

SOME PARTING SHOTS

I don't care to go into the argument of "Picking a college because it has a great Mathematics Department" vs. "Picking a school because the school overall is great (Yeah Harvard!) and you'll probably change your major anyway." The fact of the matter is that parents, career educators, and other educators are telling 16-year-olds (and younger) to have a career and a major all mapped out and I bet will continue to do so. I'm sure high school counselors will continue to be asked to help Suzy find a list of quality schools with "excellent majors in mathematics." Personally, I see nothing wrong with a high school senior, who loves mathematics, trying to pick a quality school where the math department at that institution is ranked by its students as one of the top majors at that school and is generally recognized as being top notch by college counselors. If Suzy changes her mind after a year or two, she's at least given it a good shot with a premier math department. And chances are excellent that if she changes her major, it was because another outstanding department at that school helped her grow and reassess her career goals. She'll probably stay with that department for her new major. No harm done.

A few other comments on this book and some random thoughts...

1. Some state universities, like Penn State, are very competitive for out-of-staters. A university such as this may be in Group II for in-staters, but, in reality, is a Group I school for "outsiders."

2. In general, a college that is competitive is that way for all majors—but there are some departments that are exceptions. For example, engineering is a tough major and must be considered "Group II" at a "Group III" school.

3. A knowledgeable observer of the college scene will note that some competitive "alternative" colleges do not appear in this work, e.g., Hampshire College (MA), St. John's (MD). The jury is not unanimous on these progressive schools, and they are not included in this book except under "Miscellaneous Majors Pages."

4. A few majors in this book, such as engineering, have *not* been broken down into subdivisions (Civil, Electrical, Mechanical, etc.). Students will have to research these majors more fully. Well, what's wrong with that? Good to have the youngsters doing some hard work and research on the college admissions process. Foreign Languages, however, is broken down.

5. Every year a few more colleges close their doors. Today, colleges are under pressure to compete and "Be Hot." We need a college guide to weed things out a bit, a consumer-oriented handbook. We hope this helps.

6. Don't overlook the *good* small liberal arts college. Too many large universities are too impersonal. But some kids love a big school. Some thrive in the anonymity of a huge lecture hall.

7. Keep in mind that weak departments at Harvard, Yale, Stanford, Princeton, etc. might be equal to or better than the strongest departments at many colleges and universities.

8. This book is an aid for counselors, parents, and kids—nothing more. It is not a guide for the colleges to compare themselves one with the other.

9. Do not be surprised if you discover that the best of the more expensive schools are actually least expensive—because they have financial aid, the part-time jobs, etc. They're able to meet a student's financial need in many cases.

10. Students should discuss with their counselors the socioeconomic factors of the colleges they are considering. Will the college of your choice have several students enrolled with your socioeconomic background?

11. When you visit a college, seek out the students who attend and ask them the following question: "When you sign up for classes, do you get 100% of your choices, or only 4 out of 10 courses, or...?" Also, does the faculty seem to be there, to like to talk to you, to meet and greet you? Or are they not to be found?

12. Most states have a "flagship" university, the leader of the system (e.g., The University of North Carolina at Chapel Hill). In this book it is listed as just "No. Carolina." The other members of the University system are listed as follows: No. Carolina (Asheville), No. Carolina (Charlotte), No. Carolina (Greensboro), No. Carolina (Pembroke), No. Carolina (Wilmington).

13. Some colleges do a great job with private school youngsters, others do a fantastic job with public school youngsters. Some colleges are outstanding with both groups. A very fine college with an outstanding record with public school youngsters is Virginia's Roanoke College.

14. A tip for the high school senior: Don't ease up in your senior year. Take a tough course load with courses such as Physics. College admissions people aren't stupid. The first thing they look at when they review your high school record is the quality of your high school courses.

15. To parents and counselors: Hang tough. The pieces will finally fit.

16. Keep in mind that a starter list of colleges to consider for your daughter #1 may be a terrible list for your daughter #2.

17. I received a phone call from a community college instructor in the Mid-West. He also consults with companies recruiting college graduates, and has found my lists to be the best. He said to me on the phone, "The true test of any college guidebook or college list is, 'Does the information work?' So if the best information comes from college janitors, you go after college janitors."

18. I give an apology now to many of the top secondary prep schools in the country. Many of you may not be happy with my recent emphasis on adding departments to the Cal States, the Mass States, Connecticut States, Pennsylvania States, Michigan and Illinois States, etc. But the public school counselors and parents need these recommendations and they are over 90% of my customer base.

19. This book is not perfect. It has never claimed to be perfect. Our study is not scientific. It has never claimed to be. But it is a good place to start and represents tens of thousands of contacts. I'll repeat that. We have never claimed to be perfect. There is no expert in the field. There never will be. The field is too big. We've even moved to many parts of the country to try to put together "the big picture." We do our best.

Frederick E. Rugg

San Diego County, California
January, 2004 (21st Edition)

SOME NOTES ON THE TWENTY-FIRST EDITION

The twenty-first edition contains over 1200 entry changes since the twentieth edition. All 100 plus majors have been revised and changed. Computer Graphics and Peace Studies - these two majors have been added.

The "Average SAT-1 Total/ACT Total/Recommended majors" pages are included mainly because of counselors' requests. School counselors wanted average score comparisons and an index of colleges showing recommended majors. In all cases, SAT-1 Total Scores are noted and the equivalent ACT score is provided. These scores are the best estimate by our staff for the entering fall class of 2004. Especially young counselors tell us this section is a quick ready reference—a marker for them. And if you're looking for schools that do not require SAT's, please see "www.fairtest.org" for the latest list.

As in the past, when a state university is noted like Wisconsin, we mean the flagship at Madison, if no other city follows in parenthesis.

Finally, in the middle of the book, you will find every college's website. You know to add the "www." up front.

Frederick E. Rugg

San Diego County, California
January, 2004 (21st Edition)

ACKNOWLEDGMENTS

I would like to thank the following for their help in the preparation of this guidebook: Phi Beta Kappa Office, Bureau of Educational Statistics, our Research Aides, Officers of Institutional Research who returned our requests, and especially the great number of secondary counselors who've filled out questionnaires and tip me off on quality departments to look at. I am independent of the colleges and these people are, too.

A "Thank You" also goes to the counselors and students I've worked with who have contributed each in their own way. At last count, I've worked 25,000 hours in five secondary school guidance cubicles with 30 counselors, and conducted over 550 workshops with over 7500 counselors. Of course I've learned from them. Together we've probably done the college admissions process a million times. Also I thank the counselors and students and university officials in the United States and abroad for their help, suggestions, and, yes, their complaints. I appreciate, too, those departments who have sent us vitae on their professors. College PR officers who write always get a reading. And the same goes for anyone who e-mails me. Seventy-nine percent of college personnel who write me and tip me off on a great major at their school find it in the next year's book!

I am also grateful to George Gibbs, Ed Wall, Reg Alexander, Arvin R. Anderson, Howard Ahlskog, Hy Kleinman, Michele M. Charles, Gary Metras, Edward Field, Betty Rossie, Horacio Rodriquez, A.P. Stevens, Madeline Field, Cyrus Benson, John Barker, Fred Ames, Matthew Jagielski, Gilbert Field, Jeff Sheehan, Charles Doebler, Joan Girard, Mrs. Fran Fisher, Ralph Strycharz, Dennis Gurn, John DeBonville, Sammy Edwards, Eric Goodhart, Kevin L. Miller, Gloria Broecker, Hoover Sutton, Francona, J.R., Rebecca Lou, Cousin Leonard, professional photographer Lynn C. Henkel of Bradenton, Florida, Dave Congalton, Steve Stassen, Dwayne Copeland, Dianne Pelletier, Art Northrop, Roger Dexter, great friend, great listener, great counselor, and to all the secretaries I've worked with over the years.

And finally, a special thanks to my wife, Barbara, for her patience and industry, and daughter, Betsie.

Inquiries and comments about this guide should be addressed to:

Rugg's Recommendations
P.O. Box 417
Fallbrook, CA 92088

SECTION ONE

RECOMMENDED UNDERGRADUATE PROGRAMS

AGRICULTURE

Author's Note: *Students in the schools of Agriculture, in general, tend to have median college test scores below the University's overall median.*

GROUP I
Most Selective

Cornell (NY)	L	Iowa State	XL
Florida, U. of	XL	Pennsylvania State	XL
Illinois, U. of (Urbana-Champaign)	XL	Rutgers (NJ)	L

GROUP II
Very Selective

Auburn (AL)	L	Michigan State	XL
California, U. of (Davis)	L	Minnesota, U. of	XL
California, U. of (Riverside)	M	Missouri, U. of	XL
Cal. Poly. State U. (San Luis Obispo)	L	New Hampshire, U. of	L
Clemson (SC)	L	North Carolina State	L
Connecticut, U. of	L	Purdue (IN)	XL
Drury (MO)	S	Texas A&M	XL
Hawaii, U. of	L	Vermont, U. of	M
Kansas State	L	Virginia Poly. Inst.	L
Maine, U. of	M	Wisconsin, U. of	XL
Maryland, U. of	XL		

GROUP III
Selective

Arizona, U. of	XL	Nevada, U. of (Reno)	M
Arkansas, U. of	L	New Mexico State U.	L
Berea (KY)	R	North Dakota State	L
Cal. Poly. State U. (Pomona)	L	Ohio State	XL
California State U. (Chico)	L	Oklahoma State	L
California State U. (Fresno)	L	Oregon State	L
Colorado State	L	Ozarks, College of the (MO)	R
Delaware Valley (PA)	R	Tennessee, U. of	XL
Dordt (IA)	S	Texas Tech U.	L
Georgia, U. of	XL	Tuskegee University (AL)	M
Idaho, U. of	M	Utah State	L
Kentucky, U. of	L	Washington State	L
Louisiana State	XL	Western Illinois	L
Mississippi State	L	Western Kentucky	L
Montana State	L	Wilmington (OH)	S
Murray State (KY)	M	Wisconsin, U. of (Platteville)	M
Nebraska, U. of	L	Wyoming, U. of	L

Enrollment Code			
■ Men Only	S = Small (less than 1000 students)	R = Moderate (1000-3000 students)	M = Medium (3000-8000 students)
▲ Women Only	L = Large (8000-20,000 students)	XL = Extra Large (over 20,000 students)	

AMERICAN STUDIES

GROUP I
Most Selective

American U. (DC)	M
Amherst (MA)	R
Buffalo (SUNY) (NY)	L
California, U. of (San Diego)	L
Franklin & Marshall (PA)	R
George Washington (DC)	M
Georgetown (DC)	M
Harvard (MA)	M
Kalamazoo (MI)	R
Maryland, U. of (Baltimore County)	M
Michigan, U. of	XL
North Carolina, U. of	L
Northwestern (IL)	M
Pennsylvania, U. of	L
Pomona (CA)	R
Sarah Lawrence (NY)	S
▲ Smith (MA)	R
St. Olaf (MN)	R
South, U. of the (TN)	R
Stanford (CA)	M
Trinity (CT)	R
Tulane (LA)	M
Virginia, U. of	L
Wake Forest (NC)	M
Wesleyan (CT)	R
William & Mary (VA)	R
Williams (MA)	R
Yale (CT)	M

GROUP II
Very Selective

Alabama, U. of	L
Arizona, U. of	XL
California State U. (Fresno)	L
California State U. (Fullerton)	L
California, U. of (Santa Cruz)	M
DePaul (IL)	L
Eastern Connecticut	M
Florida State	L
Fredonia (SUNY)(NY)	M
George Mason (VA)	L
Hawaii, U. of	L
Hillsdale (MI)	R
Hobart & Wm. Smith (NY)	R
▲ Hollins (VA)	S
Mary Washington (VA)	R
Massachusetts, U. of (Boston)	M
Minnesota, U. of	XL
New Mexico, U. of	L
▲ Pine Manor (MA)	S
Rider (NJ)	R
Skidmore (NY)	R
South Florida, U. of	L
Texas, U. of	XL
Wagner (NY)	R
Washington College (MD)	S
▲ Wells (NY)	S
▲ Wesleyan College (GA)	S
Western Connecticut	M
Wyoming, U. of	L

Enrollment Code
■ Men Only ▲ Women Only S = Small (less than 1000 students) R = Moderate (1000-3000 students) M = Medium (3000-8000 students) L = Large (8000-20,000 students) XL = Extra Large (over 20,000 students)

ANTHROPOLOGY

GROUP I
Most Selective

American (DC)	M	Kenyon (OH)	R
Albany (SUNY) (NY)	L	Lafayette (PA)	R
▲ Barnard (NY)	R	Macalester (MN)	R
Binghamton (SUNY)(NY)	L	Michigan, U. of	XL
Boston U. (MA)	L	New College (FL)	S
Bowdoin (ME)	R	North Carolina, U. of	L
Brandeis (MA)	R	Northwestern (IL)	M
▲ Bryn Mawr (PA)	S	Notre Dame (IN)	M
Buffalo (SUNY) (NY)	L	Pennsylvania, U. of	L
California, U. of (Berkeley)	XL	Pitzer (CA)	S
California, U. of (Los Angeles)	XL	Pomona (CA)	R
Case Western Reserve (OH)	R	Rice (TX)	R
Chicago, U. of (IL)	M	Rutgers (NJ)	L
Colorado College	R	Skidmore (NY)	R
Columbia (NY)	M	▲ Smith (MA)	R
Dartmouth (NH)	M	Southern Methodist (TX)	M
Duke (NC)	M	South, U. of the (TN)	R
Emory (GA)	R	Stanford (CA)	M
Florida, U. of	XL	Tulane (LA)	M
Georgetown (DC)	M	Vanderbilt (TN)	M
Grinnell (IA)	R	Washington U. (MO)	M
Harvard (MA)	M	Yale (CT)	M
Illinois, U. of (Urbana-Champaign)	XL		

GROUP II
Very Selective

Alabama, U. of	L	Kansas, U. of	L
Arizona, U. of	XL	Knox (IL)	R
Arizona State	XL	Maryland, U. of	XL
Beloit (WI)	R	Oregon, U. of	L
California State U. (Chico)	L	Pittsburgh, U. of (PA)	L
California, U. of (Santa Cruz)	M	Principia (IL)	S
California, U. of (Davis)	L	Rhode Island, U. of	L
City College (CUNY)(NY)	L	St. Mary's College of Maryland	R
Colorado State	L	Sonoma State (CA)	M
Colorado, U. of	L	South Florida, U. of	L
Earlham (IN)	R	Stony Brook (SUNY)(NY)	L
George Mason (VA)	L	Tulsa, U. of (OK)	M
George Washington (DC)	M	Washington State	L
Grand Valley (MI)	L	Washington, U. of	XL
Hamline (MN)	R	William Paterson (NJ)	M
Hofstra (NY)	M	Wisconsin, U. of	XL
Hunter (CUNY)(NY)	L	Wisconsin, U. of (Milwaukee)	L
Indiana (PA)	L		

Enrollment Code

■ Men Only	S = Small (less than 1000 students) R = Moderate (1000-3000 students) M = Medium (3000-8000 students)
▲ Women Only	L = Large (8000-20,000 students) XL = Extra Large (over 20,000 students)

ANTHROPOLOGY, continued

GROUP III
Selective

Ball State (IN) L	Mercyhurst (PA) .... R
California State U. (Channel Islands) .. R	New Mexico State U. L
California State U. (Fullerton) L	New Mexico, U. of L
California State U. (Long Beach) L	Pittsburgh, U. of (Greensburg) .... R
California State U. (Sacramento) .... M	Queens (CUNY) (NY) L
Fort Lewis (CO) .... M	Tennessee, U. of XL
Hawaii, U. of L	Western Connecticut .... M
Louisiana State Xl	

ARCHITECTURE

GROUP I
Most Selective

▲Barnard (NY) .... R
Buffalo (SUNY) (NY) L
California, U. of (Berkeley) XL
Carnegie Mellon (PA) .... M
Columbia (NY) .... M
Cooper Union (NY) .... S
Cornell (NY) L
Florida, U. of XL
Georgia Inst. of Tech. L
Illinois Inst. of Tech. .... R
Illinois, U. of (Urbana-Champaign) ... XL
Lehigh (PA) .... M
Maryland, U. of XL

Miami U. (OH) L
Michigan, U. of XL
MIT (MA) .... M
New Jersey Inst. of Tech .... M
Notre Dame (IN) .... M
Princeton (NJ) .... M
Rensselaer (NY) .... M
Rice (TX) .... R
Temple (PA) XL
Tulane (LA) .... M
Virginia, U. of L
Washington U. (MO) .... M
Yale (CT) .... M

GROUP II
Very Selective

Arizona State XL
Arizona, U. of XL
Auburn (AL) L
Boston Arch. Center (MA) .... S
California College of Art & Crafts .... S
Cal. Poly. State U. (San Luis Obispo)... L
Catholic U. (DC) .... M
Cincinnati, U. of (OH) L
Clemson (SC) L
Detroit Mercy, U. of (MI) .... M
Drexel (PA) .... M
Drury (MO) .... S
Florida International L
Kentucky, U. of L
Houston, U. of (TX) L
Illinois, U. of (Chicago) L
Kansas State L
Kansas, U. of L
Kentucky, U. of L

Miami, U. of (FL) L
Milwaukee Sch. of Engineering (WI) .... R
Montana State L
Nebraska, U. of L
North Carolina State L
Oklahoma, U. of L
Oregon, U. of L
Pennsylvania State XL
Rhode Island School of Design (RI) ..... R
Southern California, U. of L
Syracuse (NY) L
Tennessee, U. of XL
Texas A&M XL
Texas Tech U. L
Texas, U. of (Austin) XL
Virginia Poly. Inst. L
Washington State L
Washington, U. of XL

GROUP III
Selective

Arkansas, U. of L
Cal. Poly. State U. (Pomona) L
City College (CUNY) (NY) L
Florida A&M .... M
Howard (DC) .... M
Idaho, U. of .... M
Kent State (OH) L
Louisiana State XL
Mississippi State L
Morgan State (MD) .... M
Nevada, U. of (Las Vegas) .... M
New York Institute of Tech .... M

North Carolina (Charlotte) L
North Dakota State L
Ohio State XL
Pratt Inst. (NY) .... R
Roger Williams (RI) .... R
Southern Polytechnic (GA) .... R
Texas, U. of (Arlington) L
Texas, U. of (San Antonio) L
Tuskegee University (AL) .... M
Wisconsin, U. of (Milwaukee) L
Woodbury (CA) .... S

ART (STUDIO)

● ━━━━━━━━━━━━━ *GROUP I* ━━━━━━━━━━━━━ ●
Most Selective

Albany (SUNY)(NY)	L	Michigan, U. of	XL
Bard (NY)	R	Middlebury (VT)	R
Bates (ME)	R	New Jersey, College of	M
Binghamton (SUNY)(NY)	L	New York U.	L
Boston U. (MA)	L	Pennsylvania, U. of	L
Brown (RI)	M	R.I. School of Design	R
▲ Bryn Mawr (PA)	S	Rhodes (TN)	R
Buffalo (SUNY)(NY)	L	Rochester, U. of (NY)	M
Carnegie Mellon (PA)	M	▲ Scripps (CA)	S
Centre (KY)	R	Skidmore (NY)	R
Colorado College	R	▲ Smith (MA)	R
Connecticut College	R	Southwestern (TX)	R
Cooper Union (NY)	S	St. Olaf (MN)	R
Cornell (NY)	L	Trinity (TX)	R
Cornish (WA)	S	Tulane (LA)	M
Dallas, U. of (TX)	R	Vassar (NY)	R
Dartmouth (NH)	M	Virginia, U. of	L
Drew (NJ)	R	Washington & Lee (VA)	R
Florida, U. of	XL	Washington U. (MO)	M
Furman (SC)	R	▲ Wellesley (MA)	R
Harvard (MA)	M	Wesleyan (CT)	R
Kenyon (OH)	R	Wheaton (IL)	R
Lafayette (PA)	R	Williams (MA)	R
Lawrence (WI)	R	Wisconsin, U. of (Madison)	XL
Macalester (MN)	R	Yale (CT)	M

●● ━━━━━━━━━━━━━ *GROUP II* ━━━━━━━━━━━━━ ●●
Very Selective

▲ Agnes Scott (GA)	S	Butler (IN)	R
Alabama, U. of	L	California College of Arts & Crafts	S
Alaska, U. of (Anchorage)	M	California Institute of the Arts	S
Alfred (NY)	R	California, U. of (Davis)	L
Alma (MI)	R	California, U. of (Irvine)	L
Arizona, U. of	XL	California, U. of (Santa Barbara)	L
Art Center College of Design (CA)	R	Clarke (IA)	S
Art Institute of Chicago (IL)	R	Cleveland Institute of Art (OH)	S
Auburn (AL)	L	Colorado State	L
Augustana (IL)	R	Connecticut, U. of	L
Belmont (TN)	R	▲ Converse (SC)	S
Birmingham-Southern (AL)	R	Creighton (NE)	R
Bowling Green (OH)	L	Delaware, U. of	L
Bradley (IL)	M		
Brigham Young (UT)	XL		

GROUP II continues next page

Enrollment Code

■ **Men Only** **S = Small** (less than 1000 students) **R = Moderate** (1000-3000 students) **M = Medium** (3000-8000 students)
▲ **Women Only** **L = Large** (8000-20,000 students) **XL = Extra Large** (over 20,000 students)

ART (STUDIO), continued

GROUP II, continued

Denison (OH)	R
Denver, U. of (CO)	M
Drake (IA)	M
East Carolina (NC)	L
Florida International	L
Florida State	L
Gordon (MA)	R
Guilford (NC)	R
Hamline (MN)	R
Hofstra (NY)	M
▲ Hollins (VA)	S
Houghton (NY)	S
Houston, U. of (TX)	L
Hunter (CUNY) (NY)	L
Illinois, U. of (Chicago)	L
Indiana (PA)	L
Iowa, U. of	XL
James Madison (VA)	R
Juniata (PA)	R
Kansas, U. of	L
Knox (IL)	R
Lake Forest (IL)	R
Loras (IA)	R
Loyola Marymount (CA)	M
Manhattanville (NY)	S
Marietta (OH)	R
Maryland Institute–College of Art	S
Maryland, U. of (Baltimore County)	M
Mass. College of Art	R
Messiah (PA)	R
▲ Mills (CA)	S
Missouri, U. of (Kansas City)	M
Montana State	L
Moore College of Art (PA)	S
Moravian (PA)	R
Muhlenberg (PA)	R
North Dakota, U. of	M
Ohio State	XL
Ohio U.	L
Oregon, U. of	L
Otis Art Institute (CA)	S
Pacific, U. of the (CA)	M
Parsons School of Design (NY)	R
Portland State (OR)	M
Principia (IL)	S
Purchase (SUNY)(NY)	R
▲ Randolph-Macon Woman's Col. (VA)	S
Redlands, U. of (CA)	R
▲ Rosemont (PA)	R
Rowan (NJ)	M
▲ St. Mary's College (IN)	R
St. Rose (NY)	R
Salisbury State (MD)	M
San Diego State (CA)	XL
San Francisco Art Institute (CA)	S
Sch. of the Art Institute of Chicago	S
Shepherd (WV)	R
Southern Methodist (TX)	M
Syracuse (NY)	L
Temple (PA)	L
Tennessee, U. of	XL
Tulsa, U. of (OK)	R
Washington & Jefferson (PA)	R
Washington, U. of	XL
▲ Wesleyan Col. (GA)	S
Western Washington U. (WA)	L
Westminster (UT)	R
West Virginia, U. of	L
Wheaton (MA)	R
Whitworth (WA)	R
Wisconsin Lutheran	S
Wisconsin, U. of (Steven's Point)	L
Wittenberg (OH)	R

Enrollment Code

■ Men Only   **S = Small** (less than 1000 students)   **R = Moderate** (1000-3000 students)   **M = Medium** (3000-8000 students)
▲ Women Only   **L = Large** (8000-20,000 students)   **XL = Extra Large** (over 20,000 students)

ART (STUDIO), continued

GROUP III
Selective

Anna Maria (MA) .... S	Memphis College of Art (TN) .... S
Arcadia (PA) .... R	Memphis, U. of (TN) L
Arizona State XL	Mercyhurst (PA) .... R
Arts, U. of the (PA) .... R	Millersville (PA) .... M
Ball State (IN) L	Millikin (IL) .... R
Belhaven (MS) .... R	Minnesota State U. (Moorhead) .... M
Bloomsburg (PA) .... M	Monmouth (NJ) .... R
Brescia (KY) .... S	Montana State (Billings) .... R
California College of Arts & Crafts .... S	Montclair State (NJ) .... M
California State U. (Channel Islands) .. R	Montevallo (AL) .... R
California State U. (Fresno) L	Montserrat (MA) .... S
California State U. (Hayward)............. M	Mount St. Joseph (OH) .... R
California State U. (Long Beach) L	Murray State (KY) .... M
California State U. (Los Angeles) L	Museum of Fine Arts, School of (MA)... R
California State U. (Monterey Bay) ...... R	Nevada, U. of (Las Vegas) .... M
California State U. (Northridge) L	New Mexico, U. of L
California State U. (San Bernardino) .. M	North Carolina (Asheville) .... R
California State U. (San Jose) L	North Carolina (Greensboro) .... M
▲ Chatham (PA) .... S	Northern Illinois U. L
Chowan (NC) .... S	Northern Iowa L
Coker (SC) .... S	Northern Michigan .... M
Colorado, U. of (Denver) .... M	Old Dominion (VA) L
East Tennessee L	Otterbein (OH) .... R
Eastern Illinois L	Pennsylvania Acad. of the Fine Arts .... S
Edgewood (WI) .... S	Potsdam (SUNY)(NY) .... R
Edinboro (PA) .... M	Roanoke (VA) .... R
Emmanuel (MA) .... S	Rockford (IL) .... S
Fairleigh Dickinson (NJ).................... M	St. Edward's (TX) .... M
Fort Hays (KS) .... M	▲ Salem College (NC) .... S
Frostburg (MD) .... M	Salem State (MA) .... M
Georgia Southern L	Santa Fe, College of (NM) .... S
Grand Valley (MI) L	▲ Seton Hill (PA) .... S
Hawaii, U. of L	Shawnee State (OH) .... R
Humboldt State (CA) .... M	Siena Heights (MI) .... S
Indiana State L	South Dakota, U. of .... M
Jacksonville (FL).............................. R	Southern Maine .... M
Judson (AL) .... S	Texas Tech. U. L
Keene State (NH) .... R	Texas, U. of (San Antonio).................. L
Kent State (OH) L	Towson (MD) L
Kutztown (PA) .... M	Union University (TN) .... R
Lambuth (TN)................................... S	Virginia Commonwealth U. L
Lewis-Clark State (ID) .... R	Visual Arts, School of (NY).................. R
Lock Haven (PA) .... M	Weber State (UT)............................... L
Long Island U. (C.W.Post)(NY) .... M	West Chester (PA) .... M
Long Island U. (Southampton) .... R	West Virginia Wesleyan .... R
Louisiana-Lafayette.......................... L	Western Connecticut .... M
Louisiana State XL	Western Michigan L
Lycoming (PA) .... R	Wingate (NC) .... R
▲ Mary Baldwin (VA) .... S	Winthrop (SC) .... M
Maryville (St. Louis) (MO) .... R	Wisconsin, U. of (Green Bay) .... M
Marywood (PA)................................. R	Youngstown State (OH) L
Massachusetts, U. of (Dartmouth) ...... M	

ART HISTORY

───────────────── **GROUP I** ─────────────────
Most Selective

Albany (SUNY)(NY) L	Pennsylvania, U. of L
▲ Barnard (NY) .... R	Pittsburgh, U. of (PA) L
Binghamton (SUNY)(NY) L	Pomona (CA) .... R
Bowdoin (ME) .... R	Princeton (NJ) .... M
Brown (RI) .... M	Reed (OR) .... R
▲ Bryn Mawr (PA) .... S	Rochester, U. of (NY) .... M
California, U. of (Los Angeles) XL	Rutgers (NJ) L
Case Western Reserve U. (OH) .... R	▲ Scripps (CA) .... S
Colorado College .... R	Skidmore (NY) .... R
Chicago, U. of (IL) .... M	▲ Smith (MA) .... R
Columbia (NY) .... M	Swarthmore (PA) .... R
Cornell (NY) L	Syracuse (NY) L
Emory (GA) .... R	Trinity (CT) .... R
George Washington (DC) .... M	Trinity (TX) .... R
Harvard (MA) .... M	Vanderbilt (TN) .... M
Johns Hopkins (MD) .... R	Vassar (NY) .... R
Michigan, U. of XL	Washington U. (MO) .... M
▲ Mount Holyoke (MA) .... R	▲ Wellesley (MA) .... R
New York U. L	Willamette (OR) .... R
North Carolina, U. of L	Williams (MA) .... R
Northwestern (IL) .... M	Wisconsin, U. of XL
Oberlin (OH) .... R	Yale (CT) .... M

───────────────── **GROUP II** ─────────────────
Very Selective

California State U. (Northridge) L	Kansas, U. of L
California, U. of (Riverside) .... M	Lake Forest (IL) .... R
California, U. of (Santa Barbara) L	Manhattanville (NY) .... S
City College (CUNY)(NY) L	Massachusetts, U. of (Lowell) .... M
Clarke (IA) .... S	Minnesota, U. of XL
College of Charleston (SC) L	Missouri, U. of XL
Colorado State L	Oregon, U. of L
Delaware, U. of L	▲ Pine Manor (MA) .... S
Denver, U. of (CO) .... M	Queens (CUNY)(NY) L
East Carolina L	▲ Rosemont (PA) .... S
Eastern Connecticut .... M	▲ Salem College (NC) .... S
Edinboro (PA) .... M	Salem State (MA) .... M
Florida State L	San Diego State U. (CA) XL
George Mason (VA) L	Sonoma State (CA) .... M
Georgia, U. of XL	Southern Methodist (TX) .... M
▲ Hollins (VA) .... S	Stony Brook (SUNY)(NY) L
Hunter (CUNY) (NY) L	▲ Sweet Briar (VA) .... S
Illinois, U. of (Chicago) L	Wheaton (MA) .... R
Indiana (PA) L	Wooster (OH) .... R

ASTRONOMY

GROUP I
Most Selective

Amherst (MA) .... R	Northwestern (IL) .... M
Boston U. L	Pennsylvania, U. of............................ L
Brigham Young (UT) XL	Pennsylvania State........................... XL
▲ Bryn Mawr (PA) .... S	Vassar (NY) .... R
California Inst. of Tech. .... S	Villanova (PA) .... M
Case Western Reserve U. (OH) .... R	Virginia, U. of L
Cornell (NY) L	▲ Wellesley (MA) .... R
Harvard (MA) .... M	Wesleyan (CT) .... R
Haverford (PA) .... S	Whitman (WA) .... R
Illinois, U. of (Urbana-Champaign) ... XL	Williams (MA) .... R
Michigan, U. of XL	Wisconsin, U. of............................... XL
MIT (MA).. M	

GROUP II
Very Selective

Arizona, U. of XL	Minnesota, U. of XL
Colorado, U. of L	North Carolina State L
Drake (IA)... M	Ohio State U. XL
Earlham (IN) .... R	Oklahoma, U. of L
Florida Inst. of Tech. .... R	Pittsburgh, U. of (PA) L
Florida, U. of XL	San Diego State XL
Georgia, U. of XL	San Francisco State U. L
Hawaii, U. of L	Southern California L
Indiana U. XL	Stony Brook (SUNY) (NY) L
Iowa, U. of XL	Texas, U. of (Austin).......................... XL
Kansas, U. of L	Washington, U. of XL
Maryland, U. of XL	Wheaton (MA) .... R
Massachusetts, U. of L	

GROUP III
Selective

Benedictine (KS) .... S	Nebraska, U. of L
Georgia State L	Northern Arizona.............................. XL
Louisiana State XL	Western Connecticut .... M
Lycoming (PA) .... R	Wisconsin, U. of (La Crosse)................ L
Montana, U. of .... M	Wyoming, U. of L

BIOCHEMISTRY (Molecular Biology)

GROUP I
Most Selective

▲ Barnard (NY)	R	Iowa, U. of	XL
Binghamton (SUNY) (NY)	L	Miami, U. of (FL)	L
Bowdoin (ME)	R	MIT (MA)	M
Brandeis (MA)	R	▲ Mount Holyoke (MA)	R
Brown (RI)	M	Pennsylvania, U. of	L
California, U. of (Berkeley)	XL	Princeton (NJ)	M
California, U. of (Los Angeles)	XL	Rice (TX)	R
California, U. of (San Diego)	L	Rutgers (NJ)	L
Case Western Reserve (OH)	R	Rochester, U. of (NY)	M
Columbia (NY)	M	Swarthmore (PA)	R
Cornell (NY)	L	Tulane (LA)	M
Dallas, U. of (TX)	R	Virginia, U. of	L
Geneseo (SUNY) (NY)	M	Worcester Poly Inst. (MA)	R
Georgia, U. of	XL	Yale (CT)	M
Harvard (MA)	M		

GROUP II
Very Selective

Albright (PA)	R	Mississippi State	L
Beloit (WI)	R	Muhlenberg (PA)	R
California Poly State U. (San Luis Obispo)	L	Ohio State	XL
California, U. of (Davis)	L	Pennsylvania State	XL
California, U. of (Riverside)	M	Pittsburgh, U. of (PA)	L
Centre (KY)	R	Purdue (IN)	XL
Clark (MA)	R	Regis (CO)	R
Colorado, U. of	L	Ripon (WI)	R
Denison (OH)	R	Sciences, U. of the (PA)	S
Florida Inst. of Tech.	R	Siena (NY)	R
Ithaca (NY)	M	Skidmore (NY)	R
Kansas State	L	St. Andrews Presbyterian (NC)	S
Knox (IL)	R	Stony Brook (SUNY) (NY)	L
Lewis & Clark (OR)	R	Susquehanna (PA)	R
Louisiana State	XL	Virginia Poly. Inst.	L
McDaniel (MD)	R	Washington State	L
Michigan State	XL	Washington, U. of	XL
Minnesota, U. of	XL	Wisconsin, U. of	XL

GROUP III
Selective

California State U. (Channel Islands)	R	Northern Illinois U.	L
California State U. (Fullerton)	L	Ohio Northern	R
Framingham (MA)	M	Oregon State	L
Misericordia, College (PA)	S	Sacred Heart (CT)	R
Nevada, U. of (Reno)	M	Temple (PA)	L

Enrollment Code

■ Men Only	S = Small (less than 1000 students)	R = Moderate (1000-3000 students)	M = Medium (3000-8000 students)
▲ Women Only	L = Large (8000-20,000 students)	XL = Extra Large (over 20,000 students)	

BIOLOGY

GROUP I
Most Selective

Albany (SUNY) (NY)	L
Amherst (MA)	R
Austin (TX)	R
Bates (ME)	R
Bethany (WV)	S
Binghampton (SUNY)(NY)	L
Boston College (MA)	L
Boston University (MA)	L
Bowdoin (ME)	R
Brandeis (MA)	R
Brown (RI)	M
▲ Bryn Mawr (PA)	S
Bucknell (PA)	R
California Inst. of Tech.	S
California, U. of (Los Angeles)	XL
California, U. of (San Diego)	L
Carleton (MN)	R
Chicago, U. of (IL)	M
Claremont McKenna (CA)	R
Colby (ME)	R
Colgate (NY)	R
Colorado Col.	R
Cornell (NY)	L
Dallas, U. of (TX)	R
Dartmouth (NH)	M
Davidson (NC)	R
De Pauw (IN)	R
Dickinson (PA)	R
Duke (NC)	M
Emory (GA)	R
Franklin & Marshall (PA)	R
Furman (SC)	R
Geneseo (SUNY) (NY)	M
Georgetown (DC)	M
Gettysburg (PA)	R
Grinnell (IA)	R
Hamilton (NY)	R
Harvard (MA)	M
Harvey Mudd (CA)	S
Haverford (PA)	S
Holy Cross (MA)	R
Illinois Wesleyan	R
Iowa State	XL
Johns Hopkins (MD)	R
Kalamazoo (MI)	R
Kenyon (OH)	R
Lafayette (PA)	R
Lawrence (WI)	R
Lehigh (PA)	M
Macalester (MN)	R
Miami, U. of (FL)	L
Middlebury (VT)	R
Minnesota, U. of (Morris)	R

Missouri, U. of (Rolla)	M
MIT (MA)	M
▲ Mount Holyoke (MA)	R
New College (FL)	S
North Carolina, U. of	L
Oberlin (OH)	R
Occidental (CA)	R
Pepperdine (CA)	R
Pitzer (CA)	S
Pomona (CA)	R
Princeton (NJ)	M
Providence (RI)	M
Reed (OR)	R
Rennselaer (NY)	M
Rhodes (TN)	R
Rice (TX)	R
Richmond, U. of (VA)	R
Rochester, U. of (NY)	M
Rutgers (NJ)	L
Skidmore (NY)	R
▲ Smith (MA)	R
South, U. of the (TN)	R
Southwestern (TX)	R
Stanford (CA)	M
St. Mary's Col. of Maryland	R
St. Olaf (MN)	R
Swarthmore (PA)	R
Trinity (CT)	R
Tufts (MA)	M
Tulane (LA)	M
Union (NY)	R
Ursinus (PA)	R
Vanderbilt (TN)	M
Vassar (NY)	R
Vermont, U. of	L
Villanova (PA)	M
Virginia, U. of	L
■ Wabash (IN)	S
Wake Forest (NC)	M
Washington & Lee (VA)	M
Washington U. (MO)	M
▲ Wellesley (MA)	R
Wesleyan (CT)	R
Wheaton (IL)	R
Whitman (WA)	R
Willamette (OR)	R
William & Mary (VA)	M
Williams (MA)	R
Worcester Poly Inst. (MA)	R
Yale (CT)	M
Yeshiva (NY)	R

BIOLOGY continues next page

BIOLOGY, continued

GROUP II
Very Selective

▲ Agnes Scott (GA) .... S	Florida Southern .... R
Albertson (ID) .... S	Georgetown (KY) .... R
Albright (PA) .... R	Georgia State L
Allegheny (PA) .... R	Georgia, U. of XL
Alma (MI) .... R	Gonzaga (WA) .... R
Arizona, U. of XL	Gordon (MA) .... R
Augustana (IL) .... R	Grove City (PA) .... R
Augustana (SD) .... R	Guilford (NC) .... R
Benedictine (IL) .... R	Gustavus Adolphus (MN) .... R
Berry (GA) .... R	Hamline (MN) .... R
Birmingham-Southern (AL) .... R	■ Hampden-Sydney (VA) .... S
California Poly State U. (San Luis Obispo) . L	Hendrix (AR) .... R
California State U. (Chico) L	Hiram (OH) .... R
California, U. of (Davis) L	Hobart & William Smith (NY) .... R
California, U. of (Irvine) L	Hood (MD) .... S
California, U. of (Riverside) .... M	Hope (MI) .... R
California, U. of (Santa Barbara) L	Houghton (NY) .... S
California, U. of (Santa Cruz) .... M	Hunter (CUNY)(NY) L
Canisius (NY) .... M	Illinois College .... S
Centenary (LA) .... S	Illinois, U. of (Chicago) L
Central (IA) .... R	Indiana (PA) L
Clark (MA) .... R	Indiana U. XL
Clarke (IA) .... S	Juniata (PA) .... R
Clemson (SC) L	Kansas State L
Coe (IA) .... R	Kentucky, U.of L
Colorado, U. of L	King's (PA) .... R
Columbia College (SC) .... R	Knox (IL) .... R
Concordia (MN) .... R	Lake Forest (IL) .... S
Connecticut, U. of L	LeMoyne (NY) .... R
Cornell Col. (IA) .... R	Lewis & Clark (OR) .... R
Creighton (NE) .... R	Linfield (OR) .... R
Delaware, U. of L	Loras (IA) .... R
Denison (OH) .... R	Loyola (IL) .... M
Denver, U. of (CO) .... M	Loyola (LA) .... R
Drake (IA) .... M	Loyola (MD) .... R
Duquesne (PA) .... M	Luther (IA) .... R
Earlham (IN) .... R	Marist (NY) .... M
Eckerd (FL) .... R	Marquette (WI) .... M
Elizabethtown (PA) .... R	Mary Washington (VA) .... R
Elon (NC) .... R	McDaniel (MD) .... R
Erskine (SC) .... S	McKendree (IL) .... R
Fairfield (CT) .... M	Michigan State XL
Florida Inst. of Tech .... R	Millersville (PA) .... M
Florida International L	

GROUP II continues next page

BIOLOGY, continued

GROUP II, continued

Millsaps (MS) .... S	Spring Hill (AL)............................ R
Minnesota, U. of (Duluth) .... M	St. John's (MN) .... R
Mobile, U. of (AL) .... R	St. Louis (MO)............................. M
Monmouth (IL)............................ S	St. Michael's (VT) .... R
Morningside (IA) .... S	St. Norbert (WI) .... R
Mount Mercy (IA) .... S	Stonehill (MA) .... R
Muhlenberg (PA) .... R	Stony Brook (SUNY) (NY) L
Murray State (KY) .... M	Susquehanna (PA) .... R
Nazareth (NY) .... R	Texas, U. of (Austin) XL
Nebraska Wesleyan .... R	Texas Christian .... M
New Hampshire, U. of L	Transylvania (KY) .... S
New Mexico State L	Truman State (MO) .... M
New Mexico, U. of L	Tulsa, U. of (OK) .... R
North Central (IL) .... R	Utah, U. of L
North Dakota, U. of........................ M	Valparaiso U. (TN) .... M
Oglethorpe (GA) .... R	Washington & Jefferson (PA) .... R
Ohio Northern .... R	Washington College (MD) .... S
Ohio Wesleyan............................ R	▲ Wells (NY) .... S
Oklahoma City U. .... R	West Chester (PA) .... M
Oklahoma, U. of L	Westminster (MO)......................... S
Presbyterian (SC) .... S	Westminster (PA) .... R
Puget Sound (WA) .... R	Westminster (UT) .... R
Randolph-Macon (VA)...................... R	Westmont (CA) .... R
▲ Randolph-Macon Woman's Col. (VA)..... S	Wheaton (MA) .... R
Ripon (WI)................................ R	William Jewell (MO) .... R
Roanoke (VA) .... R	Winona State U. (MN) .... M
Rochester Inst. of Tech. (NY) L	Winthrop (SC) .... M
Salisbury State (MD) .... M	Wisconsin, U. of (Milwaukee) L
Sciences in Philadelphia (PA).............. R	Wisconsin, U. of (Stevens Point) .... M
Scranton, U. of (PA) .... M	Wittenberg (OH).......................... R
▲ Scripps (CA) .... S	Wofford (SC) .... R
Seattle Pacific (WA) .... R	Wooster (OH) .... R
Siena (NY) .... R	Xavier (OH) .... R

GROUP III
Selective

Arcadia (PA) .... R	College of Charleston (SC).................. L
Aquinas (MI) .... R	Colorado, U. of (Denver) .... M
Azusa Pacific (CA) .... R	Daemen (NY) .... R
Ball State (IN) L	Delaware Valley (PA) .... R
Berea (KY) .... R	DeSales (PA) .... S
Blackburn (IL) .... S	Dillard (LA) .... R
Brooklyn (CUNY)(NY) L	D'Youville (NY) .... R
California Poly State U. (Pomona) L	East Stroudsburg (PA) .... M
California State U. (Channel Islands) .. R	Eastern Connecticut .... M
California State U. (Monterey Bay) ...... R	Eastern Oregon............................ R
Carroll (MT).............................. R	
Central Michigan L	*GROUP III continues next page*

GROUP III continues next page

BIOLOGY, continued

GROUP III, Continued

Emmanuel (MA)	S
Fitchburg (MA)	R
Fort Lewis (CO)	M
Framingham (MA)	M
Gwynedd-Mercy (PA)	S
Hardin-Simmons (TX)	R
Heidelberg (OH)	S
Houston Baptist (TX)	R
Jacksonville (FL)	R
Kentucky Wesleyan	S
Lambuth (TN)	S
Lewis-Clark State (ID)	R
Lock Haven (PA)	M
Long Island U. (Southampton Col.)(NY)	R
Louisiana - Lafayette	L
Lycoming (PA)	R
Lynchburg (VA)	R
Lyndon State (VT)	R
Maryville (TN)	S
▲ Meredith (NC)	R
Millersville (PA)	M
Milligan (TN)	S
Misericordia, College (PA)	S
Morgan State (MD)	M
Mount St. Mary's (CA)	R
Nichols State (LA)	M
North Carolina (Pembroke)	R
North Carolina (Wilmington)	M
Northern Illinois U.	L
Northern Michigan	M
Northland (WI)	S
Northwestern (IA)	R

▲ Pine Manor (MA)	S
Pittsburgh, U. of (Bradford)	S
Point Park (PA)	R
Puerto Rico (Cayey), U. of	M
Reinhardt (GA)	S
Rhode Island College	M
Rider (NJ)	R
Rockford (IL)	S
Shippensburg (PA)	M
South Alabama	M
South Dakota, U. of	M
▲ Spelman (GA)	R
Saint Scholastica (MN)	R
St. Vincent (PA)	R
Temple (PA)	L
Texas Lutheran	S
Texas, U. of (San Antonio)	L
Thomas More (KY)	R
Tougaloo (MS)	S
Virginia Wesleyan	R
Wartburg (IA)	R
Western Colorado	R
Western Kentucky	L
West Chester (PA)	M
West Virginia Wesleyan	R
Wheeling Jesuit (WV)	R
Wilkes (PA)	R
Wisconsin, U. of (Eau Claire)	L
Wisconsin, U. of (Platteville)	M
Wyoming, U. of	L
Xavier University of Louisiana	R

BOTANY / PLANT SCIENCE

GROUP I
Most Selective

California, U. of (Berkeley) XL
Connecticut College .... R
Cornell (NY) L
Duke (NC) .... M

Florida, U. of XL
Miami U. (OH) L
Michigan, U. of XL
North Carolina, U. of L

GROUP II
Very Selective

California, U. of (Davis) L
California, U. of (Riverside) .... M
Connecticut, U. of L
Delaware, U. of L
Maine, U. of .... M
Maryland, U. of L
Michigan State XL
Montana, U. of .... M
North Carolina State L

Ohio U. L
Ohio Wesleyan .... R
Pennsylvania State XL
Purdue (IN) XL
Tennessee, U. of L
Texas, U. of (Austin) XL
Vermont, U. of L
Washington, U. of XL
Wisconsin, U. of XL

GROUP III
Selective

Alabama, U. of L
Ball State (IN) L
Colorado State L
Eastern Connecticut .... M
Eastern Illinois L
Hawaii, U. of L

Humboldt State (CA) .... M
Louisiana State XL
Northern Arizona XL
Oregon State L
Southern Illinois U. (Carbondale) L
Wyoming, U. of L

Enrollment Code		
■ Men Only	**S = Small** (less than 1000 students)	**R = Moderate** (1000-3000 students)	**M = Medium** (3000-8000 students)
▲ Women Only	**L = Large** (8000-20,000 students)	**XL = Extra Large** (over 20,000 students)	

BUSINESS ADMINISTRATION

GROUP I
Most Selective

Albany (SUNY) (NY) L	Miami U. (OH) L
American (DC) .... M	Michigan, U. of XL
Babson (MA) .... R	Missouri, U. of XL
Binghamton (SUNY) (NY) L	MIT (MA) .... M
Boston College (MA) L	Muhlenberg (PA) .... R
Boston U. (MA) L	New York U. L
Bucknell (PA) .... R	North Carolina, U. of L
Buffalo (SUNY) (NY) L	Notre Dame (IN) .... M
California, U. of (Berkeley) XL	Pennsylvania, U. of L
California, U. of (Los Angeles) XL	Rensselaer (NY) .... M
Carnegie Mellon (PA) .... M	Rhodes (TN) .... R
Case Western Reserve U. (OH) .... R	Richmond, U. of (VA) .... R
Claremont McKenna (CA) .... R	Rutgers (NJ) L
Clarkson (NY) .... M	Shippensburg (PA) .... M
➤Colby (ME) .... R	Southern California, U. of L
DePauw (IN) .... R	Southwestern (TX) .... R
Emory (GA) .... R	Syracuse (NY) L
Fairfield (CT) .... R	Trinity (TX) .... R
Florida, U. of XL	Tulane (LA) .... M
Florida State L	U.S. Air Force Academy (CO) .... M
Franklin & Marshall (PA) .... R	Vermont, U. of L
Furman (SC) .... R	Villanova (PA) .... M
Geneseo (SUNY) (NY) .... M	Virginia Poly. Institute L
Georgetown (DC) .... M	Virginia, U. of L
George Washington (DC) .... M	Wake Forest (NC) .... M
Georgia Inst. of Tech L	Washington U. (MO) .... M
Gettysburg (PA) .... R	Washington & Lee (VA) .... M
Gustavus Adolphus (MN) .... R	William & Mary (VA) .... M
Illinois, U. of (Urbana-Champaign) ... XL	Wisconsin, U. of XL
Indiana U. XL	Worcester Poly Inst. (MA) .... R
Lafayette (PA) .... R	Yeshiva (NY) .... R
Lehigh (PA) .... M	➤ *Administrative Science*

GROUP II
Very Selective

Adrian (MI) .... S	Belmont (TN) .... R
▲Agnes Scott (GA) .... S	Bentley (MA) .... M
Alabama, U. of L	Berry (GA) .... R
Alabama, U. of (Huntsville) .... M	Birmingham Southern (AL) .... R
Alaska Pacific .... S	Bowling Green (OH) L
Albertson (ID) .... S	Bradley (IL) .... M
Albright (PA) .... R	Brigham Young (UT) XL
Alfred (NY) .... R	Bryant (RI) .... R
Alma (MI) .... R	Buena Vista (IA) .... R
Arizona, U. of XL	Butler (IN) .... R
Arizona State XL	California Poly State U. (San Luis Obispo) L
Asbury (KY) .... R	California State (Fullerton) L
Auburn (AL) L	California, U. of (Riverside) .... M
Augustana (IL) .... R	California, U. of (Santa Barbara) L
Austin (TX) .... R	
Baylor (TX) .... M	*GROUP II continues next page*

BUSINESS ADMINISTRATION, cont.

── *GROUP II, Continued* ──

College	Code
Capital U. (OH)	R
Centenary (LA)	S
Central Florida, U. of	L
Charleston, College of (SC)	L
Christian Brothers (TN)	R
Clark (MA)	R
Clemson (SC)	L
Coe (IA)	R
Colorado, U. of	L
Colorado, U. of (Col. Springs)	M
Columbia College (SC)	R
Concordia (MN)	R
Connecticut, U. of	L
Dayton, U. of (OH)	M
Delaware, U. of	L
Denver, U. of (CO)	M
DePaul (IL)	L
Dominican (IL)	S
Drake (IA)	M
Dubuque, U. of (IA)	S
Duquesne (PA)	M
Eastern Michigan	L
Eckerd (FL)	R
Elizabethtown (PA)	R
Elon (NC)	R
Erskine (SC)	S
Flagler (FL)	R
Florida Atlantic	L
Florida Gulf Coast U.	R
Florida Inst. of Tech.	R
Florida International	M
Fredonia (SUNY) (NY)	M
George Mason (VA)	L
Georgetown College (KY)	R
Gonzaga (WA)	R
Goucher (MD)	S
Grove City (PA)	R
Guilford (NC)	R
Hampton (VA)	M
Hanover (IN)	R
Harding (AR)	M
Hendrix (AR)	R
Hillsdale (MI)	R
Hofstra (NY)	M
Hood (MD)	S
Houston, U. of (TX)	L
Idaho, U. of	M
Illinois College	S
Illinois, U. of (Chicago)	L
Indiana U. of Pennsylvania	L
Iowa State	XL
Iowa, U. of	XL
Ithaca (NY)	M
James Madison (VA)	M
John Carroll (OH)	M
▲Judson (AL)	S
Juniata (PA)	R
Kansas State	L
Kentucky, U. of	L
LaSalle (PA)	M
Lebanon Valley (PA)	R
LeMoyne (NY)	R
LeTourneau (TX)	R
Lewis & Clark (OR)	R
Longwood (VA)	R
Loras (IA)	R
Lowell, U. of (MA)	L
Loyola (MD)	R
Loyola (LA)	R
Loyola Marymount (CA)	M
Luther (IA)	R
Manhattan (NY)	M
Manhattanville (NY)	R
Marietta (OH)	R
Marist (NY)	M
Marquette (WI)	M
Maryland, U. of	XL
Mary Washington (VA)	R
Massachusetts, U. of	L
Master's (CA)	R
McDaniel (MD)	R
Messiah (PA)	R
Michigan, U. of (Dearborn)	M
Michigan State	XL
Michigan Tech	M
Millersville (PA)	M
Millsaps (MS)	S
Minnesota, U. of	XL
Mississippi College	R
Mississippi, U. of	M
Mississippi U. for Women	R
Missouri, U. of (St. Louis)	M
Mobile, U. of (AL)	R
Monmouth (IL)	S
Moravian (PA)	R

GROUP II continues next page

Enrollment Code

■ Men Only　　S = Small (less than 1000 students)　　R = Moderate (1000-3000 students)　　M = Medium (3000-8000 students)
▲ Women Only　　L = Large (8000-20,000 students)　　XL = Extra Large (over 20,000 students)

BUSINESS ADMINISTRATION, cont.

GROUP II, Continued

Nazareth (NY) .... R	Shaw (NC) .... R
New Hampshire, U. of L	Shepherd (WV) .... M
Newman University (KS) .... S	Siena (NY) .... R
New Mexico State L	▲Simmons (MA) .... R
New Paltz (SUNY) (NY) .... M	Skidmore (NY) .... R
North Carolina, U. of (Greensboro) ..... M	Southern Methodist (TX) .... M
North Dakota, U. of .... M	Spring Hill (AL) .... R
Northeastern (MA) L	St. Bonaventure (NY) .... R
North Florida .... M	▲St. Catherine (MN) .... R
Oglethorpe (GA) .... R	St. John's (MN) .... R
Ohio U. L	St. Joseph's U. (PA) .... R
Oklahoma City U. (OK) .... R	St. Mary's Col. of CA .... R
Oklahoma State L	▲St. Mary's Col. (IN) .... R
Oklahoma, U. of L	St. Mary's Col. (MN) .... R
Old Dominion (VA) L	St. Michael's Col. (VT) .... R
Oregon, U. of L	St. Norbert (WI) .... R
Oswego (SUNY) (NY) .... M	Southern Oregon State U. .... M
Pacific Lutheran (WA) .... R	Stetson (FL) .... R
Pacific, U. of the (CA) .... M	Stonehill (MA) .... R
Pacific University (OR) .... R	Susquehanna U. (PA) .... R
Palm Beach Atlantic (FL) .... R	Temple (PA) L
Pennsylvania State XL	Texas A&M XL
Pepperdine (CA) .... R	Texas A&M at Galveston .... S
Pittsburgh, U. of (PA) L	Texas Christian .... M
Plattsburgh (SUNY) (NY) .... M	Texas Tech U. L
Portland State (OR) .... M	Texas, U. of (Austin) XL
Portland, U. of (OR) .... R	Texas, U. of (Dallas) .... M
Presbyterian (SC) .... S	Transylvania (KY) .... S
Principia (IL) .... S	▲Trinity (DC) .... S
Providence (RI) .... M	Truman State (MO) .... M
Puerto Rico, U. of L	Tulsa, U. of (OK) .... R
Puget Sound (WA) .... R	Ursinus (PA) .... R
Purdue (IN) XL	Utah, U. of L
Queens (NC) .... S	Valparaiso (IN) .... M
Randolph-Macon (VA) .... R	Virginia Military Inst. .... R
Redlands, U. of (CA) .... R	Washington College (MD) .... S
Richard Stockton (NJ) .... M	Washington State L
Ripon (WI) .... R	Washington, U. of XL
Roanoke (VA) .... R	▲Wells (NY) .... S
Rochester Inst. of Tech (NY) L	▲Wesleyan College (GA) .... S
Rockhurst (MO) .... R	Western Michigan L
Rowan (NJ) .... M	Westminster (UT) .... R
Salem College (NC) .... S	West Virginia U. L
Samford (AL) .... R	Wilberforce (OH) .... S
San Diego State U. (CA) XL	William Jewell Col. (MO) .... R
San Diego, U. of (CA) .... M	Wisconsin, U. of (Milwaukee) L
San Francisco, U. of (CA) .... M	Wisconsin, U. of (Stevens Point) ... M
Santa Clara U. (CA) .... M	Wittenberg (OH) .... R
Sciences, U. of the (PA) .... S	Wofford (SC) .... R
Scranton, U. of (PA) .... M	Wyoming, U. of L
Seton Hall (NJ) .... M	Xavier (OH) .... R

BUSINESS ADMINISTRATION, cont.

GROUP III
Selective

Abilene Christian (TX)	M
Akron, U. of (OH)	L
Alabama, U. of (Birmingham)	M
Alaska, U. of (Anchorage)	M
Alaska, U. of (Fairbanks)	M
Alderson-Broaddus (WV)	S
▲Alverno (WI)	R
American International (MA)	R
Appalachian State (NC)	L
Arkansas, U. of	L
Ashland (OH)	R
Assumption (MA)	R
Averett (VA)	S
Azusa Pacific (CA)	R
Baker (KS)	S
Baldwin-Wallace (OH)	R
Barry (FL)	R
Baruch (CUNY) (NY)	L
Belhaven (MS)	R
Bellarmine (KY)	R
Belmont Abbey (NC)	S
Benedictine (KS)	S
Benedictine (IL)	R
▲Bennett (NC)	S
Berea (KY)	R
Bethel (MN)	R
Blackburn (IL)	S
Bluffton (OH)	S
Brescia (KY)	S
Bridgewater (VA)	R
Brockport (SUNY) (NY)	M
Caldwell (NJ)	S
California Lutheran	R
California Maritime Academy	S
Cal. Poly. State U. (Pomona)	L
California State U. (Bakersfield)	M
California State U. (Channel Islands)	R
California State U. (Dominguez Hills)	M
California State U. (Fresno)	L
California State U. (Fullerton)	L
California State U. (Hayward)	M
California State U. (Los Angeles)	L
California State U. (Sacramento)	M
California State U. (San Bernardino)	M
California State U. (San Marcos)	M
California State U. (Stanislaus)	M
Campbell (NC)	R
Canisius (NY)	M
Carthage (WI)	R
Castleton (VT)	R
Catawba (NC)	S
Cedarville (OH)	R
Central Arkansas	M
Central Connecticut	M
Champlain (VT)	R
Chapman (CA)	R
▲Chatham (PA)	S
Chowan (NC)	S
Christopher Newport (VA)	M
Citadel, The (SC)	R
Clark Atlanta (GA)	M
Coastal Carolina (SC)	M
Coker (SC)	S
Colorado State	L
Colorado, U. of (Denver)	M
Concordia (CA)	R
Concordia (NE)	R
Daemen (NY)	R
Delaware Valley (PA)	R
Dillard (LA)	R
Doane (NE)	S
East Tennessee	L
Eastern (PA)	R
Eastern Connecticut	M
Eastern Illinois	L
Eastern Nazarene (MA)	R
Eastern Oregon	R
Edgewood (WI)	S
Elmhurst (IL)	R
Elmira (NY)	R
Emory & Henry (VA)	S
Eureka (IL)	S
Fairleigh Dickinson (NJ)	M
Fairmont State (WV)	M
Faulkner (AL)	R
Ferris State (MI)	L
Fisk (TN)	S

GROUP III continues next page

Enrollment Code

■ Men Only ▲ Women Only | S = Small (less than 1000 students) | R = Moderate (1000-3000 students) | M = Medium (3000-8000 students) | L = Large (8000-20,000 students) | XL = Extra Large (over 20,000 students)

BUSINESS ADMINISTRATION, cont.

••• ────── *GROUP III, Continued* ────── •••

Florida A&M	M
Framingham (MA)	M
Freed-Hardeman (TN)	R
Frostburg (MD)	M
Gannon (PA)	M
George Fox (OR)	S
Georgia Southern	L
Georgia State	L
Graceland (IA)	R
Grambling (LA)	M
Green Mountain (VT)	S
Hartford, U. of (CT)	M
Hartwick (NY)	R
Hastings (NE)	S
Hawaii Pacific	M
Heidelberg (OH)	S
Henderson State (AR)	M
Hillsdale (MI)	R
Howard (DC)	M
Husson (ME)	S
▲ Immaculata (PA)	S
Indiana Institute of Tech.	S
Indiana State U.	L
Iona (NY)	M
Jacksonville (FL)	R
Kennesaw State (GA)	R
Kentucky Wesleyan (KY)	S
King's (PA)	R
LaSell (MA)	S
LaVerne, U. of (CA)	R
Lenoir-Rhyne (NC)	R
▲ Lesley (MA)	S
Linfield (OR)	R
Long Island U. (Southampton)	R
Louisiana-Lafayette	L
Louisville (KY)	L
Maine (Farmington)	R
Maine, U. of	M
Malone (OH)	R
Manchester (IN)	R
Marshall (WV)	M
▲ Mary Baldwin (VA)	S
Marygrove (MI)	R
Mass. Col. of Lib. Arts (N. Adams)	R
Massachusettes, U. of (Boston)	M
McMurray (TX)	R

Mercer (GA)	R
Mercyhurst (PA)	R
▲ Meredith (NC)	R
Merrimack (MA)	R
Middle Tennessee	L
Milligan (TN)	S
Mississippi State	L
Monmouth (NJ)	R
Montana, U. of	M
Montclair State (NJ)	M
Montreat (NC)	S
■ Morehouse (GA)	R
Mount Mercy (IA)	S
Mount St. Joseph (OH)	R
Mount St. Mary's (CA)	R
Mount St. Mary's (MD)	R
Mount Union (OH)	S
Muskingum (OH)	R
Nebraska, U. of	L
Nevada, U. of (Las Vegas)	M
Nevada, U. of (Reno)	M
New Orleans, U. of	L
Niagara (NY)	R
North Carolina, U. of (Charlotte)	L
North Carolina, U. of (Pembroke)	R
North Carolina, U. of (Wilmington)	M
North Georgia	R
Northern Arizona	L
Northern Colorado	L
Northern Illinois	L
Northern Iowa, U. of	L
Northern Kentucky	L
Northwestern U. of Louisiana	L
Northwood University (MI)	R
Nova Southeastern (FL)	R
Nyack (NY)	R
Oakland U. (MI)	M
Oakland City U. (IN)	R
Ohio Northern	R
Ohio State	XL
Oregon Inst. of Tech.	R
Ozarks, College of the (MO)	R
Pace (NY)	R

GROUP III continues next page

BUSINESS ADMINISTRATION, cont.

GROUP III, Continued

Penn State (Erie)(PA)	M
Philadelphia U. (PA)	R
▲ Pine Manor (MA)	S
Pittsburgh, U. of (Greensburg)	R
Pittsburgh, U. of (Johnstown)	R
Point Loma (CA)	R
Potsdam (SUNY) (NY)	M
Puerto Rico (CAYEY), U. of	M
Quincy (IL)	R
Quinnipiac (CT)	R
Phillips (OK)	R
Radford (VA)	M
Ramapo (NJ)	M
Regis (CO)	R
Reinhardt (GA)	S
Rider (NJ)	M
Robert Morris (PA)	M
Rockford (IL)	S
Roger Williams (RI)	R
Roosevelt (IL)	R
Sacred Heart (CT)	R
San Jose State (CA)	L
Schreiner (TX)	S
Seattle U. (WA)	R
Shippensburg (PA)	M
Silver Lake (WI)	S
Simpson (IA)	S
Sonoma State (CA)	M
South Alabama	M
South Carolina, U. of	L
South Dakota, U. of	M
Southern Illinois	L
Southern Maine	M
Southern Mississippi	L
South Florida, U. of	XL
Southwest Texas State	L
▲ Stephens (MO)	S
St. Andrews Presbyterian (NC)	S
St. Edward's (TX)	M
St. Francis (NY)	R
St. John Fisher (NY)	L

St. John's (NY)	L
St. Joseph's (IN)	S
St. Joseph's (NY)	R
St. Mary's (TX)	R
St. Rose (NY)	R
St. Thomas (MN)	M
St. Vincent's (PA)	R
Suffolk (MA)	R
Tampa, U. of (FL)	R
Taylor (IN)	R
Tennessee, U. of	L
Texas Lutheran	S
Texas Wesleyan	R
Texas, U. of (San Antonio)	L
Thomas More (KY)	R
Toledo, U. of	L
Towson (MD)	L
Utica College (NY)	R
Virginia Commonwealth	L
Virginia Wesleyan	R
Visual Arts, School of (NY)	R
Wagner (NY)	R
Washington & Jefferson (PA)	R
West Chester (PA)	M
West Florida, U. of	M
Western Connecticut State	M
Western New England (MA)	R
Western State (CO)	R
Whittier (CA)	R
Wichita State (KS)	M
Widener (PA)	R
Winthrop (SC)	M
Wisconsin, U. of (Eau Claire)	L
Wisconsin, U. of (Green Bay)	M
Wisconsin, U. of (LaCrosse)	L
Wisconsin, U. of (Stout)	M
Woodbury (CA)	S
Worcester State (MA)	M
Xavier U. of Louisiana	R
York (PA)	M
Youngstown State (OH)	L

Enrollment Code

■ Men Only	S = Small (less than 1000 students)	R = Moderate (1000-3000 students)	M = Medium (3000-8000 students)
▲ Women Only	L = Large (8000-20,000 students)	XL = Extra Large (over 20,000 students)	

CHEMISTRY

GROUP I
Most Selective

Albany (SUNY)(NY)	L		Lafayette (PA)	R
Amherst (MA)	R		Lawrence (WI)	R
▲ Barnard (NY)	R		Macalester (MN)	R
Bates (ME)	R		MIT (MA)	M
Binghamton (SUNY)(NY)	L		Michigan, U. of	XL
Boston College (MA)	L		Missouri, U. of (Rolla)	M
Bowdoin (ME)	R		▲ Mount Holyoke (MA)	R
Brandeis (MA)	M		New College (FL)	S
Brown (RI)	M		North Carolina, U. of	L
▲ Bryn Mawr (PA)	S		Northwestern (IL)	M
Bucknell (PA)	M		Notre Dame (IN)	M
Buffalo (SUNY)(NY)	L		Oberlin (OH)	R
California Inst. of Tech.	S		Occidental (CA)	R
California, U. of (Berkeley)	XL		Pennsylvania State	XL
California, U. of (Los Angeles)	XL		Pomona (CA)	R
California, U. of (San Diego)	L		Princeton (NJ)	M
Carleton (MN)	R		Puget Sound (WA)	R
Carnegie Mellon (PA)	M		Reed (OR)	R
Case Western Reserve U. (OH)	R		Rennselaer (NY)	M
Centre (KY)	R		Rhodes (TN)	R
Claremont McKenna (CA)	R		Rice (TX)	R
Colby (ME)	R		Richmond (VA)	R
Colgate (NY)	R		Rochester, U. of (NY)	M
Colorado College	R		Rose-Hulman (IN)	R
Columbia (NY)	M		Rutgers (NJ)	L
Cornell (NY)	L		Siena (NY)	R
Dartmouth (NH)	M		Skidmore (NY)	R
Davidson (NC)	R		South, U. of the (TN)	R
DePauw (IN)	R		Southwestern (TX)	R
Drew (NJ)	R		St. Olaf (MN)	R
Duke (NC)	M		Stanford (CA)	M
Emory (GA)	R		Trinity (CT)	R
Franklin & Marshall (PA)	R		Trinity (TX)	R
Furman (SC)	R		Tufts (MA)	M
Georgetown (DC)	M		Union (NY)	R
Georgia Inst. of Tech	L		United States Naval Academy (MD)	M
Grinnell (IA)	R		Virginia, U. of	L
Gustavus Adolphus (MN)	R		■ Wabash (IN)	S
Hamilton (NY)	R		Wake Forest (NC)	M
Harvard (MA)	M		Washington U. (MO)	M
Harvey Mudd (CA)	S		▲ Wellesley (MA)	R
Haverford (PA)	S		Wesleyan (CT)	R
Holy Cross (MA)	R		Wheaton (IL)	R
Illinois Wesleyan	R		Whitman (WA)	R
Illinois, U. of (Urbana-Champaign)	XL		Willamette (OR)	R
Iowa State	XL		Williams (MA)	R
Johns Hopkins (MD)	R		Wisconsin, U. of	XL
Kalamazoo (MI)	R		Worcester Poly Inst.(MA)	R
Kenyon (OH)	R			

CHEMISTRY continues next page

Enrollment Code

■ Men Only	S = Small (less than 1000 students)　R = Moderate (1000-3000 students)　M = Medium (3000-8000 students)
▲ Women Only	L = Large (8000-20,000 students)　XL = Extra Large (over 20,000 students)

CHEMISTRY, continued

GROUP II
Very Selective

Albertson (ID)	S	Linfield (OR)	R
Alma (MI)	R	Loras (IA)	R
Arcadia (PA)	R	Louisiana State	XL
Austin (TX)	R	Louisiana-Lafayette	L
Baylor (TX)	M	Louisville (KY)	L
Berea (KY)	R	Loyola (LA)	R
Birmingham-Southern (AL)	R	Lycoming (PA)	R
Bradley (IL)	M	Marquette (WI)	M
Brooklyn College (CUNY)(NY)	L	Maryland, U. of (Baltimore County)	M
Butler (IN)	R	Massachusetts, U. of	L
California, U. of (Davis)	L	McKendree (IL)	R
California, U. of (Irvine)	L	Michigan State	XL
California, U. of (Santa Cruz)	M	Michigan, U. of (Dearborn)	M
Carroll (WI)	R	Millsaps (MS)	S
Centenary (LA)	S	Minnesota, U. of (Morris)	R
Central (IA)	R	Monmouth (IL)	S
Citadel, The (SC)	R	Murray State (KY)	M
City College (CUNY)(NY)	L	New Hampshire, U. of	L
Clark (MA)	R	New Mexico State	L
Clarke (IA)	S	North Carolina State	L
Clemson (SC)	L	North Central (IL)	R
Coe (IA)	R	North Dakota, U. of	M
Colorado, U. of	L	Ohio Northern	R
Converse (SC)	S	Ohio State	XL
Creighton (NE)	R	Ohio University	L
Delaware, U. of	L	Ohio Wesleyan	R
Denver, U. of (CO)	M	Oklahoma, U. of	L
DePaul (IL)	L	Oregon, U. of	L
Duquesne (PA)	M	Otterbein (OH)	R
Earlham (IN)	R	Pittsburgh, U. of (PA)	L
Eastern Michigan	L	Providence (RI)	M
Florida Inst. of Tech	R	Puerto Rico, U of (Mayaguez)	L
Florida Southern	R	Puget Sound (WA)	R
Florida State	L	Purdue (IN)	XL
Georgetown (KY)	R	Richard Stockton (NJ)	M
George Washington (DC)	M	Ripon (WI)	S
Georgia, U. of	XL	Roanoke (VA)	R
Goucher (MD)	S	Rochester, U. of (NY)	M
Hamline (MN)	R	Rockhurst (MO)	R
Hendrix (AR)	R	Rollins (FL)	R
Hiram (OH)	R	St. John's (MN)	R
Hobart & William Smith (NY)	R	St. Louis (MO)	M
Hope (MI)	R	St. Michael's (VT)	R
Houghton (NY)	S	St. Thomas (TX)	R
Hunter (CUNY)(NY)	L	St. Vincent (PA)	R
Huntingdon (AL)	S	San Diego State U. (CA)	XL
Indiana U.	XL	Sciences in Philadelphia (PA)	R
Ithaca Col.	M	Shepherd (WV)	M
Juniata (PA)	R	South Florida, U. of	L
Kansas, U. of	L	▲Spelman (GA)	R
Knox (IL)	R	Spring Hill (AL)	R
Lake Forest (IL)	R	Stetson (FL)	R
LaSalle (PA)	R		
Lehigh (PA)	M		

GROUP II continues next page

CHEMISTRY, continued

GROUP II, Continued

Stonehill (MA)	R
Stony Brook (SUNY) (NY)	L
Temple (PA)	L
Texas A&M	XL
Transylvania (KY)	S
Truman State (MO)	M
Ursinus (PA)	R
Utah State	L
Utah, U. of	L
Vermont, U. of	L
Virginia Military Inst.	R
Virginia Poly Inst.	L
Viterbo (WI)	R
Washington & Jefferson (PA)	R
Washington, U. of	XL
▲ Wells (NY)	S
Westminster (UT)	R
Westmont (CA)	R
Whitworth (WA)	R
Winthrop (SC)	M
Wisconsin Lutheran	S
Wisconsin, U. of (Milwaukee)	L
Wittenberg (OH)	R
Wofford (SC)	R
Wooster (OH)	R

GROUP III
Selective

Akron, U. of (OH)	L
Alabama, U. of (Birmingham)	M
Aquinas (MI)	R
Ashland (OH)	R
Baldwin-Wallace (OH)	R
Bluffton (OH)	S
California State U. (Channel Islands)	R
California State U. (Chico)	L
California State U. (Fresno)	L
California State U. (Long Beach)	L
California State U. (San Jose)	L
Carson-Newman (TN)	R
College of Charleston (SC)	L
Cumberland (KY)	R
Delaware Valley (PA)	R
DeSales (PA)	S
Framingham (MA)	M
Georgia State	L
Houston Baptist (TX)	R
Kennesaw State (GA)	R
Kentucky Wesleyan	R
King's (PA)	R
Lock Haven (PA)	M
Long Island U. (Brooklyn)(NY)	M
Long Island U. (Southampton)(NY)	R
Marshall (WV)	M
▲ Mary Baldwin (VA)	S
Maryville (TN)	R
Massachusetts, U. of (Dartmouth)	M
Millersville (PA)	M
Milligan (TN)	S
Mount St. Joseph (OH)	R
Muskingum (OH)	R
Nichols State (LA)	M
North Carolina, U. of (Charlotte)	L
North Carolina, U. of (Wilmington)	M
Northern Illinois U.	L
Northern Michigan	M
Northwestern (IA)	R
Oakland U. (MI)	M
Puerto Rico, U. of (Cayey)	L
Rider (MJ)	R
St. Mary's (MN)	R
St. Scholastica (MN)	R
Salem State (MA)	M
Shippensburg (PA)	M
Shorter (GA)	R
Sonoma State (CA)	M
Southern Connecticut	M
Southern Maine	M
▲ Sweet Briar (VA)	S
Tennessee, U. of	XL
Texas Lutheran	S
Thomas More (KY)	R
Towson (MD)	L
Union (TN)	R
Washington & Lee (VA)	R
West Chester (PA)	M
Western Illinois	L
Wheeling Jesuit (WV)	R
Whittier (CA)	R
Wisconsin, U. of (Eau Claire)	L
Wisconsin, U. of (LaCrosse)	L
Wisconsin, U. of (Platteville)	M
Wisconsin, U. of (Stevens Point)	M
Worcester State (MA)	M
Wyoming, U. of	L
Xavier (OH)	R
Xavier U. of Louisiana	R

Enrollment Code

■ Men Only ▲ Women Only   S = Small (less than 1000 students)   R = Moderate (1000-3000 students)   M = Medium (3000-8000 students)   L = Large (8000-20,000 students)   XL = Extra Large (over 20,000 students)

CLASSICS

GROUP I
Most Selective

Amherst (MA)	R		Michigan, U. of	XL
▲ Barnard (NY)	R		Middlebury (VT)	R
Brown (RI)	M		New York U.	M
▲ Bryn Mawr (PA)	S		North Carolina, U. of	L
Buffalo (SUNY)(NY)	L		Northwestern (IL)	M
California, U. of (Berkeley)	XL		Oberlin (OH)	R
Case Western Reserve (OH)	M		Pennsylvania, U. of	L
Centre (KY)	R		Pittsburgh, U. of (PA)	L
Chicago, U. of (IL)	M		Princeton (NJ)	M
Columbia (NY)	M		Rhodes (TN)	R
Dallas, U. of (TX)	R		Skidmore (NY)	R
Dartmouth (NH)	M		Stanford (CA)	M
Drew (NJ)	R		Swarthmore (PA)	R
Duke (NC)	M		Texas, U. of (Austin)	XL
Emory (GA)	R		Trinity (TX)	R
Georgetown (DC)	M		Tufts (MA)	M
Gustavus Adolphus (MN)	R		Vanderbilt (TN)	M
Harvard (MA)	M		Virginia, U. of	L
Holy Cross (MA)	R		■ Wabash (IN)	S
Johns Hopkins (MD)	R		Whitman (WA)	R
Kalamazoo (MI)	R		Williams (MA)	R
Kenyon (OH)	R		Wisconsin, U. of	XL
Macalester (MN)	R		Yale (CT)	M
Maryland, U. of (Baltimore County)	M			

GROUP II
Very Selective

▲ Agnes Scott (GA)	S		Massachusetts, U. of (Boston)	M
Beloit (WI)	R		Millsaps (MS)	S
Brooklyn College (CUNY)(NY)	L		Misericordia, College (PA)	S
California State U. (Long Beach)	L		Montana, U. of	L
California, U. of (Santa Barbara)	L		Montclair State (NJ)	M
Catholic U. (DC)	M		North Carolina (Asheville)	R
Cincinnati, U. of	L		North Carolina (Greensboro)	M
Coe(IA)	R		Ohio State	XL
Duquesne (PA)	M		Oklahoma, U. of	L
Florida State	L		▲ Randolph-Macon Woman's Col. (VA)	S
Florida, U. of	XL		Rollins (FL)	R
Fordham (NY)	L		St. Anselm (NH)	R
Georgia, U. of	L		St. John's/St. Benedict (MN)	R
■ Hampden-Sydney (VA)	S		Tennessee, U. of	XL
Hunter (CUNY)(NY)	L		Virginia Poly. Inst.	L
Illinois, U. of (Chicago)	L		Wooster, College of the (OH)	R
Kentucky, U. of	L		Xavier (OH)	R

Enrollment Code

■ **Men Only**	**S = Small** (less than 1000 students)	**R = Moderate** (1000-3000 students)	**M = Medium** (3000-8000 students)
▲ **Women Only**	**L = Large** (8000-20,000 students)	**XL = Extra Large** (over 20,000 students)	

COMPUTER SCIENCE

GROUP I
Most Selective

Albany, (SUNY)(NY)	L
Binghamton (SUNY)(NY)	L
Brandeis (MA)	R
Brown (RI)	M
Bucknell (PA)	R
California, U. of (Berkeley)	XL
California, U. of (Los Angeles)	XL
Carnegie Mellon (PA)	M
Case Western Reserve U. (OH)	M
Colorado School of Mines	R
Cornell (NY)	L
Dallas, U. of (TX)	R
Dartmouth (NH)	M
DePauw (IN)	R
Dickinson (PA)	R
Furman (SC)	R
George Washington (DC)	M
Georgia Institute of Tech.	M
Grinnell (IA)	R
Harvard (MA)	M
Harvey Mudd (CA)	S
Illinois, U. of	XL
Iowa State	XL
Lafayette (PA)	R
Lehigh (PA)	M
Maryland, U. of (Baltimore County)	M
Maryland, U. of	XL
Michigan, U. of	XL
MIT (MA)	M
Missouri, U. of (Rolla)	M
Pennsylvania State	XL
Princeton (NJ)	M
Rensselaer (NY)	M
Rice (TX)	R
Rochester, U. of (NY)	M
Rose-Hulman (IN)	R
Stanford (CA)	M
Stevens Inst. of Tech (NJ)	R
United States Air Force Academy (CO)	M
Vassar (NY)	R
Washington, U. of	XL
Washington U. (MO)	M
William & Mary (VA)	M
Williams (MA)	R
Wisconsin, U. of	XL
Worcester Poly. Tech. (MA)	R
Yeshiva (NY)	R

GROUP II
Very Selective

Alabama, U. of (Huntsville)	M
Alfred (NY)	R
Allegheny (PA)	R
Alma (MI)	R
Bradley (IL)	M
Brooklyn College (CUNY)(NY)	L
Bryant (RI)	R
Butler (IN)	R
Cal. Poly. State U. (San Luis Obispo)	L
California, U. of (Irvine)	L
California, U. of (San Diego)	L
California, U. of (Santa Barbara)	L
California, U. of (Santa Cruz)	M
Capital (OH)	R
Central (IA)	R
Central Florida, U. of	L
Clarke (IA)	S
Clemson (SC)	L
Cogswell (CA)	S
Colorado State	L
Denver, U. of (CO)	M
DePaul (IL)	L
Drexel (PA)	M
Eckerd (FL)	R
Embry-Riddle (FL)	M
Florida Inst. of Tech	M
Florida State	L
George Mason (VA)	L
Goucher (MD)	R
Hendrix (AR)	R
Hiram (OH)	R
Hunter (CUNY) (NY)	L
Illinois College	S
James Madison (VA)	M

GROUP II continues next page

COMPUTER SCIENCE, continued

GROUP II, Continued

Kent State (OH)	L
LaSalle (PA)	M
Maine, U. of	M
Marist (NY)	M
Marquette (WI)	M
Mary Washington (VA)	R
Massachusetts, U. of	L
Massachusetts, U. of (Lowell)	M
McKendree (IL)	R
Michigan, U. of (Dearborn)	M
Millsaps (MS)	S
Minnesota, U. of (Morris)	R
Missouri, U. of (Kansas City)	M
Mobile, U. of (AL)	R
Montana College of Min. Sci. & Tech.	R
Montana, U. of	M
Moravian (PA)	R
Murray State (KY)	M
New Jersey Inst. of Tech	M
New Mexico State	L
North Central (IL)	R
Northeastern (MA)	L
Oklahoma City U.	R
Oregon, U. of	L
Pace (NY)	M
Pacific Lutheran (WA)	R
Pepperdine (CA)	R
Pittsburgh, U. of (Johnstown)	R
Portland State (OR)	M
Potsdam (SUNY) (NY)	M
Queens (CUNY)(NY)	L
Regis (CO)	R
Rhode Island, U. of	L
Rochester Inst. of Tech (NY)	L
Rowan (NJ)	M
Rutgers (Camden) (NJ)	M
Santa Clara U. (CA)	M
St. Ambrose (IA)	R
St. Edward's (TX)	M
St. John's (MN)	R
St. Norbert (WI)	R
Sciences, U. of the (PA)	S
Shippensburg (PA)	M
South Carolina, U. of	L
Stetson (FL)	R
Stonehill (MA)	R
Stony Brook (SUNY) (NY)	L
Syracuse (NY)	L
Taylor (IN)	R
Texas, U. of	XL
Texas, U. of (Dallas)	M
Transylvania (KY)	S
Tulsa, U of (OK)	R
Utah, U. of	L
Westminster (PA)	R
Westminster (UT)	R
Wofford (SC)	R

COMPUTER SCIENCE continues next page

Enrollment Code

■ Men Only	
▲ Women Only	

S = Small (less than 1000 students)　R = Moderate (1000-3000 students)　M = Medium (3000-8000 students)
L = Large (8000-20,000 students)　XL = Extra Large (over 20,000 students)

COMPUTER SCIENCE, continued

GROUP III
Selective

Arizona State XL	■ Morehouse (GA) .... R
Ball State (IN) L	Mount St. Joseph (OH) .... R
Baruch (CUNY)(NY) L	Mount Union (OH) .... S
Brockport (SUNY) (NY) .... M	Muskingum (OH) .... R
Cal. Poly. State U. (Pomona) L	Northeastern Illinois .... M
California State U. (Chico) L	Northern Michigan .... M
California State U. (Hayward) .... M	Northwestern Louisiana L
California State U. (Monterey Bay) ...... R	North Carolina (Greensboro) .... M
California State U. (San Bernardino) .. M	North Florida .... M
California State U. (San Jose) L	Oakland U. (MI) .... M
California State U. (San Marcos) .... M	Oswego (SUNY)(NY) .... M
California State U. (Stanislaus) .... M	Ozarks, College of the (MO) .... R
Canisius (NY) .... M	Pittsburgh, U. of (Bradford) .... R
Catawba (NC) .... S	Quinnipiac (CT) .... R
Charleston Southern (SC) .... R	Ramapo (NJ) .... M
Christopher Newport (VA) .... M	Rider (NJ) .... M
Chowan (NC) .... S	Robert Morris (PA) .... R
Clark Atlanta (GA) .... M	St. Joseph's (NY) .... R
Coastal Carolina (SC) .... M	St. Mary's (MN) .... R
Colorado, U. of (Col. Springs) .... M	Salem State (MA) .... M
Colorado, U. of (Denver) .... M	San Jose State U. (CA) L
East Stroudsburg (PA) .... M	Southeastern Louisiana L
Eastern Connecticut .... M	Southern Connecticut .... M
Eastern Michigan L	Southern Maine .... M
Eureka (IL) .... S	Southern Polytechnic (GA) .... R
Evansville (IN) .... R	▲ Spelman (GA) .... R
Ferris State (MI) L	Temple (PA) L
Florida Gulf Coast U. .... R	Texas, U. of (Arlington) L
Frostburg (MD) .... M	Texas, U. of (Tyler) .... R
Georgia State L	Thomas More (KY) .... R
Hawaii Pacific .... M	Weber State (UT) L
High Point (NC) .... R	West Chester (PA) .... M
Husson (ME) .... S	West Florida, U. of .... M
Jacksonville State (AL) .... M	West Virginia Wesleyan .... R
Jamestown (ND) .... R	Western Kentucky L
Louisiana-Lafayette L	Western Michigan L
Loyola U. (LA) .... M	Western New England (MA) .... R
Marygrove (MI) .... R	Wilkes (PA) .... R
Millersville (PA) .... M	William Paterson (NJ) .... M
Mississippi State L	Wisconsin (LaCrosse) L
Monmouth (NJ) .... M	

Enrollment Code

■ Men Only   **S = Small** (less than 1000 students)   **R = Moderate** (1000-3000 students)   **M = Medium** (3000-8000 students)

▲ Women Only   **L = Large** (8000-20,000 students)   **XL = Extra Large** (over 20,000 students)

DANCE/DRAMA/THEATER

GROUP I
Most Selective

Allegheny (PA) .... R
American Acad. of Dramatic Arts (NY) . S
Amherst (MA) .... R
▲ Barnard (NY) .... R
Binghamton (SUNY)(NY) L
Boston U. (MA) L
Brandeis (MA) .... R
California, U. of (Los Angeles) XL
California, U. of (San Diego) L
Carleton (MN) .... R
Carnegie Mellon (PA) .... M
Case Western Reserve (OH) .... R
Columbia (NY) .... M
Connecticut College .... R
Cornell (NY) L
Dartmouth (NH) .... M
Denison (OH) .... R
Drew (NJ) .... R
Gettysburg (PA) .... R
Illinois, U. of.......................... XL
Illinois Wesleyan .... R
Juilliard (NY) .... S
Kenyon (OH) .... R
Lawrence (WI) .... R

Macalester (MN) .... R
Maryland, U. of (Baltimore County) .... M
Miami, U. of (FL) L
Middlebury (VT) .... R
Milliken (IL) .... R
▲ Mount Holyoke (MA) .... R
New School U. (Eugene Lang)(NY) .... S
New York U. L
North Carolina, U. of.................... L
Northwestern (IL) .... M
Oberlin (OH) .... R
Princeton (NJ) .... M
Rutgers (NJ) L
Sarah Lawrence (NY) .... S
Skidmore (NY) .... R
South, U. of the (TN) .... R
Southwestern (TX)........................ R
Tufts (MA) .... M
Tulane (LA) .... M
Vassar (NY) .... R
Wesleyan (CT) .... R
Whitman (WA) .... R
William & Mary (VA) .... R
Yale (CT) .... M

GROUP II
Very Selective

Alabama, U. of L
Arizona, U. of XL
Arizona State XL
Bard (NY) .... R
Baylor (TX) .... M
Beloit (WI) .... R
Bennington (VT) .... S
Birmingham-Southern (AL) .... R
Brooklyn College (CUNY)(NY) L
Butler (IN) .... R
California Institute of the Arts .... S
California, U. of (Irvine) L
California, U. of (Riverside) L
Catholic U. (DC) .... M
Central Florida, U. of L
Clarke (IA) .... S
Columbia College (IL) .... M
Columbia College (SC) .... R
Cornish (WA)............................. S
Creighton (NE) .... R
DePaul (IL) L
π Elon (NC) .... R
Florida, U. of XL
Florida State L

Florida Southern .... R
Fordham (NY)............................. L
George Mason (VA)........................ L
Georgia, U. of........................... L
Goucher (MD) .... S
Grand Valley (MI) L
Hanover (IN)............................. R
Hawaii, U. of L
Hofstra (NY) .... M
Hunter (CUNY)(NY) L
Indiana U. XL
Iowa, U. of XL
James Madison (VA) .... M
Kansas, U. of L
LeMoyne (NY) .... R
Linfield (OR) .... R
Long Island U.(Southampton Col.)(NY) . R
Loyola (IL).............................. M
Lyon (AR) .... S
Maine, U. of............................. M
Manhattanville (NY) .... R

π *Music Theatre*

DANCE/DRAMA/THEATER continues next page

DANCE/DRAMA/THEATER, cont.

GROUP II, Continued

Minnesota, U. of XL	Southern Methodist (TX) .... M
Manhattanville (NY) .... R	Susquehanna (PA) .... R
McDaniel (MD) .... R	Syracuse (NY) L
Minnesota, U. of XL	Texas Christian .... M
Muhlenberg (PA) .... R	Texas, U. of XL
Nevada, U. of (Las Vegas) .... M	Utah State L
New Hampshire, U. of .... R	Utah, U. of L
No. Carolina School of the Arts .... S	Virginia Commonwealth U. L
Ohio U. L	Viterbo (WI) .... R
Oklahoma City U. .... R	Washington, U. of XL
Oklahoma State L	▲ Wells (NY) .... S
Purchase (SUNY) (NY) .... R	Western Maryland .... R
Rollins (FL) .... R	West Virginia U. L
▲ Scripps (CA) .... S	Wheaton (MA) .... R
Seattle Pacific (WA) .... R	Wisconsin, U. of XL
Shepherd (WV) .... R	Wisconsin, U. of (Milwaukee) L
South Carolina, U. of L	Wisconsin, U. of (Stevens Point) .... M
Southern California L	Wooster (OH) .... R

GROUP III
Selective

++ Akron, U. of (OH) L	Northwestern College (IA) .... R
Alaska, U. of (Fairbanks) .... M	Ohio State XL
Arcadia (PA) .... R	Otterbein (OH) .... R
Arts, U. of the (PA) .... R	# Point Park (PA) .... R
Barry (FL) .... R	Rockford (IL) .... S
Bethany (WV) .... S	Salem State (MA) .... M
Brenau (GA) .... R	San Francisco State (CA) L
Brockport (SUNY)(NY) .... M	Santa Fe, College of (NM) .... S
California State U. (Long Beach) L	Seattle U. (WA) .... R
California State U. (Northridge) L	▲ Seton Hill (PA) .... S
California State U. (Sacramento) .... M	++ Slippery Rock (PA) .... M
Catawba (NC) .... S	Southern Maine .... M
Central Michigan L	Southern Missippi L
Coker (SC) .... S	Southern Utah .... M
Converse College (SC) .... S	South Florida, U. of L
Dana (NB) .... S	Southwest Missouri L
DeSales (PA) .... S	St. Edward's (TX) .... M
Emerson (MA) .... R	St. Mary's (MN) .... R
Evansville (IN) .... R	Stephens (MO) .... S
Fontbonne (MO) .... R	Temple (PA) L
Franklin (IN) .... S	Towson (MD) L
Greensboro College (NC) .... S	Wagner (NY) .... R
Illinois State L	Weber State (UT) L
Indiana State L	Webster (MO) .... R
Jacksonville (FL) .... R	Western Michigan L
Johnson State (VT) .... R	* Western St. Coll. of Colorado .... R
Keene State (NH) .... R	π West Virginia Wesleyan .... R
Lewis-Clark State (ID) .... R	++ Winthrop(SC) .... M
Longwood (VA) .... R	
▲ Mary Baldwin (VA) .... S	π *Music Theatre*
Montana, U. of .... M	# *Musical Theater and Dance*
Niagara (NY) .... R	++ *Especially Dance*
	* *Communication and Theatre - One Major*

ECONOMICS

GROUP I
Most Selective

Albany (SUNY)(NY)	L	Miami, U. of (OH)	L
American U. (DC)	M	Michigan, U. of	XL
Amherst (MA)	R	MIT (MA)	M
Babson (MA)	R	Middlebury (VT)	R
▲ Barnard (NY)	R	▲ Mount Holyoke (MA)	R
Bates (ME)	R	New York U.	L
Boston University (MA)	L	Northwestern (IL)	M
Bowdoin (ME)	R	Occidental (CA)	R
Brandeis (MA)	R	Pennsylvania, U. of	L
Brown (RI)	M	Pomona (CA)	R
▲ Bryn Mawr (PA)	S	Princeton (NJ)	M
Bucknell (PA)	M	Rhodes (TN)	R
California, U. of (Los Angeles)	XL	Richmond (VA)	R
California, U. of (San Diego)	L	Rochester, U. of (NY)	M
Carleton (MN)	R	Rose-Hulman (IN)	R
Case Western Reserve (OH)	R	Rutgers (NJ)	L
Chicago, U. of (IL)	M	▲ Smith (MA)	R
Claremont McKenna (CA)	R	St. Mary's Col. of Maryland	R
Colby (ME)	R	St. Olaf (MN)	R
Colorado College	R	South, U. of the (TN)	R
Colorado School of Mines	R	Southwestern (TX)	R
Columbia (NY)	M	Stanford (CA)	M
Connecticut College	R	Swarthmore (PA)	R
Cornell (NY)	L	Trinity (CT)	R
Dallas, U. of (TX)	R	Trinity (TX)	R
Dartmouth (NH)	M	Tufts (MA)	M
Davidson (NC)	R	U.S. Military Academy (NY)	M
DePauw (IN)	R	Vanderbilt (TN)	M
Drew (NJ)	R	Vassar (NY)	R
Duke (NC)	M	Villanova (PA)	M
Emory (GA)	R	Virginia, U. of	L
George Washington (DC)	M	■ Wabash (IN)	S
Georgetown (DC)	M	Wake Forest (NC)	M
Georgia Inst. of Tech.	M	Washington & Lee (VA)	R
Grinnell (IA)	R	▲ Wellesley (MA)	R
Hamilton (NY)	R	Wesleyan (CT)	R
Harvard (MA)	M	Whitman (WA)	R
Haverford (PA)	S	Willamette (OR)	R
Holy Cross (MA)	R	Williams (MA)	R
Kalamazoo (MI)	R	Worcester Poly. Inst. (MA)	R
Kenyon (OH)	R	Yale (CT)	M
Lafayette (PA)	R		
Macalester (MN)	R		

ECONOMICS continues next page

Enrollment Code

■ **Men Only**	**S = Small** (less than 1000 students)	**R = Moderate** (1000-3000 students)	**M = Medium** (3000-8000 students)
▲ **Women Only**	**L = Large** (8000-20,000 students)	**XL = Extra Large** (over 20,000 students)	

ECONOMICS, continued

▲Agnes Scott (GA) .... S	Maryland, U. of XL
Albion (MI) .... R	Maryland, U. of (Baltimore County) .... M
Allegheny (PA) .... R	Mary Washington (VA) .... R
Auburn (AL) .... M	Massachusetts, U. of L
Baruch (CUNY)(NY) L	Michigan State XL
Beloit (WI) .... R	Michigan, U. of (Dearborn) .... M
Bethany (WV) .... S	Minnesota, U. of XL
California State U. (Long Beach) L	Nebraska, U. of L
California State U. (Santa Barbara) L	North Carolina State L
Centre (KY) .... R	Oglethorpe (GA) .... R
City College (CUNY)(NY) L	Ohio State XL
Clark (MA) .... R	Ohio Wesleyan (OH) .... R
Clemson (SC) L	Oneonta (SUNY) (NY) .... M
Colorado, U. of L	Randolph-Macon (VA) .... R
Connecticut, U. of L	Richard Stockton (NJ) .... M
Delaware, U. of L	Ripon (WI) .... S
Denison (OH) .... R	▲Salem Col. (NC) .... S
Florida State L	San Francisco, U. of .... M
George Mason (VA) L	St. John's (MN) .... R
Georgia State L	St. Lawrence (NY) .... R
Georgia, U. of XL	▲Spelman (GA) .... R
Grove City (PA) .... R	Texas A&M XL
Guilford (NC) .... R	Ursinus (PA) .... R
■ Hampden-Sydney (VA) .... S	Vermont, U. of L
Hendrix (AR) .... R	Virginia Military Inst. .... R
Hobart & William Smith (NY) .... R	Washington & Jefferson (PA) .... R
Illinois Col. .... S	Washington, U. of XL
Illinois, U. of (Chicago) L	Westminster Col. (MO) .... S
Lake Forest (IL) .... R	Westmont Col. (CA) .... R
Linfield (OR) .... R	Wheaton (MA) .... R
Loyola (LA) .... R	Wofford (SC) .... R
Maine, U. of .... M	Wooster (OH) .... R
Manhattanville (NY) .... R	Xavier (OH) .... R

Enrollment Code			
■ Men Only	**S = Small** (less than 1000 students)	**R = Moderate** (1000-3000 students)	**M = Medium** (3000-8000 students)
▲ Women Only	**L = Large** (8000-20,000 students)	**XL = Extra Large** (over 20,000 students)	

ECONOMICS, continued

GROUP III
Selective

Baldwin-Wallace (OH)	R	Oakland U. (MI)	M
Bellarmine (KY)	R	Old Dominion (VA)	L
California State U. (Channel Islands)	R	Northern Colorado	L
California State U. (Chico)	L	Queens (CUNY)(NY)	L
California State U. (Northridge)	L	Rhode Island College	M
East Carolina	L	St. Anselm (NH)	R
East Tennessee	L	Southern Connecticut	M
Eastern Connecticut	M	Toledo, U. of (OH)	L
Framingham (MA)	M	Washington State	L
Hawaii Pacific	M	Whittier (CA)	R
Heidelberg (OH)	S	Wilson (PA)	S
Indiana U.-Purdue U.-Indianapolis (IN)	L	Wisconsin, U. of (Milwaukee)	L
Louisiana State	XL	Wright State (OH)	L
Monmouth (IL)	S	Wyoming, U. of	L

Enrollment Code		
■ Men Only	**S = Small** (less than 1000 students)	**R = Moderate** (1000-3000 students)	**M = Medium** (3000-8000 students)
▲ Women Only	**L = Large** (8000-20,000 students)	**XL = Extra Large** (over 20,000 students)

EDUCATION

GROUP I
Most Selective

Albany (SUNY)(NY)	L
Boston U. (MA)	L
Bucknell (PA)	R
Buffalo (SUNY) (NY)	L
Connecticut Col.	R
Dallas, U. of (TX)	R
Dickinson (PA)	R
Earlham (IN)	R
Geneseo (SUNY) (NY)	M
Illinois, U. of	XL
Iowa, U. of	XL
Miami, U. of (FL)	M
Miami U. (OH)	L
Michigan, U. of	XL
New Jersey, College of	M

New School U. (Lang)(NY)	S
North Carolina, U. of	L
Pittsburgh, U. of (PA)	L
Occidental (CA)	R
Rutgers (NJ)	L
Skidmore (NY)	R
Southern California	L
Swarthmore (PA)	S
Trinity (TX)	R
➤ Tufts (MA)	M
Vanderbilt (TN)	M
▲Wellesley (MA)	R
Wheaton (IL)	R
William & Mary (VA)	M

➤ *Child Study*

GROUP II
Very Selective

Adelphi (NY)	M
Adrian (MI)	S
Alaska Pacific	S
Albertson (ID)	S
Alfred (NY)	R
Alma (MI)	R
Arizona, U. of	XL
Auburn (AL)	L
Augustana (IL)	R
Augustana (SD)	R
Austin (TX)	R
Baylor (TX)	L
Berry (GA)	R
π Bethel (IN)	R
Biola (CA)	R
Birmingham Southern (AL)	R
Bradley (IL)	M
Bridgewater (MA)	M
Brigham Young (UT)	XL
Bryan (TN)	S
Buena Vista (IA)	R
Butler (IN)	R
California, U. of (Santa Barbara)	L
Calvin (MI)	M
Capital U. (OH)	R
Carroll (WI)	R
Centenary (LA)	S
Central (IA)	R
Centre (KY)	R
Chestnut Hill (PA)	S
Christian Brothers (TN)	R
Cincinnati, U. of (OH)	L
Clarke (IA)	S
Clemson (SC)	L
Coe (IA)	R

Columbia College (SC)	R
Concordia (MN)	R
Connecticut, U. of	L
Cornell College (IA)	R
Creighton (NE)	R
Dayton, U. of (OH)	M
Delaware, U. of	L
DePaul (IL)	L
Drake (IA)	M
Duquesne (PA)	M
Eastern Michigan	L
Elizabethtown (PA)	R
Elon (NC)	R
Erskine (SC)	S
π Flagler (FL)	R
Florida International	L
Florida Southern	R
Florida State	L
Fredonia (SUNY) (NY)	M
Georgetown College (KY)	R
Georgia, U. of	XL
Gonzaga (WA)	R
Goucher (MD)	R
Grove City (PA)	R
Guilford (NC)	R
Gustavus Adolphus (MN)	R
Hanover (IN)	R
Harding (AR)	M
Hillsdale (MI)	R
Hiram (OH)	R
Hood (MD)	S
Houghton (NY)	S

π *Especially Deaf Education*

GROUP II continues next page

EDUCATION, continued

_____ *GROUP II, Continued* _____

Hunter (CUNY) (NY)	L	Providence (RI)	M
Illinois College	S	Puerto Rico, U. of	L
Indiana, U.	XL	Queens (CUNY) (NY)	L
Indiana, U. of (PA)	L	Redlands, U. of (CA)	R
Iowa State	XL	Regis (CO)	R
James Madison (VA)	M	Rowan (NJ)	M
Juniata (PA)	R	St. Bonaventure (NY)	R
Kansas State	L	St. Catherine (MN)	R
Kentucky, U. of	L	St. John's/ St. Benedict (MN)	R
Lake Forest (IL)	R	St. Louis (MO)	M
Lindenwood (MO)	S	St. Mary's Col. (CA)	R
Loras (IA)	R	▲St. Mary's Col. (IN)	R
Luther (IA)	R	St. Mary's Col. (MN)	R
Lyon (AR)	S	St. Michael's (VT)	R
Manhattan (NY)	M	St. Norbert (WI)	R
Manhattanville (NY)	R	Salisbury State (MD)	M
Maryland, U. of	XL	San Diego State U. (CA)	XL
McDaniel (MD)	R	Shepherd (WV)	M
Mercer (GA)	R	Shippensburg (PA)	M
Messiah (PA)	R	▲Simmons (MA)	R
Michigan State	XL	South Carolina, U. of	L
Millersville (PA)	M	South Florida, U. of	L
▲Mills (CA)	S	Southwest Missouri	L
Minnesota, U. of	XL	Stetson (FL)	R
Minnesota, U. of (Duluth)	M	Tennessee, U. of	XL
Minnesota, U. of (Morris)	R	Tennessee Tech	M
Mississippi U. for Women	R	Texas A&M	XL
Missouri, U. of (St. Louis)	M	Texas Christian	M
Moravian (PA)	R	Texas, U. of (Austin)	XL
Mount St. Mary's (MD)	R	Transylvania (KY)	R
Nazareth (NY)	R	Truman State (MO)	M
New Hampshire, U. of	L	Ursinus (PA)	R
New Mexico State	L	Valparaiso (IN)	R
New Orleans (LA)	L	Washington & Jefferson (PA)	R
New Paltz (SUNY) (NY)	M	Washington State	L
North Carolina, U. of (Asheville)	R	Washington, U. of	XL
North Carolina, U. of (Greensboro)	M	▲Wells (NY)	S
North Dakota, U. of	M	Western Michigan	L
North Florida	M	Western Washington U.	L
Ohio U.	L	Whitworth (WA)	R
Oklahoma State	L	William Jewell Col. (MO)	R
Oneonta (SUNY)(NY)	M	Wisconsin Lutheran	S
Oregon, U. of	L	Wisconsin, U. of	XL
Oswego (SUNY)(NY)	M	Wisconsin, U. of (Milwaukee)	L
Pacific, U. of the (CA)	M	Wisconsin, U. of (Stevens Point)	M
Palm Beach Atlantic (FL)	R	Wittenberg (OH)	R
Pennsylvania State	XL	Wofford (SC)	R
Potsdam (SUNY) (NY)	R	York (PA)	M
Principia (IL)	S		

EDUCATION continues next page

Enrollment Code

■ Men Only   **S = Small** (less than 1000 students)   **R = Moderate** (1000-3000 students)   **M = Medium** (3000-8000 students)
▲ Women Only   **L = Large** (8000-20,000 students)   **XL = Extra Large** (over 20,000 students)

EDUCATION, continued

GROUP III
Selective

Akron, U. of (OH) L	Catawba (NC) .... S
Alaska, U. of (Anchorage) .... M	Cedarville (OH) .... R
Alderson-Broaddus (WV) .... S	Central Connecticut .... M
Anderson (IN) .... R	Central Michigan U. L
Appalachian State (NC) L	Charleston Southern (SC) .... R
Arcadia (PA) .... R	Citadel, The (SC) .... R
Arkansas, U. of L	City College (CUNY) (NY) L
Arizona State XL	Clark Atlanta (GA) .... M
Ashland (OH) .... R	Coker (SC) .... S
Assumption (MA) .... R	College of Charleston (SC) .... M
Augsburg (MN) .... R	Colorado, U. of (Colorado Springs) ..... M
Averett (VA) .... S	Concordia (NE) .... R
Avila (MO) .... S	▲ Converse (SC) .... S
Baldwin-Wallace (OH) .... R	Cumberland (KY) .... R
Ball State (IN) L	Daemen (NY) .... R
Belhaven (MS) .... R	Dana (NB) .... S
Bellarmine (KY) .... R	Dominican (CA) .... S
▲ Bennett (NC) .... S	Dordt (IA) .... S
Berea (KY) .... R	Dubuque, U. of (IA) .... S
Bethany (WV) .... S	D'Youville (NY) .... R
Bethel (MN) .... R	East Carolina (NC) L
Blackburn (IL) .... S	Eastern Connecticut .... M
Bluffton (OH) .... S	Eastern Illinois L
Bowling Green (OH) L	Eastern Kentucky L
Bloomsburg (PA) .... M	Eastern Mennonite (VA) .... R
Brescia (KY) .... S	Eastern Oregon .... R
Brockport (SUNY) (NY) .... M	Edgewood (WI) .... S
Brooklyn College (CUNY)(NY) L	Edinboro (PA) .... M
Caldwell (NJ) .... S	Elmira (NY) .... R
California Lutheran .... R	Elms (MA) .... S
California State U. (Bakersfield) .... M	Eureka (IL) .... S
California State U. (Channel Islands) .. R	Fairmont (WV) .... M
California State U. (Fresno) L	Florida A&M .... M
California State U. (Monterey Bay) ...... R	Florida Atlantic L
California State U. (Los Angeles) L	Florida Gulf Coast U. .... R
California State U. (Sacramento) .... M	Fontbonne (MO) .... R
California State U. (San Bernardino) .. M	Franklin (IN) .... S
California State U. (San Marcos) .... M	Freed-Hardeman (TN) .... R
California State U. (Stanislaus) .... M	Frostburg (MD) .... M
California (PA) .... M	Geneva (PA) .... R
Canisius (NY) .... M	
Carson-Newman (TN) .... R	***GROUP III continues next page***

Enrollment Code

■ **Men Only**   **S = Small** (less than 1000 students)   **R = Moderate** (1000-3000 students)   **M = Medium** (3000-8000 students)

▲ **Women Only**   **L = Large** (8000-20,000 students)   **XL = Extra Large** (over 20,000 students)

EDUCATION, continued

GROUP III, Continued

George Fox (OR)	S
Georgia Southern	L
Georgia Southwestern	R
Georgia State	L
Gordon (MA)	R
Graceland (IA)	R
Grambling (LA)	M
Hardin-Simmons (TX)	R
Hastings (NE)	S
Heidelberg (OH)	S
Henderson State (AR)	M
Herbert Lehman (CUNY) (NY)	L
Holy Names (CA)	S
Huntingdon (AL)	S
Huntington (IN)	S
Husson (ME)	S
Illinois State	L
Indiana State U.	L
Indiana U.-Purdue U.-Indianapolis (IN)	L
Jacksonville State (AL)	M
Jamestown (ND)	R
Johnson State (VT)	R
▲ Judson (AL)	S
Kean (NJ)	M
Keene State (NH)	R
Kent State (OH)	L
Kentucky Wesleyan	S
King (TN)	S
Kutztown (PA)	M
Lamar (TX)	M
Lambuth (TN)	S
Lasell (MA)	S
Laverne, U. of (CA)	R
▲ Lesley (MA)	S
Lewis-Clark State (ID)	R
Linfield (OR)	R
Lock Haven (PA)	M
Long Island U. (Southampton)(NY)	R
Long Island U. (C.W.Post)(NY)	M
Longwood (VA)	R
Louisiana College	R
Louisiana-Lafayette	L
Maine (Farmington)	R
Manchester (IN)	R
Mansfield (PA)	R
Marshall (WV)	M
Maryville (St. Louis) (MO)	R
Marywood (PA)	R
Mass. St. Col. System	M
Memphis, U. of (TN)	L
Middle Tennessee	L
Millikin (IL)	R
Misericordia, College (PA)	S
Mississippi College	R
Mississippi State	L
Mobile, U. of (AL)	R
Monmouth (IL)	S
Montana, U. of	M
Montana State (Billings)	R
Montclair State (NJ)	M
Montevallo (AL)	R
Mount St. Joseph (OH)	R
Mount Mercy (IA)	S
Mount Union (OH)	R
Murray State (KY)	M
Muskingum (OH)	R
Nevada, U. of (Las Vegas)	M
Nevada, U. of (Reno)	M
New Mexico, U. of	L
Nichols State (LA)	M
North Dakota State	L
Northeastern Illinois	M
Northern Arizona	L
Northern Colorado	L
Northern Illinois U.	L
Northern Iowa	L
Northern Kentucky	L
Northern Michigan	M
Northwestern (IA)	R
Northwestern (MN)	R
Northwestern Louisiana	L
Nyack (NY)	R
Oakland City U. (IN)	R
Ohio State	L
Oklahoma Baptist	R
Olivet Nazarene (IL)	R
Ouachita Baptist (AR)	R
Ozarks, College of the (MO)	R

GROUP III continues next page

EDUCATION, continued

GROUP III, Continued

Peru State (NE)	R	Southern Oregon State U.	M
Philadelphia Biblical (PA)	S	Southern Utah	M
Pittsburgh, U. of (Johnstown)	R	Southwest Baptist (MO)	R
Plymouth State (NH)	M	Southwest Texas State	L
Point Loma (CA)	R	Southwestern Oklahoma	M
Puerto Rico (Cayey), U. of	L	Tabor (KS)	S
Radford (VA)	M	Texas Tech. U.	L
Robert Morris (PA)	R	Texas Wesleyan	R
Rhode Island College	M	Tougaloo (MS)	S
Rider (NJ)	R	Utah State	L
Roger Williams (RI)	R	Wagner (NY)	R
Saginaw Valley (MI)	M	Walsh (OH)	R
St. Andrews Presbyterian (NC)	S	Wartburg (IA)	R
St. Cloud (MN)	L	Weber State (UT)	L
Saint Rose (NY)	R	Western Connecticut	M
St. Joseph's (IN)	S	Western Illinois	L
St. Joseph's (ME)	S	Western Kentucky	L
St. Joseph's (NY)	R	Western New England (MA)	R
▲St. Joseph Col. (CT)	S	Westfield State (MA)	M
St. Scholastica (MN)	R	West Florida, U. of	M
St. Thomas Aquinas (NY)	R	West Virginia Wesleyan	R
Seton Hall (NJ)	M	▲Wheelock (MA)	S
Shawnee State (OH)	R	Whittier (CA)	R
Shorter (GA)	R	Widener (PA)	R
Silver Lake (WI)	S	Wilmington (OH)	S
Simpson (IA)	S	Winthrop (SC)	M
Slippery Rock (PA)	M	Wisconsin, U. of (Platteville)	M
Southeastern Louisiana	L	Worcester State (MA)	M
Southern Connecticut	M	Wyoming, U. of	L
Southern Illinois U. (Edwardsville)	L	Xavier U. of Louisiana	R
Southern Mississippi	L		

Enrollment Code

■ **Men Only**   **S = Small** (less than 1000 students)   **R = Moderate** (1000-3000 students)   **M = Medium** (3000-8000 students)
▲ **Women Only**   **L = Large** (8000-20,000 students)   **XL = Extra Large** (over 20,000 students)

ENGINEERING

GROUP I
Most Selective

Binghamton (SUNY)(NY) L
Boston U. (MA) L
Brown (RI) .... M
Bucknell (PA) .... M
Buffalo (SUNY) (NY) L
California Inst. of Tech. .... S
California, U. of (Berkeley) XL
California, U. of (Davis) L
California, U. of (Los Angeles) XL
California, U. of (San Diego) L
California, U. of (Santa Barbara) L
Carnegie Mellon (PA) .... M
Case Western Reserve U. (OH) .... R
Clarkson (NY) .... M
Colorado School of Mines .... R
Columbia (NY) .... M
Cooper Union (NY) .... S
Cornell (NY) L
Dartmouth (NH) .... M
Duke (NC) .... M
Florida, U. of XL
Georgia Inst. of Tech. .... M
Harvey Mudd (CA) .... S
Illinois Inst. of Tech. .... R
Illinois, U. of (Urbana-Champaign) ... XL
Iowa State XL
Iowa, U. of XL
Johns Hopkins (MD) .... R
Kettering (MI) .... R
Lafayette (PA) .... R
Lehigh (PA) .... M
Maryland, U. of XL
MIT (MA) .... M
Michigan, U. of XL

Missouri, U. of (Rolla) .... M
New Mexico Inst. of Mining & Tech. .... S
New Jersey, College of .... M
Northwestern (IL) .... M
Notre Dame (IN) .... M
Olin (MA) .... S
Pennsylvania State XL
Pennsylvania, U. of L
Princeton (NJ) .... M
Rensselaer (NY) .... M
Rice (TX) .... R
Rochester, U. of .... M
Rose-Hulman (IN) .... R
Rutgers (NJ) L
▲ Smith (MA) .... R
Southern California, U. of L
Stanford (CA) .... M
Stevens Inst. of Tech. (NJ) .... R
Swarthmore (PA) .... R
Texas, U. of (Austin) XL
Trinity (CT) .... R
Tufts (MA) .... M
Tulane (LA) .... M
Union (NY) .... R
U.S. Air Force Academy (CO) .... M
U.S. Coast Guard Academy (CT) .... S
U.S. Military Academy (NY) .... M
U.S. Naval Academy (MD) .... M
Vanderbilt (TN) .... M
Villanova (PA) .... M
Virginia, U. of L
Washington U. (MO) .... M
Washington, U. of L
Worcester Poly. Tech. (MA) .... R

GROUP II
Very Selective

Akron, U. of (OH) L
Alabama, U. of L
Alabama, U. of (Birmingham) .... M
Alabama, U. of (Huntsville) .... M
Alfred (NY) .... R
Arizona, U. of XL
Arizona State XL

Arkansas, U. of L
Auburn (AL) L
Bradley (IL) .... M
Butler (IN) .... R
California State U. (Fresno) L

GROUP II continues next page

ENGINEERING, continued

GROUP II, Continued

California State U. (Fullerton)	L	
California, U. of (Irvine)	L	
California, U. of (Riverside)	M	
California, U. of (Santa Cruz)	M	
California Maritime Academy	S	
Cal. Poly State U. (Pomona)	L	
Cal. Poly. State U. (San Luis Obispo)	L	
Calvin (MI)	M	
Catholic U. (DC)	M	
Central Connecticut	M	
Central Florida, U. of	L	
Christian Brothers (TN)	R	
Cincinnati, U. of (OH)	L	
Citadel, The (SC)	R	
City College (CUNY)(NY)	L	
Clemson (SC)	L	
Cogswell (CA)	S	
Colorado State	L	
Colorado, U. of	L	
Colorado, U. of (Col. Springs)	R	
Connecticut, U. of	L	
Dayton, U. of (OH)	M	
Delaware, U. of	L	
Denver, U. of (CA)	M	
Detroit Mercy (MI)	M	
Dordt (IA)	S	
Drexel (PA)	M	
East Carolina (NC)	L	
Embry-Riddle (FL)	M	
Florida A&M	M	
Florida Atlantic	L	
Florida Inst. of Tech.	R	
Florida International	L	
Gannon (PA)	R	
Geneva (PA)	R	
Gonzaga (WA)	R	
Grand Valley (MI)	L	
Grove City (PA)	R	
Hartford, U. of (CT)	M	
Houston, U. of (TX)	L	
Howard (DC)	M	
Idaho, U. of	M	

Illinois, U. of (Chicago)	L	
Kansas, U. of	L	
Kansas State	L	
Kentucky, U. of	L	
Lamar (TX)	M	
Letourneau College (TX)	S	
Louisiana-Layafette	L	
Louisiana State	XL	
Louisville (KY)	L	
Lowell, U. of (MA)	L	
Loyola (MD)	R	
Loyola Marymount (CA)	M	
Maine, U. of	M	
Manhattan (NY)	M	
π Marietta (OH)	R	
Maritime College (SUNY)(NY)	S	
Marquette (WI)	M	
Massachusetts, U. of	L	
# Massachusetts, U. of (Dartmouth)	M	
Massachusetts, U. of (Lowell)	M	
Mass. Maritime Academy	S	
Memphis, U. of (TN)	L	
Mercer (GA)	R	
Messiah (PA)	R	
Michigan State	XL	
Michigan Tech.	M	
Michigan, U. of	XL	
Michigan, U. of (Dearborn)	M	
Milwaukee Sch. of Engine (WI)	R	
Minnesota, U. of	XL	
Minnesota, U. of (Duluth)	M	
Mississippi State	L	
Mississippi, U. of	M	
Montana College of Min. Sci. & Tech.	R	
Montana State	L	
Morgan State (MD)	M	
Nevada, U. of (Las Vegas)	M	
Nevada, U. of (Reno)	M	
New Hampshire, U. of	L	

π *Petroleum Engineering*
Also, Textile Science / Industry

GROUP II continues next page

ENGINEERING, continued

GROUP II, Continued

New Jersey Inst. of Tech.	M
New Mexico State U.	L
New Orleans, U. of	L
New Paltz (SUNY)(NY)	M
New York Institute of Tech	M
North Carolina State	L
North Dakota State	L
North Dakota, U. of	M
Northeastern (MA)	L
Northern Illinois U.	L
Oakland U. (MI)	M
Ohio Northern	R
Ohio State	XL
Ohio U.	L
Oklahoma, U. of	L
Oklahoma State	L
Old Dominion (VA)	L
Oregon Inst. of Tech.	R
Oregon State	L
Pacific, U. of the (CA)	R
Pittsburgh, U. of	L
Pittsburgh, U. of (Johnstown)	R
Polytechnic Univ. of NY	R
Portland, U. of (OR)	R
Puerto Rico, U. of (Mayaguez)	L
Purdue (IN)	XL
+ Rhode Island, U. of	L
Rochester Inst. of Tech. (NY)	L
Roger Williams (RI)	R
Rowan (NJ)	M
San Diego State (CA)	XL
Santa Clara U. (CA)	M
Seattle Pacific (WA)	R
Seattle U. (WA)	R
South Carolina, U. of	L
So. Dakota School of Mines	R
South Dakota State U.	M
Southern Illinois U. (Carbondale)	L

Southern Illinois U. (Edwardsville)	L
Southern Maine, U. of	M
Southern Methodist (TX)	L
Southern Polytechnic (GA)	R
South Florida, U. of	L
Stony Brook (SUNY) (NY)	L
Syracuse (NY)	L
Tennessee Tech	M
Tennessee, U. of	XL
Texas A&M	XL
Texas Tech U.	L
Texas, U. of (Arlington)	L
Texas, U. of (Dallas)	M
Texas, U. of (San Antonio)	L
Texas, U. of (Tyler)	R
Toledo, U. of (OH)	L
Tri-State (IN)	R
Tulsa, U. of (OK)	R
Tuskegee University (AL)	M
Utah, U. of	L
Valparaiso (IN)	M
Virginia Commonwealth	L
Virginia Military Inst.	R
Virginia Poly. Inst.	L
Walla Walla (WA)	R
Washington State	L
Wayne State (MI)	L
West Virginia U.	L
Western Michigan	L
Western New England (MA)	R
Westminster (UT)	R
Widener (PA)	R
Wilkes (PA)	R
Wisconsin, U. of	XL
Wisconsin, U. of (Platteville)	M
Wright State (OH)	L
Wyoming, U. of	L

+ *And International Engineering*

Enrollment Code

■ Men Only	S = Small (less than 1000 students) R = Moderate (1000-3000 students) M = Medium (3000-8000 students)
▲ Women Only	L = Large (8000-20,000 students) XL = Extra Large (over 20,000 students)

ENGLISH

GROUP I
Most Selective

Allegheny (PA)	R	Lawrence (WI)	R
Amherst (MA)	R	Lehigh (PA)	m
Bard (NY)	R	Macalester (MN)	R
▲ Barnard (NY)	R	Miami U. (OH)	L
Bates (ME)	R	Michigan, U. of	XL
Binghamton (SUNY)(NY)	L	Middlebury (VT)	R
Boston Col. (MA)	L	▲ Mount Holyoke (MA)	R
Bowdoin (ME)	R	New (FL)	S
Brandeis (MA)	R	North Carolina, U. of	L
Brown (RI)	M	New Jersey, College of	M
▲ Bryn Mawr (PA)	S	New School U. (Lang)(NY)	S
Bucknell (PA)	M	Northwestern (IL)	M
Buffalo (SUNY) (NY)	L	Notre Dame (IN)	M
California, U. of (Berkeley)	XL	Oberlin (OH)	R
California, U. of (Los Angeles)	XL	Pennsylvania, U. of	L
Carleton (MN)	R	Pitzer (CA)	S
Centre (KY)	R	Pomona (CA)	R
Chicago, U. of (IL)	M	Princeton (NJ)	M
Claremont McKenna (CA)	R	Puget Sound, U. of (WA)	R
Colby (ME)	R	Reed (OR)	R
Colgate (NY)	R	Rhodes (TN)	R
Colorado College	R	Rice (TX)	R
Columbia (NY)	M	Richmond, U. of (VA)	R
Connecticut Col.	R	Rochester, U. of (NY)	M
Cornell (NY)	L	Rutgers (NJ)	L
Dallas, U. of (TX)	R	Sarah Lawrence (NY)	S
Dartmouth (NH)	M	Skidmore (NY)	R
Davidson (NC)	R	▲ Smith (MA)	R
DePauw (IN)	R	South, U. of the (TN)	R
Dickinson (PA)	R	Southwestern (TX)	R
Drew (NJ)	R	Stanford (CA)	M
Duke (NC)	M	St. Olaf (MN)	R
Emory (GA)	R	Swarthmore (PA)	R
Florida, U. of	XL	Trinity (CT)	R
Franklin & Marshall (PA)	R	Trinity (TX)	R
Geneseo (SUNY)(NY)	M	Tufts (MA)	M
Georgetown (DC)	M	Vanderbilt (TN)	M
Gettysburg (PA)	R	Vassar (NY)	R
Grinnell (IA)	R	Virginia, U. of	L
Gustavus Adolphus (MN)	R	■ Wabash (IN)	S
Hamilton (NY)	R	Wake Forest (NC)	M
Harvard (MA)	M	Washington & Lee (VA)	R
Haverford (PA)	S	Washington U. (MO)	M
Holy Cross (MA)	R	▲ Wellesley (MA)	R
Illinois, U. of	XL	Wesleyan (CT)	R
Illinois Wesleyan	R	Wheaton (IL)	R
Iowa, U. of	XL	Whitman (WA)	R
Kalamazoo (MI)	R	Willamette (OR)	R
Kenyon (OH)	R	Williams (MA)	R
Knox (IL)	R	Wisconsin, U. of	XL
Lafayette (PA)	R	Yale (CT)	M

ENGLISH, continued

GROUP II
Very Selective

▲Agnes Scott (GA) .... S
Alabama, U. of.................................. L
Albertson (ID)................................... S
Albion (MI)....................................... R
Alfred (NY) .... R
Arizona, U. of XL
Auburn (AL) L
Augustana (IL) .... R
Baylor (TX) .... M
Belmont (TN) .... R
Beloit (WI) .... R
Bennington (VT) .... S
Berea (KY) .... R
Bethany (WV) .... S
Birmingham-Southern (AL) .... R
Brigham Young (UT) XL
Bryn Athyn (PA) .... S
California, U. of (Davis) L
Cal Poly State U. (San Luis Obispo) L
Calvin (MI) .... M
Canisius (NY) .... M
Catholic (DC) .... M
Centenary (LA) .... S
Central (IA) .... R
Central Florida L
Central Michigan L
Chapman (CA) .... R
Cincinnati, U. of (OH) L
Clark (MA) .... R
Clemson (SC) L
Coe (IA) .... R
Colorado, U. of L
Cornell Col. (IA) .... R
Denison (OH) .... R
DePaul (IL) L
Denver, U. of (CO) .... M
Drury (MO) .... S
Earlham (IN) .... R
Eckerd (FL) .... R
Elizabethtown (PA) .... R
Emerson (MA) .... R
Florida State L
Franciscan U. of Steubenville (OH) ...... R
Fredonia (SUNY)(NY) .... M
Fordham (NY) L
George Mason (VA) L
Georgetown College (KY) .... R
Georgia, U. of XL
Gonzaga (WA) .... R
Gordon (MA) .... R

Goucher (MD) .... R
Grand Valley (MI) L
Grove City (PA) .... R
Guilford (NC) .... R
Hamline (MN) .... R
■ Hampton-Sydney (VA) .... S
Hanover (IN) .... R
Hendrix (AR) .... R
Hiram (OH) .... R
Hobart & Wm. Smith (NY) .... R
▲Hollins (VA) .... S
▲Hood (MD) .... S
Hunter (CUNY) (NY) L
Illinois, U. of (Chicago) L
John Carroll (OH) .... M
▲Judson (AL) .... S
Juniata (PA) .... R
Kansas State L
Kentucky, U. of L
Kentucky Wesleyan .... S
Lake Forest (IL) .... R
LaSalle (PA) .... M
LeMoyne (NY) .... R
Lewis & Clark (OR) .... R
Loras (IA) .... R
Loyola (LA) .... R
Lycoming (PA) .... R
Lyon (AR) .... S
Manhattanville (NY) .... R
Marietta (OH) .... R
Marquette (WI) .... M
Massachusetts, U. of L
Master's (CA) .... R
Messiah (PA) .... R
Michigan State XL
Millsaps (MS) .... S
Minnesota, U. of (Morris) .... R
Mississippi, U. of .... M
Mississippi U. for Women .... R
Missouri, U. of XL
Mount Mercy (IA) .... S
Muhlenberg (PA) .... R
Murray State (KY) .... M
Nazareth (NY) .... R
New Hampshire, U. of L
New Orleans (LA) L
New Paltz (SUNY)(NY) .... M
North Dakota, U. of.......................... M
Northeastern (MA) L

GROUP II continues next page

ENGLISH, continued

GROUP II, Continued

Oglethorpe (GA)	R	San Diego State (CA)	XL
Ohio State	XL	Santa Clara U. (CA)	M
Ohio U.	L	▲Scripps (CA)	S
Oklahoma City U.	R	Seattle Pacific (WA)	R
Oklahoma, U. of	L	Shepherd (WV)	R
Oneonta (SUNY)(NY)	M	South Carolina, U. of	L
Otterbein (OH)	R	Spring Hill (AL)	R
Pacific University (OR)	R	Stetson (FL)	R
Pittsburgh, U. of (PA)	L	Stony Brook (SUNY) (NY)	L
Portland State (OR)	M	Truman State (MO)	M
Presbyterian (SC)	S	Tulsa, U. of (OK)	R
Principia (IL)	S	Utah State	L
Providence (RI)	M	Virginia Poly. Institute	L
Purchase (SUNY) (NY)	R	Warren Wilson (NC)	S
Queens (NC)	S	Wartburg (IA)	R
Queens (CUNY)(NY)	L	Washington & Jefferson (PA)	R
Randolph-Macon (VA)	R	Washington State	L
▲Randolph-Macon Woman's Col. (VA)	S	▲Wells (NY)	S
Redlands, U. of (CA)	R	Western Michigan	L
Ripon (WI)	S	Western Washington U.	L
Roanoke (VA)	R	Westminster (MO)	S
Rollins (FL)	R	Westminster (UT)	R
Rutgers (Camden) NJ	M	Wheaton (MA)	R
St. Anselm (NH)	R	Whitworth (WA)	R
St. Bonaventure (NY)	R	William Jewell (MO)	R
St. Joseph's U. (PA)	R	Winona State U. (MN)	M
St. Lawrence (NY)	R	Winthrop (SC)	M
▲St. Mary's Col. (IN)	R	Wittenberg (OH)	R
St. Mary's College of Maryland	R	Wofford (SC)	S
St. Norbert (WI)	R	Wooster (OH)	R

GROUP III
Selective

Adrian (MI)	S	California State U. (Bakersfield)	M
Alabama, U. of (Birmingham)	M	California State U. (Channel Islands)	R
Appalachian State (NC)	L	California State U. (Fresno)	L
Aquinas (MI)	R	California State U. (Monterey Bay)	R
Arkansas, U. of	L	California State U. (Northridge)	L
Arcadia (PA)	R	California State U. (Sacramento)	M
Augsburg (MN)	R	Campbell (NC)	R
Augusta (GA)	M	Carson-Newman (TN)	R
Azusa Pacific (CA)	R	Charleston Southern (SC)	R
Baldwin-Wallace (OH)	R	Chestnut Hill (PA)	S
Bellarmine (KY)	R	Chowan (NC)	S
Brescia (KY)	S		
California (PA)	M		

GROUP III continues next page

Enrollment Code

■ Men Only
▲ Women Only

S = Small (less than 1000 students)   R = Moderate (1000-3000 students)   M = Medium (3000-8000 students)
L = Large (8000-20,000 students)   XL = Extra Large (over 20,000 students)

ENGLISH, continued

───── *GROUP III, Continued* ─────

Christopher Newport (VA) .... M	Montevallo (AL) .... R
Citadel, The (SC) .... R	Mount St. Joseph (OH) .... R
City College (CUNY)(NY) L	Niagara (NY) .... R
Daemen (NY) .... R	North Carolina, U. of (Wilmington) .... M
Dana (NB) .... S	Northeastern Illinois .... M
DeSales (PA) .... S	Northern Kentucky L
D'Youville (NY) .... R	Northern Michigan .... M
East Carolina L	Penn State (Erie)(PA) .... M
Eastern Illinois L	Pittsburgh, U. of (Greensburg) .... R
Eastern Michigan L	Point Park (PA) .... R
Eastern Nazarene (MA) .... R	Plymouth State (NH) .... M
Edinboro (PA) .... M	▲ Regis (MA) .... S
Eureka (IL) .... S	Rhode Island, U. of L
Fairleigh Dickinson (NJ) .... M	Robert Morris (PA) .... R
Florida A&M .... M	Rockford (IL) .... S
Florida Gulf Coast U. .... R	▲ Rosemont (PA) .... S
Fort Hays (KS) .... M	St. Mary (KS) .... S
Fort Lewis (CO) .... M	St. Mary's U. of San Antonio (TX) .... R
Georgia Southwestern .... R	St. Peter's (NJ) .... R
Goshen (IN) .... R	▲ Salem Col. (NC) .... S
Gwynedd-Mercy (PA) .... S	San Francisco State (CA) L
Howard (DC) .... M	Seattle U. (WA) .... R
Jamestown (ND) .... R	Slippery Rock (PA) .... M
Johnson State (VT) .... R	South Alabama .... M
Keene State (NH) .... R	Southeastern Louisiana L
Kennesaw State (GA) .... R	Southern Connecticut .... M
King (TN) .... S	▲ Spelman (GA) .... R
Illinois College .... S	Temple (PA) L
Long Island U. (Brooklyn)(NY) .... MR	Tennessee, U. of XL
Long Island U. (Southampton)(NY) ..... R	Utah, U. of L
Longwood (VA) .... R	Walsh (OH) .... R
Louisiana College .... R	Western Connecticut .... M
Louisiana-Lafayette L	Western Illinois L
Louisiana State XL	Western St. Coll. of Colorado .... R
Lyndon State (VT) .... R	Westfield (MA) .... M
Mansfield (PA) .... R	West Virginia Wesleyan .... R
Mass. Coll. of Lib. Arts (N. Adams) .... R	Wheeling Jesuit (WV) .... R
Massachusetts, U. of (Boston) .... M	Wichita State (KS) .... M
Memphis, U. of (TN) L	Whittier (CA) .... R
Mercyhurst (PA) .... R	Wilkes (PA) .... R
▲ Meredith (NC) .... R	William Paterson (NJ) .... M
Merrimack (MA) .... R	Wilmington (OH) .... S
Middle Tennessee L	Wisconsin, U. of (Eau Claire) L
Millersville (PA) .... M	Wisconsin, U. of (Milwaukee) .... R
Misericordia (PA) .... S	Wisconsin, U. of (Platteville) .... M
Montclair State (NJ) .... M	

Enrollment Code

■ **Men Only**   **S = Small** (less than 1000 students)   **R = Moderate** (1000-3000 students)   **M = Medium** (3000-8000 students)
▲ **Women Only**   **L = Large** (8000-20,000 students)   **XL = Extra Large** (over 20,000 students)

FOREIGN LANGUAGES

GROUP I
Most Selective

College	Code	College	Code
Albany (SUNY)(NY)	L	Kalamazoo (MI)	R
Allegheny (PA)	R	Lawrence (WI)	R
Bard (NY)	R	Michigan, U. of	XL
▲ Barnard (NY)	R	Middlebury (VT)	R
Binghamton (SUNY)(NY)	L	▲ Mt. Holyoke (MA)	R
Boston College (MA)	L	New York U.	M
Bowdoin (ME)	R	North Carolina, U. of	L
Brown (RI)	M	Pennsylvania, U. of	L
▲ Bryn Mawr (PA)	S	Pomona (CA)	R
California, U. of (Berkeley)	XL	Princeton (NJ)	M
California, U. of (Los Angeles)	XL	Rhodes (TN)	R
Carleton (MN)	R	Rochester, U. of (NY)	M
Chicago, U. of (IL)	M	Rutgers (NJ)	L
Colby (ME)	R	▲ Scripps (CA)	S
Columbia (NY)	M	Skidmore (NY)	R
Dallas, U. of	R	▲ Smith (MA)	R
Dartmouth (NH)	M	South, U. of the (TN)	R
DePauw (IN)	R	Southwestern (TX)	R
Dickinson (PA)	R	Trinity (TX)	R
Drew (NJ)	R	Tulane (LA)	M
Emory (GA)	R	Virginia, U. of	L
Florida, U. of	XL	Wake Forest (NC)	M
Georgetown (DC)	M	Washington & Lee (VA)	R
Grinnell (IA)	R	Washington U. (MO)	M
Gustavus Adolphus (MN)	R	▲ Wellesley (MA)	R
Harvard (MA)	M	Whitman (WA)	R
Haverford (PA)	S	William & Mary (VA)	M
Illinois, U. of (Urbana-Champaign)	XL	Yale (CT)	M

FOREIGN LANGUAGES continues next page

Enrollment Code

■ **Men Only**   **S = Small** (less than 1000 students)   **R = Moderate** (1000-3000 students)   **M = Medium** (3000-8000 students)
▲ **Women Only**   **L = Large** (8000-20,000 students)   **XL = Extra Large** (over 20,000 students)

FOREIGN LANGUAGES, cont.

GROUP II
Very Selective

▲Agnes Scott (GA) .... S
Alabama, U. of L
Beloit (WI) .... R
Brigham Young (UT) XL
California, U. of (Santa Barbara) L
Calvin (MI) .... M
Catholic (DC) .... M
Central (IA) .... R
Centre (KY) .... R
Clark (MA) .... R
Clemson (SC) L
Concordia (MN) .... R
Drake (IA) .... M
Earlham (IN) .... R
Eckerd (FL) .... R
Georgia, U. of XL
Grand Valley (MI) L
Gustavus Adolphus (MN) .... R
Hawaii, U. of L
Herbert Lehman (CUNY)(NY) .... M
▲Hollins (VA) .... S
Illinois College .... S
Illinois, U. of (Chicago) L
Indiana U. XL
Iowa, U. of XL
James Madison (VA) L
Kansas, U. of L
Lake Forest (IL) .... R
Lewis & Clark (OR) .... R
Linfield (OR) .... R

Lyon (AR) .... S
▲Mills (CA) .... S
Minnesota, U. of (Morris) .... R
Moravian (PA) .... R
Nazareth (NY) .... R
New Paltz (SUNY)(NY) .... M
North Carolina (Charlotte) L
Ohio State XL
Pacific University (OR) .... R
Pepperdine (CA) .... R
Pittsburgh, U. of (PA) L
Puerto Rico, U. of (Mayaguez) L
▲Rosemont (PA) .... S
St. Anselm (NH) .... R
South Carolina, U. of L
Stony Brook (SUNY)(NY) L
▲Sweet Briar (VA) .... S
Temple (PA) L
Texas, U. of (Austin) XL
▲Trinity (DC) .... S
Truman State (MO) .... M
Utah, U. of L
Valparaiso U. (IN) .... M
Vermont, U. of L
Virginia Commonwealth L
▲Wells (NY) .... S
West Chester (PA) .... M
Wheaton (MA) .... R
Wisconsin, U. of XL
Wofford (SC) .... R

GROUP III
Selective

Bethany (WV) .... S
California State U. (Sacramento) .... M
Carthage (WI) .... R
Emory & Henry (VA) .... S
Lewis-Clark State (ID) .... R
Mansfield (PA) .... R
Montana State L
New Mexico, U. of L

Slippery Rock (PA) .... M
South Alabama .... M
South Florida, U. of L
Southern Oregon State U. .... M
Wayne State (MI) L
Western Michigan L
Wisconsin, U. of (Milwaukee) L

FOREIGN LANGUAGES continues next page

Enrollment Code		
■ Men Only	**S = Small** (less than 1000 students)	**R = Moderate** (1000-3000 students)	**M = Medium** (3000-8000 students)
▲ Women Only	**L = Large** (8000-20,000 students)	**XL = Extra Large** (over 20,000 students)

FOREIGN LANGUAGES, cont.

Some Recommendations by Specific Departments
Compiled initially with the help of Minnesota's Jeff Sheehan, Secondary School Counselor

FRENCH

Arizona, U. of XL	▲Mount Holyoke (MA) .... R
California, U. of (Berkeley) XL	North Carolina, U. of............................ L
Central (IA) .... R	Northwestern (IL) .... M
Colby (ME) .... R	Princeton (NJ) .... M
Columbia (NY) .... M	Rhodes (TN) .... R
Dartmouth (NH) .... M	San Diego State U. (CA) L
Emory (GA) .... R	▲Scripps (CA) .... S
Georgetown (DC) .... M	Tufts (MA) .... M
Harvard (MA) .... M	Tulane (LA) .... M
Holy Cross (MA) .... M	Vassar (NY) .... R
Indiana U. XL	Washington U. (MO) .... M
Indiana (PA) L	▲Wellesley (MA) .... R
▲Mills (CA)... S	Wittenberg (OH)................................. R

GERMAN

Brown (RI) .... M	Penn State XL
California, U. of (Berkeley) XL	Pennsylvania, U. of............................. L
California, U. of (Santa Barbara) L	Princeton (NJ) .... M
Colorado, U. of L	Rhode Island., U. of L
Hunter (CUNY)(NY) L	Stanford (CA) .... M
Illinois, U. of (Urbana-Champaign) ... XL	Texas, U. of (Austin)........................... XL
Indiana U. XL	Williams (MA) .... R
Indiana (PA) L	Wisconsin, U. of................................. XL
Michigan State................................... XL	Wofford (SC) .... R

JAPANESE

Brigham Young (UT) XL	Pacific University (OR) .... R
Harvard (MA) .... M	Pennsylvania, U. of............................. L
Hawaii, U. of (Manoa) L	Pittsburgh, U. of (PA) L
Ohio State L	Washington, U. of XL
Oregon, U. of L	Wisconsin, U. of................................ XL

SPANISH

Bradley (IL) .... M	Maryland, U. of XL
Brigham Young (UT) XL	Massachusetts, U. of (Dartmouth) ...... M
Buffalo (SUNY) (NY) L	Messiah (PA) .... R
California State U. (San Marcos) .... M	Pittsburgh, U. of L
California, U. of (Irvine) .... M	Puerto Rico, U. of (Mayaguez)............. L
California, U. of (San Diego) L	Rutgers (NJ) L
California, U. of (Santa Barbara) L	San Diego State U. (CA) L
Central (IA) .... R	▲Scripps (CA) .... S
Colby (ME) .... R	Southern Connecticut......................... M
George Washington (DC).................... M	Texas, U. of XL
Greensboro College (NC).................... S	Utah, U. of L
Indiana U. XL	Vanderbilt (TN) .... M
Kansas, U. of L	Wisconsin, U. of................................ XL
Lyon (AR) .... S	Worcester State (MA) .... M

FORESTRY

GROUP I
Most Selective

Florida, U. of XL	North Carolina State L
Illinois, U. of XL	SUNY Coll. of Env. Sci. & Forestry .... R

GROUP II
Very Selective

Arizona, U. of XL	Montana State L
Auburn (AL) L	Oklahoma State L
Berry (GA) .... R	Pennsylvania State XL
Clemson (SC) L	Purdue (IN) XL
Colorado State L	South, U. of the (TN) .... R
Georgia, U. of L	Syracuse (NY) L
Iowa State XL	Tennessee, U. of XL
Maine, U. of .... M	Texas A&M XL
Michigan State XL	Virginia Poly. Inst. L
Michigan Tech .... M	Washington, U. of XL
Minnesota, U. of XL	West Virginia U. L
Mississippi State L	Wisconsin, U. of XL
Missouri, U. of XL	

GROUP III
Selective

Humboldt State (CA) .... M	Oregon State L
Idaho, U. of .... M	Southern Illinois (Carbondale) L
Montana, U. of .... M	Stephen F. Austin (TX) L
Northern Arizona XL	Utah State L

Enrollment Code

■ Men Only
▲ Women Only

S = Small (less than 1000 students) R = Moderate (1000-3000 students) M = Medium (3000-8000 students)
L = Large (8000-20,000 students) XL = Extra Large (over 20,000 students)

GEOGRAPHY

GROUP I
Most Selective

Buffalo (SUNY)(NY) L	George Washington (DC) .... M
California, U. of (Berkeley) XL	Johns Hopkins (MD) .... R
Chicago, U. of (IL) .... M	Macalester (MN) .... R
Clark (MA) .... R	Michigan, U. of XL
Colgate (NY) .... R	Middlebury (VT) .... R
Dartmouth (NH) .... M	Minnesota, U. of XL
Florida, U. of XL	Sarah Lawrence (NY) .... S

GROUP II
Very Selective

Arizona State XL	Ohio State XL
Bemidji State (MN) .... M	Oklahoma, U. of L
California, U. of (Santa Barbara) L	Oklahoma State L
Colorado, U. of L	Oregon, U. of L
Colorado, U. of (Colorado Springs) ..... M	Oneonta (SUNY)(NY) .... M
Denver, U. of (CO) .... M	Pennsylvania State XL
Florida International L	Radford (VA) .... M
Georgia, U. of L	San Diego State U. (CA) L
Hunter (CUNY)(NY) L	South Carolina, U. of L
Indiana U. XL	Texas, U. of (Austin) XL
Kansas, U. of L	Vermont, U. of L
Louisiana State XL	Virginia Poly. Institute L
Mary Washington (VA) .... R	Western Washington U. L
Michigan State XL	Wisconsin, U. of (Madison) XL
New Paltz (SUNY)(NY) .... M	Wittenberg (OH) .... R

GROUP III
Selective

Ball State (IN) .... M	Keene State (NH) .... R
Bloomsburg (PA) .... M	Maine (Farmington) .... R
Bridgewater (MA) .... M	Mansfield (PA) .... R
California State U. (Chico) L	Massachusetts, U. of (Boston) .... M
California State U. (Long Beach) L	New Orleans (LA) L
California State U. (Northridge) L	North Carolina (Charlotte) L
California State U. (Stanislaus) .... M	Salem State (MA) .... M
Carthage (WI) .... R	Sonoma State (CA) .... M
Central Connecticut .... M	Southern Connecticut .... M
Central Michigan L	Southern Illinois U. (Carbondale) L
Edinboro (PA) .... M	Western Illinois L
Frostburg (MD) .... M	Wisconsin, U. of (LaCrosse) L
++Indiana (PA) L	Wyoming, U. of L
Indiana State L	

++ *Especially Regional Planning*

GEOLOGY

GROUP I
Most Selective

Amherst (MA) .... R	Geneseo (SUNY) (NY) .... M
▲ Barnard (NY) .... R	Gustavus Adolphus (MN)..................... R
Bates (ME) .... R	Harvard (MA) .... M
Binghamton (SUNY)(NY) L	Lafayette (PA) .... R
Bowdoin (ME) .... R	Lehigh (PA) .... M
Brown (RI) .... M	MIT (MA).. M
▲ Bryn Mawr (PA) .... R	Pennsylvania, U. of L
California Inst. of Tech. .... S	Pomona (CA) .... R
California, U. of (Berkeley) XL	Princeton (NJ) .... M
Carleton (MN) .... R	Rennselaer (NY) .... M
Chicago, U. of (IL)............................ M	Rochester, U. of (NY) .... M
Colgate (NY) .... R	Skidmore (NY) .... R
Colorado Col. .... R	▲ Smith (MA) .... R
Colorado School of Mines .... R	Vanderbilt (TN) .... M
Columbia (NY) .... M	Washington & Lee (VA) .... R
Dartmouth (NH) .... M	Washington U. (MO) .... M
Franklin & Marshall (PA) .... R	Whitman (WA) .... R
Furman (SC) .... R	William & Mary (VA) .... M

GROUP II
Very Selective

Albany (SUNY) (NY) L	Millsaps (MS) .... S
Alabama, U. of.................................. L	Minnesota, U. of XL
Allegheny (PA) .... R	Minnesota, U. of (Duluth) .... M
Arizona State XL	Minnesota, U. of (Morris) .... R
Arizona, U. of XL	New Hampshire, U. of L
Beloit (WI) .... R	New Mexico Inst. of Mining & Tech. .... S
Bowling Green (OH) L	New Mexico, U. of L
Brigham Young (UT) XL	Oklahoma, U. of L
California, U. of (Davis) L	Oklahoma State L
California, U. of (Santa Barbara) L	Purdue (IN)..................................... XL
Centenary College (LA) .... S	St. Lawrence (NY) .... R
College of Charleston (SC) L	St. Thomas (MN) .... M
Colorado State L	San Diego State (CA).......................... L
Colorado, U. of L	South Carolina, U. of L
Cornell Col. (IA) .... R	South Dakota School of Mines .... R
Dayton, U. of (OH) .... M	Stony Brook (SUNY) (NY) L
Denison (OH) .... R	Texas A&M XL
Denver, U. of (CO) .... M	Texas Christian .... M
Earlham (IN) .... R	Texas, U. of (Austin) XL
Guilford (NC).................................... R	Tulsa, U. of (OK) .... M
Hanover (IN) .... R	Vermont, U. of .... M
Hope (MI) .... R	Washington, U. of............................ XL
Idaho, U. of .... M	Wisconsin, U. of............................... XL
Indiana U. XL	Wooster, College of (OH).................... R
Juniata (PA) .... R	
Michigan Tech .... M	

GEOLOGY continues next page

Enrollment Code		
■ **Men Only** **S = Small** (less than 1000 students)	**R = Moderate** (1000-3000 students)	**M = Medium** (3000-8000 students)
▲ **Women Only** **L = Large** (8000-20,000 students)	**XL = Extra Large** (over 20,000 students)	

GEOLOGY, continued

Bloomsburg (PA)	M	Louisiana State	XL
Brockport (SUNY)(NY)	M	Muskingum (OH)	R
Brooklyn College (CUNY) (NY)	L	North Carolina (Wilmington)	M
California State U. (Bakersfield)	M	Northland (WI)	S
California State U. (Chico)	L	Northern Illinois U	L
California State U. (Hayward)	M	Oneonta (SUNY)(NY)	M
California State U. (Sacramento)	M	Plattsburgh (SUNY)(NY)	M
Edinboro (PA)	M	West Chester (PA)	M
Fort Lewis (CO)	M	Western State Coll. of Colorado	R
Hartwick (NY)	R	Wright State (OH)	L
Lamar (TX)	M	Wyoming, U. of	L
Louisiana-Lafayette	L		

HISTORY

GROUP I
Most Selective

Albertson (ID) .... S	Lafayette (PA) .... R
Albion (MI) .... R	Lawrence (WI) .... R
American (DC) .... M	Lehigh (PA) .... M
Amherst (MA) .... R	Macalester (MN) .... R
▲ Barnard (NY) .... R	Miami, U. of L
Bates (ME) .... R	Michigan, U. of XL
Binghamton (SUNY)(NY) L	Middlebury (VT) .... R
Boston Col. (MA) L	Missouri, U. of (Rolla) .... M
Boston U. (MA) L	▲ Mount Holyoke (MA) .... R
Bowdoin (ME) .... R	North Carolina, U. of L
Brandeis (MA) .... R	Northwestern (IL) .... M
Brown (RI) .... M	Notre Dame (IN) .... M
▲ Bryn Mawr (PA) .... S	Oberlin (OH) .... R
Bucknell (PA) .... M	Pennsylvania, U. of L
Buffalo (SUNY)(NY) L	Pitzer (CA) .... S
California, U. of (Berkeley) XL	Pomona (CA) .... R
California, U. of (Los Angeles) XL	Princeton (NJ) .... M
Carleton (MN) .... R	Reed (OR) .... R
Case Western (OH) .... R	Rhodes (TN) .... R
Centre (KY) .... R	Rice (TX) .... R
Chicago, U. of (IL) .... M	Richmond, U. of (VA) .... R
Claremont McKenna (CA) .... R	Rutgers (NJ) L
Colgate (NY) .... R	▲ Smith (MA) .... R
Colorado Col. .... R	South, U. of the (TN) .... R
Columbia (NY) .... M	Southwestern (TX) .... R
Connecticut Col. .... R	Swarthmore (PA) .... R
Cornell (NY) L	Texas Christian U. (TX) .... M
Dallas, U. of (TX) .... R	Trinity (TX) .... R
Dartmouth (NH) .... M	Tufts (MA) .... M
Davidson (NC) .... R	Tulane (LA) .... M
Dickinson (PA) .... R	Union (NY) .... R
Drew (NJ) .... R	U.S. Military Academy (NY) .... M
Duke (NC) .... M	Vanderbilt (TN) .... R
Emory (GA) .... R	Vassar (NY) .... R
Florida, U. of XL	Virginia, U. of L
Furman (SC) .... R	■ Wabash (IN) .... S
George Washington (DC) .... M	Wake Forest (NC) .... M
Georgetown (DC) .... M	Washington & Lee (VA) .... R
Georgia Institute of Tech. L	▲ Wellesley (MA) .... R
Gettysburg (PA) .... R	Wesleyan U. (CT) .... R
Grinnell (IA) .... R	Wheaton (IL) .... R
Hamilton (NY) .... R	Whitman (WA) .... R
Harvard (MA) .... M	William & Mary (VA) .... M
Haverford (PA) .... S	Williams (MA) .... R
Holy Cross (MA) .... R	Yale (CT) .... M
Illinois, U. of (Urbana-Champaign) ... XL	Yeshiva (NY) .... R
Kalamazoo (MI) .... R	
Kenyon (OH) .... R	

HISTORY continues next page

HISTORY, continued

GROUP II
Very Selective

▲ Agnes Scott (GA)	S	
Albion (MI)	R	
Alfred (NY)	R	
Allegheny (PA)	R	
Alma (MI)	R	
Austin (TX)	R	
Baylor (TX)	M	
Birmingham-Southern (AL)	R	
Bryn Athyn (PA)	S	
California, U. of (Davis)	L	
California, U. of (Riverside)	L	
Calvin (MI)	M	
Canisius (NY)	M	
Christendom (VA)	S	
City College (CUNY)(NY)	L	
Coe (IA)	R	
Colorado U. of	L	
Connecticut U. of	L	
Cornell College (IA)	R	
Covenant (GA)	S	
Denison (OH)	R	
Denver, U. of (CO)	M	
East Carolina	L	
Eastern Michigan	L	
Elmira (NY)	R	
Erskine (SC)	S	
Florida Atlantic	L	
Florida State	L	
Georgetown College (KY)	R	
Georgia, U. of	L	
Gonzaga (WA)	R	
Goucher (MD)	S	
Guilford (NC)	R	
■ Hampden-Sydney (VA)	S	
Hanover (IN)	R	
Hillsdale (MI)	R	
Hiram (OH)	R	
Hobart & William Smith (NY)	R	
▲ Hollins (VA)	S	
Hood (MD)	S	
Illinois College	S	
Illinois, U. of (Chicago)	L	
Indiana U.	XL	
Juniata (PA)	R	
Kansas, U. of	L	
Kentucky, U. of	L	
Kentucky Wesleyan	S	
Knox (IL)	R	

Lake Forest (IL)	R
Loras (IA)	R
Loyola (LA)	R
Manhattanville (NY)	R
Marquette (WI)	M
Maryland, U. of	XL
+ Mary Washington (VA)	R
Massachusetts, U. of	L
Miami, U. of (FL)	M
Michigan State	XL
Millersville (PA)	M
Millsaps (MS)	S
Minnesota, U. of (Morris)	R
Missouri, U. of	XL
■ Morehouse (GA)	R
Muhlenberg (PA)	R
North Carolina (Asheville)	R
Northeastern (MA)	L
Ohio State	XL
Ohio U.	L
Oklahoma, U. of	L
Pittsburgh, U. of (PA)	L
Portland, U. of (OR)	R
Providence (RI)	M
Queens (NC)	S
Ripon (WI)	S
Roanoke (VA)	R
▲ Rosemont (PA)	S
Rowan (NJ)	M
Rutgers (Camden) (NJ)	M
St. Joseph's (PA)	R
St. John's/ St. Benedict (MN)	R
St. Mary's College of Maryland	R
St. Norbert (WI)	R
San Diego State U. (CA)	XL
Santa Clara U. (CA)	M
Shepherd (WV)	M
South Carolina, U. of	L
Spring Hill (AL)	R
Stetson (FL)	R
Stony Brook (SUNY)(NY)	L
Tennessee, U. of	XL
Texas Tech U.	L
Texas, U. of (Austin)	XL
Texas, U. of (Dallas)	M

+ And Historic Preservation Major

HISTORY continues next page

HISTORY, continued

GROUP II, *Continued*

Trinity (CT) .... R	Westminster (MO) .... S
Vermont, U. of L	Westminster (UT) .... S
Virginia Poly Inst. L	Wheaton (MA) .... R
Virginia Military Institute .... R	Willamette (OR) .... R
Warren Wilson (NC) .... S	William Paterson (NJ) .... M
Wartburg (IA) .... R	Winthrop (SC) .... M
Washington College (MD) .... S	Wisconsin, U. of XL
Washington, U. of XL	Wittenberg (OH) .... R
Washington & Jefferson (PA) .... R	Wofford (SC) .... R
▲Wells (NY) .... S	Wooster (OH) .... R
Western Michigan L	Xavier (OH) .... R

GROUP III
Selective

Akron, U. of (OH) L	Massachusetts U. of (Boston) .... M
Alabama, U. of L	Middle Tennessee L
Appalachian State (NC) L	Milligan (TN) .... S
Baldwin-Wallace (OH) .... R	Misericordia (PA) .... S
Bellarmine (KY) .... R	Murray State (KY) .... M
Bridgewater (MA) .... M	Muskingum (OH) .... R
Bridgewater (VA) .... R	Nevada, U. of (Las Vegas) .... M
Brockport (SUNY)(NY) .... M	New Mexico, U. of L
California State U. (Fullerton) L	Northern Colorado L
California State U. (Hayward) .... M	Northwestern (IA) .... S
California State U. (Long Beach) L	Northwestern Louisiana L
California State U. (San Marcos) .... M	Quincy (IL) .... R
Campbell (NC) .... R	Ramapo (NJ) .... M
Capital U. (OH) .... R	Regis (CO) .... R
Carroll (MT) .... R	Rhode Island College .... M
Carson-Newman (TN) .... R	St. Joseph's (NY) .... R
Central Connecticut .... M	St. Mary's (MN) .... R
Charleston, U. of (WV) .... S	Salem State (MA) .... M
Cumberland (KY) .... R	Southern Illinois U. (Carbondale) L
Delaware State .... R	Southern Mississippi L
East Tennessee L	Toledo, U. of L
Eastern Connecticut .... M	Western St. Col. of Colorado .... R
Fairmont State (WV) .... M	West Kentucky L
Fredonia (SUNY)(NY) .... M	West Virginia Wesleyan .... R
Georgia Southern L	Wheeling Jesuit (WV) .... R
Heidelberg (OH) .... S	Wilkes (PA) .... R
Indiana (PA) L	Wilmington (OH) .... S
Kennesaw State (GA) .... R	Wingate (NC) .... R
Lambuth (TN) .... S	Wisconsin, U. of (Green Bay) .... M
Louisiana State XL	Wisconsin, U. of (Milwaukee) L
▲Mary Baldwin (VA) .... S	

HOME ECONOMICS/FAMILY STUDIES

GROUP I
Most Selective

Florida State L
Iowa state XL

Wisconsin, U. of XL

GROUP II
Very Selective

\# Bradley (IL) .... M
Connecticut, U. of............................. L
Georgia, U. of XL
➤ Kansas State L
Michigan State.................................. XL
Northern Illinois U............................. L

Oneonta (SUNY) (NY) .... M
π Seattle Pacific (WA) .... M
Utah State L
Western Michigan.............................. L
Wisconsin, U. of (Stout) .... M

\# *Family & Consumer Science*
π *Apparel Design, also Clothing*
➤ *Nutritional & Exercise Sciences*

GROUP III
Selective

Akron, U. of (OH)............................. L
Berea (KY) .... R
California State U. (Fresno) L
California State U. (Sacramento) .... M
Central Michigan L
Eastern Illinois L
Framingham State (MA) .... M
Georgia Southern L

Marywood (PA)................................. R
Montclair State (NJ) .... M
Montevallo (AL) .... R
Oregon State..................................... L
Point Loma (CA)................................ R
Texas Tech. U. L
Washington State.............................. L

JOURNALISM/COMMUNICATIONS

GROUP I
Most Selective

American U. (DC) .... M
Boston U. (MA) L
California, U. of (Los Angeles) XL
California, U. of (San Diego) L
Creighton (NE) .... R
DePauw (IN) .... R
Florida, U. of XL
Gettysburg (PA) .... R
Illinois, U. of (Urbana-Champaign) ... XL
Macalester (MN) .... R
Miami, U. of (FL) L
Michigan, U. of XL
New York U L

North Carolina, U. of......................... L
Northwestern (IL) .... M
Ohio U. L
Southern California L
Southwestern (TX)............................ R
Stanford (CA) .... M
Syracuse (NY).................................. L
Trinity (TX) .... R
Villanova (PA) .... M
Washington & Lee (VA) .... R
Wheaton (IL) .... R
Wisconsin, U. of............................... XL

GROUP II
Very Selective

Alabama, U. of L
Alabama, U. of (Huntsville) .... M
Arizona State XL
Arizona, U. of XL
Asbury (KY)..................................... R
Auburn (AL) L
California Poly. State U. (SLO) L
Canisius (NY) .... M
Central Florida, U. of L
Chapman (CA) .... R
Charleston, College of (SC)................ L
Clark (MA) .... R
Colorado, U. of L
Columbia College (IL)....................... M
Delaware, U. of L
Denver, U. of (CO) .... M
DePaul (IL) L
Drake (IA)....................................... M
Dubuque, U. of (IA) .... S
Duquesne (PA) .... M
Fairfield (CT) .... M
Flagler (FL) .... R
Florida Inst. of Tech. .... R
Fordham (NY) .... M
Fredonia (SUNY) (NY) .... M

Geneva (PA) .... R
Georgetown College (KY) .... R
Georgia State L
Georgia, U. of XL
Gonzaga (WA) .... R
Hanover (IN).................................... R
Hastings (NE) .... S
Houston, U. of (TX) L
Illinois College .... S
Indiana State L
Indiana U. XL
Indiana U. of Pennsylvania L
Iowa, U. of XL
Ithaca (NY) .... M
James Madison (VA) .... M
John Carroll (OH) .... M
Juniata (PA) .... R
Kansas, U. of L
Kansas State L
Kentucky, U. of L
LeMoyne (NY).................................. R
Linfield (OR) .... R
Loras (IA) .... R
Louisiana State XL

GROUP II continues next page

Enrollment Code
■ Men Only ▲ Women Only | S = Small (less than 1000 students) R = Moderate (1000-3000 students) M = Medium (3000-8000 students) L = Large (8000-20,000 students) XL = Extra Large (over 20,000 students)

JOURNALISM/COMMUNICATIONS, cont.

GROUP II, *Continued*

Loyola (MD) .... R	St. Bonaventure (NY) .... R
Loyola Marymount (CA) .... M	St. Cloud (MN) L
Mansfield (PA) .... M	St. Louis (MO) .... M
Marist (NY) .... M	St. Mary's (IN) .... R
π Marquette (WI) .... M	St. Michael's (VT) .... R
Marshall (WV) .... M	St. Norbert (WI) .... R
Mary Baldwin (VA) .... S	St. Thomas (MN) .... M
Maryland, U. of XL	San Diego State U. (CA) XL
Massachusetts, U. of L	Santa Clara U. (CA) .... M
Master's (CA) .... R	Scranton, U. of (PA) .... M
Memphis, U. of (TN) L	▲Simmons (MA) .... R
Michigan State L	South Alabama .... M
Milligan (TN) .... S	South Carolina, U. of L
▲Mills College (CA) .... S	Southern Illinois U. (Carbondale)........ L
Minnesota, U. of XL	Southern Methodist (TX) .... M
Minnesota, U. of (Duluth) .... M	Spring Hill (AL)...................................... R
Mississippi, U. of .... M	▲Stephens (MO) .... S
Missouri, U. of XL	Suffolk (MA) .... R
Montana, U. of .... M	Susquehanna U. (PA) .... R
Moravian (PA) .... R	Temple (PA) L
Muhlenberg (PA) .... R	Texas A&M (Galveston)........................ S
Nevada, U. of (Reno) .... M	Texas Christian U. .... M
New Hampshire, U. of L	Texas, U. of (Arlington) L
North Central (IL) .... R	Texas, U. of (Austin)............................ XL
North Florida .... M	Tulsa, U. of (OK) .... R
North Texas.. L	Wartburg (IA) .... R
Ohio Wesleyan...................................... R	Washington State L
Oklahoma, U. of L	West Virginia U. L
Oregon, U. of L	Western Michigan.................................. L
Oswego (SUNY)(NY) .... M	Western Washington U. L
Pepperdine (CA) .... R	Westminster (UT) .... R
Pittsburgh, U. of (PA) L	Whitworth (WA) .... R
Plattsburgh (SUNY)(NY) .... M	William Paterson (NJ) .... M
Purchase (SUNY)(NY)............................ R	Winona State U. (MN) L
Quinnipiac (CT) .... R	Wisconsin Lutheran .... S
▲Randolph-Macon Woman's Col. (VA)..... S	Wisconsin, U. of (Stevens Point)........ M
Rowan (NJ) .... M	Xavier (OH) .... R
St. Ambrose (IA) .... R	York (PA) .... R

π *Especially Broadcasting*

JOURNALISM/COMMUNICATIONS **continues next page**

Enrollment Code		
■ **Men Only**	**S = Small** (less than 1000 students)	**R = Moderate** (1000-3000 students)	**M = Medium** (3000-8000 students)
▲ **Women Only**	**L = Large** (8000-20,000 students)	**XL = Extra Large** (over 20,000 students)	

JOURNALISM/COMMUNICATIONS, cont.

GROUP III
Selective

Appalachian State (NC) L	Missouri, U. of (St. Louis) .... M
Arkansas, U. of L	Monmouth (NJ) .... R
Augsburg (MN) .... R	Montana, U. of .... M
+ Azusa Pacific (CA) .... R	Morningside (IA) .... S
Ball State (IN) L	Montevallo (AL) .... R
Bemidji State (MN) .... M	Muskingum (OH) .... R
Bethany (WV) .... S	Murray State (KY) .... M
Bridgewater State (WA) .... M	Nebraska, U. of L
Brockport (SUNY) (NY) .... M	North Carolina, U. of (Greensboro) ..... M
Buena Vista (IA) .... R	North Carolina, U. of (Pembroke) .... R
Butler (IN) .... R	North Dakota, U. of .... M
California Lutheran .... R	Northern Illinois U. L
California State U. (Fullerton) L	Northern Kentucky L
California State U. (Long Beach) L	Oakland U. (MI) .... M
California State U. (Northridge) L	Oklahoma City U. .... R
California State U. (Sacramento) .... M	Otterbein (OH) .... R
California State U. (San Bernardino) .. M	▲ Pine Manor (MA) .... S
▲ Chatham (PA) .... S	Regis (CO) .... R
Eastern Connecticut .... M	▲ Regis (MA) .... S
Eastern Kentucky L	Reinhardt (GA) .... S
Elon (NC) .... R	Rider (NJ) .... R
Fitchburg (MA) .... R	Robert Morris (PA) .... R
Florida A&M .... M	Roger Williams (RI) .... R
Florida Southern .... R	St. Edward's (TX) .... M
Fontbonne (MO) .... R	St. John Fisher (NY) .... R
Franklin (IN) .... S	St. Mary's College (MN) .... R
Gwynedd-Mercy (PA) .... S	Samford (AL) .... R
Hardin-Simmons (TX) .... R	San Jose State (CA) L
Hawaii Pacific .... M	Santa Fe, College of (NM) .... S
Hofstra (NY) .... M	Seton Hall (NJ) .... M
Howard (DC) .... M	Southeastern Louisiana L
Hunter (CUNY) (NY) L	Southern Connecticut......................... M
Idaho, U. of .... M	Southern Maine .... M
Jacksonville (FL) .... R	Tampa, U. of (FL) .... R
Johnson C. Smith (NC) .... R	Texas Wesleyan .... R
▲ Judson (AL) .... S	Towson (MD) L
Keene State (NH) .... R	Virginia Wesleyan.............................. R
Kent State (OH) L	Weber State (UT)............................... L
Kentucky Wesleyan .... S	West Chester (PA) .... M
Loyola (IL)....................................... M	Western Illinois L
Loyola U. (LA) .... M	Wichita State (KS) .... M
Lynchburg (VA) .... R	Wingate (NC) .... R
• Lyndon State (VT) .... R	Wisconsin, U. of (LaCrosse) L
Massachusetts Col. of Lib. Arts (N. Adams) R	Worcester State (MA) .... M
Minnesota, U. of (Duluth) .... M	
Misericordia, College (PA) .... S	

+ *Media Studies*

• *Also Broadcasting, also Television Studies*

MATHEMATICS

Albany (SUNY)(NY) L	▲ Mount Holyoke (MA) .... R
American U. (DC) .... M	New College (FL) .... S
▲ Barnard (NY) .... R	New Jersey, College of .... M
Bates (ME) .... R	New York U. L
Binghamton (SUNY) (NY) L	Northwestern (IL) .... M
Boston U. (MA) L	Oberlin (OH) .... R
Bowdoin (ME) .... R	Occidental (CA) .... R
Brandeis (MA) .... R	Pennsylvania, U. of L
Bucknell (PA) .... M	Pomona (CA) .... R
Buffalo (SUNY)(NY) L	Princeton (NJ) .... M
California Inst. of Tech. .... S	Reed (OR) .... R
California, U. of (Berkeley) XL	Rensselaer (NY) .... M
California, U. of (Los Angeles) XL	Rice (TX) .... R
California, U. of (San Diego) L	Rose-Hulman (IN) .... R
Carleton (MN) .... R	Stanford (CA) .... M
Case Western Reserve U. (OH) .... R	St. Mary's Col. of Maryland .... R
Chicago, U. of (IL) .... M	St. Olaf (MN) .... R
Colgate (NY) .... R	Trinity (CT) .... R
Colorado School of Mines .... R	Tulane (LA) .... M
Columbia (NY) .... M	Union (NY) .... R
Dartmouth (NH) .... M	United States Air Force Academy (CO).. M
Davidson (NC) .... R	Villanova (PA) .... M
Dickinson (PA) .... R	■ Wabash (IN) .... S
Duke (NC) .... M	Wake Forest (NC) .... M
Florida, U. of XL	Washington & Lee (VA) .... R
Georgia Inst. of Tech. L	Washington U. (MO) .... M
Harvard (MA) .... M	▲ Wellesley (MA) .... R
Harvey Mudd (CA) .... S	Wesleyan (CT) .... R
Holy Cross (MA) .... R	Wheaton (IL) .... R
Illinois Inst. of Tech. .... R	Whitman (WA) .... R
Illinois, U. of (Urbana-Champaign) ... XL	Willamette (OR) .... R
Kenyon (OH) .... R	Wisconsin, U. of XL
Michigan, U. of XL	Worcester Poly Inst. (MA) .... R
MIT (MA) .... M	Yale (CT) .... M

MATHEMATICS continues next page

MATHEMATICS, continued

GROUP II
Very Selective

Alabama, U. of (Huntsville)	M	Millsaps (MS)	S
Albion (MI)	R	Muhlenberg (PA)	R
Arizona State	XL	New Mexico State	L
Bellarmine (KY)	R	Newman U. (KS)	S
Birmingham-Southern (AL)	R	North Carolina State	L
Bryant (RI)	R	Ohio State	XL
California, U. of (Irvine)	L	Ohio U.	L
California, U. of (Riverside)	M	Oregon, U. of	L
California, U. of (Santa Cruz)	M	Otterbein (OH)	R
Cincinnati, U. of (OH)	L	Potsdam (SUNY) (NY)	R
College of Charleston (SC)	L	Puerto Rico, U. of (Mayaguez)	L
Colorado, U. of	L	Rochester Inst. of Tech.	L
Concordia (MN)	R	Rockhurst (MO)	R
DePaul (IL)	L	▲Simmons (MA)	R
Earlham (IN)	R	South Dakota School of Mines	R
Fairfield (CT)	M	Southern California, U. of	L
Florida Atlantic	L	Southwest Missouri	L
George Mason (VA)	L	Stetson (FL)	R
Hendrix (AR)	R	▲Sweet Briar (VA)	S
Hiram (OH)	R	Texas, U. of (Austin)	XL
Illinois College	S	▲Trinity (DC)	S
Illinois, U. of (Chicago)	L	Valparaiso (IN)	M
Kansas State	L	Vassar (NY)	R
Knox (IL)	R	Virginia Poly. Institute	L
LaSalle (PA)	M	Washington, U. of	XL
Lebanon Valley (PA)	R	Wheaton (MA)	R
Lyon (AR)	S	Winthrop (SC)	M
Massachusetts, U. of (Lowell)	M	Wisconsin Lutheran	S
Michigan State	XL	Wofford (SC)	R
Michigan, U. of (Dearborn)	M	Wooster (OH)	R

GROUP III
Selective

Ball State (IN)	L	Malone (OH)	R
Bloomsburg (PA)	M	Mount St. Joseph (OH)	R
Bluffton (OH)	S	Murray State (KY)	M
California State U. (Dominguez Hills)	M	Northern Michigan	M
California State U. (Monterey Bay)	R	Ozarks, College of the (MO)	R
California State U. (San Jose)	L	Penn State (Erie)(PA)	M
Christopher Newport (VA)	M	St. Joseph's (NY)	R
Clark Atlanta (GA)	M	Simpson (IA)	S
Colorado, U. of (Denver)	M	Southern Polytechnic (GA)	R
East Carolina	L	Southwest Texas State	L
Eastern Connecticut	M	Texas Tech. U.	L
Fisk (TN)	S	Weber State (UT)	L
Fontbonne (MO)	R	Wheeling Jesuit (WV)	R
Georgia State	L	Wilkes (PA)	R
Louisiana-Lafayette	L	Wisconsin, U. of (Eau Claire)	L
Louisiana State	XL	Wisconsin, U. of (Stevens Point)	M
Lynchburg (VA)	R		

MUSIC

GROUP I
Most Selective

▲ Barnard (NY) .... R
Beloit (WI) .... R
Binghamton (SUNY)(NY) L
Boston College (MA) L
Boston U. (MA) L
Bowdoin (ME) .... R
Brandeis (MA) .... R
Bucknell (PA) .... R
Buffalo (SUNY)(NY) L
California, U. of (Berkeley) XL
California, U. of (Los Angeles) XL
California, U. of (San Diego) L
Carnegie-Mellon (PA) .... M
Case Western Reserve U. (OH) .... R
Chicago, U. of (IL) .... M
Cleveland Inst. of Music (OH) .... S
Columbia (NY) .... M
Connecticut College .... R
π DePauw (IN) .... R
Florida, U. of XL
Furman (SC) .... R
Geneseo (SUNY) (NY) .... M
Gustavus Adolphus (MN) .... R
Harvard (MA) .... M
Illinois, U. of (Urbana-Champaign) ... XL
Illinois Wesleyan .... R
Indiana U. XL
Iowa, U. of XL
Johns Hopkins (MD) .... M
Juilliard (NY) .... S

Kenyon (OH) .... R
Lawrence (WI) .... R
Miami, U. of (FL) L
Miami U. (OH) L
Michigan, U. of XL
New York U. L
Northwestern (IL) .... M
Oberlin (OH) .... R
Pomona (CA) .... R
Princeton (NJ) .... M
Rhodes (TN) .... R
Rice (TX) .... R
Rochester, U. of (NY) .... M
Rutgers (NJ) L
Skidmore (NY) .... R
▲ Smith (MA) .... R
Southern California, U. of L
Southwestern (TX) .... R
Stanford (CA) .... M
St. Mary's College of Maryland............ R
St. Olaf (MN)...................................... R
Texas, U. of (Austin)......................... XL
Vanderbilt (TN) .... M
Vassar (NY) .... R
Virginia, U. of.................................... L
Wheaton (IL) .... R
Whitman (WA) .... R
Willamette (OR) .... R
Wisconsin, U. of................................. XL
Yale (CT) .... M

π Music and Music Business

MUSIC continues next page

MUSIC, continued

GROUP II
Very Selective

Alabama, U. of	L
Alaska Pacific	S
Albertson (ID)	S
Arizona State	XL
Asbury (KY)	R
Augustana (IL)	R
Augustana (SD)	M
Bard (NY)	R
Berklee College of Music (MA)	R
Birmingham-Southern (AL)	R
Boston Conservatory	S
Bryan (TN)	S
Butler (IN)	R
Cal. Inst. of the Arts	S
California, U. of (Riverside)	M
California, U. of (Santa Barbara)	L
California, U. of (Santa Cruz)	M
Capital (OH)	R
Catholic U. (DC)	M
Centenary (LA)	S
Central Florida	L
Chapman (CA)	R
Cincinnati, U. of	L
Clark (MA)	R
Clarke (IA)	S
Coe (IA)	R
Colorado, U. of	L
Concordia (CA)	R
Concordia (MN)	R
▲ Converse (SC)	S
Cornish (WA)	S
Covenant (GA)	S
Creighton (NE)	R
Curtis Institute of Music (PA)	S
Denison (OH)	R
Denver, U. of	R
DePaul (IL)	L
Drake (IA)	M
Drury (MO)	S
Florida State	L
Florida Southern	R
π Fredonia (SUNY) (NY)	M
Georgia State	L
Georgia, U. of	L
Gordon (MA)	R
Harding (AR)	M
Hiram (OH)	R
Hofstra (NY)	M
Hope (MI)	R
Houghton (NY)	S
Houston, U. of (TX)	L
Illinois, U. of (Chicago)	L

Ithaca (NY)	M
James Madison (VA)	L
▲ Judson (AL)	S
Kentucky, U. of	L
Lake Forest (IL)	R
Lebanon Valley (PA)	R
Louisiana State	XL
Loyola (IL)	M
Luther (IA)	R
Maine, U. of	M
Manhattanville (NY)	R
Manhattan School of Music (NY)	S
Maryland, U. of	XL
Maryville (TN)	S
McDaniel (MD)	R
Mercer (GA)	R
Michigan State	XL
Milliken (IL)	R
▲ Mills (CA)	S
Millsaps (MS)	S
Missouri, U. of (Kansas City)	M
Mobile, U. of (AL)	R
Moravian (PA)	R
Murray State (KY)	M
Nebraska, U. of	L
New England Conservatory (MA)	S
New Hampshire, U. of	L
North Carolina School of the Arts	S
North Florida	M
North Texas	L
Ohio State	XL
Ohio U.	L
π Oklahoma City U.	R
π Oneonta (SUNY)(NY)	M
Oregon, U. of	L
Pacific Lutheran (WA)	R
Pacific, U. of the (CA)	R
Portland State (OR)	M
Potsdam (SUNY) (NY)	M
Purchase (SUNY) (NY)	R
π Puget Sound (WA)	R
Queens (NC)	R
Queens (CUNY)(NY)	L
Redlands, U. of (CA)	R
Roanoke (VA)	R
Rowan (NJ)	M
San Francisco Conservatory (CA)	S
Santa Clara U. (CA)	M
Shepherd (WV)	R
▲ St. Catherine (MN)	R

GROUP II continues next page

MUSIC, continued

GROUP II, Continued

Stetson (FL) .... R
Stony Brook (SUNY)(NY) L
Susquehanna (PA) .... R
Syracuse (NY) L
Temple (PA) .... M
Utah State L
Valparaiso (IN) .... R
Wartburg (IA) .... R
▲ Wells (NY) .... S

West Chester (PA) .... M
West Virginia, U. of L
Western Michigan L
Whitworth (WA) .... R
William Jewell Col. (MO) .... R
Wisconsin Lutheran .... S
Wittenberg (OH) .... R
Wooster, College of (OH) .... R

GROUP III
Selective

Anderson (IN) .... R
Anna Maria (MA) .... S
Arkansas, U. of L
Arts, U. of the (PA) .... R
➤ Azusa Pacific (CA) .... R
π Baldwin-Wallace (OH) .... R
Belhaven (MS) .... S
➤ Belmont (TN) .... R
Bethany (WV) .... R
Bowling Green (OH) L
Bluffton (OH) .... S
Brenau (GA) .... R
Bridgewater (VA) .... R
California State U. (Fresno) L
California State U. (Fullerton) L
California State U. (Hayward) .... M
California State U. (Long Beach) L
California State U. (Northridge) L
California State U. (Sacramento) .... M
California State U. (San Jose) L
Carson-Newman (TN) .... R
Carthage (WI) .... R
Cedarville (OH) .... R
Central Connecticut .... M
Central Michigan L
Central Washington L
Charleston Southern (SC) .... R
Christopher Newport (VA) .... M
Coker (SC) .... S
Cumberland (KY) .... R
Duquesne (PA) .... M
East Carolina L
Eastern Michigan L
➤ Five Towns College (NY) .... S

Fort Hays (KS) .... M
Goshen (IN) .... R
Hardin-Simmons (TX) .... R
Hartford, U. of (CT) .... M
Hartwick (NY) .... R
Hastings (NE) .... S
Heidelberg (OH) .... S
Huntingdon (AL) .... S
Indiana State L
Jacksonville (FL) .... R
John Brown (AR) .... R
Johnson State (VT) .... R
Keene State (NH) .... R
Kent State (OH) L
Lock Haven (PA) .... M
Longwood (VA) .... R
Louisiana College .... R
Louisiana-Lafayette L
Louisville (KY) L
π Loyola (LA) .... M
Marywood (PA) .... R
Massachusetts, U. of (Boston) .... M
Massachusetts, U. of (Lowell) .... M
Memphis, U. of (TN) L
▲ Meredith (NC) .... R
Minnesota State U. (Moorhead) .... M
Minnesota, U. of (Duluth) .... M
Mississippi College .... R
π Monmouth (NJ) .... R
Montevallo (AL) .... R
Mount St. Joseph (OH) .... R
Mount St. Mary's (CA) .... R
Muskingum (OH) .... R

GROUP III continues next page

MUSIC, continued

GROUP III, *Continued*

Nevada, U. of (Las Vegas) .... M
Nevada, U. of (Reno) .... M
Northern Colorado L
Northwestern College (IA) .... R
Northwestern Louisiana L
Nyack (NY) .... R
Oklahoma Baptist .... R
Otterbein (OH) .... R
Ouachita (AR) .... R
Philadelphia Biblical (PA) .... S
Rhode Island College .... M
Rider (NJ) .... M
Roosevelt (IL) .... R
Samford (AL) .... R
▲ Seton Hill (PA) .... S
Shenandoah (VA) .... R
Shorter (GA) .... R
Simpson (IA) .... S
Slippery Rock (PA) .... M
Sonoma State (CA) .... M

South Florida, U. of L
π Southern Illinois U. (Carbondale) L
Southern Maine .... M
Southern Mississippi L
Southwest Baptist (MO) .... R
Tampa, U. of (FL) .... R
Texas Lutheran .... S
Towson (MD) L
Union University (TN) .... R
Virginia Commonwealth L
Viterbo (WI) .... R
Weber State (UT) L
Western Connecticut .... M
π Western Illlinois L
Western St. Coll. of Colorado .... R
Westfield (MA) .... M
π William Paterson (NJ) .... M
Wingate (NC) .... R
π Wisconsin, U. of (Stevens Point) .... M
Xavier U. of Louisiana .... R

➤ *Music Business*
π *Music and Music Business*

NURSING

GROUP I
Most Selective

▲ Barnard (NY)	R		Johns Hopkins (MD)	M
Binghamton (SUNY) (NY)	L		Missouri, U. of (Rolla)	M
Boston Col. (MA)	L		New York U.	L
Buffalo (SUNY)(NY)	L		North Carolina, U. of	L
Case Western Reserve U. (OH)	R		Northern Michigan	M
Colorado, U. of	L		Pennsylvania, U. of	L
Columbia (NY)	M		St. Olaf (MN)	R
Duke (NC)	M		Vanderbilt (TN)	M
Emory (GA)	R		Villanova (PA)	M
Florida, U. of	XL		Virginia, U. of	L
Gustavus Adolphus (MN)	R		Washington, U. of	XL
Illinois, U. of	XL		Wisconsin, U. of	L
Illinois Wesleyan	R			

NURSING continues next page

NURSING, continued

Adelphi (NY)	M
Alabama, U. of (Huntsville)	M
Arizona, U. of	XL
Augustana (SD)	R
Barry (FL)	R
Baylor (TX)	M
Belmont (TN)	R
Bethel (MN)	R
Bradley (IL)	M
Calvin (MI)	R
Capital (OH)	R
Carroll (WI)	R
Catholic U. (DC)	M
Cincinnati, U. of (OH)	L
Clarke (IA)	S
Connecticut, U. of	L
Creighton (NE)	R
Daemen (NY)	R
Delaware, U. of	L
Detroit Mercy (MI)	M
Duquesne (PA)	M
Elmira (NY)	R
Evansville (IN)	R
Fairfield (CT)	M
Florida Gulf Coast U.	R
Florida International	L
Franciscan U. of Steubenville (OH)	R
George Mason (VA)	M
Georgetown (DC)	M
Gwynedd-Mercy (PA)	S
Harding (AR)	M
Hunter (CUNY) (NY)	I
Illinois, U. of (Chicago)	L
Indiana U.	XL
Indiana U. of Pennsylvania	L
Iowa, U. of	XL
Lebanon Valley (PA)	R
Loyola (IL)	M
Luther (IA)	R
Marquette (WI)	M
➤ Maryland, U. of (Baltimore County)	M
Massachusetts, U. of	L
McKendree (IL)	R
McMurry (TX)	R
Michigan, U. of	XL
Milwaukee Sch. of Engine (WI)	R
Minnesota, U. of	XL

Mississippi U. for Women	R
Mobile, U. of (AL)	R
Moravian (PA)	R
Morningside (IA)	S
Mount Mercy (IA)	S
New Jersey, College of	M
New Mexico, U. of	L
North Dakota, U. of	M
North Florida	M
Northeastern (MA)	L
Ohio State	XL
Pace (NY)	M
Pacific Lutheran (WA)	R
Pennsylvania State	XL
Pittsburgh, U. of (PA)	L
Portland, U. of (OR)	R
Purdue (IN)	XL
Samford (AL)	R
San Diego, U. of (CA)	M
San Francisco, U. of (CA)	M
Seattle Pacific (WA)	R
Seton Hall (NJ)	M
▲Simmons (MA)	R
South Carolina, U. of	L
South Dakota School of Mines	R
St. Anselm's (NH)	R
▲St. Catherine (MN)	R
St John's/St. Benedict (MN)	R
St. Louis (MO)	M
▲St. Mary's College (IN)	R
Texas Christian U.	M
Truman State (MO)	M
Union University (TN)	R
Valparaiso U. (IN)	M
Vermont, U. of	M
Viterbo (WI)	R
Virginia Commonwealth	L
Webster (MD)	R
Western Michigan	L
Westminster (UT)	R
William Jewell (MO)	R
Wisconsin, U. of (Milwaukee)	XL
Wyoming, U. of	M
York (PA)	M

➤ *Health Policy, also*

NURSING continues next page

NURSING, continued

Akron, U. of (OH)	L	Georgia Southern	L
Alabama, U. of (Birmingham)	M	Georgia Southwestern	R
Alaska, U. of (Fairbanks)	M	Georgia State	L
Alderson-Broaddus (WV)	S	Goshen (IN)	R
▲Alverno (WI)	R	Graceland (IA)	R
Andrews (MI)	R	Grambling (LA)	M
Arizona State	XL	Hartwick (NY)	R
Avila (MO)	S	Hawaii Pacific	M
Azusa Pacific (CA)	R	Henderson State (AR)	M
Ball State (IN)	L	Howard (DC)	M
Bellarmine (KY)	R	Husson (ME)	S
Berea (KY)	R	▲Immaculata (PA)	S
Bethel (IN)	R	Ind.U.-Purdue U.-Indianapolis (IN)	L
Bloomsburg (PA)	M	Jacksonville (FL)	R
Brockport (SUNY)(NY)	M	Jacksonville State (AL)	M
California State U. (Bakersfield)	M	Jamestown (ND)	R
California State U. (Chico)	L	Kennesaw State (GA)	R
California State U. (Dominguez Hills)	M	Kent State (OH)	L
California State U. (Fresno)	L	King (TN)	S
California State U. (Fullerton)	L	Lewis-Clark State (ID)	R
California State U. (Los Angeles)	L	Long Island U. (Brooklyn)(NY)	M
California State U. (San Jose)	L	Louisiana College	R
Carroll (MT)	R	Louisiana-Lafayette	L
Carson-Newman (TN)	R	MacMurray (IL)	S
▲Cedar Crest (PA)	S	Malone (OH)	R
Cedarville (OH)	R	Marshall (WV)	M
Central Arkansas	M	Marymount (VA)	R
Charleston, U. of (WV)	S	Maryville (St. Louis) (MO)	R
Colby-Sawyer (NH)	S	Massachusetts, U. of (Boston)	M
Colorado, U. of (Colorado Springs)	M	Massachusetts, U. of (Dartmouth)	M
Dillard (LA)	R	Memphis, U. of (TN)	L
Dominican (CA)	S	Mercy (NY)	M
D'Youville (NY)	R	Midwestern State U. (TX)	M
East Carolina (NC)	L	Milligan (TN)	R
East Tennessee	L	Misericordia, College (PA)	S
Eastern (PA)	R	Mississippi College	R
Eastern Kentucky	L	Molloy (NY)	R
Eastern Mennonite (VA)	R	Mount St. Joseph (OH)	R
Eastern Michigan	L	Mount St. Mary's (CA)	R
Edgewood (WI)	S	Mount St. Mary's (NY)	S
Elms (MA)	S	Murray State (KY)	M
Fairmont State (WV)	M	Nevada, U. of (Las Vegas)	M
Ferris State (MI)	L	Nevada, U. of (Reno)	M
Fitchburg (MA)	R		
Gannon (PA)	M		

GROUP III continues next page

NURSING, continued

GROUP III, Continued

Nichols State (LA) .... M	South Alabama .... M
North Carolina, U. of (Charlotte) L	South Dakota, U. of .... M
North Carolina, U. of (Greensboro) ..... M	South Florida, U. of L
Northern Colorado L	Southern Illinois U. (Edwardsville)...... L
Northern Illinois U. L	Southern Mississippi L
Northwestern Louisiana L	Southern Maine, U. of .... M
Oakland (MI) .... M	St. Anselm (NH) .... R
Oklahoma Baptist .... R	Texas, U.of (Tyler) .... R
Olivet Nazarene (IL) .... R	Towson (MD) L
Pittsburgh, U. of (Bradford) .... R	Tuskegee University (AL).................... M
Plattsburgh (SUNY) (NY) .... M	Union University (TN) .... R
Point Loma (CA) .... R	Villa Julie (MD) .... R
Regis (CO) .... R	Walla Walla (WA)................................ R
Rhode Island, U. of L	Walsh (OH) .... R
Rockford (IL) .... S	Wayne State (MI) L
Russell Sage (The Sage Colleges)(NY) .. R	Western Connecticut State .... M
Saginaw Valley (MI) .... M	Western Kentucky............................... L
St. Scholastica (MN) .... R	Wheeling Jesuit (WV) .... R
St. Joseph's (ME) .... S	Widener (PA) .... R
San Diego State (CA).......................... L	Wilkes (PA) .... R
Seattle U. (WA) .... R	Wisconsin, U. of (Eau Claire).............. L
Shenandoah (VA) .... R	Worcester State (MA) .... M
Sonoma State (CA) .... M	Wright State (OH) L

Enrollment Code		
■ **Men Only**	**S = Small** (less than 1000 students)	**R = Moderate** (1000-3000 students)	**M = Medium** (3000-8000 students)
▲ **Women Only**	**L = Large** (8000-20,000 students)	**XL = Extra Large** (over 20,000 students)

PHARMACY

GROUP I
Most Selective

Buffalo (SUNY) (NY)	L	Michigan, U. of	XL
Butler (IN)	R	North Carolina, U. of	L
Creighton (NE)	R	Purdue (IN)	XL
Florida, U. of	XL	Rutgers (NJ)	L
Illinois, U. of	XL	Wisconsin, U. of	L
Iowa, U. of	XL		

GROUP II
Very Selective

Albany Col. of Pharmacy (NY)	S	Ohio State	XL
Auburn (AL)	L	Pacific, U. of the (CA)	R
Cincinnati, U. of (OH)	L	Palm Beach Atlantic (FL)	R
Connecticut, U. of	L	Pittsburgh, U. of	L
Drake (IA)	M	Rhode Island, U. of	L
Duquesne (PA)	M	Samford (AL)	R
Ferris State (MI)	L	+ Sciences in Philadelphia, U. of (PA)	R
Florida A&M	L	South Carolina, U. of	L
Georgia, U. of	L	Southern California, U. of	L
Illinois, U. of (Chicago)	L	Southwestern Oklahoma	M
Kansas, U. of	L	St. John's (NY)	L
Kentucky, U. of	L	St. Louis Col. of Pharmacy (MO)	S
Maryland, U. of	XL	Temple (PA)	L
Mass. College of Pharmacy	R	Texas, U. of (Austin)	XL
Mercer (GA)	R	Toledo, U. of	L
Minnesota, U. of	XL	Utah, U. of	L
Mississippi, U. of	M	Virginia Commonwealth U.	L
Montana, U. of	M	Washington State	L
New Mexico, U. of	L	Wayne State (MI)	L
Northeastern (MA)	L	West Virginia U.	L
Northwestern Louisiana	L	Wyoming, U. of	L
North Dakota State	L	Xavier (LA)	R
Ohio Northern U.	R		

+ Also Pharmaceutical Marketing

PHILOSOPHY

GROUP I
Most Selective

Albany (SUNY)(NY)	L	Lawrence (WI)	R
Austin (TX)	R	Macalester (MN)	R
▲ Barnard (NY)	R	Michigan, U. of	XL
Bates (ME)	R	New College (FL)	S
Binghamton (SUNY) (NY)	L	New York U.	L
Boston Col. (MA)	L	North Carolina, U. of	L
Boston U. (MA)	L	Notre Dame (IN)	M
Bowdoin (ME)	R	Oberlin (OH)	R
Brown (RI)	M	Ohio State	XL
Bucknell (PA)	M	Pennsylvania, U. of	L
California, U. of (Berkeley)	XL	Pittsburgh, U. of (PA)	L
California, U. of (Los Angeles)	XL	Pomona (CA)	R
Centre (KY)	R	Princeton (NJ)	M
Chicago, U. of (IL)	M	Reed (OR)	R
Claremont McKenna (CA)	R	Rochester, U. of (NY)	M
Colby (ME)	R	Rutgers (NJ)	L
Colgate (NY)	R	▲ Smith (MA)	R
Colorado Col.	R	Southwestern (TX)	R
Columbia (NY)	M	St. Olaf (MN)	R
Connecticut Col.	R	Swarthmore (PA)	R
Cornell (NY)	L	Texas, U. of (Austin)	XL
Dallas, U. of (TX)	R	Trinity (CT)	R
Davidson (NC)	R	Trinity (TX)	R
DePauw (IN)	R	Tufts (MA)	M
Duke (NC)	M	Tulane (LA)	M
Florida State	L	Vanderbilt (TN)	M
Florida, U. of	XL	Vassar (NY)	R
Geneseo (SUNY)(NY)	M	Villanova (PA)	M
George Washington (DC)	M	■ Wabash (IN)	S
Georgetown (DC)	M	Washington U. (MO)	M
Hamilton (NY)	R	Washington, U. of	XL
Harvard (MA)	M	Wheaton (IL)	R
Haverford (PA)	S	Whitman (WA)	R
Holy Cross (MA)	R	Wisconsin, U. of	XL
Johns Hopkins (MD)	R	Yale (CT)	M
Kenyon (OH)	R		

PHILOSOPHY continues next page

Enrollment Code

■ **Men Only**
▲ **Women Only**

S = Small (less than 1000 students)   **R = Moderate** (1000-3000 students)   **M = Medium** (3000-8000 students)
L = Large (8000-20,000 students)   **XL = Extra Large** (over 20,000 students)

PHILOSOPHY, continued

GROUP II
Very Selective

Alabama, U. of (Birmingham)	M	Mansfield (PA)	R
Allegheny (PA)	R	Marquette (WI)	M
Albion (MI)	R	Maryland, U. of	XL
Arizona, U. of	XL	Mass. College of Lib. Arts (N.Adams)	R
Asbury (KY)	R	Massachusetts, U. of (Boston)	M
Bellarmine (KY)	R	Messiah (PA)	R
Belmont (TN)	R	Milligan (TN)	S
Bethel (IN)	R	Mount Mercy (IA)	S
Biola (CA)	R	Muhlenberg (PA)	R
California, U. of (Santa Barbara)	L	New Hampshire, U. of	L
California State U. (Dominguez Hills)	M	North Carolina, U. of (Charlotte)	L
California State U. (Fresno)	L	Northeastern (MA)	L
California State U. (Northridge)	L	Northern Illinois	`L
Calvin (MI)	R	Oneonta (SUNY)(NY)	M
Central Florida	L	Ozarks, College of the (MO)	R
Christendom (VA)	S	Portland, U. of (OR)	R
Christopher Newport (VA)	M	Providence (RI)	M
Clarke (IA)	S	Regis (CO)	R
Coastal Carolina (SC)	M	Rhode Island College	M
Cornell Col. (IA)	R	Richard Stockton (NJ)	M
Denison (OH)	R	Rowan (NJ)	M
DePaul (IL)	L	St. Andrews Presbyterian (NC)	S
DeSales (PA)	S	St. Bonaventure (NY)	R
Detroit Mercy (MI)	M	St. John's/St. Benedict (MN)	R
Doane (NB)	S	St. Louis (MO)	M
Earlham (IN)	R	▲St. Mary's College (IN)	R
Elon (NC)	R	St. Mary's (MN)	R
Frostburg (MD)	M	St. Thomas (MN)	M
Fordham (NY)	L	St. Thomas, U. of (TX)	R
Franciscan U. of Steubenville (OH)	R	Salisbury State (MD)	M
George Mason (VA)	L	Santa Clara U. (CA)	M
Georgia State	L	Seton Hall (NJ)	M
Georgia, U. of	L	Skidmore (NY)	R
Gonzaga (WA)	E	South Alabama	M
Hanover (IN)	R	South Florida, U. of	L
Hood (MD)	S	Stony Brook (SUNY) (NY)	L
Illinois, U. of (Chicago)	L	Transylvania (KY)	R
Indiana (PA)	L	Westminster (UT)	R
Indiana U.	XL	Wheeling Jesuit (WV)	R
Louisiana State	XL	Wofford (SC)	R
Loyola (IL)	M	Worcester State (MA)	
Loyola (LA)	M	Xavier (OH)	R
Lycoming (PA)	R		

PHYSICS

GROUP I
Most Selective

Albany (SUNY)(NY)	L	Macalester (MN)	R
Amherst (MA)	R	MIT (MA)	M
▲ Barnard (NY)	R	Michigan, U. of	XL
Bates (ME)	R	Michigan, U. of (Dearborn)	M
Binghamton (SUNY) (NY)	L	Middlebury (VT)	R
Boston U. (MA)	L	New College (FL)	S
Brandeis (MA)	M	New Mexico Inst. of Mining & Tech.	S
▲ Bryn Mawr (PA)	S	New York U.	L
California Inst. of Tech.	S	Notre Dame (IN)	M
California, U. of (Berkeley)	XL	Oberlin (OH)	R
California, U. of (San Diego)	L	Occidental (CA)	R
Carleton (MN)	R	Pennsylvania, U. of	L
Case Western Reserve U. (OH)	R	Pomona (CA)	R
Centre (KY)	R	Princeton (NJ)	M
Chicago, U. of (IL)	M	Reed (OR)	R
Colorado School of Mines	R	Rensselaer (NY)	M
Columbia (NY)	M	Rhodes (TN)	R
Cornell (NY)	L	Rice (TX)	R
Dartmouth (NH)	M	Rose-Hulman (IN)	R
DePauw (IN)	R	Rutgers (NJ)	L
Dickinson (PA)	R	St. Olaf (MN)	R
Florida, U. of	XL	▲ Smith (MA)	R
Franklin & Marshall (PA)	R	South, U. of the (TN)	R
Geneseo (SUNY) (NY)	M	Stanford (CA)	M
Georgetown (DC)	M	Swarthmore (PA)	R
Georgia Inst. of Tech.	M	Texas, U. of (Dallas)	M
Grinnell (IA)	R	Trinity (TX)	R
Gustavus Adolphus (MN)	R	United States Air Force Academy (CO)	M
Harvard (MA)	M	Vanderbilt (TN)	M
Harvey Mudd (CA)	S	Wake Forest (NC)	M
Haverford (PA)	S	Washington, U. of	XL
Illinois, U. of (Urbana-Champaign)	XL	Washington U. (MO)	M
Illinois Wesleyan	R	▲ Wellesley (MA)	R
Iowa State	XL	Wheaton (IL)	R
Iowa, U. of	XL	Whitman (WA)	R
Kenyon (OH)	R	William & Mary (VA)	M
Kalamazoo (MI)	R	Worcester Poly. Inst. (MA)	R
Lawrence (WI)	R	Yeshiva (NY)	R

PHYSICS continues next page

Enrollment Code		
■ **Men Only**	**S = Small** (less than 1000 students) **R = Moderate** (1000-3000 students)	**M = Medium** (3000-8000 students)
▲ **Women Only**	**L = Large** (8000-20,000 students) **XL = Extra Large** (over 20,000 students)	

PHYSICS, continued

GROUP II
Very Selective

Adelphi (NY) .... M	Marietta (OH) .... R
▲ Agnes Scott (GA) .... S	Maryland, U. of XL
Augsburg (MN) .... R	Maryland, U. of (Baltimore County) .... M
Beloit (WI) .... R	Massachusetts, U. of (Lowell) .... M
Bethany (WV) .... S	Mississippi, U. of .... M
Bradley (IL) .... M	New Hampshire, U. of L
California Poly. State U. (San Luis Obispo).L	New Orleans (LA) L
California, U. of (Irvine) L	North Carolina State L
California, U. of (Santa Barbara) L	Ohio State XL
California, U. of (Santa Cruz) .... M	Ohio U. L
Calvin (MI) .... R	Oklahoma State L
Clemson (SC) L	Oregon State L
Coe (IA) .... R	Pacific University (OR) .... R
Colorado, U. of L	Rollins (FL) .... R
Colorado, U. of (Colorado Springs) ..... M	Rowan (NJ) .... M
Creighton (NE) .... R	St. John's (MN) .... R
Denver, U. of (CO) .... M	Santa Clara U. (CA) .... M
Evansville, U. of (IN) .... R	Shippensburg (PA) .... M
Fairfield (CT) .... M	Sonoma State (CA) .... M
Florida Inst. of Tech .... R	South Carolina, U. of L
Florida State L	South Dakota School of Mines .... R
George Mason (VA) L	Stockton State (NJ) .... M
Guilford (NC) .... R	Stony Brook (SUNY) (NY) L
Hamline (MN) .... R	Tennessee, U. of XL
Hanover (IN) .... R	Texas, U. of (Austin) XL
Hendrix (AR) .... R	Ursinus (PA) .... R
Kansas State L	Vermont, U. of .... M
Kent State (OH) L	Westminster (UT) .... R
Knox (IL) .... R	Whitworth (WA) .... R
Lewis & Clark (OR) .... R	Wisconsin, U. of XL
Loras (IA) .... R	Xavier (OH) .... R
Loyola (IL) .... M	

PHYSICS, continued

GROUP III
Selective

Ball State (IN) L

Brooklyn Col. (CUNY) (NY) L

California Poly. State U. (Pomona) L

California State U. (Dominguez Hills) . M

California State U. (Northridge) L

California State U. (San Jose) L

Christopher Newport (VA) .... M

City Col. (CUNY) (NY) L

Clark Atlanta (GA) .... M

Eastern Michigan L

Edinboro (PA) .... M

Fisk (TN) .... S

Florida A&M .... M

Fort Lewis (CO) .... M

Georgia State L

Goshen (IN) .... R

Hastings (NE) .... S

Indiana State L

Jacksonville (FL) .... R

Louisiana-Lafayette............................. L

Louisiana State XL

▲ Mary Baldwin (VA) .... S

Mass. College of Lib. Arts (N. Adams).. R

Massachusetts, U. of (Boston)............ M

Muskingum (OH) .... R

Nevada, U. of (Reno) .... M

Northern Illinois U............................. L

Northern Michigan .... M

Northwestern (IA) .... R

Ozarks, College of the (MO)................ R

Penn State (Erie)(PA) .... M

Southern Connecticut......................... M

Thomas More (KY) .... R

Tuskegee (AL) .... M

Union (TN) .... R

Weber State (UT)............................... L

π West Virginia Wesleyan .... R

Western Kentucky............................... L

Western Michigan L

Wisconsin, U. of (Milwaukee) L

π Engineering Physics

POLITICAL SCIENCE

GROUP I
Most Selective

American U. (DC) .... M	Miami, U. of (OH) L
Amherst (MA)............................ R	Michigan, U. of........................... XL
Binghamton (SUNY)(NY).............. L	Middlebury (VT)........................... R
▲ Barnard (NY)........................... R	▲ Mount Holyoke (MA)................. R
Bates (ME) .... R	North Carolina, U. of.................. L
Boston College (MA) L	Northwestern (IL) .... M
Boston U. (MA) L	Notre Dame (IN) .... M
Brandeis (MA) .... R	Oberlin (OH) .... R
Brown (RI) .... M	Occidental (CA) .... R
California, U. of (Berkeley) XL	Pennsylvania, U. of.................... L
California, U. of (Los Angeles) XL	Pomona (CA) .... R
California, U. of (San Diego) L	Princeton (NJ) .... M
Carleton (MN) .... R	Rhodes (TN) .... R
Centre (KY) .... R	Richmond, U. of (VA) .... M
Chicago, U. of (IL) .... M	Rochester, U. of (NY) .... M
Claremont McKenna (CA) .... R	Rutgers (NJ) L
Colby (ME) .... R	▲ Smith (MA) .... R
Colgate (NY) .... R	South, U. of the (TN) .... R
Colorado Col. .... R	Southwestern (TX)..................... R
Columbia (NY) .... M	Stanford (CA) .... M
Connecticut Col. .... R	Swarthmore (PA) .... R
Connecticut, U. of...................... L	Texas A&M XL
Dallas, U. of (TX) .... R	Texas, U. of (Austin).................. XL
Dartmouth (NH) .... M	Trinity (TX) .... R
Davidson (NC) .... M	Tufts (MA) .... M
DePauw (IN) .... R	Tulane (LA) .... M
Dickinson (PA) .... R	Union (NY) .... R
Drew (NJ) .... R	U.S. Air Force Academy (CO) .... M
Duke (NC) .... M	U.S. Military Academy (NY) .... M
Emory (GA) .... R	U.S. Naval Academy (MD) .... M
Florida, U. of XL	Ursinus (PA) .... R
Franklin & Marshall (PA) .... R	Vanderbilt (TN) .... M
Furman (SC) .... R	Villanova (PA) .... M
Georgetown (DC) .... M	Virginia, U. of......................... L
George Washington (DC)................. M	■ Wabash (IN) .... S
Grinnell (IA) .... R	Wake Forest (NC)....................... M
Hamilton (NY) .... R	Washington & Lee (VA) .... R
Harvard (MA) .... M	▲ Wellesley (MA)........................ R
Holy Cross (MA) .... R	Wesleyan (CT) .... R
Illinois, U. of........................... XL	Whitman (WA) .... R
Johns Hopkins (MD) .... R	Willamette (OR) .... R
Kenyon (OH) .... R	William & Mary (VA) .... M
Lehigh (PA) .... M	Williams (MA) .... R
Macalester (MN)......................... R	Yale (CT) .... M
MIT (MA)................................. M	Yeshiva (NY) .... R

POLITICAL SCIENCE, continued

GROUP II
Very Selective

▲Agnes Scott (GA) .... S	Manhattan (NY) .... M
Albany (SUNY)(NY) L	Manhattanville (NY) .... R
Albion (MI) .... R	Marist (NY) .... M
Alma (MI) .... R	Marquette (WI) .... M
Auburn (AL) L	Maryland, U. of XL
Austin (TX) .... R	Maryland, U. of (Baltimore County) .... M
Belmont (TN) .... R	Massachusetts, U. of L
California, U. of (Davis) L	Millersville (PA) .... M
California, U. of (Riverside) .... M	Minnesota, U. of XL
California, U. of (Santa Barbara) L	North Carolina (Charlotte) L
Catholic U. (DC) .... M	North Central (IL) .... R
Clark (MA) .... R	Oglethorpe (GA) .... S
Clemson (SC) L	Ohio State XL
Colorado State L	Ohio U. L
College of Charleston (SC) L	Ohio Wesleyan .... R
Cornell College (IA) .... R	Oklahoma City U. .... R
Creighton (NE) .... R	Oklahoma, U. of L
Dayton, U. of (OH) .... M	Oklahoma State L
Denison (OH) .... R	Portland, U. of (OR) .... R
DePaul (IL) L	Presbyterian (SC) .... S
Drake (IA) .... M	Providence (RI) .... M
Elon (NC) .... R	Purchase (SUNY)(NY) .... R
Florida International L	Randolph Macon (VA) .... R
George Mason (VA) L	Redlands, U. of (CA) .... R
Georgia, U. of Xl	Richard Stockton (NJ) .... M
Gonzaga (WA) .... R	Ripon (WI) .... S
Grove City (PA) .... R	Roanoke (VA) .... R
Guilford (NC) .... R	St. Bonaventure (NY) .... R
Hampden-Sydney (VA) .... S	St. John's (MN) .... R
Hawaii, U. of L	St. Joseph's (PA) .... R
Hillsdale (MI) .... R	St. Lawrence (NY) .... R
Hobart & William Smith (NY) .... R	St. Mary's College of Maryland .... R
Hofstra (NY) .... M	Santa Clara U. (CA) .... M
Hope (MI) .... R	Siena (NY) .... R
Howard (DC) .... M	Skidmore (NY) .... R
Illinois College .... S	South Carolina L
Illinois, U. of (Chicago) L	Spring Hill (AL) .... R
Iowa, U. of XL	Stonehill (MA) .... R
James Madison (VA) .... M	Stony Brook (SUNY)(NY) L
John Carroll (OH) .... R	Syracuse (NY) L
Knox (IL) .... R	
Lake Forest (IL) .... R	*GROUP II continues next page*

GROUP II continues next page

Enrollment Code

■ **Men Only** **S = Small** (less than 1000 students)   **R = Moderate** (1000-3000 students)   **M = Medium** (3000-8000 students)
▲ **Women Only**   **L = Large** (8000-20,000 students)   **XL = Extra Large** (over 20,000 students)

POLITICAL SCIENCE, continued

GROUP II, Continued

Tennessee, U. of XL	Wilberforce (OH) .... S
▲ Trinity (DC) .... S	Winthrop (SC) .... M
Utah, U. of L	Wisconsin, U. of................................ XL
Vermont, U. of L	Wittenberg (OH)................................. R
Washington & Jefferson (PA) .... R	Wofford (SC) .... R
Westchester (PA) .... M	Wooster, College of the (OH) .... R
Westminster (UT) .... R	Wyoming, U. of L
Wheaton (MA) .... R	

GROUP III
Selective

Adrian (MI) .... S	Heidelburg (OH) .... S
Albright (PA) .... R	Illinois State L
Appalachian State (NC) L	John Jay (CUNY)(NY) .... M
Arizona State XL	Kutztown (PA) .... M
Azusa Pacific (CA)............................. R	Lock Haven (PA) .... M
Baldwin-Wallace (OH) .... R	Louisiana State XL
Ball State (IN) L	Louisville (KY) L
Belmont Abbey (NC) .... S	▲ Mary Baldwin (VA) .... S
Bridgewater (MA) .... M	Massachusetts, U. of (Boston)............ M
Brockport (SUNY)(NY) .... M	Mercyhurst (PA) .... R
California State U. (Chico) L	Michigan State................................. XL
California State U. (Fullerton)............. L	Mt. St. Mary's (MD) .... R
California State U. (Long Beach) L	▲ Pine Manor (MA) .... S
California State U. (Northridge) L	Radford (VA) .... M
California State U. (Sacramento) .... M	Rhode Island, U. of............................ L
California State U. (San Marcos) .... M	St. Mary's (TX) .... R
California State U. (Stanislaus) .... M	Southern Connecticut........................ M
Campbell (NC) .... R	Southern Illinois U. (Carbondale)........ L
▲ Chatham (PA)................................. S	Southern Illinois U. (Edwardsville)...... L
Christopher Newport (VA)................... M	Southwest Missouri L
City College (CUNY)(NY) L	▲ Spelman (GA) .... R
▲ Converse (SC)................................ S	Suffolk (MA) .... R
Eastern Connecticut .... M	Texas, U. of (Arlington) L
Eastern Kentucky L	Virginia Wesleyan............................... R
Eastern Michigan.............................. L	Westfield (MA) .... M
Grambling (LA) .... M	Whittier (CA) .... R
Hartwick (NY) .... R	Wisconsin, U. of (Milwaukee) L

PRE-LAW

Author's Note: *Law School Associations usually recommend that a student choose a major dependent upon one's own individual intellectual interests and upon "the quality of undergraduate education" provided by various departments and colleges. The following recommended colleges have been taken primarily from our recommended departments in English, Economics, and Political Science.*

GROUP I
Most Selective

Albany (SUNY) (NY)	L		Franklin & Marshall (PA)	R
Allegheny (PA)	R		Furman (SC)	R
American U. (DC)	M		Georgetown (DC)	M
Amherst (MA)	R		George Washington (DC)	M
Bard (NY)	R		Gettysburg (PA)	R
▲ Barnard (NY)	R		Grinnell (IA)	R
Bates (ME)	R		Hamilton (NY)	R
Binghamton (SUNY) (NY)	L		Harvard (MA)	M
Boston Col. (MA)	L		Haverford (PA)	S
Boston U. (MA)	L		Holy Cross (MA)	R
Bowdoin (ME)	R		Illinois, U. of (Chicago)	L
Brandeis (MA)	R		Illinois, U. of (Urbana-Champaign)	XL
Brown (RI)	M		Illinois Wesleyan	R
▲ Bryn Mawr (PA)	S		Iowa, U. of	XL
Bucknell (PA)	M		Johns Hopkins (MD)	R
Buffalo (SUNY) (NY)	L		Kalamazoo (MI)	R
California, U. of (Berkeley)	XL		Kenyon (OH)	R
California, U. of (Los Angeles)	XL		Lafayette (PA)	R
California, U. of (San Diego)	L		Macalester (MN)	R
Carleton (MN)	R		Maryland, U. of (Baltimore County)	M
Centre (KY)	R		MIT (MA)	M
Chicago, U. of (IL)	M		Miami, U. of (OH)	L
Claremont McKenna (CA)	R		Michigan, U. of	XL
Clark (MA)	R		Middlebury (VT)	R
Colby (ME)	R		▲ Mount Holyoke (MA)	R
Colgate (NY)	R		Muhlenberg (PA)	R
Colorado Col.	R		New Jersey, College of	M
Columbia (NY)	M		North Carolina, U. of	L
Connecticut Col.	R		Northwestern (IL)	M
Dallas, U. of (TX)	R		Notre Dame (IN)	M
Dartmouth (NH)	M		Oberlin (OH)	R
Davidson (NC)	R		Occidental (CA)	R
DePauw (IN)	R		Pennsylvania, U. of	L
Dickinson (PA)	R		Pitzer (CA)	S
Drew (NJ)	R		Pomona (CA)	R
Duke (NC)	M		Princeton (NJ)	M
Emory (GA)	R		Providence (RI)	M
Florida, U. of	XL			

GROUP I continues next page

Enrollment Code

■ Men Only	**S = Small** (less than 1000 students)	**R = Moderate** (1000-3000 students)	**M = Medium** (3000-8000 students)
▲ Women Only	**L = Large** (8000-20,000 students)	**XL = Extra Large** (over 20,000 students)	

PRE-LAW, continued

GROUP I, Continued

Reed (OR)	R	Tulane (LA)	M
Rhodes (TN)	R	Union (NY)	R
Richmond, U. of (VA)	M	Vanderbilt (TN)	M
Rice (TX)	R	Vassar (NY)	R
Richmond, U. of (VA)	M	Villanova (PA)	M
Rochester, U. of (NY)	M	Virginia, U. of	L
Rutgers (NJ)	L	■ Wabash (IN)	S
Sarah Lawrence (NY)	S	Wake Forest (NC)	M
Skidmore (NY)	R	Washington & Lee (VA)	R
▲ Smith (MA)	R	Washington U. (MO)	M
South, U. of the (TN)	R	▲ Wellesley (MA)	R
Southwestern (TX)	R	Wesleyan U. (CT)	R
Stanford (CA)	M	Wheaton (IL)	R
St. Olaf (MN)	R	Whitman (WA)	R
Swarthmore (PA)	R	Williams (MA)	R
Trinity (CT)	R	Wisconsin, U. of	XL
Trinity (TX)	R	Worcester Poly. Inst. (MA)	R
Tufts (MA)	M	Yale (CT)	M

GROUP II
Very Selective

▲ Agnes Scott (GA)	S	Creighton (NE)	R
Alabama, U. of	L	Dayton, U. of (OH)	M
Albertson (ID)	S	Denison (OH)	R
Albion (MI)	R	Denver, U. of (CO)	M
Alfred (NY)	R	DePaul (IL)	L
Alma (MI)	R	Drake (IA)	M
Arizona, U. of	XL	Evansville (IN)	R
Augsburg (MN)	R	Elizabethtown (PA)	R
Augustana (IL)	R	Flagler (FL)	R
Baylor (TX)	R	Fordham (NY)	L
Belmont (TN)	R	George Mason (VA)	L
Bennington (VT)	S	Georgetown College (KY)	R
Birmingham-Southern (AL)	R	Georgia, U. of	XL
Brigham Young (UT)	XL	Gonzaga (WA)	R
Butler (IN)	R	Goucher (MD)	R
California, U. of (Davis)	L	Grand Valley (MI)	L
California, U. of (Irvine)	L	Guilford (NC)	R
California, U. of (Riverside)	M	Hamline (MN)	R
California, U. of (Santa Barbara)	L	■ Hampden-Sydney (VA)	S
Calvin (MI)	M	Hartwick (NY)	R
Catholic (DC)	R	Hendrix (AR)	R
Chapman (CA)	R	Hiram (OH)	R
City College (CUNY)(NY)	L	Hobart & Wm. Smith (NY)	R
Clark (MA)	R	Hofstra (NY)	M
Columbia Col. (SC)	R	Hope (MI)	R
Cornell Col. (IA)	R		

GROUP II continues next page

PRE-LAW, continued

GROUP II, *Continued*

Howard (DC)	M	Purchase (SUNY) (NY)	R
Hunter (CUNY) (NY)	L	Queens (NC)	S
Illinois College	S	Randolph-Macon (VA)	R
Illinois, U. of (Chicago)	L	▲ Randolph-Macon Woman's Col. (VA)	S
Indiana (PA)	L	Redlands, U. of (CA)	R
James Madison (VA)	L	Ripon (WI)	S
Juniata (PA)	R	Rutgers (Camden) (NJ)	M
Kansas State	L	▲ Salem College (NC)	S
Knox (IL)	R	Salisbury State (MD)	M
Lake Forest (IL)	R	San Diego, U. of	M
LaSalle (PA)	M	San Francisco, U. of (CA)	M
Lawrence (WI)	R	Santa Clara U. (CA)	R
Loras (IA)	R	▲ Scripps (CA)	S
Loyola (LA)	R	Seton Hall (AL)	M
Loyola (MD)	M	Siena (NY)	R
Manhattan (NY)	M	South Carolina, U. of	L
Marietta (OH)	R	Spring Hill (AL)	R
Marquette (WI)	M	St. Bonaventure (NY)	R
Maryland, U. of	XL	St. John's (MN)	R
Massachusetts, U. of	L	St. Lawrence (NY)	R
Mercyhurst (PA)	R	▲ St. Mary's Col. (IN)	R
Michigan State	XL	Stetson (FL)	R
Michigan, U. of (Dearborn)	M	Stonehill (MA)	R
Millersville (PA)	M	Stony Brook (SUNY) (NY)	L
Millsaps (MS)	S	Syracuse (NY)	L
Minnesota, U. of	XL	▲ Trinity (DC)	S
Minnesota, U. of (Morris)	R	Tuskegee (AL)	M
Mississippi, U. of	M	Ursinus (PA)	R
Nebraska, U. of	L	Vermont, U. of	L
New Hampshire, U. of	L	Virginia Commonwealth U.	L
North Carolina State	L	Virginia Military Inst.	R
North Central (IL)	R	Warren Wilson (NC)	S
Oglethorpe (GA)	S	Washington & Jefferson (PA)	R
Ohio State	XL	Washington, U. of	XL
Ohio U.	L	▲ Wells (NY)	S
Ohio Wesleyan	R	West Chester (PA)	M
Oklahoma City U.	R	Western Washington U.	L
Oklahoma, U. of	L	Westminster Col. (MO)	S
Oneonta (SUNY) (NY)	M	Westmont (CA)	R
Oswego (SUNY)(NY)	M	Wheaton (MA)	R
Pittsburgh, U. of (PA)	L	Wilberforce (OH)	S
Portland State (OR)	M	Wittenberg (OH)	R
Presbyterian (SC)	S	Wofford (SC)	R
Principia (IL)	S	Wooster (OH)	R
Puget Sound (WA)	R		

PRE-LAW continues next page

PRE-LAW, continued

GROUP III
Selective

Adrian (MI)	S	Lynchburg (VA)	R
Albright (PA)	R	Massachusetts, U. of (Boston)	M
Arkansas, U. of	L	Mount St. Joseph (OH)	R
Baldwin-Wallace (OH)	R	Mount St. Mary's (MD)	R
Belmont Abbey (NC)	S	Niagara (NY)	R
▲Bennett (NC)	S	North Carolina, U. of (Wilmington)	M
California State U. (Long Beach)	L	Radford (VA)	M
California State U. (Monterey Bay)	R	Rhode Island, U. of	L
California State U. (Northridge)	L	Roanoke (VA)	R
Campbell (NC)	R	Rockford (IL)	S
▲Chatham (PA)	S	▲Rosemont (PA)	S
Chestnut Hill (PA)	S	San Francisco State (CA)	L
Emerson (MA)	R	Seattle U. (WA)	R
Fairleigh Dickinson (NJ)	M	Southwest Missouri	L
Fisk (TN)	S	▲Spelman (GA)	R
Florida A&M	M	St. Anselm (NH)	R
Fort Lewis (CO)	M	St. Mary's (TX)	R
Gwynedd-Mercy (PA)	S	Temple (PA)	L
Hawaii, U. of	L	Tennessee, U. of	XL
Heidelberg (OH)	S	Utah, U. of	L
▲Hollins (VA)	S	Virginia Wesleyan	R
Illinois State	L	Whittier (CA)	R
Longwood (VA)	R	Wilson (PA)	S
Louisiana-Lafayette	L	Wisconsin, U. of (Milwaukee)	L
Louisiana State	Xl	Wyoming, U. of	L

PRE-MED/PRE-DENTAL

Author's Note: *In addition to general college requirements and requirements of their major department, premedical and predental students must usually pass with a good grade the following: general chemistry, zoology, organic chemistry, general biology, English composition or literature, and general physics.*

Other required or highly recommended courses are: advanced biology, psychology or sociology, physical chemistry, calculus, and quantitative chemistry. Of course, the wise path to follow is to consult the exact course requirements of the school you expect to apply to. The recommended colleges below are taken primarily from our recommended departments in biology and chemistry.

GROUP I
Most Selective

Albany (SUNY) (NY)	L	Georgetown (DC)	M
Allegheny (PA)	R	Gettysburg (PA)	R
Amherst (MA)	R	Grinnell (IA)	R
Bates (ME)	R	Hamilton (NY)	R
Binghamton (SUNY) (NY)	L	Harvard (MA)	M
Boston Col. (MA)	L	Harvey Mudd (CA)	S
Bowdoin (ME)	R	Haverford (PA)	S
Brandeis (MA)	R	Holy Cross (MA)	R
Brown (RI)	M	Illinois, U. of (Urbana-Champaign)	XL
▲ Bryn Mawr (PA)	S	Illinois Wesleyan	R
Bucknell (PA)	M	Iowa State	XL
Buffalo (SUNY) (NY)	L	Iowa, U. of	XL
California Inst. of Tech.	S	Johns Hopkins (MD)	R
California, U. of (Berkeley)	XL	Kalamazoo (MI)	R
California, U. of (Los Angeles)	XL	Kenyon (OH)	R
California, U. of (San Diego)	L	Knox (IL)	R
Carleton (MN)	R	Lafayette (PA)	R
Carnegie-Mellon (PA)	M	Lawrence (WI)	R
Case Western Reserve U. (OH)	R	Macalester (MN)	R
Centre (KY)	R	Miami, U. of (FL)	L
Chicago, U. of (IL)	M	Miami, U. of (OH)	L
Citadel, The (SC)	R	MIT (MA)	M
Claremont McKenna (CA)	R	Michigan, U. of	XL
Clark (MA)	R	Middlebury (VT)	R
Colby (ME)	R	▲ Mount Holyoke (MA)	R
Colgate (NY)	R	New College (FL)	S
Colorado Col.	R	New Jersey, College of	M
Colorado School of Mines	R	North Carolina, U. of	L
Cornell (NY)	L	Northwestern (IL)	M
Dallas, U. of (TX)	R	Notre Dame (IN)	M
Dartmouth (NH)	M	Oberlin (OH)	R
Davidson (NC)	R	Occidental (CA)	R
DePauw (IN)	R	Pitzer (CA)	S
Dickinson (PA)	M	Pomona (CA)	R
Drew (NJ)	R	Princeton (NJ)	M
Duke (NC)	R	Puget Sound (WA)	R
Emory (GA)	R	Reed (OR)	R
Fairfield (CT)	M	Rhodes (TN)	R
Florida, U. of	XL	Rice (TX)	R
Franklin & Marshall (PA)	R	Richmond, U. of (VA)	R
Furman (SC)	R	Rochester, U. of (NY)	M
Geneseo (SUNY) (NY)	M		

GROUP I continues next page

PRE-MED/PRE-DENTAL, cont.

GROUP I, continued

Rutgers (NJ)	L
Skidmore (NY)	R
▲ Smith (MA)	R
South, U. of the (TN)	R
Southwestern (TX)	R
Stanford (CA)	M
Stetson (FL)	R
St. Mary's College of Maryland	R
St. Olaf (MN)	R
Susquehanna (PA)	R
Swarthmore (PA)	S
Texas, U. of (Austin)	XL
Trinity (CT)	R
Trinity (TX)	R
Tufts (MA)	M
Tulane (LA)	M
Union (NY)	R
Ursinus (PA)	R
Vanderbilt (TN)	M
Vassar (NY)	R
Villanova (PA)	M
Virginia, U. of	L
■ Wabash (IN)	S
Wake Forest (NC)	M
Washington & Lee (VA)	M
Washington U. (MO)	M
▲ Wellesley (MA)	R
Wesleyan (CT)	R
Wheaton (IL)	R
Whitman (WA)	R
Willamette (OR)	R
William & Mary (VA)	M
Williams (MA)	R
Yale (CT)	M
Yeshiva (NY)	R

GROUP II
Very Selective

▲ Agnes Scott (GA)	S
Alabama, U. of	l
Albertson (ID)	S
Albright (PA)	R
Alma (MI)	R
Arizona State	XL
Arizona, U. of	XL
Augustana (SD)	M
Austin (TX)	R
Baylor (TX)	M
Berry (GA)	R
Bethany (WV)	S
Birmingham-Southern (AL)	R
Brigham Young (UT)	XL
Butler (IN)	R
California, U. of (Davis)	L
California, U. of (Irvine)	L
California, U. of (Riverside)	M
California, U. of (Santa Barbara)	L
California, U. of (Santa Cruz)	M
Canisius (NY)	M
Carroll (WI)	R
Chapman (CA)	R
City College (CUNY)(NY)	L
College of Charleston (SC)	L
Columbia Col. (SC)	R
Colorado, U. of	L
Concordia (MN)	R
Connecticut, U. of	L
Cornell (IA)	R
Creighton (NE)	R
Delaware, U. of	L
DePaul (IL)	L
Denison (OH)	R
Denver, U. of (CO)	M
Duquesne (PA)	M
Earlham (IN)	R
Eckerd (FL)	R
Erskine (SC)	S
Evansville (IN)	R
Florida State	L
Fordham (NY)	M
Franklin (IN)	S
Georgia, U. of	XL
Gonzaga (WA)	R
Guilford (NC)	R
Hamline (MN)	R
■ Hampden-Sydney (VA)	S
Hendrix (AR)	R
Hiram (OH)	R
Hobart & Wm. Smith (NY)	R
Hofstra (NY)	M
Hood (MD)	S
Hope (MI)	R

GROUP II continues next page

PRE-MED/PRE-DENTAL, cont.

GROUP II, *Continued*

Houghton (NY)	S
Houston Baptist (TX)	R
Howard (DC)	M
Huntingdon (AL)	S
Illinois, U. of (Chicago)	L
Indiana U.	XL
Ithaca Col. (NY)	M
James Madison (VA)	L
Juniata (PA)	R
Kansas, U. of	L
Kansas State	L
Kentucky, U. of	L
Knox (IL)	R
Lake Forest (IL)	R
Lewis & Clark (OR)	R
Loyola (IL)	M
Loyola (LA)	R
Loyola (MD)	M
Lycoming (PA)	R
Marquette (WI)	M
Mary Washington (VA)	R
Massachusetts, U. of	L
McDaniel (MD)	R
Michigan State	XL
Michigan, U. of (Dearborn)	M
Millsaps (MS)	R
Minnesota, U. of (Morris)	R
Mississippi State	L
Monmouth (IL)	S
Morningside (IA)	S
Muhlenberg (PA)	R
Nebraska Wesleyan	R
Nevada, U. of (Reno)	L
New Hampshire, U. of	L
New York U.	L
North Central (IL)	R
Ohio State	XL
Ohio Wesleyan	R
Pacific Lutheran (OR)	R
Pennsylvania State	XL
Pittsburgh, U. of (PA)	L
Presbyterian (SC)	S
Randolph-Macon (VA)	R

▲Randolph-Macon Woman's Col. (VA)	S
Redlands, U. of (CA)	R
Regis (CO)	R
Richard Stockton (NJ)	M
Ripon (WI)	S
San Diego, U. of (CA)	M
San Francisco, U. of (CA)	M
Scranton, U. of (PA)	M
▲Scripps (CA)	S
Seton Hall (NJ)	M
Siena (NY)	R
Spring Hill (AL)	R
St. John's (MN)	R
St. Joseph's U. (PA)	R
St. Louis (MO)	M
St. Louis Col. of Pharmacy (MO)	S
St. Thomas, U. of (MN)	S
St. Thomas, U. of (TX)	R
Stetson (FL)	R
Stony Brook (SUNY) (NY)	L
Tennessee, U. of	XL
Texas A&M	XL
Transylvania (KY)	S
Truman State (MO)	M
Tuskegee (AL)	M
Utah, U. of	L
Valparaiso U. (IN)	M
Vermont, U. of	L
Washington College (MD)	S
Washington & Jefferson (PA)	R
Washington, U. of	XL
▲Wells (NY)	S
Westminster (MO)	S
Westminster (PA)	R
Westmont (CA)	R
Wheaton (MA)	R
Winona State U. (MN)	M
Wisconsin, U. of	XL
Wittenberg (OH)	R
Wofford (SC)	R
Wooster (OH)	R
Wyoming, U. of	L

PRE-MED/PRE-DENTAL continues next page

Enrollment Code		
■ Men Only	**S = Small** (less than 1000 students)	**R = Moderate** (1000-3000 students)	**M = Medium** (3000-8000 students)
▲ Women Only	**L = Large** (8000-20,000 students)	**XL = Extra Large** (over 20,000 students)

PRE-MED/PRE-DENTAL, cont.

GROUP III
Selective

American International (MA) .... R
Benedictine (IL) .... R
▲ Bennett (NC) .... S
Blackburn (IL) .... S
Brooklyn Col. (SUNY) (NY) L
California State U. (Channel Islands) .. R
California State U. (Fullerton) L
California State U. (Monterey Bay) ...... R
California State U. (San Jose) L
Carroll (MT) .... R
Carson-Newman (TN) .... R
Delaware Valley (PA) .... R
Dillard (LA) .... R
East Carolina (NC) L
Florida A&M .... M
Florida Southern .... R
Freed-Hardeman (TN) .... R
Heidelberg (OH) .... S
Ind.U.-Purdue U.-Indianapolis (IN) L
Jacksonville (FL) .... R
Kentucky Wesleyan .... S

Louisiana-Lafayette L
Louisiana State XL
Lynchburg (VA) .... R
Mount St. Joseph (OH) .... R
Mount St. Mary's (MD) .... R
Nova Southeastern (FL) .... R
Rider (NJ) .... R
▲ Spelman (GA) .... R
St. Mary's (TX) .... R
St. Vincent (PA) .... R
South Dakota, U. of .... M
Temple (PA) L
Texas, U. of (San Antonio) L
Thomas More (KY) .... R
Virginia Commonwealth L
Virginia Wesleyan .... R
Walla Walla (WA) .... R
Wartburg (IA) .... R
Wayne State (MI) L
Wilkes (PA) .... R
Xavier U. of Louisiana .... R

PSYCHOLOGY

GROUP I
Most Selective

Allegheny (PA)	R	Miami U. (OH)	L
Amherst (MA)	R	Michigan, U. of	XL
▲ Barnard (NY)	R	▲ Mount Holyoke (MA)	R
Bates (ME)	R	New College (FL)	S
Binghamton (SUNY) (NY)	L	New Jersey, College of	M
Boston U. (MA)	L	New York U.	L
Brandeis (MA)	R	North Carolina, U. of	L
▲ Bryn Mawr (PA)	S	Northwestern (IL)	M
Bucknell (PA)	M	Notre Dame, U of (IN)	M
California, U. of (Berkeley)	XL	Pennsylvania, U. of	L
California, U. of (Los Angeles)	XL	Pitzer (CA)	S
California, U. of (San Diego)	L	Pomona (CA)	S
Carnegie-Mellon (PA)	M	Reed (OR)	R
Case Western Reserve U. (OH)	R	Richmond, U. of (VA)	R
Centre (KY)	R	Rhodes (TN)	R
Chicago, U. of (IL)	M	Rochester, U. of (NY)	M
Claremont McKenna (CA)	R	Rutgers (NJ)	L
Colby (ME)	R	▲ Scripps (CA)	S
Colorado College	R	▲ Simmons (MA)	R
Columbia (NY)	M	Skidmore (NY)	R
Connecticut Col.	R	▲ Smith (MA)	R
DePauw (IN)	R	Southwestern (TX)	R
Dickinson (PA)	R	Stanford (CA)	M
Drew (NJ)	R	St. Mary's College of Maryland	R
Duke (NC)	M	St. Olaf (MN)	R
Emory (GA)	R	Swarthmore (PA)	R
Franklin & Marshall (PA)	R	Tufts (MA)	M
Furman (SC)	R	Tulane (LA)	M
Georgetown (DC)	M	Union (NY)	R
George Washington (DC)	M	Vanderbilt (TN)	M
Georgia Institute of Tech.	L	Vassar (NY)	R
Gettysburg (PA)	R	Virginia, U. of	L
Grinnell (IA)	R	■ Wabash (IN)	S
Gustavus Adolphus (MN)	R	Wake Forest (NC)	M
Harvard (MA)	M	Wesleyan (CT)	R
Haverford (PA)	S	Wheaton (IL)	R
Illinois, U. of (Urbana-Champaign)	XL	Whitman (WA)	R
Illinois Wesleyan	R	Willamette (OR)	R
James Madison (VA)	L	Williams (MA)	R
Kenyon (OH)	R	Yale (CT)	M
Lafayette (PA)	R	Yeshiva (NY)	M
Macalester (MN)	R		

PSYCHOLOGY continues next page

Enrollment Code

■ Men Only	S = Small (less than 1000 students)	R = Moderate (1000-3000 students)	M = Medium (3000-8000 students)
▲ Women Only	L = Large (8000-20,000 students)	XL = Extra Large (over 20,000 students)	

PSYCHOLOGY, continued

═══════════════ **GROUP II** ═══════════════
Very Selective

▲ Agnes Scott (GA) .... S	Herbert Lehman (CUNY) (NY) L
Albany (SUNY) (NY) L	Hobart & Wm. Smith (NY) .... R
Albright (PA) .... R	Hood (MD) .... S
Alfred (NY) .... R	Hope (MI) .... R
Arizona State XL	Houghton (NY) .... S
Arizona, U. of XL	Houston, U. of (TX) L
Belmont (TN) .... R	Hunter (CUNY) (NY) L
Beloit (WI) .... R	Illinois, U. of (Chicago) L
Berry (GA) .... R	Indiana U. XL
California, U. of (Santa Barbara) L	Iowa, U. of XL
California, U. of (Riverside) .... M	John Carroll (OH) .... R
California, U. of (Santa Cruz) .... M	Kean (NJ) .... M
Carroll (WI) .... R	Kentucky, U. of L
Central Florida, U. of L	Lake Forest (IL) .... R
Chapman (CA) .... R	LaSalle (PA) .... M
Cincinnati, U. of L	Lebanon Valley (PA) .... R
Clark (MA) .... R	LeMoyne (NY) .... R
Colorado State L	Loras (IA) .... R
Concordia (MN) .... R	Louisiana State U. L
Cornell Col. (IA) .... R	Loyola (IL) .... M
Creighton (NE) .... R	Luther (IA) .... R
Denison (OH) .... R	Lycoming (PA) .... R
Denver, U. of (CO) .... M	Manhattanville (NY) .... R
DePaul (IL) L	Marist (NY) .... M
Dubuque, U. of (IA) .... S	Marquette (WI) .... R
Earlham (IN) .... R	Maryville (TN) .... S
Eastern Michigan L	Mary Washington (VA) .... R
Elmira (NY) .... R	Massachusetts, U. of L
Elon (NC) .... R	Mercer (GA) .... R
Fairfield (CT) .... M	Merrimack (MA) .... R
Fairmont (WV) .... M	Michigan State XL
Flagler (FL) .... R	Millersville (PA) .... M
Florida Atlantic L	▲ Mills (CA) .... S
Florida Inst. of Tech. .... R	Minnesota, U. of (Morris) .... R
Florida International L	Minnesota, U. of XL
Florida State L	Missouri, U. of XL
George Mason (VA) L	Missouri, U. of (Kansas City) .... M
Georgia State .... `L	Missouri, U. of (St. Louis) .... M
Grand Valley (MI) L	Moravian (PA) .... R
Guilford (NC) .... R	Muhlenberg (PA) .... R
Hamline (MN) .... R	Nebraska Wesleyan .... R
Hampton (VA) .... M	Nevada, U. of (Las Vegas) .... M
Hanover (IN) .... R	New Paltz (SUNY) (NY) .... M
Hendrix (AR) .... R	*GROUP II continues next page*

Enrollment Code
■ Men Only | S = Small (less than 1000 students) | R = Moderate (1000-3000 students) | M = Medium (3000-8000 students)
▲ Women Only | L = Large (8000-20,000 students) | XL = Extra Large (over 20,000 students)

PSYCHOLOGY, continued

GROUP II, Continued

New Mexico, U. of L
Newman U. (KS) .... S
North Carolina (Asheville) .... R
Ohio State XL
Ohio U. L
Ohio Wesleyan .... R
Oklahoma City U. .... R
Oklahoma, U. of L
Oregon, U. of L
Oswego (SUNY) (NY) .... M
Pace (NY) .... M
Pittsburgh, U. of (PA) L
Portland State (OR) .... M
Queens (CUNY) (NY) L
Randolph-Macon (VA) .... R
▲ Randolph-Macon Woman's Col. (VA) ..... S
Roanoke (VA) .... R
Rockhurst (MO) .... R
Rollins (FL) .... R
Salisbury State (MD) .... M
San Francisco, U. of (CA) .... M
Santa Clara, U. of (CA) .... M
Shepherd (WV) .... R
Siena (NY) .... R
Southern California L
St. Lawrence (NY) .... R
St. Mary's College (CA) .... R
St. Thomas, U. of (TX) .... R
Stetson (FL) .... R

Stonehill (MA) .... R
Stony Brook (SUNY) (NY) L
Susquehanna (PA) .... R
▲ Sweet Briar (VA) .... S
Syracuse (NY) L
Texas, U. of (Austin) XL
Transylvania (KY) .... R
Tulsa, U. of (OK) .... R
Valparaiso U. (IN) .... M
Vermont, U of L
Virginia Poly. Inst. L
Virginia, U. of L
Washington College (MD) .... S
Washington & Jefferson (PA) .... R
Washington, U. of XL
Webster (MO) .... R
▲ Wells (NY) .... S
Western Michigan L
Westminster (MO) .... S
Westminster (UT) .... R
Westmont (CA) .... R
Wheaton (MA) .... R
Whitworth (WA) .... R
Winthrop (SC) .... M
Wisconsin, U. of XL
Wittenberg (OH) .... R
Wofford (SC) .... R
Xavier, (OH) .... R

GROUP III
Selective

Alabama, U. of (Birmingham) .... M
American International (MA) .... R
Aquinas (MI) .... R
Arcadia (PA) .... R
Baker (KS) .... S
Bethel (MN) .... R
Biola (CA) .... R
Blackburn (IL) .... S
Bridgewater (MA) .... M
Bridgewater (VA) .... R
Brockport (SUNY)(NY) .... M
Caldwell (NJ) .... S
California Lutheran .... R
California State U. (Bakersfield) .... M
California State U. (Chico) L
California State U. (Dominguez Hills). M

California State U. (Chico) L
California State U. (Long Beach) L
California State U. (Los Angeles) L
California State U. (Northridge) L
California State U. (Sacramento) .... M
California State U. (San Bernardino) .. M
California State U. (San Marcos) .... M
California State U. (Stanislaus) .... M
Canisius (NY) .... M
Carson-Newman (TN) .... R
Carthage (WI) .... R
Castleton State (VT) .... R
▲ Cedar Crest (PA) .... S
Central Connecticut .... M

GROUP III continues next page

PSYCHOLOGY, continued

GROUP III, Continued

Central Michigan	L	
Chapman (CA)	R	
Coker (SC)	S	
Colorado, U. of (Colorado Springs)	M	
Colorado, U. of (Denver)	M	
Delaware State	R	
Dominican (CA)	S	
Dominican (IL)	S	
D'Youville (NY)	R	
East Carolina	L	
Eastern Connecticut	M	
Eastern Illinois	L	
Edgewood (WI)	S	
Fitchburg (MA)	R	
Framingham (MA)	M	
Franciscan U. of Steubenville (OH)	R	
▲Hollins (VA)	S	
Holy Names (CA)	S	
John Jay College (CUNY)(NY)	M	
▲Judson (AL)	S	
Keene State (NH)	R	
Kentucky Wesleyan	S	
Lindenwood (MO)	S	
Long Island U. (C.W.Post)(NY)	M	
Long Island U. (Southampton)(NY)	R	
Longwood (VA)	R	
Lyndon State(VT)	R	
Lyon (AR)	S	
Maine, U. of (Farmington)	R	
Manchester (IN)	R	
▲Mary Baldwin (VA)	S	
Marymount (VA)	R	
Massachusetts, U. of (Dartmouth)	M	
Mercy (NY)	M	
▲Meredith (NC)	R	
Middle Tennessee	L	
Millersville (PA)	M	
Molloy (NY)	R	
Montclair State (NJ)	M	
Muskingum (OH)	R	
New Hampshire, U. of	L	
North Carolina (Greensboro)	M	
North Carolina (Wilmington)	M	
Northern Arizona	L	
Northwestern (IA)	R	
Nyack (NY)	R	
Oakland City U. (IN)	R	
Oklahoma Baptist	R	

Otterbein (OH)	R	
Ozarks, College of the (MO)	R	
Palm Beach Atlantic (FL)	R	
▲Pine Manor (MA)	S	
Point Park (PA)	R	
Potsdam (SUNY)(NY)	R	
Purchase (SUNY) (NY)	R	
Regis (CO)	R	
Rockford (IL)	S	
Roger Williams (RI)	R	
▲Rosemont (PA)	S	
Sacred Heart (CT)	R	
St. Anselm (NH)	R	
St. Edward's (TX)	M	
St. Francis (NY)	R	
St. Joseph's (IN)	S	
St. Joseph's (NY)	R	
St. Martin's (WA)	S	
St. Scholastica (MN)	R	
St. Thomas Aquinas (NY)	R	
St. Vincent (PA)	R	
Seton Hall (NJ)	M	
Siena Heights (MI)	S	
Shippensburg (PA)	M	
Simpson (IA)	S	
Sonoma State (CA)	M	
Southern Connecticut	M	
Southern Illinois U. (Carbondale)	L	
Springfield (MA)	R	
▲Stephens (MO)	S	
Taylor (IN)	R	
Texas, U. of (Tyler)	R	
Texas Wesleyan	R	
Virginia Commonwealth U.	L	
Virginia Wesleyan	R	
West Florida	M	
Western Kentucky	L	
Western New England (MA)	R	
Westfield (MA)	M	
Wheeling Jesuit (WV)	R	
Wilkes (PA)	R	
William Paterson (NJ)	M	
Wilson (PA)	S	
Wisconsin, U. of (Green Bay)	M	
Wisconsin, U. of (Stout)	M	
Worcester State (MA)	M	
Wyoming, U. of	L	
Xavier University of Louisiana	R	

RELIGIOUS STUDIES

GROUP I
Most Selective

▲ Barnard (NY) .... R	Northwestern (IL) .... M
Bates (ME) .... R	Notre Dame (IN) .... M
Brown (RI) .... M	Oberlin (OH) .... R
California, U. of (Berkeley) XL	Occidental (CA) .... R
Case Western (OH) .... R	Pittsburgh, U. of (PA) L
Centre (KY) .... R	Pomona (CA) .... R
Chicago, U. of (IL) .... M	Princeton (NJ) .... M
Claremont McKenna (CA) .... R	Rhodes (TN) .... R
Colby (ME) .... R	Richmond, U. of (VA) .... R
Colgate (NY) .... R	Rutgers (NJ) L
Columbia (NY) .... M	St. Joseph's (PA) .... R
Dartmouth (NH) .... M	South, U. of the (TN) .... R
Davidson (NC) .... R	Southwestern (TX) .... R
DePauw (IN) .... R	Stanford (CA) .... M
Dickinson (PA) .... R	Trinity (CT) .... R
Drew (NJ) .... R	Virginia, U. of L
Duke (NC) .... M	■ Wabash (IN) .... S
Emory (GA) .... R	Wake Forest (NC) .... M
Furman (SC) .... R	▲ Wellesley (MA) .... R
Georgetown (DC) .... M	Wesleyan (CT) .... R
Hamilton (NY) .... R	Wheaton (IL) .... R
Haverford (PA) .... S	William & Mary (VA) .... M
Kenyon (OH) .... R	Wisconsin Lutheran .... S
Lawrence (WI) .... R	Yale (CT) .... M
North Carolina, U. of L	

GROUP II
Very Selective

Alaska Pacific .... S	Detroit Mercy (MI) .... M
Arizona State XL	Drury (MO) .... S
Austin (TX) .... R	Duquesne (PA) .... M
Baylor (TX) .... M	Earlham (IN) .... R
Birmingham-Southern (AL) .... R	Eckerd (FL) .... R
Brigham Young (UT) XL	Elizabethtown (PA) .... R
Bryan (TN) .... S	Florida State L
Bryn Athyn (PA) .... S	Fordham (NY) .... M
California, U. of (Santa Barbara) L	Gordon (MA) .... R
Catholic U. (DC) .... M	Guilford (NC) .... R
Christendom (VA) .... S	Harding (AR) .... M
Concordia (CA) .... R	Hendrix (AR) .... R
Creighton (NE) .... R	Hiram (OH) .... R
Denver, U. of (CO) .... M	
DePaul (IL) L	

GROUP II continues next page

Enrollment Code		
■ **Men Only**	**S = Small** (less than 1000 students)	**R = Moderate** (1000-3000 students)	**M = Medium** (3000-8000 students)
▲ **Women Only**	**L = Large** (8000-20,000 students)	**XL = Extra Large** (over 20,000 students)

RELIGIOUS STUDIES, continued

GROUP II, Continued

Houghton (NY) .... S	St. Thomas, U. of (TX) .... R
Iowa, U. of XL	Sanford (AL) .... R
John Carroll (OH) .... R	San Diego, U. of (CA) .... M
LaSalle (PA) .... M	Santa Clara U. (CA) .... M
Loyola (LA) .... R	Southern Methodist (TX) L
Lycoming (PA) .... R	Stetson (FL) .... R
Marquette)WI) .... M	Stony Brook (SUNY) (NY) L
Master's (CA) .... R	Syracuse (NY) L
Muhlenberg (PA) .... R	Tennessee, U. of XL
Newman U. (KS) .... S	Texas Christian U. .... M
North Carolina (Charlotte).................... L	Valparaiso U. (IN) .... M
Portland, U. of (OR) .... R	Vermont, U. of L
Roanoke (VA) .... R	Wartburg (IA) .... R
Rockhurst (MO) .... R	Westmont (CA) .... R
Rollins (FL) .... R	Whitworth (WA) .... R
Rowan (NJ) .... M	Wittenberg (OH) .... R
St. Bonaventure (NY) .... R	Wofford (SC) .... R
St. John's (MN) .... R	Wooster (OH) .... R
▲St. Mary's College (IN) .... R	Xavier (OH) .... R
St. Mary's (MN) .... R	

GROUP III
Selective

Brescia (KY) .... S	Muskingum (OH) .... R
California State U. (Chico) L	Northwestern (IA) .... S
California State U. (Fullerton) L	Northwestern (MN) .... R
California State U. (Long Beach) L	Nyack (NY) .... R
Carthage (WI) .... R	Oakland City U. (IN) .... R
Cumberland (KY) .... R	Oklahoma Baptist .... R
De Sales (PA) .... S	Olivet Nazarene (IL) .... R
Doane (NE) .... S	Ouachita Baptist (AR) .... R
Eastern Mennonite (VA) .... R	Regis (CO).. R
Franciscan U. of Steubenville (OH)...... R	▲St. Catherine (MN) .... R
Freed-Hardeman (TN) .... R	Saint Peter's (NJ) .... R
John Brown (AR)..................................... R	St. Vincent (PA) .... R
Kentucky Wesleyan .... R	Seton Hall (NJ) .... M
King (TN) .... S	Silver Lake (WI) .... S
Louisiana College .... R	Southwest Baptist (MO) .... R
Louisiana State XL	Taylor (IN) .... R
Marywood (PA) .... R	Union University (TN) .... R
Mercyhurst (PA) .... R	Virginia Commonwealth U. L
Milligan (TN).. S	Virginia Wesleyan................................. R
Mississippi College .... R	Wheeling Jesuit (WV) .... R
■ Morehouse (GA) .... R	

Enrollment Code		
■ Men Only	S = Small (less than 1000 students)	R = Moderate (1000-3000 students)	M = Medium (3000-8000 students)
▲ Women Only	L = Large (8000-20,000 students)	XL = Extra Large (over 20,000 students)

SOCIOLOGY

GROUP I
Most Selective

Amherst (MA) .... R	Illinois, U. of (Urbana-Champaign) ... XL
▲ Barnard (NY) .... R	Kalamazoo (MI) .... R
Binghamton (SUNY)(NY) .... M	Lycoming (PA) .... R
▲ Bryn Mawr (PA) .... S	Michigan, U. of XL
Bucknell (PA) .... M	North Carolina, U. of L
California, U. of (Berkeley) XL	Northwestern (IL) .... M
California, U. of (Los Angeles) XL	Notre Dame (IN) .... M
Chicago, U. of (IL) .... M	Oberlin (OH) .... R
Clarkson (NY) .... M	Pennsylvania, U. of L
Colorado College .... R	Pitzer (CA) .... S
Columbia (NY) .... M	Pomona (CA) .... R
Dartmouth (NH) .... M	Princeton (NJ) .... M
Florida, U. of XL	Southwestern (TX) .... R
Franklin & Marshall (PA) .... R	Stanford (CA) .... M
Geneseo (SUNY)(NY) .... M	Trinity (TX) .... R
Georgetown (DC) .... M	Virginia, U. of L
Gettysburg (PA) .... S	Wheaton (IL) .... R
Grinnell (IA) .... R	Willamette (OR) .... R
Harvard (MA) .... M	Yale (CT) .... M

GROUP II
Very Selective

Albany (SUNY) (NY) L	Knox (IL) .... R
Arizona, U. of XL	Lake Forest (IL) .... R
Asbury (KY) .... R	Lewis & Clark (OR) .... R
Beloit (WI) .... R	Manhattanville (NY) .... R
California, U. of (Santa Barbara) L	McDaniel (MD) .... R
College of Charleston (SC) L	Merrimack (MA) .... R
Clemson(SC) L	Minnesota, U. of XL
Colorado, U. of L	Mississippi State L
Concordia (MN) .... R	Moravian (PA) .... R
Cornell Col. (IA) .... R	■ Morehouse (GA) .... R
Covenant (GA) .... S	Mount Mercy (IA) .... S
Dayton, U. of (OH) .... M	New Mexico, U. of L
Denison (OH) .... R	North Carolina (Asheville) .... R
Earlham (IN) .... R	North Texas L
Florida International L	Oklahoma State L
Georgetown College (KY) .... R	Pace (NY) .... M
Gordon (MA) .... R	Principia (IL) .... S
Hamline (MN) .... R	Puget Sound (WA) .... R
Hanover (IN) .... R	Queens (CUNY)(NY) L
Hendrix (AR) .... R	Regis (CO) .... R
Hofstra (NY) .... M	Roanoke (VA) .... R
Howard (DC) .... M	Rutgers (Camden) (NJ) .... M
Illinois College .... S	▲ Salem Col. (NC) .... S
Indiana U. XL	San Diego State U. (CA) XL
Iowa State XL	▲ Simmons (MA) .... R
James Madison (VA) .... M	

GROUP II continues next page

SOCIOLOGY, continued

GROUP II, *Continued*

St. Lawrence (NY)	R
St. Mary's Col. (CA)	R
South Dakota School of Mines	R
Syracuse (NY)	L
▲Trinity (DC)	S
Washington State	L
▲Wells (NY)	S
Westminster (PA)	R
Western Washington U.	L
Wheaton (MA)	R
Winona State U. (MN)	M
Wisconsin, U. of	XL
Wisconsin, U. of (Stevens Point)	M
Wofford (SC)	R
Wooster (OH)	R

GROUP III
Selective

Adrian (MI)	S
Akron, U. of (OH)	L
Augusta (GA)	M
Belmont Abbey (NC)	S
Benedictine (KS)	S
Biola (CA)	R
Bridgewater (VA)	R
Bridgewater State (MA)	M
California State U. (Fresno)	L
California State U. (Fullerton)	L
California State U. (Hayward)	M
California State U. (Los Angeles)	L
California State U. (Northridge)	L
California State U. (Sacramento)	M
California State U. (San Bernardino)	M
California State U. (San Marcos)	M
Central Connecticut	M
Coker (SC)	S
Doane (NE)	S
D'Youville (NY)	R
Eastern (PA)	R
Eastern Connecticut	M
Eastern Michigan	L
Fisk (TN)	S
Framingham State (MA)	M
George Fox (OR)	S
Georgia State	L
Grambling (LA)	M
Hartwick (NY)	R
Johnson C. Smith (NC)	R
Kean (NJ)	M
Indiana (PA)	L
Indiana U.-Purdue U.-Indianapolis (IN)	L
Lamar (TX)	M
Lenoir-Rhyne (NC)	R
Louisville (KY)	L
Lynchburg (VA)	R
Manchester (IN)	R
▲Mary Baldwin (VA)	S
Massachusetts Col. of Lib. Arts. (N. Adams)	R
Massachusetts, U. of (Boston)	M
Massachusetts, U. of (Dartmouth)	M
Michigan State	XL
Minnesota, U. of (Duluth)	m
Nevada, U. of (Reno)	M
New Orleans (LA)	L
North Carolina, U. of (Wilmington)	M
Northern Colorado	L
Northern Illinois	L
Northern Michigan	M
Old Dominion (VA)	L
Quincy (IL)	R
St. Anselm (NH)	R
▲St. Catherine (MN)	R
St. Mary's U. of San Antonio (TX)	R
St. Rose (NY)	R
San Francisco State (CA)	L
Shaw (NC)	R
Shippensburg (PA)	M
Sonoma State (CA)	M
South Alabama	M
Southern Connecticut	M
Southern Oregon State U.	M
▲Spelman (GA)	R
Suffolk (MA)	R
Temple (PA)	L
Virginia Wesleyan	R
Wagner (NY)	R
West Chester (PA)	M
Western Connecticut State	M
Western Illinois	L
Western Kentucky	L
Western Michigan	L
Whitman (WA)	R
William Paterson (NJ)	M
Wilson (PA)	S
Wisconsin, U. of (LaCrosse)	L

ZOOLOGY

GROUP I
Most Selective

California, U. of (Berkeley)	XL	Michigan, U. of	XL
Cornell (NY)	L	North Carolina, U. of	L
Florida, U. of	XL	Pennsylvania State	XL
Miami, U. of (OH)	L	Wisconsin, U. of	XL

GROUP II
Very Selective

Albertson (ID)	S	Maryland, U. of	XL
Arizona State	XL	Massachusetts, U. of	L
Brigham Young (UT)	XL	North Carolina State	L
California, U. of (Davis)	L	North Central (IL)	R
California, U. of (Santa Barbara)	L	Ohio Wesleyan	R
Clemson (SC)	L	Ohio U.	L
Connecticut, U. of	L	Oklahoma, U. of	L
Georgia, U. of	L	Oswego (SUNY)(NY)	M
Hawaii, U. of	L	Texas A&M	XL
Indiana U.	XL	Texas, U. of (Austin)	XL
Iowa State	XL	Vermont, U. of	L
Kansas, U. of	L	Washington State	L
Kentucky, U. of	XL	Washington, U. of	XL

GROUP III
Selective

Cal. Poly. State U. (Pomona)	L	Montana, U. of	M
California State U. (San Jose)	L	Oregon State	L
Colorado State	I	San Jose State (CA)	L
Eastern Illinois	L	Southern Illinois U. (Carbondale)	L
Howard (DC)	M	Tennessee, U. of	XL
Louisiana-Lafayette	L	Weber State (UT)	L
Louisiana State	XL	Wyoming, U. of	L

Enrollment Code			
■ Men Only	S = Small (less than 1000 students)	R = Moderate (1000-3000 students)	M = Medium (3000-8000 students)
▲ Women Only	L = Large (8000-20,000 students)	XL = Extra Large (over 20,000 students)	

SECTION TWO

MISCELLANEOUS MAJORS

AFRICANA STUDIES

Albany (SUNY) (NY)
Bates (ME)
Brooklyn (CUNY) (NY)
California, U. of (Berkeley)
California, U. of (Santa Barbara)
Chicago, U. of (IL)
City (CUNY)(NY)
Coe (IA)
Columbia (NY)
Denison (OH)
Duke (NC)
Earlham (IN)
Eastern Illinois
Emory (GA)
Harvard (MA)
Howard (DC)
Illinois, U. of (Chicago)
Loyola Marymount (CA)
Luther (IA)
Mercer (GA)
New York U.

North Carolina (Chapel Hill)
Northwestern (IL)
Oberlin (OH)
Ohio State U.
Pennsylvania, U. of
Pittsburgh, U. of (PA)
Princeton (NJ)
Rutgers (NJ)
San Diego State (CA)
San Francisco State (CA)
Stanford (CA)
Stony Brook (SUNY)(NY)
Toledo, U. of (OH)
Vassar (NY)
Washington U. (MO)
▲ Wellesley (MA)
Wesleyan (CT)
Wooster (OH)
Wisconsin, U. of
Yale (CT)

ALTERNATIVE COLLEGES (see page ix)

Antioch (OH)
Atlantic, College of the (ME)
Berea (WV)
Deep Springs (CA)
Eugene Lang (NY)
Evergreen (WA)
Hampshire (MA)
Marlboro (VT)
New College (FL)

New School U.-Eugene Lang College (NY)
Prescott (AZ)
St. John's (MD) (NM)
Shimer (IL)
Simon's Rock (MA)
Sterling (VT)
Thomas Aquinas (CA)
Unity (ME)
Warren Wilson (NC)

ANIMAL SCIENCES

Arizona, U. of
Arkansas, U. of
Auburn (AL)
Berry (GA)
Brigham Young (UT)
Cal Poly (Pomona)
Cal Poly (SLO)
Cal State U. (Fresno)
California, U. of (Davis)
Clemson (SC)
Colorado State
Connecticut, U. of
Cornell (NY)
Delaware Valley (PA)
Delaware, U. of
Florida, U. of
Georgia U. of
Hampshire (MA)
Hawaii, U. of
Idaho, U. of

Illinois, U. of
Iowa State
Kansas State
Kentucky, U. of
Louisiana State U.
Maine, U. of
Maryland, U. of
Massachusetts, U. of
Michigan State
Minnesota, U. of
Mississippi State
Missouri, U. of
Montana, U. of (Bozeman)
Nebraska, U. of
Nevada, U of (Reno)
New Hampshire, U. of
New Mexico State
North Carolina State
North Dakota State U.

■ Men Only
▲ Women Only

ANIMAL SCIENCES continues next page

ANIMAL SCIENCES CONTINUED

Ohio State
Oklahoma State
Oregon State
Ozarks, College of the (MO)
Pennsylvania State
Purdue (IN)
Rhode Island, U. of
Rutgers (NJ)
South Dakota State
Southern Illinois (Carbondale)
Southwest Missouri

Tennessee
Texas A&M
Texas Tech
Utah State
Vermont, U. of
Virginia Poly
Washington State
West Virginia U.
Wisconsin, U.of
Wyoming, U. of

APPLIED MATHEMATICS

American (DC)
Auburn (AL)
▲ Barnard (NY)
Boston U. (MA)
Brown (RI)
Cal Tech
California, U. of (Berkeley)
California, U. of (Los Angeles)
California, U. of (San Diego)
Carnegie-Mellon (PA)
Case Western (OH)
Chicago, U. of (IL)
Colgate (NY)
Colorado, U. of
Columbia (NY)
Connecticut, U. of
Florida State
George Washington (DC)
Georgia Tech
Harvard (MA)
Idaho, U. of

Illinois Inst. of Tech
Michigan, U. of
Missouri, U. of (Rolla)
New Jersey Inst of Tech.
Northwestern (IL)
Pitzer (CA)
Rice (TX)
Rochester, U. of (NY) .
Rutgers (NJ)
San Jose State (CA)
Stony Brook (SUNY)(NY)
Tulane (LA)
Tulsa (OK)
Virginia, U. of
Wake Forest (NC)
Washington U. (MO)
Western Michigan
Western Washington
Wisconsin
Worcester Poly (MA)
Yale (CT)

ARCHAEOLOGY

Baylor (TX)
Boston U. (MA)
Bowdoin (ME)
Brown (RI)
▲ Bryn Mawr (PA)
Cornell (NY)
Dartmouth (NH)
Dickinson (PA)
Evansville (IN)
Florida State
George Washington (DC)
Hamilton (NY)
Harvard (MA)
Haverford (PA)
Hunter (CUNY) (NY)
Kent State (OH)
Maryland, U. of

Michigan, U. of
Missouri, U. of
North Carolina, U. of (Greensboro)
New York U.
Oberlin (OH)
Rhode Island College
Texas, U. of
Virginia
Washington & Lee (VA)
Washington U. (MO)
▲ Wellesley (MA)
Wesleyan (CT)
West Florida
Wheaton (IL)
Wisconsin (La Crosse)
Wooster (OH)
Yale (CT)

■ Men Only
▲ Women Only

ART THERAPY

Alverno (WI)
Anna Maria (MA)
Arcadia (PA)
Art Institute of Chicago (IL)
Avila (MO)
Barat (IL)
Bowling Green (OH)
Brescia (KY)
Capital U. (OH)
Carlow (PA)
▲ Converse (SC)
▲ Edgewood (WI)
Harding (AR)
Indianapolis, U. of
▲ Lesley (MA)

Long Island U. (CW Post)(NY)
Marygrove (MI)
Marian Col. of Fond du Lac (WI)
▲ Meredith (NC)
Millikin (IL)
Pittsburg (KS)
Russell Sage (NY)
Santa Fe, Col. of (NM)
▲ Seton Hill (PA)
South Illinois (Edwardsville)
Spring Hill (AL)
Springfield (MA)
St. Thomas Aquinas (NY)
Wisconsin (Superior)

ATMOSPHERIC SCIENCES

Albany (SUNY) (NY)
Arizona, U. of
Brockport (SUNY) (NY)
California, U. of (Davis)
Cornell (NY)
Embry-Riddle (FL)
Florida Inst. of Tech.
Florida State
Hawaii
Iowa State
Kansas
Lyndon State (VT)
Metropolitan State (CO)
Millersville (PA)
Nebraska
North Carolina State
North Dakota, U. of
Northern Illinois

Northland (WI)
Oklahoma, U. of
Oneonta (SUNY) (NY)
Pennsylvania State
Purdue (IN)
San Francisco State (CA)
San Jose State (CA)
St. Louis University (MO)
South Alabama
Stony Brook (SUNY)(NY)
Texas A&M
Utah, U. of
Valparaiso (IN)
Washington, U. of
Western Illinois
Western Connecticut
Wisconsin, U. of
Wisconsin, U. of (Milwaukee)

AUDIOLOGY/SPEECH/LANGUAGE THERAPY

Akron, U. of (OH)
Arizona
Arizona State
Ball State (IN)
Boston U.
Buffalo (SUNY) (NY)
California State U. (Fresno)
California State U. (Hayward)
Clarion (PA)
Colorado
East Stroudsburg (PA)
Eastern Illinois
Elmira (NY)
Florida
Florida State

Geneseo (SUNY) (NY)
Geneva (PA)
George Washington (DC)
Hardin-Simmons (TX)
Hawaii
Hofstra (NY)
Illinois, U. of
Iowa, U. of
James Madison (VA)
Kansas
Kean (NJ)
Longwood (VA)
Loyola (MD)
Maryville (TN)

■ Men Only
▲ Women Only

AUDIOLOGY / SPEECH / LANGUAGE THERAPY continues next page

AUDIOLOGY/SPEECH/LANGUAGE THER. cont.

Michigan State
Misericordia, College (PA)
Montevallo (AL)
Moorhead (MN)
Nazareth (NY)
Nebraska
New Hampshire, U. of
New Paltz (SUNY) (NY)
No. Colorado
No. Iowa
No. Michigan
Oklahoma
Pace (NY)
Plattsburg (SUNY) (NY)
Portland State (OR)
Purdue (IN)
Richard Stockton (NJ)
Rhode Island
St. John's (NY)

S. Alabama
S. Dakota, U. of
S. Florida
Southeastern Louisiana
Syracuse (NY)
Tennessee
Texas
Texas (Dallas)
Texas Christian
Towson (MD)
Tulsa (OK)
Utah State
Washington, U. of
Wayne State (MI)
Western Michigan
Western Washington
Worcester State (MA)
Wisconsin
Wyoming

AVIATION MANAGEMENT

Aeronautics, College of (NY)
Auburn (AL)
Daniel Webster (NH)
Dowling (NY)
Dubuque, U. of (IA)
Eastern Kentucky
Eastern Michigan
Embry-Riddle (FL)
Fairmont (WV)
Farmingdale (SUNY)(NY)
Florida Inst. of Tech.
Hampton (VA)
Henderson (AR)

Jacksonville (FL)
Lewis (IL)
Lynn (FL)
Metropolitan State (CO)
Minnesota State U. (Mankato)
New Haven (CT)
North Dakota, U. of
Purdue (IN)
Robert Morris (PA)
St. Francis (NY)
St. Louis (MO)
Southern Illinois U.

AVIATION SCIENCE

Andrews (MI)
Averett (VA)
Baylor (TX)
Bowling Green (OH)
Daniel Webster (NH)
Dowling (NY)
Embry-Riddle (FL)
Fairmont (WV)
Florida Inst. of Tech.
Geneva (PA)
Georgia Institute of Technology
Grace (NE)
Hampton (VA)
Henderson State (AR)
Kansas State
Kent State (OH)

Lewis (IL)
Metropolitan State (CO)
North Dakota, U. of
Ohio State
Ohio University
Oklahoma State
Purdue (IN)
St. Cloud State (MN)
St. Louis U. (MO)
Salem State (MA)
Salem-Teikyo (WV)
San Jose State (CA)
Southern Illinois
Walla Walla (WA)
Western Michigan
Westminster (UT)

■ Men Only
▲ Women Only

BIOPHYSICS

Brown (RI)
Buffalo (SUNY)(NY)
California, U. of (Irvine)
Centenary (LA)
Chicago U. of (IL)
Columbia (NY)
Connecticut, U. of
Geneseo (SUNY)(NY)
Harvard (MA)
Houston, U. of (TX)
Illinois, U. of

Iowa State
Johns Hopkins (MD)
Michigan, U. of
Oregon State
Pennsylvania, U. of
Rensselaer (NY)
St. Bonaventure (NY)
Scranton, U. of (PA)
Walla Walla (WA)
Washington U. (MO)

CERAMICS

Alfred (NY)
Arcadia (PA)
Bennington (VT)
Bowling Green (OH)
Cleveland Institute of Art (OH)
Colorado State
East Carolina (NC)
Hartford, U. of (CT)
Kansas City Art Institute (MO)
Maryland Inst. College of Art
Massachusetts College of Art

Miami (FL)
Montevallo (AL)
Moore (PA)
North Texas
Oklahoma, U. of
Rhode Island School of Design
San Jose State (CA)
Syracuse (NY)
Temple (PA)
Washington, U. of

CINEMATOGRAPHY/FILM STUDIES/VIDEO PRODUCTION

* Arts, U. of the (PA)
Bard (NY)
Bennington (VT)
Bowling Green (OH)
Boston U. (MA)
Brooklyn (CUNY) (NY)
California College of Arts & Crafts
California State U. (Long Beach)
California, U. of (Berkeley)
California, U. of (Irvine)
California, U. of (Los Angeles)
California, U. of (Santa Barbara)
California, U. of (Santa Cruz)
California Institute of the Arts
Central Florida
Chapman (CA)
Chicago, U. of (IL)
Claremont-McKenna (CA)
Clark (MA)
Cogswell (CA)
Columbia (Hollywood)(CA)
Colorado State

Colorado, U. of
Columbia (IL)
Columbia (NY)
Columbus College of Art & Design (OH)
Denison (OH)
DeSales (PA)
Eastern Washington
Emerson (MA)
Emory (GA)
Florida
Florida State
Georgia State
Hampshire (MA)
Hofstra (NY)
▲ Hollins
Howard (DC)
Hunter (CUNY) (NY)
Iowa
Ithaca (NY)

* *and Writing for Media Performance*

CINIMA/FILM/VIDEO continues next page

■ Men Only
▲ Women Only

CINEMATOGRAPHY/FILM STUD./VIDEO PROD.   CONT.

Kansas
Loyola-Marymount (CA)
Massachusetts College of Art
Memphis (TN)
Michigan
New Orleans, U. of (LA)
New York U.
North Carolina, U. of (Greensboro)
North Carolina, U. of (Wilmington)
North Texas
Northern Michigan
Northwestern (IL)
Oklahoma
Pennsylvania State
Pittsburgh, U. of (PA)
Pitzer (CA)
Point Park (PA)
Purchase (SUNY) (NY)
Purdue (IN)
Rhode Island College

Rhode Island School of Design
Rochester Inst. of Tech. (NY)
San Francisco Art Institute (CA)
San Francisco State (CA)
Santa Fe (NM)
Sarah Lawrence (NY)
Southern California
Southern Methodist (TX)
Syracuse (NY)
Temple (PA)
Texas Christian
Texas, U. of
Toledo (OH)
Towson (MD)
Visual Arts, School of (NY)
Wayne State (MI)
Webster (MO)
Wesleyan (CT)
Wisconsin (Milwaukee)
Woodbury (CA)

COMPUTER GRAPHICS

Allegheny (PA)
American (DC)
Andrews (MI)
Arts, U. of the (PA)
Champlain (VT)
Cogswell (CA)
Columbia (IL)
Columbus College of Art & Design (OH)
Dominican (IL)
Dubuque (IA)
E. Michigan
Embry-Riddle (FL)
Fashion Institute of Tech. (NY)
Huntingdon (AL)
Jacksonville (FL)

LaSalle (PA)
Lewis (IL)
Loyola Marymount (CA)
Monmouth (NJ))
New York Institute of Tech.
Pratt Institute (NY)
Purdue (IN)
Ringling (FL)
Rochester Institute of Tech (NY)
Springfield (MA)
Syracuse (NY)
Taylor (IN)
Tampa (FL)
Woodbury (CA)

■ Men Only
▲ Women Only

CREATIVE WRITING

▲ Agnes Scott (GA)
Alabama, U. of
Albertson (ID)
Bard (NY)
Belmont (TN)
Beloit (WI)
Bennington (VT)
California Institute of the Arts
California, U. of (Riverside)
Carlow (PA)
Carnegie Mellon (PA)
Chapman (CA)
Columbia (NY)
Creighton (NE)
Dana (NE)
Dominican (CA)
East Carolina (NC)
Eckerd (FL)
Emerson (MA)
Florida State
Hamilton (NY)
Iowa
Kenyon (OH)
Knox (IL)

Lewis-Clark State (ID)
Linfield (OR)
Long Island U. (Southampton)(NY)
Lycoming (PA)
Maine (Farmington)
Michigan, U. of
New Paltz (SUNY)(NY)
New School U. (Lang) (NY)
North Carolina (Wilmington)
Oberlin (OH)
Oregon, U. of
Pacific U. (OR)
Pittsburgh, U. of (PA)
Redlands (CA)
St. Andrews (NC)
San Francisco State (CA)
Santa Fe, College of (NM)
Sarah Lawrence (NY)
▲ Stephens (MO)
Susquehanna (PA)
▲ Sweet Briar (VA)
Wheaton (MA)
Wichita State (KS)

CRIMINAL JUSTICE

Albany (SUNY) (NY)
Anna Maria (MA)
Bloomsburg (PA)
Bowling Green (OH)
Brockport (SUNY) (NY)
California State U. (Bakersfield)
California State U. (Fresno)
California State U. (Fullerton)
California State U. (Long Beach)
California State U. (Los Angeles)
California State U. (Sacramento)
California State U. (San
    Bernardino)
California, U. of (Irvine)
Castleton (VT)
Dayton, U. of (OH)
Delaware, U. of
Dillard (LA)
East Tennessee
Eastern Kentucky
Edinboro (PA)

Elmira (NY)
Fairmont State (WV)
Florida Gulf Coast U.
Florida International
Florida Southern
Florida State
Gannon (PA)
George Washington (DC)
Georgia State
Grambling (LA)
Guilford (NC)
Hamline (MN)
Illinois (Chicago)
Indiana
Iona (NY)
Jacksonville State (AL)
John Jay (CUNY) (NY)
Juniata (PA)
Kentucky Wesleyan
Lindenwood (MO)

■ Men Only
▲ Women Only

CRIMINAL JUSTICE continues next page

CRIMINAL JUSTICE CONT.

Loras (IA)
Lycoming (PA)
Madonna (MI)
Mansfield (PA)
Marist (NY)
Marshall (WV)
Maryland
Massachusetts State College
   (Westfield)
Mercy (NY)
Mercyhurst (PA)
Michigan State
Minnesota State U. (Mankato)
Minnesota State U. (Moorhead)
Missouri, U. of (St. Louis)
Mitchell (CT)
Mount Mercy (IA)
New Haven (CT)
New Mexico State
North Carolina (Charlotte)
North Carolina Wesleyan
North Florida
North Michigan
Northeastern (MA)
Ohio Northern
Pittsburgh (Bradford)
Portland, U. of (OR)
Potsdam (SUNY) (NY)
Quinnipiac (CT)
Radford (VA)
Regis (CO)
Richard Stockton (NJ)
Richmond (VA)

Roanoke (VA)
Roger Williams (RI)
Rowan (NJ)
Sacred Heart (CT)
Saginaw Valley (MI)
St. Anselm (NH)
St. Edward's (TX)
St. Francis (NY)
St. John's (NY)
St. Leo (FL)
Salem State (MA)
Salve Regina-The Newport College (RI)
Sam Houston State (TX)
San Diego State (CA)
San Jose State (CA)
Seton Hall (NJ)
Simpson (IA)
South Dakota, U. of
South Florida
Southern Illinois U. (Carbondale)
Southern Oregon
Southwest Texas
Texas (Tyler)
Toledo (OH)
Weber State (UT)
Western Connecticut
Western Illinois
West Virginia Wesleyan
Wilmington (OH)
Wisconsin (Milwaukee)
Wisconsin (Platteville)
York (PA)
Youngstown State (OH)

■ Men Only
▲ Women Only

DESIGN/COMMERCIAL ART

Alfred (NY)
Art Center College of Design (CA)
Arts, U. of the (PA)
Brenau (GA)
Brigham Young (UT)
California College of Arts & Crafts
California Inst. of the Arts
California Poly (SLO)
Carthage (WI)
Champlain (VT)
Chowan (NC)
Cincinnati, U. of (OH)
Cleveland Institute of Art (OH)
Columbia (IL)
Columbus College of Art & Design (OH)
Cornish (WA)
Creighton (NE)
Drake (IA)
Edgewood (WI)
Fashion Inst. of Tech. (NY)
Flagler (FL)
Florida A&M
Fort Hays (KS)
Grand Valley (MI)
Illinois, U. of
Iowa State
Kansas City Art Institute (MO)
Kean (NJ)

Kendall Coll. of Art & Design (MI)
Kent State (OH)
Long Island U. (Southampton)(NY)
Lyndon State (VT)
Maryland Institute - College of Art
Maryland, U. of
Massachusetts College of Art
Massachusetts, U. of (Dartmouth)
Memphis College of Art
Milliken (IL)
Montserrat (MA)
Moore (PA)
Moravian (PA)
Morningside (IA)
New York Institute of Technology
North Carolina State
Ohio State
Otis College of Art and Design (CA)
Parsons School of Design (NY)
Rhode Island School of Design
Ringling (FL)
Rochester Inst. of Tech. (NY)
St. Mary's (MN)
San Jose State (CA)
Southern Illinois U.
Texas Christian
Visual Arts, School of (NY)

EAST ASIAN STUDIES

Berea (KY)
Binghamton (SUNY) (NY)
▲ Bryn Mawr (PA)
Bucknell (PA)
California, U. of (Davis)
California, U. of (Los Angeles)
California, U. of (San Diego)
Chicago, U. of (IL)
Coe (IA)
Colorado College
Columbia (NY)
Cornell (NY)
Denison (OH)
DePauw (IN)
Furman (SC)
George Washington (DC)
Hamline (MN)
Harvard (MA)
Hawaii, U. of
Illinois, U. of
Indiana
Lawrence (WI)
Lewis & Clark (OR)
Macalester (MN)

Manhattanville (NY)
Maryland, U. of
Middlebury (VT)
Oberlin (OH)
Ohio State
Pennsylvania, U. of
Pomona (CA)
Puget Sound (WA)
Redlands (CA)
Reed (OR)
Rutgers (NJ)
Sarah Lawrence (NY)
Stanford (CA)
Ursinus (PA)
Vassar (NY)
Washington & Lee (VA)
Washington, U. of
▲ Wellesley (MA)
Wesleyan (CT)
Western Washington
Westmont (CA)
Wisconsin, U. of
Wittenberg (OH)

■ Men Only
▲ Women Only

E-COMMERCE

Bellevue (NE)
California State U. (Monterey Bay)
Castleton State (VT)
Champlain (VT)
Christopher Newport (VA)
DePaul (IL)
Emory (GA)
Jacksonville State (AL)

▲ Judson (AL)
Northwestern Oklahoma
Old Dominion (VA)
San Jose State (CA)
Scranton (PA)
Seattle U. (WA)
Southern Alabama
Thomas (ME)

ENTOMOLOGY

Auburn (AL)
California, U. of (Davis)
California, U. of (Riverside)
Colorado State
Cornell (NY)
Delaware, U. of
Florida A & M
Georgia, U. of
Harvard (MA)
Hawaii, U. of
Idaho, U. of
Illinois, U. of
Iowa State

Michigan State
Ohio State
Oklahoma State
Oregon State
Purdue (IN)
Rutgers (NJ)
San Jose State (CA)
Texas A & M
Texas Tech
Washington State
Wisconsin, U. of
Wyoming, U. of

■ Men Only
▲ Women Only

ENTREPRENEUR STUDIES

American (DC)
American International (MA)
Arizona, U. of
Babson (MA)
Baylor (TX)
Black Hills State U. (SD)
Bradley (IL)
Brown (RI)
Buena Vista (IA)
California State U. (San Bernardino)
California, U. of (Riverside).
Canisius (NY)
Case Western Reserve (OH)
Catawba (NC)
Central Connecticut
Chowan (NC)
Colorado State
Columbia College (SC)
Creighton (NE)
Dayton (OH)
Eastern Michigan
Fairleigh Dickinson (NJ)
Ferris State U. (MI)
Florida State
Gannon (PA)
Gonzaga (WA)
Hampton (VA)
Hartford, U. of (CT)
Hawaii Pacific
Hofstra (NY)
Houston, U. of (TX)
Illinois
Indiana

Juniata (PA)
Louisiana State U.
Lourdes (OH)
Lyndon State (VT)
Lynn (FL)
Maryland, U. of
Miami (FL)
Middle Tennessee
Mississippi U. for Women
Muhlenberg (PA)
New Mexico
Northeastern (MA)
North Carolina (Greensboro)
North Dakota
North Texas
Ohio University
Palm Beach Atlantic (FL)
Pennsylvania, U. of
Reinhardt (GA)
Rensselaer (NY)
St. Mary's (TX)
▲ Seton Hill (PA)
Syracuse (NY)
Virginia Commonwealth
Washington & Jefferson (PA)
Washington State
Waynesburg (PA)
Wheeling Jesuit (WV)
Wichita State (KS)
Winthrop (SC)
Wyoming
Xavier (LA)
Xavier (OH)

■ Men Only
▲ Women Only

ENVIRONMENTAL STUDIES

Adelphi (NY)
Alaska Pacific
Allegheny (PA)
Antioch (OH)
Atlantic, College of the (ME)
Bates (ME)
Berry (GA)
Bowdoin (ME)
Brenau (GA)
Brown (RI)
California, U. of (Davis)
California, U. of (Merced)
California, U. of (Riverside)
California, U. of (Santa Barbara)
California, U. of (Santa Cruz)
Case Western Reserve
Centenary (LA)
Central (IA)
Chestnut Hill (PA)
Chicago, U. of (IL)
Clark (MA)
Colby (ME)
Colorado, U. of
Connecticut College
Dartmouth (NH)
Davis & Elkins (WV)
Delaware Valley (PA)
Denison (OH)
Dickinson (PA)
Doane (NE)
Dordt (IA)
Drake (IA)
Dubuque (IA)
Earlham (IN)
Eastern Connecticut
Eastern Kentucky
Eckerd (FL)
Elizabethtown (PA)
Evergreen State (WA)
Florida Gulf Coast
Florida, U. of
Florida Institute of Technology
Georgetown College (KY)
Georgia
Green Mountain (VT)
Harvard (MA)
Hawaii Pacific
Idaho
Johnson State (VT)
Juniata (PA)
Lake Forest (IL)
Long Island U. (Southampton)(NY)
Loyola (IL)
Lynchburg (VA)

Lyndon (VT)
Macalester (MN)
Marietta (OH)
Maritime College (SUNY)(NY)
Michigan, U. of
Michigan State
Middlebury (VT)
Minnesota, U. of
Monmouth (IL)
Montreat (NC)
New Hampshire, U. of
New Mexico Inst. of Min. & Tech.
π New Mexico State
North Carolina (Asheville)
North Carolina (Greensboro)
Northland (WI)
* Northwestern (IA)
Oberlin (OH)
Ohio Wesleyan
Oregon State
Pacific U. (OR)
Pennsylvania State
Pennsylvania, U. of
Pittsburgh (Bradford)
Pittsburgh, U. of (PA)
Pitzer (CA)
Plattsburgh (SUNY)(NY)
Prescott (AZ)
Purchase (SUNY) (NY)
Ramapo (NJ)
Randolph-Macon (VA)
Rensselaer (NY)
Rhode Island, U. of
Richard Stockton (NJ)
Ripon (WI)
Rutgers (NJ)
Sacred Heart (CT)
St. Anselm (NH)
St. Lawrence (NY)
St. Michael's (VT)
St. Norbert (WI)
Salisbury State (MD)
Santa Fe, College of (NM)
Sarah Lawrence (NY)
Shepherd (WV)
South, U. of the (TN)
South Florida
Southwestern (TX)
Stanford (CA)
Stockton State (NJ)

■ Men Only
▲ Women Only

π *Environmental & Occupational Health*

* *Environmental Science*

ENVIRONMENTAL STUDIES continues next page

ENVIRONMENTAL STUDIES   CONTINUED

SUNY Coll. of Env. Sci. & Forestry
Susquehanna (PA)
Valparaiso (IN)
Vermont, U. of
Virginia, U. of
Warren Wilson (NC)
Washington State
Washington, U. of
Wesleyan (CT)
Western Washington

West Virginia Wesleyan
Westfield State (MA)
Westminster (MO)
Whitman (WA)
Wilson (PA)
Wisconsin
Wisconsin (Green Bay)
Worcester Poly (MA)
Yale (CT)

EQUESTRIAN STUDIES

Averett (VA)
Centenary (NJ)
Colorado State
Delaware Valley (PA)
Findlay (OH)
▲ Judson (AL)
Lake Erie (OH)
Otterbein (OH)

Puerto Rico, U. of (Rio Piedras)
St. Andrews (NC)
Salem-Teikyo (WV)
▲ Stephens (MO)
Truman State (MO)
Virginia Intermont
William Woods (MO)
Wilson (PA)

EXERCISE SCIENCE/WELLNESS/MOVEMENT

Abilene Christian (TX)
Adrian (MI)
Alma (MI)
Austin (TX)
Ball State (IN)
Bloomsburg (PA)
Bluffton (OH)
Boston U.
Bridgewater (VA)
Cal Poly (SLO)
California State U. (Fresno)
California State U. (Fullerton)
California State U. (Long Beach)
California State U. (San Bernardino)
Carthage (WI)
Castleton (VT)
Chapman (CA)
Colby-Sawyer (NH)
Concordia (NE)
Cumberland (KY)
Dayton (OH)
Drury (MO)
Eastern Nazarene (MA)
Evansville (IN)
Fitchburg (MA)
Florida Atlantic
Fort Lewis (CO)
Georgetown (KY)
George Washington (DC)
Gordon (MA)
Greensboro (NC)
Houston (TX)
Humboldt State (CA)
High Point (NC)
Idaho, U. of

Illinois, U. of (Chicago)
▲ Immaculata (PA)
James Madison (VA)
Kennesaw State (GA)
Linfield (OR)
Lynchburg (VA)
Massachusetts, U. of
▲ Meredith (NC)
Miami U. (OH)
Millersville (PA)
Mississippi U. for Women
Nevada, U. of (Las Vegas)
North Texas
New Hampshire, U. of
Otterbein (OH)
Pacific U. (OR)
▲ St. Catherine (MN)
San Francisco State (CA)
Shaw (NC)
Slippery Rock (PA)
Southwestern (TX)
Springfield (MA)
Stetson (FL)
Tampa, U. of (FL)
Tennessee, U. of
Toledo (OH)
Transylvania(KY)
Texas Lutheran
Texas Women's
Utah
Westfield (MA)
Willamette (OR)
Western State College of Colorado
Western Maryland
Wyoming

■ Men Only
▲ Women Only

FASHION DESIGN / MERCHANDISING

Akron, U. of (OH)
Auburn (AL)
Baylor (TX)
Bowling Green (OH)
Brenau (GA)
California Coll. of Arts & Crafts
California State U. (Fresno)
California State U. (Sacramento)
Central Washington
Champlain (VT)
Cincinnati (OH)
Colorado State
Columbus College of Art & Design (OH)
Davis & Elkins (WV)
Delaware, U. of
Dominican (IL)
Drexel (PA)
Florida State
Framingham (MA)
Eastern Michigan
Harding (AR)

Hawaii, U. of
High Point (NC)
Illinois, U. of
Indiana (PA)
Iowa State
Kansas State
Kent State (OH)
Lasell (MA)
Lynn (FL)
▲ Meredith (NC)
New Hampshire College
Oregon State
Pratt (NY)
Rhode Island School of Design
Rhode Island, U. of
▲ Stephens (MO)
Texas Christian
Virginia Commonwealth U.
Washington State
Wisconsin, U. of
Wisconsin, U. of (Stout)

 # Especially Interior Design

FORENSIC SCIENCES / TECHNOLOGY

▲ Bay Path (MA)
Central Florida
Defiance (OH)
Duquesne (PA)
Eastern Kentucky
Edinboro (PA)
Florida Gulf Coast U.
Hamline (MN)

John Jay (CUNY)(NY)
Kansas State
Miami, U. of (FL)
Mississippi, U. of
New Haven, U. of (Connecticut)
Virginia Commonwealth U.
West Virginia

GENETICS

Ball State (IN)
California, U. of (Berkeley)
California, U. of (Davis)
California, U. of (Irvine)
California, U. of (Los Angeles)
Carnegie Mellon (PA)
▲ Cedar Crest (PA)
Chicago, U. of (IL)
Connecticut, U. of
Cornell (NY)
Florida State
Fredonia (SUNY)(NY)
Georgia, U. of
Harvard (MA)
Illinois, U. of
Illinois, U. of (Chicago)

Iowa State
Kansas
Maryland, U. of
Minnesota
Ohio State
Ohio Wesleyan
Otterbein (OH)
Purdue (IN)
Rochester, U. of (NY)
Rutgers (NJ)
Texas A & M
Vermont, U. of
Washington State
Western Kentucky
Wisconsin, U. of

■ Men Only
▲ Women Only

GERONTOLOGY/GERIATRIC SERVICES

Alfred (NY)
Arkansas, U. of (Pine Bluff)
Bethune-Cookman (FL)
Cal State (Sacramento)
California (PA)
Case Western (OH)
Central Washington
Florida Gulf Coast U.
Gwynedd-Mercy (PA)
Kent State (OH)
King's (PA)
Langston (OK)
Lindenwood (VA)
Lourdes (OH)
Madonna (MI)
Massachusetts (Boston)
Mount St. Mary's (CA)
Mount St. Joseph (OH)

North Carolina (Greensboro)
North Colorado
North Texas
Oneonta (SUNY)(NY)
Quinnipiac (CT)
Roosevelt (IL)
Richard Stockton (NJ)
St. Mary's (CA)
San Diego State (CA)
Scranton (PA)
Shaw (NC)
South Florida
Southern California
Springfield (MA)
Stephen F. Austin (TX)
Wagner (NY)
Weber State (UT)

HEALTH SERVICES ADMINISTRATION

Alfred (NY)
Appalachian State (NC)
Arizona
Detroit Mercy (MI)
Eastern Michigan
Herbert Lehman (CUNY) (NY)
Kentucky
Madonna (MI)
▲ Mary Baldwin (VA)
Michigan (Dearborn)
Missouri, U. of
Mount Mercy (IA)

North Carolina (Chapel Hill)
Northeastern (MA)
Oregon State
Pennsylvania State
Providence College (RI)
Quinnipiac (CT)
Saint Scholastica (MN)
Scranton (PA)
Springfield (MA)
Stonehill (MA)
Washington, U. of
Wisconsin (Eau Claire)

HISPANIC STUDIES/LATIN AMERICAN STUDIES

American (DC)
Arizona, U. of
Austin (TX)
California, U. of (Berkeley)
California, U. of (Santa Barbara)
California, U. of (Santa Cruz)
California State (Long Beach)
City (CUNY) (NY)
DePaul (IL)
Flagler (FL)
Gettysburg (PA)
Hunter (CUNY)(NY)
Loyola Marymount (CA)
Michigan, U. of
▲ Mount Holyoke (MA)
New Mexico, U. of
North Carolina
Northern Colorado
Northridge State (CA)

Northwestern (IL)
Pomona (CA)
Rice (TX)
Rollins (FL)
Rutgers (NJ)
San Diego State (CA)
San Francisco State (CA)
▲ Scripps (CA)
▲ Smith (MA)
Sonoma State (CA)
Stetson (FL)
Texas, U. of
Tulane (LA)
Virginia, U. of
Wheaton (MA)
Whittier (CA)
Wisconsin, U. of
Wisconsin (Eau Claire)

■ Men Only
▲ Women Only

HORTICULTURE

Auburn (AL)
Arkansas, U. of
Berry (GA)
Brigham Young (UT)
Cal Poly (Pomona)
Cal Poly (San Luis Obispo)
California, U. of (Davis)
Christopher Newport
Clemson (SC)
Colorado State
Connecticut, U. of
Cornell (NY)
Delaware Valley (PA)
Delaware, U. of
Florida, U. of
Georgia, U. of
Hawaii, U. of
Illinois, U. of
Iowa State
Kansas State
Maine, U. of
Maryland, U. of
Michigan State
Mississippi State
Montana State (Bozeman)

Nebraska, U. of
New Hampshire, U. of
North Carolina State
North Dakota State
Northwest Missouri
Ohio State
Oklahoma State
Oregon State
Pennsylvania State
Purdue (IN)
Rhode Island, U. of
Rutgers (NJ)
South Dakota State
Southwest Missouri
Temple (PA)
Tennessee Tech
Tennessee, U. of
Texas A & M
Texas Tech
Utah State
Vermont, U. of
Virginia Poly
Washington State
Washington, U. of
Wisconsin, U. of

HOTEL AND RESTAURANT MANAGEMENT

Ashland (OH)
Auburn (AL)
Berea (KY)
Bowling Green (OH)
Cal Poly (Pomona)
Central Florida
Champlain (VT)
Colorado State
Cornell (NY)
Delaware
Denver, U. of (CO)
Fairleigh Dickinson (NJ)
Florida International U.
Florida State
Georgia Southern
Georgia State
Houston, U. of (TX)
Illinois, U. of
Indiana (PA)
Iowa State
Kansas State
Lasell (MA)
● Lyndon State (VT)
Massachusetts, U. of
Michigan State
Missouri, U. of
Nebraska
Nevada (Las Vegas)

New Hampshire College
New Hampshire, U. of
New Haven (CT)
New Orleans, U. of (LA)
New York University
Niagara (NY)
North Dakota State
Northern Arizona
Northern Michigan
North Texas
Oklahoma State
Ozarks (MO)
Penn State
Plattsburgh (SUNY)(NY)
Purdue (IN)
Rochester Inst. of Tech. (NY)
Siena Heights (MI)
South Carolina, U. of
South Dakota State U.
Southern Illinois (Carbondale)
Southern New Hampshire, U. of
Texas Tech
Virginia Poly. Inst.
Washington State
Western Illinois
Western Kentucky
Widener (PA)
Wisconsin (Stout)

■ Men Only
▲ Women Only

● *Ski Resort Management*

HUMAN RESOURCES MANAGEMENT

American (DC)
Baylor (TX)
Birmingham-Southern (AL)
Boston College (MA)
Bowling Green (OH)
Cabrini (PA)
Cal. Poly. State U. (Pomona)
Cal. State (Los Angeles)
DeSales (PA)
Duquesne (PA)
Florida State
Hastings (NE)
Hawaii Pacific
Holy Names (CA)
Houston (TX)
Indiana (PA)
Loras (IA)
LeMoyne (NY)
Lindenwood (MO)
Marietta (OH)

Michigan State
Muhlenberg (PA)
Nevada, U. of (Las Vegas)
New Mexico, U. of
Northeastern (MA)
Oakland (MI)
Ohio State
Ohio University
Point Park (PA)
Puerto Rico, U. of (Rio Piedras)
Rider (NJ)
Rockhurst (MO)
St. Leo (FL)
St. Mary's (TX)
Utah State
Washington U. (MO)
Western Illinois
Wichita State (KS)
Widener (PA)
Wisconsin (Oshkosh)

INDUSTRIAL ARTS

Auburn (AL)
Berea (KY)
California (PA)
π California State U. (Fresno)
Cal. Poly. (Pomona)
Central Michigan
Cincinnati, U. of (OH)
Clemson (SC)
Colorado State
Ferris State (MI)
Fitchburg (MA)
Florida A & M
Idaho
Indiana State
Iowa State
Louisiana State U.

Millersville (PA)
Montclair (NJ)
Nebraska, U. of
New Mexico, U. of
North Carolina State
Northern Colorado
Northern Illinois
Oklahoma State
Oswego (SUNY) (NY)
Pittsburgh, U. of (PA)
Purdue (IN)
Southern Illinois
Texas A&M
Western Michigan
Wisconsin, U. of (Stout)
Wyoming

π Also Construction Management

■ **Men Only**
▲ **Women Only**

INTERNATIONAL RELATIONS/STUDIES

▲ Agnes Scott (GA)
American U. (DC)
+ Arcadia (PA)
Austin (TX)
Beloit (WI)
● Bentley (MA)
Bethany (WV)
☎ Bethune-Cookman (FL)
Boston U. (MA)
Brown (RI)
▲ Bryn Mawr (PA)
Bucknell (PA)
☎ Butler (IN)
☎ Caldwell (NJ)
California State U. (Chico)
California State U. (Long Beach)
California, U. of (Davis)
π Central (IA)
▲ Chatham (PA)
City (CUNY) (NY)
Claremont McKenna (CA)
Colby (ME)
Colgate (NY)
Colorado
Connecticut College
☎ Cornell (IA)
Davidson (NC)
Dayton (OH)
Denison (OH)
Denver, U. of (CO)
DePaul (IL)
☎ Dickinson (PA)
Dominican (CA)
☎ Drake (IA)
π D'Youville (NY)
✪ Earlham (IN)
Eckerd (FL)
☎ Elizabethtown (PA)
☎ Elmira (NY)
Emory (GA)
Evansville (IN)
☎ Florida International
George Mason (VA)
+ George Washington (DC)
+ Georgetown (DC)
π Georgia
π Georgia Tech.
Goucher (MD)
Grand Valley (MI)
Hamline (MN)
☎ Hawaii

+ Hawaii Pacific
☎ Hiram (OH)
☎ Husson (ME)
Johns Hopkins (MD)
Juniata (PA)
☎ Illinois
Indiana
Kalamazoo (MI)
★ Kansas State
Kenyon (OH)
Knox (IL)
☎ Lenoir-Rhyne (NC)
Lewis & Clark (OR)
Linfield (OR)
Macalester (MN)
Maine (Farmington)
Manhattanville (NY)
▲ Mary Baldwin (VA)
☎ Marygrove (MI)
Massachusetts, U. of
▲ Meredith (NC)
Miami, U. of (FL)
☎ Michigan, U. of
Middlebury (VT)
Mississippi, U. of
☎ Moravian (PA)
Mt. Holyoke (MA)
Mt. St. Mary's (MD)
Muhlenberg (PA)
Nebraska
North Carolina (Chapel Hill)
π Northeastern (MA)
Oglethorpe (GA)
Ohio U.
Ohio Wesleyan
π Oklahoma City U.
Pacific, U. of the (CA)
Pennsylvania, U. of
Pepperdine (CA)
Pittsburgh, U. of
Pitzer (CA)
Pomona (CA)
Princeton (NJ)

★ *International Economics*
☎ *International Business*
★ *International Marketing*
✪ *Peace & Global Studies*
● *International Culture and Economy*
π *International Business and Global Affairs*
+ *International Relations, also International Business*

■ **Men Only**
▲ **Women Only**

INTERNATIONAL RELATIONS continues next page

INTERNATIONAL RELATIONS/STUDIES, cont.

▲ Randolph-Macon Woman's Col. (VA)
Redlands (CA)
Richmond (VA)
Rhodes (TN)
☎ Rochester Inst. of Tech. (NY)
San Diego, U. of (CA)
Scranton, U. of (PA)
▲ Scripps (CA)
☎ South Carolina, U. of
☎ Southern California, U. of
Southwestern (TX)
Spring Hill (AL)
☎ St. Andrews (NC)
▲ St. Catherine (MN)
☎ St. Louis U. (MO)
☎ St. Mary's (MN)
St. Mary's (TX)
St. Michael's (VT)
☎ St. Norbert (WI)
St. Olaf (MN)
☎ St. Peter's (NJ)
☎ Stetson (FL)

▲ Sweet Briar (VA)
▲ Trinity (DC)
Tufts (MA)
Tulane (LA)
U. S. Military Academy (NY)
Vassar (NY)
Virginia Poly. Institute
Virginia Wesleyan
Washington College (MD)
Washington, U. of
☎▲ Wesleyan (GA)
Westminster (MO)
π Westmont (CA)
☎ Westminster (UT)
Wheaton (MA)
Wheeling Jesuit (WV)
Whittier (CA)
William & Mary (VA)
William Jewell (MO)
Wilson (PA)
Wisconsin, U. of
Wisconsin (Oshkosh)

* *International Economics*
☎ *International Business*
★ *International Marketing*
✪ *Peace & Global Studies*
● *International Culture and Economy*
π *International Business and Global Affairs*
+ *International Relations, also International Business*

JAPANESE STUDIES

Bucknell (PA)
California, U. of (Los Angeles)
California, U. of (Santa Barbara)
Case Western (OH)
Dillard (LA)
Earlham (IN)
Georgetown (DC)
Hawaii, U. of
Macalester (MN)
Michigan, U. of

Minnesota, U. of
North Central (IL)
Oberlin (OH)
Oregon, U. of
Pacific, U. of the (CA)
San Francisco State (CA)
Stanford (CA)
Washington, U. of
Washington U. (MO)

■ **Men Only**
▲ **Women Only**

JAZZ

Alabama
Arizona State
Arizona, U. of
Auburn (AL)
Augustana (IL)
Bennington College (VT)
Berklee College of Music (MA)
Bowling Green (OH)
California Institute of the Arts
California State U. (Los Angeles)
California State U. (Northridge)
Cincinnati
Delaware
Denver, U. of
DePaul U. (IL)
Duquesne U. (PA)
Five Towns College (NY)
Florida Atlantic
Georgia State
Hampshire College (MA)
Hartford (CT)
Idaho
Iowa
Indiana U.
Indiana U. (PA)
Long Island U. (Brooklyn)(NY)
Loyola U. (New Orleans) (LA)
Manhattan School of Music (NY)
Mannes College of Music (NY)
Marlboro College (VT)

Miami (FL)
Michigan State
Middle Tennessee
Minnesota (Duluth)
Minnesota
New England Conservatory of
    Music (MA)
New York U. (NY)
North Florida
North Texas
Oberlin College (OH)
Ohio State U. (OH)
Rochester (NY)
Rowan (NJ)
Rutgers (NJ)
San Diego State (CA)
Shenandoah U. (VA)
South Florida
Southern California
Temple U. (PA)
Tennessee
Texas (Arlington)
Virginia Commonwealth
Washington, U. of
Webster U. (MO)
Western Maryland
Western Michigan U.
Western Washington
Westfield State (MA)
William Patterson (NJ)

■ **Men Only**
▲ **Women Only**

LINGUISTICS

Arizona, U. of
Beloit (WI)
Boston U. (MA)
Brandeis (MA)
Brown (RI)
Buffalo (SUNY) (NY)
California State U. (Fresno)
California, U. of (Berkeley)
California, U. of (Los Angeles)
California, U. of (San Diego)
California, U. of (Santa Barbara)
Chicago, U. of (IL)
Clemson (SC)
Colorado, U. of
Connecticut, U. of
Cornell (NY)
Florida State
Florida, U. of
Georgetown (DC)
Georgia, U. of
Harvard (MA)
Illinois, U. of
Indiana U.
Iowa, U. of
Kansas, U. of
Kentucky, U. of
Lawrence (WI)
Maryland, U. of
Massachusetts, U. of
MIT (MA)

Michigan, U. of
Minnesota, U. of
Mississippi, U. of
New York U.
North Carolina, U. of
Northeastern (MA)
Ohio State U.
Oklahoma, U. of
Oregon, U. of
Pennsylvania, U. of
Pittsburgh, U. of (PA)
Pitzer (CA)
Pomona (CA)
Queens (CUNY) (NY)
Rice (TX)
Rochester, U. of
Rutgers (NJ)
San Jose State (CA)
▲ Scripps (CA)
Southern California, U. of
Southern Maine, U. of
Stanford (CA)
Tennessee, U. of
Texas, U. of
Tulane (LA)
Virginia, U. of
Washington, U. of
▲ Wellesley (MA)
Wisconsin, U. of
Yale (CT)

MARINE SCIENCE

Alaska Pacific
Atlantic, College of the (ME)
Barry (FL)
Brown (RI)
California State U. (Long Beach)
California State U. (Stanislaus)
California, U. of (Santa Barbara)
California, U. of (Santa Cruz)
Coastal Carolina (SC)
College of Charleston (SC)
Eckerd (FL)
Fairleigh Dickinson (NJ)
Florida Inst. of Technology
Hawaii Pacific
Idaho, U. of
Jacksonville U. (FL)
▲ Judson (AL)
Juniata (PA)
Kutztown (PA)
Long Island U. (Southampton)(NY)

Maine, U. of
★ Maritime College (SUNY)(NY)
Miami, U. of (FL)
North Carolina, U. of (Wilmington)
Northern Michigan
Rhode Island, U. of
Richard Stockton (NJ)
Roger Williams (RI)
Samford (AL)
South Alabama
South Carolina
South Florida
Spring Hill (AL)
Tampa, U. of (FL)
Texas A&M
Texas A&M (Galveston)
U. S. Coast Guard Academy (CT)
Washington, U. of
West Florida

■ Men Only
▲ Women Only

★ *and Marine Environmental Science*

MEDICAL TECHNOLOGY

Alabama, U. of (Birmingham)
American International (MA)
Avila (MO)
Bowling Green (OH)
Bradley (IL)
Buffalo (SUNY) (NY)
Carroll (WI)
Cincinnati (OH)
Connecticut
Edgewood (WI)
Elon (NC)
Fairmont (WV)
Florida Atlantic
Florida International
Gwynedd-Mercy (PA)
▲ Hood (MD)
Houston (TX)
Humboldt (CA)
Loma Linda (CA)
▲ Mary Baldwin (VA)
Massachusetts, U. of (Boston)
Mercy (NY)

Miami U. (OH)
Michigan
Michigan State
Minnesota, U. of
North Carolina (Greensboro)
Pacific U. (OR)
Pittsburgh (PA)
St. Leo (FL)
St. Mary's (NE)
▲ St. Mary's (IN)
Salisbury (MD)
Sciences, U. of the (PA)
Scranton (PA)
Springfield (MA)
Stetson (FL)
Suffolk (MA)
Texas
Tuskegee (AL)
Virginia Commonwealth
Washington, U. of
Western Connecticut
Wisconsin, U. of

MIDDLE EASTERN STUDIES

Arizona, U. of
Arkansas, U. of
Barnard (NY)
Brandeis (MA)
Brigham Young (UT)
Brown (RI)
California, U. of (Berkeley)
California, U. of (Los Angeles)
California, U. of (Santa Barbara)
Chicago, U. of
Columbia (NY)
Connecticut, U. of
Cornell (NY)
Emory (GA)
Fordham (NY)
George Washington (DC)
Hampshire (MA)
Harvard (MA)

Indiana, U. of
Johns Hopkins (MD)
Lycoming (PA)
Massachusetts, U. of
Michigan, U. of
Minnesota, U. of
New York U.
Princeton (NJ)
Rutgers (NJ)
Southwest Texas State
Texas, U. of
Toledo, U. of (OH)
United States Military Academy (NY)
Utah, U. of
Washington, U. of
Washington U (MO)
Wooster (OH)
Yale (CT)

■ Men Only
▲ Women Only

MORTUARY SCIENCE / FUNERAL SERVICES

Central Oklahoma
Cincinnati Coll. of Mort. Sci.
π District of Columbia, U. of the
π Ferris State (MI)
Gannon (PA)
π Lynn (FL)

Minnesota, U. of
Mount Ida (MA)
Point Park (PA)
Southern Illinois
St. John's (NY)
Wayne State (MI)

π Two Year Only

MUSIC THERAPY

Alabama, U. of
Alverno (WI)
Anna Maria (MA)
Arizona State
Augsburg (MN)
Baldwin-Wallace (OH)
Berklee Coll. of Music (MA)
Charleston Southern (SC)
Colorado State
Dayton (OH)
Duquesne (PA)
East Carolina (NC)
Eastern Michigan (MI)
Elizabethtown (PA)
Evansville (IN)
Florida State
Fredonia (SUNY)(NY)
Georgia
Howard (DC)
▲ Immaculata (PA)
Incarnate Word (TX)
Iowa
Kansas
Loyola (LA)
Mansfield (PA)

Maryville, U. of (St. Louis)(MO)
Miami, U. of (FL)
Michigan State
Minnesota
Mississippi U. for Women
Montclair (NJ)
Nazareth (NY)
New Paltz (SUNY)(NY)
Ohio U.
Pacific, U. of the (CA)
Queens (NC)
Shenandoah (VA)
Slippery Rock (PA)
Southern Methodist (TX)
Southwestern Oklahoma
Temple (PA)
Texas Women's
Utah State
Wartburg (IA)
Western Illinois
Western Michigan
Wisconsin, U. of (Eau Claire)
Wisconsin, U. of (Oshkosh)
Wooster (OH)

MUSICAL THEATER

American Academy of Dramatic
   Arts (NY)
Arizona, U. of
California State (Fullerton)
Carnegie Mellon (PA)
Catholic U. (DC)
Central Florida
Central Michigan
Cincinnati, U. of (OH)
Elon (NC)
Florida
Florida State
Fredonia (SUNY)(NY)
Illinois Wesleyan
James Madison (VA)
Miami, U. of (FL)
Muhlenberg (PA)

North Colorado
Northwestern (IL)
New York U.
Otterbein (OH)
Point Park (PA)
Russell Sage (NY)
Santa Clara (CA)
Sarah Lawrence (NY)
Southern Illinois U. (Carbondale)
Southwest Missouri State
Syracuse (NY)
Texas Christian
West Virginia Wesleyan
Weber State (UT)
Western Illinois
Wilkes (PA)
Wisconsin (Stevens Point)

NAVAL ARCHITECTURE

California Maritime Academy
Michigan, U. of
New Orleans, U. of (LA)
SUNY Maritime College (NY)
Texas A&M (Galveston)

U.S. Coast Guard Academy (CT)
U.S. Merchant Marine Academy (NY)
U.S. Naval Academy
Webb Institute (NY)

NEUROSCIENCE

Allegheny (PA)
Amherst (MA)
Bowling Green (OH)
Bowdoin (ME)
Brown (RI)
California, U. of (Los Angeles)
Carthage (WI)
Central Michigan
Colgate (NY)
Drew (NJ)
Emory (GA)
Florida State

Michigan
Muskingum (OH)
New College (FL)
Northwestern (IL)
Oberlin (OH)
Pittsburgh (PA)
Pomona (CA)
Regis (CO)
Rochester, U. of (NY)
Texas, U. of (Dallas)
Ursinus (PA)
Wesleyan (CT)

■ Men Only
▲ Women Only

NUTRITIONAL SCIENCE

Alabama, U. of
Arizona, U. of
Ball State (IN)
Bridgewater (VA)
Cal Poly (SLO)
California, U. of (Berkeley)
California, U. of (Davis)
Case Western Reserve (OH)
Chapman (CA)
Clemson (SC)
Colorado State
Connecticut, U. of
Cornell (NY)
Delaware
Dominican (IL)
Florida, U. of
Framingham State (MA)
Georgia, U. of
Hawaii, U. of
Illinois
Kansas State
Long Island U. (C.W. Post)(NY)
Marygrove (MI)
Marywood (PA)
Minnesota, U. of

Mississippi State
Missouri, U. of
Nebraska, U. of
New Hampshire, U. of
New York Inst. of Technology
North Carolina, U. of
North Carolina, U. of (Greensboro)
Ohio State
Oklahoma State
Oregon State
Purdue (IN)
Rutgers (NJ)
▲ Sage Colleges (Russell Sage)(NY)
San Jose State
Seattle Pacific (WA)
▲ Simmons (MA)
Tennessee Tech
Tennessee, U. of
Texas A&M
Texas Tech
Virginia Poly
Viterbo (WI)
Winthrop (SC)
Wisconsin, U. of
Wisconsin, U. of (Stout)

OCCUPATIONAL THERAPY

American International (MA)
Boston U. (MA)
Brenau (GA)
Buffalo (SUNY) (NY)
Cleveland State (OH)
Colorado State
Dominican (CA)
Eastern Carolina
Eastern Kentucky
Elizabethtown (PA)
Findlay (OH)
Florida Gulf Coast
Florida, U. of
Illinois (Chicago)
I.U. - P.U. - Indianapolis (IN)
Kansas, U. of
Maryville (St. Louis)(MO)
McKendree (IL)
Minnesota, U. of
Missouri
New England, U. of (ME)
New Hampshire, U. of
New Mexico, U. of
Newman (KS)
New York Inst. of Technology
North Carolina, U. of

North Dakota, U. of
Ohio State
Penn State
Puget Sound (WA)
St. Ambrose (IA)
▲ St. Catherine (MN)
St. Louis U. (MO)
San Jose State (CA)
Sciences, U. of the (PA)
Scranton (PA)
Southern California
Stony Brook (SUNY)(NY)
Temple (PA)
▲ Texas Woman's
Towson (MD)
Tuskegee (AL)
Utica College (NY)
Washington U. (MO)
Washington, U. of
Wayne State (MI)
Western Michigan
Wisconsin, U. of
Wisconsin, U. of (La Crosse)
Wisconsin, U. of (Milwaukee)
Worcester State (MA)
Xavier (OH)

■ Men Only
▲ Women Only

ORTHOTICS / PROSTHETICS

California State (Dominguez Hills)
Florida International

Texas, U. of, S.W. Med Ctr. (Dallas)
Washington, U. of

PARKS AND RECREATION SERVICES

π Alaska Pacific
Alderson-Broaddus (WV)
Arizona State
Aurora (IL)
Bowling Green (OH)
Cal. Poly. State U. (Pomona)
Cal. Poly. State U. (San Luis Obispo)
California State (Dominguez Hills)
California State (Fresno)
California State (Los Angeles)
California State (Northridge)
California State (Sacramento)
Catawba (NC)
Central Michigan
Clemson (SC)
Colorado State
Connecticut
Florida International
Florida State
Franklin (IN)
Georgia State
Georgia, U. of
Gordon (MA)
Idaho
Illinois State
Illinois, U. of
Indiana U.
Kansas State
Kean (NJ)
Lock Haven (PA)
● Lyndon (VT)
Maine, U. of
Maryland, U. of

Mesa State (CO)
Michigan State
Minnesota
Missouri
Montana
Nevada (Reno)
New York U.
North Carolina (Greensboro)
North Carolina State
Northern Arizona
Northern Iowa
π Northland (WI)
Ohio U.
Pfeiffer (NC)
Pittsburgh (Bradford)
Purdue (IN)
San Diego State (CA)
San Jose State (CA)
Shepherd (WV)
Slippery Rock (PA)
Southern Conneccticut
Southwest Missouri
Springfield College (MA)
Taylor (IN)
Texas A&M
Virginia Wesleyan
West Virginia U.
Western State College of Colorado
Western Washington
Wingate (NC)
Winona State (MN)
Wisconsin (LaCrosse)

π *Outdoor Studies*
● *Also Ski Resort Management*

PEACE AND CONFLICT STUDIES

American (DC)
Bethel (KS)
Bluffton (OH)
California, U. of (Berkeley)
Chapman (CA)
Clark (MA)
Colgate (NY)
DePauw (IN)
Earlham (IN)
Eastern Mennonite (PA)
Goshen (IN)
Guilford (NC)
Hamline (MN)
Hampshire (MA)
Juniata (PA)

Kent State (OH)
Manchester (IN)
Manhattan (NY)
Molloy (NY)
Mount St. Clair (IA)
North Carolina, U. of
Northland (WI)
Norwich (VT)
Quincy (IL)
St. Benedict / St. John's (MN)
St. Thomas (MN)
Washington, U. of
▲ Wellesley (MA)
Whitworth (WA)
Youngstown State (OH)

PHOTOJOURNALISM

Boston U. (MA)
Indiana U.
Missouri, U. of
Northern Illinois U.
Ohio U.
Rochester Inst. of Tech. (NY)

\# St. Edward's (TX)
San Jose State (CA)
Southern Illinois
Texas
Western Kentucky

\# *Photocommunications*

PHYSICAL EDUCATION

Alderson-Broaddus (WV)
Asbury (KY)
Augsburg (MN)
Bemidji State (MN)
Berea (KY)
Blackburn (IL)
Bridgewater (MA)
Brockport (SUNY) (NY)
Castleton (VT)
Chowan (NC)
Coe (IA)
Colorado, U. of
Colorado State
Cortland State (NY)
Dana (NE)
Davis & Elkins (WV)
Denison (OH)
Doane (NE)
East Stroudsburg (PA)
Elon (NC)
Eureka (IL)
Faulkner (AL)
Florida Southern
Florida State
Florida, U. of
Franklin (IN)
Georgia, U. of
Goshen (IN)
Grambling (LA)
Hamline (MN)
Hanover (IN)
Hardin-Simmons (TX)
Illinois College
Illinois, U. of (Chicago)
Indiana (PA)
Iowa, U. of
Ithaca (NY)
Jacksonville (FL)
Jamestown (ND)
Johnson C. Smith (NC)
Kansas State
Kansas, U. of

Kean (NJ)
Kennesaw State (GA)
Kentucky Wesleyan
King (TN)
LeTourneau (TX)
Longwood (VA)
Linfield (OR)
Luther (IA)
Maine, U. of
Michigan State
Monmouth (IL)
Nebraska, U. of
Nevada (Reno)
North Carolina, U. of
Norwich (VT)
Occidental (CA)
Ohio U.
Oregon State
Otterbein (OH)
Pacific U. (OR)
Pennsylvania State
Plymouth State (NH)
Puerto Rico, U. of (Mayaguez)
Purdue (IN)
Rockford (IL)
St. Leo (FL)
Skidmore (NY)
Slippery Rock (PA)
South Florida, U. of
Springfield (MA)
Texas, U. of
Union (TN)
Ursinus (PA)
Walsh (OH)
Washington State
Western Illinois
Western Washington
Westmont (CA)
West Virginia U.
William & Mary (VA)
Wisconsin (LaCrosse)
Wisconsin, U. of

■ Men Only
▲ Women Only

PHYSICAL THERAPY

American International (MA)	Maryville (St. Louis) (MO)
Azusa Pacific (CA)	Miami, U. of (FL)
Barry (FL)	Minnesota, U. of
Bowling Green (OH)	Missouri, U. of
Bradley (IL)	Mount St. Joseph (OH)
Buffalo (SUNY) (NY)	Mt. St. Mary's (CA)
California State U. (Fresno)	Nazareth (NY)
California State U. (Sacramento)	Nebraska, U. of
Clarke (IA)	Nevada (Reno)
Connecticut, U. of	New England, U. of (ME)
Dayton (OH)	New Mexico, U. of
D'Youville (NY)	New York Inst. of Technology
Daemen (NY)	North Dakota, U. of
Duquesne (PA)	Northeastern (MA)
Evansville (IN)	Northern Illinois
Fairmont State (WV)	Ohio State U.
Florida Gulf Coast U.	Ohio University
Florida International	Pittsburgh, U. of (PA)
Florida, U. of	Regis (CO)
Grambling (LA)	Russell Sage (NY)
Grand Valley (MI)	Sacramento State (CA)
Hartford (CT)	St. Francis (PA)
Houston, U. of (TX)	St. Louis U. (MO)
Hunter (CUNY) (NY)	Saint Scholastica (MN)
Huntington (AL)	Sciences, U. of the (PA)
Husson (ME)	Scranton, U. of (PA)
Illinois (Chicago)	Slippery Rock (PA)
Indiana State	Springfield College (MA)
I.U. - P.U. - Indianapolis (IN)	Toledo (OH)
Ithaca (NY)	Utah
Kentucky, U. of	Washington U. (MO)
Louisiana-Lafayette	Waynesburg (PA)
Louisville, U. of (KY)	West Virginia U.
Manhattan (NY)	Wisconsin, U. of

PHYSICIAN ASSISTANT

Alderson-Broaddus (WV)	New York Inst. of Technology
Augsburg (MN)	Nova Southeastern (FL)
Butler (IN)	Pace (NY)
Daeman (NY)	Rochester Inst. of Tech. (NY)
DeSales (PA)	St. Francis (NY)
D'Youville (NY)	St. Francis (PA)
East Carolina	St. Louis (MO)
Gannon (PA)	Sciences, U. of the (PA)
George Washington (DC)	▲ Seton Hill (PA)
High Point (NC)	South Dakota
Hofstra (NY)	Southern California
Howard (DC)	Springfield (MA)
Idaho State	Stony Brook (SUNY)(NY)
Kentucky	Wichita State (KS)
King's (PA)	Wisconsin
Miami, U. of (FL)	

■ Men Only
▲ Women Only

PRE-VETERINARY

Auburn (AL)
California, U. of (Davis)
Cal. Poly. State U. (San Luis Obispo)
Clemson (SC)
Colorado State
Delaware Valley (PA)
Evansville, U. of (IN)
Fort Lewis (CO)
Georgia, U. of
Humboldt State (CA)
Idaho, U. of
Iowa State
Juniata (PA)
Kansas State
Lawrence (WI)
Louisiana-Lafayette
Loyola (CA)
MacMurray (IL)
Maryland, U. of
Michigan State
Minnesota, U. of
Montana, U. of
Moravian (PA)
Murray State (KY)
Muskingum (OH)

Nevada, U. of (Reno)
New Hampshire, U. of
New Mexico State
Northland (WI)
Oklahoma State
Purdue (IN)
▲ Russell Sage (The Sage Colleges)(NY)
▲ Salem (NC)
South Dakota State U.
Southern Mississippi, U. of
Susquehanna (PA)
Tennessee, U. of
Texas A & M
Tuskegee (AL)
Utah State
Vermont, U. of
Virginia Wesleyan
Warren Wilson (NC)
Washington & Jefferson (PA)
Washington State
West Virginia Wesleyan
Wilmington (OH)
Wingate (NC)
Winona State (MN)

PUBLIC HEALTH

American (DC)
Baylor (TX)
Bethel (MN)
Brown (RI)
Central Oklahoma
Central State (OH)
Central Washington
Delaware State
Dillard (LA)
Florida State
Hofstra (NY)
Holy Family (PA)
Idaho, U. of
Indiana U.
Ind. U.-Pur U.-Ind U. (IN)
Johns Hopkins(MD)
Kansas, U. of
Kent State (OH)
Moorhead State (MN)
New Mexico State
New Orleans, U. of (LA)
Northern Illinois

Ohio U.
Purdue (IN)
Richard Stockton (NJ)
Rutgers (NJ)
St. Cloud (MN)
St. Joseph's (NY)
Salem-Teikyo (WV)
San Francisco State (CA)
San Jose State (CA)
▲ Simmons (MA)
Southern Connecticut State
Texas Women's
Utah State
Virginia Commonwealth
West Chester (PA)
Western Illinois
Western Kentucky
Western Michigan
Western Washington
Wisconsin (Eau Claire)
Worcester State (MA)

■ Men Only
▲ Women Only

SOCIAL AND REHABILITATION SERVICES

Arizona, U. of
Assumption (MA)
Boston U. (MA)
California State (Los Angeles)
Gustavus Adolphus (MN)
Iowa, U. of
Louisiana State
Maine (Farmington)
Marshall (WV)
Montana, U. of
Northern Colorado
North Texas

Ohio State
Seattle (WA)
South Florida, U. of
Southern Mississippi
Springfield College (MA)
Texas, U. of (Austin)
Virginia Commonwealth
West Virginia Wesleyan
Wilberforce (OH)
Wisconsin
Wright State (OH)

SOCIAL WORK

Alabama, U. of
Alaska, U. of (Anchorage)
Alaska, U. of (Fairbanks)
Andrews (MI)
Arizona State
Ashland (OH)
Augsburg (MN)
Azusa Pacific (CA)
Ball State (IN)
Baylor (TX)
Belmont (TN)
Bemidji State (MN)
▲ Bennett (NC)
Bethany (WV)
Boise State (ID)
Brescia (KY)
Brockport (SUNY) (NY)
Buena Vista (IA)
California (Berkeley)
California State U. (Chico)
California State U. (Fresno)
California State U. (Fullerton)
California State U. (Los Angeles)
California State U. (Sacramento)
California State U. (San Bernardino)
Carroll (WI)
Castleton (VT)
Clarke (IA)
Colorado State
Creighton (NE)
Cumberland (KY)
Dana (NE)
David Lipscomb (TN)
Dillard (LA)
Eastern Michigan
Eastern Nazarene (MA)
Elizabethtown (PA)

Elmira (NY)
Elms (MA)
Ferris State (MI)
Florida Atlantic
Florida International
Florida State
Franciscan U. of Steubenville (OH)
Fredonia (SUNY) (NY)
Georgia State
Georgia U. of
Gordon (MA)
Hawaii Pacific
▲ Hood (MD)
Hope (MI)
Humboldt State (CA)
Illinois, U. of
Illinois, U. of (Chicago)
Indiana
Indiana U.-Purdue U.-Indianapolis (IN)
Juniata (PA)
Kansas State
Kansas, U. of
Kean (NJ)
Kentucky
Lindenwood (MO)
Longwood (VA)
Loras (IA)
Lourdes (OH)
Madonna (MI)
Maine, U. of
Manchester (IN)
Marquette (WI)
▲ Mary Baldwin (VA)
Marygrove (MI)
Maryland (Baltimore County)

■ Men Only
▲ Women Only

SOCIAL WORK continues next page

SOCIAL WORK, continued

▲ Meredith (NC)
Michigan State
Michigan, U. of
Middle Tennessee
Millersville (PA)
Minnesota State U. (Moorhead)
Missouri, U. of
Mount St. Joseph (OH)
Nazareth (NY)
Nevada, U. of (Reno)
New Mexico State
New York University
Niagara (NY)
North Carolina (Greensboro)
North Carolina (Pembroke)
North Carolina State
Northwestern State (LA)
Pittsburgh, U. of (PA)
Portland, U. of (OR)
Providence (RI)
Radford (VA)
Rhode Island College
Richard Stockton (NJ)
Rochester Inst. of Tech. (NY)
Rockford (IL)
Sacramento State (CA)
Sacred Heart (CT)
Saginaw Valley (MI)
St. Edward's (TX)
St. Leo (FL)
St. Louis (MO)

St. Olaf (MN)
St. Scholastica (MN)
Salem State (MA)
Salisbury State (MD)
San Francisco State (CA)
Shepherd (WV)
Shippensburg U. of (PA)
South Connecticut
South Florida, U. of
Southern Connecticut
Tennessee, U. of
Texas, U. of (Arlington)
Texas, U. of (Austin)
Texas Women's
Utah State
Valparaiso (IN)
Vermont, U. of
Warren Wilson (NC)
Washington U. (MO)
Washington, U. of
Wayne State (MI)
West Florida
Western Maryland
Western Michigan
Western New England (MA)
William Woods (MO)
Winthrop (SC)
Wisconsin, U. of
Wisconsin, U. of (Milwaukee)
Wyoming, U. of

■ **Men Only**
▲ **Women Only**

SPECIAL EDUCATION

Alabama, U. of
Alderson-Broaddus (WV)
American International (MA)
Arizona State
Arizona, U. of
Arkansas
Auburn (AL)
Augustana (SD)
π Bethel (IN)
Boston U. (MA)
Brenau (GA)
Bridgewater State (MA)
California State (Fresno)
π California State (Northridge)
Central (CT)
Clarke (IA)
Clarion (PA)
Connecticut, U. of
▲ Converse (SC)
Curry (MA)
Dana (NE)
Delaware State
Doane (NE)
Eastern Kentucky
Eastern Michigan
Edinboro (PA)
π Flagler (FL)
Florida Gulf Coast
Florida, U. of
Geneseo (SUNY) (NY)
Georgia Southwestern
Georgia, U. of
Gonzaga (WA)
Hartford (CT)
Hofstra (NY)
▲ Hood (MD)
Idaho, U. of
Illinois State
Indiana U.
Juniata (PA)
Kansas State
Kean (NJ)
Keene (NH)
Kentucky, U. of
Kutztown (PA)
Landmark College (VT)
Lasell (MA)
Lesley (MA)
Lindenwood (MO)
Loras (IA)
Louisiana State U.

Lyndon State (VT)
Maine, U. of (Farmington)
Marygrove (MI)
Maryland, U. of
Miami, U. of (FL)
Michigan State
Michigan, U. of
Millersville (PA)
Montana State (Billings)
Muskingum (OH)
Nebraska
New Mexico State
Nevada (Reno)
North Florida
North Texas
Northern Colorado, U. of
Northern Illinois
Northern Iowa
Oklahoma, U. of
Old Dominion (VA)
Pennsylvania State
Presbyterian (SC)
Providence (RI)
Quincy (IL)
Rhode Island College
Rowan (NJ)
St. Elizabeth (NJ)
▲ St. Joseph (CT)
St. Louis U. (MO)
Silver Lake (WI)
▲ Simmons (MA)
Southern Connecticut
Southern Florida
Southern Illinois U. (Carbondale)
Southern Utah
Tennessee, U. of
Texas, U. of
▲ Trinity (DC)
Vanderbilt (TN)
Walsh (OH)
West Chester (PA)
Westfield (MA)
Wisconsin, U. of
Wisconsin, U. of (Eau Claire)
Wisconsin, U. of (Milwaukee)
Wisconsin, U. of (Oshkosh)
Winona (MN)
Wittenberg (OH)
Wyoming, U. of
Xavier (LA)

■ **Men Only**
▲ **Women Only**

π *Also Deaf Studies*

SPORTS MEDICINE/ATHLETIC TRAINING

Alderson-Broaddus (WV)
Baldwin Wallace (OH)
Ball State (IN)
Boise State (ID)
Bryan (TN)
California (PA)
California Lutheran
Canisius (NY)
Carthage (WI)
Castleton (VT)
Catawba (NC)
Charleston, U. of (WV)
Chowan (NC)
Clarke (IA)
Coe (IA)
Colorado State
East Stroudsburg (PA)
Eastern Nazarene (MA)
Elon (NC)
Eureka (IL)
Evansville (IN)
Florida Southern
Gustavus Adolphus (MN)
Heidelberg (OH)
High Point (NC)
Illinois (Chicago)
Indiana U.
LaSell (MA)
Lees-McCrae (NC)
Lindenwood (MO)
Linfield (OR)
Lynchburg (VA)
Manchester (IN)
Manhattan (NY)
Marietta (OH)

McKendree (IL)
Merrimack (MA)
Mercyhurst (PA)
Mount Union (OH)
Nevada, U. of (Las Vegas)
New Mexico State
North Dakota
Northeastern (MA)
Northwestern (IA)
Norwich (VT)
Ohio Northern
Otterbein (OH)
Palm Beach Atlantic (FL)
Pepperdine (CA)
Quincy (IL)
Quinnipiac (CT)
Roanoke (VA)
St. Andrews (NC)
Samford (AL)
Slippery Rock (PA)
Southern Maine
Springfield (MA)
Taylor (IN)
Texas (Arlington)
Tusculum (TN)
Tulsa (OK)
Union (TN)
Waynesburg (PA)
West Virginia Wesleyan
West Chester (PA)
Whitworth (WA)
Wilmington (OH)
Wingate (NC)
Xavier (OH)

■ Men Only
▲ Women Only

SPORTS SCIENCES / MANAGEMENT

Alabama, U. of
Alderson-Broaddus (WV)
Arizona State
Averett (VA)
Belmont Abbey (NC)
Bemidji (MN)
Berry (GA)
Bowling Green (OH)
Buena Vista (IA)
Cabrini (PA)
Carthage (WI)
Central Washington
Chowan (NC)
✳ Coastal Carolina (SC)
Colby-Sawyer (NH)
Concordia (CA)
Connecticut, U. of
Dallas, U. of (TX)
Eastern Connecticut
Elon (NC)
Faulkner (AL)
Flagler (FL)
Florida Southern
Florida, U. of
Guilford (NC)
High Point (NC)
Husson (ME)
Idaho, U. of
Incarnate Word (TX)
Indiana U.
Ithaca (NY)
Kansas, U. of
Kentucky Wesleyan
Louisville (KY)
Lynchburg (VA)
Lynn (FL)
MacMurray (IL)
Malone (OH)
Marian (WI)

Massachusetts, U. of
Michigan, U. of
Millersville (PA)
Misericordia (PA)
Mount Union (OH)
North Carolina State
North Michigan
Ohio Northern
Ohio State
Oklahoma
Oregon, U. of
Pfeiffer (NC)
Richmond (VA)
Robert Morris (PA)
Rutgers (NJ)
Seton Hall (NJ)
Shepherd (WV)
Simpson (IA)
South Carolina, U. of
Southern New Hampshire, U. of
Springfield (MA)
St. Ambrose (IA)
St. John's (NY)
St. Leo (FL)
St. Olaf (MN)
St. Thomas U. (FL)
Stetson (FL)
Southwest Baptist (MO)
Tampa, U. of (FL)
Taylor (IN)
Temple (PA)
Tennessee
Texas Christian
Tulsa (OK)
Union (TN)
West Virginia U.
Western New England (MA)
Wingate (NC)
Xavier (OH)

✳ *Professional Golf Management*

URBAN STUDIES

Akron, U. of (OH)
Albany (SUNY)(NY)
Aquinas (MI)
Augsburg (MN)
▲ Barnard (NY)
Boston U. (MA)
Brown (RI)
California State U. (Northridge)
California, U. of (San Diego)
Canisius (NY)

Cleveland State (OH)
College of Charleston (SC)
Columbia (NY)
Connecticut College
Connecticut, U. of
Cornell (NY)
David Lipscomb (TN)
DePaul (IL)
Florida International

■ **Men Only**
▲ **Women Only**

URBAN STUDIES continues next page

URBAN STUDIES CONTINUED

Florida, U. of
Furman (SC)
Georgia State
Grambling (LA)
Hamline (MN)
Hampshire (MA)
Harvard (MA)
Hunter (CUNY)(NY)
Illinois (Chicago)
Indiana State
Lehigh (PA)
Loyola Marymount (CA)
Macalester (MN)
Malone (OH)
Manhattan (NY)
Maryland, U. of
Minnesota, U. of
■ Morehouse (GA)
Mount Mercy (IA)
Nebraska, U. of
New York U.
Northwestern (IL)
Ohio State
Pennsylvania, U. of
Pittsburgh, U. of

Rockford (IL)
Rutgers (NJ)
St. Louis (MO)
St. Peter's (NJ)
San Francisco State U. (CA)
Shippensburg (PA)
Stanford (CA)
Tampa, U. of (FL)
Towson State (MD)
Trinity (TX)
Vanderbilt (TN)
Vassar (NY)
Virginia Commonwealth
Virginia Poly
Washington U. (MO)
Wayne State (MI)
Western Washington
π Westfield State (MA)
Wisconsin, U. of (Green Bay)
Wittenberg (OH)
Wooster (OH)
Worcester State (MA)
Wright State (OH)

π Regional Planning

WILDLIFE/WILDLANDS MANAGEMENT

Alaska (Fairbanks)
Arizona, U. of
Auburn (AL)
Ball State (IN)
Brevard (NC)
California, U. of (Davis)
Clemson (SC)
Colorado State
Cornell (NY)
Eastern Kentucky
Eastern New Mexico
Florida, U. of
Frostburg State (MD)
Georgia, U. of
π Grand Valley (MI)
Humboldt State (CA)
Idaho, U. of
Kansas State
Louisiana State
Maine, U. of
Massachusetts, U. of
Michigan State
Michigan, U. of
Mississippi State
Missouri, U. of
Montana, U. of

Nebraska, U. of
New Hampshire, U. of
New Mexico State
North Carolina State
Ohio State
Oklahoma State
Penn State
Purdue (IN)
Rhode Island, U. of
Rutgers (NJ)
South Dakota State
Tennessee Tech
Tennessee, U. of
Texas A&M
Texas Tech.
Unity (ME)
Utah State
Vermont, U. of
Virginia Poly Tech
Washington State
Washington, U. of
West Virginia, U. of
Wisconsin, U. of
Wisconsin, U. of (Stevens Point)
Wyoming, U. of

■ Men Only
▲ Women Only

π Natural Resources Management

WOMEN'S STUDIES

▲ Agnes Scott (GA)
Antioch (OH)
Arizona State
Arizona, U. of
▲ Barnard (NY)
Bates (ME)
Beloit (WI)
Bowling Green (OH)
Brandeis (MA)
Brown (RI)
Cal Poly (Pomona)
California State U. (Fresno)
California State U. (Long Beach)
California, U. of (Berkeley)
California, U. of (Davis)
California, U. of (Riverside)
California, U. of (Santa Barbara)
California, U. of (Santa Cruz)
Carleton (MN)
Colorado College
Colorado, U. of
Connecticut College
Connectut, U. of
Delaware, U. of
Denver, U. of (CO)
DePauw (IN)
Drew (NJ)
Duke (NC)
Emory (GA)
Florida, U. of
Florida International
Florida State
Franklin & Marshall (PA)
Goucher (MD)
Harvard (MA)
Hawaii, U. of
Hobart & William Smith (NY)
▲ Hollins (VA)
Iowa State
Kansas, U. of
Kalamazoo (MI)
Louisville (KY)
Macalester (MN)
Maine, U. of
Maryland, U. of

Massachusetts, U. of
Michigan, U. of
Middlebury (VT)
▲ Mills (CA)
▲ Mt. Holyoke (MA)
Nebraska, U. of
New College (FL)
Northwestern (IL)
Ohio State
Oklahoma, U. of
Oregon, U. of
Pennsylvania, U. of
Pittsburgh, U. of (PA)
Pitzer (CA)
Portland State (OR)
Regis (CO)
Rice (TX)
Rochester, U. of (NY)
▲ Rosemont (PA)
Rutgers (NJ)
San Francisco State (CA)
Sarah Lawrence (NY)
▲ Scripps (CA)
▲ Simmons (MA)
▲ Smith (MA)
Southern California
Southern Maine
Southwestern (TX)
▲ Spelman (GA)
Stanford (CA)
Syracuse (NY)
Towson (MD)
Vassar (NY)
Washington State
Washington U. (MO)
Washington, U. of
▲ Wellesley (MA)
▲ Wells (NY)
Wesleyan (CT)
West Chester (PA)
Wheaton (MA)
Wisconsin, U. of
Wisconsin, U. of (Milwaukee)
Wooster (OH)
Wyoming, U. of
Yale (CT)

■ **Men Only**
▲ **Women Only**

SECTION THREE

AVERAGE SAT-1/ACT TOTALS
RECOMMENDED MAJORS

ABILENE CHRISTIAN UNIVERSITY (TX) .... acu.edu 1095/24
Bus Admin

ADELPHI COLLEGE (NY) .... adelphi.edu 1070/23
Ed, Nurs, Physics

ADRIAN COLLEGE (MI) .... adrian.edu 1035/22
Bus Admin, Ed, English, Poli Sci, Pre-Law, Soc

AGNES SCOTT COLLEGE (GA) .... agnesscott.edu 1199/26
*Art, Bio, Bus Admin, Classics, Econ, English, For Lang, Hist, Physics, Poli Sci, Pre-Law, Pre-Med/
Pre-Dental, Psych*

AKRON, UNIVERSITY OF (OH) .... uakron.edu 1000/21
Bus Admin, Chem, Drama, Ed, Engine, Hist, Home Ec, Nurs, Soc

ALABAMA, UNIVERSITY OF (AL) .... ua.edu 1105/24
*Amer St, Anthro, Art, Bot, Bus Admin, Communic, Drama, Engine, English, For Lang, Geol, Hist,
Music, Pre-Law, Pre-Med/Pre-Dental*

ALABAMA, UNIVERSITY OF (BIRMINGHAM) .... uab.edu 1040/22
Bus Admin, Chem, Engine, English, Nurs, Philo, Psych

ALABAMA, UNIVERSITY OF (HUNTSVILLE) .... uah.edu 1125/25
Bus Admin, Communic, Comp Sci, Engine, Math, Nurs

ALASKA PACIFIC UNIVERSITY (AK) .... alaskapacific.edu 1100/24
Bus Admin, Ed, Music, Reli Stu

ALASKA, UNIVERSITY OF (ANCHORAGE) (AK) .... uaa.alaska.edu 1000/21
Art, Bus Admin, Ed

ALASKA, UNIVERSITY OF (FAIRBANKS) (AK) .... uaf.edu 1020/22
Bus Admin, Drama, Nurs

ALBANY COLLEGE OF PHARMACY (NY) .... acp.edu 1130/25
Pharm

ALBERTSON COLLEGE OF IDAHO (ID) .... albertson.edu 1160/25
Bio, Bus Admin, Chem, Ed, English, hist, Music, Pre-Law, Pre-Med/Pre-Dental, Zoo

ALBION COLLEGE (MI) .... albion.edu 1140/25
Econ, English, Hist, Math, Philo, Poli Sci, Pre-Law

ALBRIGHT COLLEGE (PA) .... albright.edu 1040/21
Biochem, Bio, Bus Admin, Poli Sci, Pre-Law, Pre-Med/Pre-Dental, Psych

ALDERSON-BROADDUS COLLEGE (WV) .... ab.edu 1000/21
Bus Admin, Ed, Nurs

ALFRED UNIVERSITY (NY) .... alfred.edu 1100/24
Art, Bus Admin, Comp Sci, Ed, Engine, English, Hist, Pre-Law, Psych

ALLEGHENY COLLEGE (PA) .... alleg.edu 1190/26
*Bio, Comp Sci, Drama, Econ, English, For Lang, Geol, Hist, Philo, Pre-Law,
Pre-Med/Pre-Dental, Psych*

ALMA COLLEGE (MI) .... alma.edu 1170/26
Art, Bio, Bus Admin, Chem, Comp Sci, Ed, Hist, Poli Sci, Pre-Law, Pre-Med/Pre-Dental

ALVERNO COLLEGE (WI) .... alverno.edu 1000/21
Bus Admin, Nurs

AMERICAN ACADEMY OF DRAMATIC ARTS (NY) .... aada.org 1205/27
Drama

AMERICAN INTERNATIONAL COLLEGE (MA) .... aic.edu 1000/21
Bus Admin, Pre-Med/Pre-Dental, Psych

AMERICAN UNIVERSITY (DC) .... american.edu 1210/27
Amer St, Anthro, Bus Admin, Econ, Communic, Hist, Math, Poli Sci, Pre-Law

AMHERST COLLEGE (MA) .... amherst.edu 1400/31
Amer St, Astro, Bio, Chem, Classics, Drama, Econ, English, Geol, Hist, Philo, Physics, Pre-Law, Pre-Med/Pre-Dental, Psych, Soc

ANDERSON UNIVERSITY (IN) .... anderson.edu 1080/23
Ed, Music

ANDREWS UNIVERSITY (MI) .... andrews.edu 1000/21
Nurs

ANNA MARIA COLLEGE (MA) .... annamaria.edu 1000/21
Art, Music

APPALACHIAN STATE UNIVERSITY (NC) .... appstate.edu 1120/24
Bus Admin, Communic, Ed, English, Hist, Poli Sci

AQUINAS COLLEGE (MI) .... aquinas.edu 1060/23
Bio, Chem, English, Psych

ARCADIA UNIVERISTY (PA) .... arcadia.edu 1080/23
Art, Bio, Chem, Ed, English, Psych

ARIZONA, UNIVERSITY OF (AZ) .... arizona.edu 1100/24
Ag, Amer St, Anthro, Arch, Art, Astro, Bio, Bus Admin, Communic, Drama, Ed, Engine, English, Forest, Geol, Nurs, Philo, Pre-Law, Pre-Med/Pre-Dental, Psych, Soc

ARIZONA STATE UNIVERSITY (AZ) .... asu.edu 1090/24
Anthro, Arch, Art, Bus Admin, Communic, Comp Sci, Drama, Ed, Engine, Geog, Geol, Math, Music, Nurs, Pre-Med, Poli Sci, Psych, Reli Sci, Zoo

ARKANSAS, UNIVERSITY OF (AR) .... uark.edu 1160/25
Ag, Arch, Bus Admin, Communic, Ed, Engine, English, Music, Pre-Law

ART CENTER COLLEGE OF DESIGN (CA) .... artcenter.edu 1100/24
Art

ART INSTITUTE OF CHICAGO (IL) .... artic.edu/saic 1100/24
Art

ARTS, UNIVERSITY OF THE (PA) .... uarts.edu 1000/21
Art, Drama, Music

ASBURY COLLEGE (KY) .... asbury.edu 1115/24
Bus Admin, Communic, Music, Philo, Soc

ASHLAND UNIVERSITY (OH) .... ashland.edu 1000/21
Bus Admin, Chem, Ed

ASSUMPTION COLLEGE (MA) .... assumption.edu 1080/23
Bus Admin, Ed

AUBURN UNIVERSITY (AL) .... auburn.edu 1120/24
Ag, Arch, Art, Bus Admin, Communic, Econ, Ed, Engine, English, Forest, Pharm, Poli Sci

AUGSBURG COLLEGE (MN) .... augsburg.edu 1080/23
Communic, Ed, English, Physics, Pre-Law

AUGUSTA STATE UNIVERSITY (GA) .... aug.edu 1000/21
English, Soc

AUGUSTANA COLLEGE (IL) .... augustana.edu 1150/25
Art, Bio, Bus Admin, Ed, English, Music, Pre-Law

AUGUSTANA COLLEGE (SD) .... augie.edu 1130/25
Bio, Ed, Music, Nurs, Pre-Med/Pre-Dental

AUSTIN COLLEGE (TX) .... austincollege.edu 1199/26
Bio, Bus Admin, Chem, Ed, Hist, Philo, Poli Sci, Pre-Med/Pre-Dental, Reli Stu

AVERETT COLLEGE (VA) .... averett.edu 1000/21
Bus Admin, Ed

AVILA UNIVERSITY (MO) ....avila.edu 1050/22
Ed, Nurs

AZUSA PACIFIC (CA) .... apu.edu 1000/21
Bio, Bus Admin, English, Music, Nurs, Poli Sci

BABSON COLLEGE (MA) .... babson.edu 1235/28
Bus Admin, Econ

BAKER UNIVERSITY (KS) .... bakeru.edu 1075/23
Bus Admin, Psych

BALDWIN-WALLACE COLLEGE (OH) .... bw.edu 1120/24
Bus Admin, Chem, Econ, Ed, English, Hist, Music, Poli Sci, Pre-Law

BALL STATE UNIVERSITY (IN) .... bsu.edu 1040/22
Anthro, Art, Bio, Botany, Communic, Comp Sci, Ed, Geog, Math, Nurs, Physics, Poli Sci

BARD COLLEGE (NY) .... bard.edu 1250/28
Art, Drama, English, For Lang, Music, Pre-Law

BARNARD COLLEGE (NY) .... barnard.edu 1320/30
Anthro, Arch, Art Hist, Biochem, Chem, Classics, Drama, Econ, Engine, English, For Lang, Geol, Hist, Math, Music, Nurs, Philo, Physics, Poli Sci, Pre-Law, Psych, Reli Stu, Soc

BARRY UNIVERSITY (FL) .... barry.edu **1100/24**
Bus Admin, Drama, Nurs

BATES COLLEGE (ME) .... bates.edu **1350/30**
Art, Bio, Chem, Econ, English, Geol, Hist, Math, Philo, Physics, Poli Sci, Pre-Law, Pre-Med/Pre-Dental, Psych, Rel Stu

BAYLOR UNIVERSITY (TX) .... baylor.edu **1145/25**
Bus Admin, Chem, Drama, Ed, English, Hist, Nurs, Pre-Law, Pre-Med/Pre-Dental, Reli Stu

BELHAVEN COLLEGE (MS) .... belhaven.edu **1160/25**
Art, Bus Admin, Ed, Music

BELLARMINE UNIVERSITY (KY) .... bellarmine.edu **1095/24**
Bus Admin, Econ, Ed, English, Hist, Math, Nurs, Philo

BELMONT ABBEY COLLEGE (NC) .... belmontabbeycollege.edu **1000/21**
Bus Admin, Poli Sci, Pre-Law, Soc

BELMONT UNIVERSITY (TN) .... belmont.edu **1120/24**
Art, Bus Admin, English, Music, Nurs, Philo, Poli Sci, Pre-Law, Psych

BELOIT COLLEGE (WI) .... beloit.edu **1240/28**
Anthro, Biochem, Classics, Drama, Econ, English, For Lang, Geol, Music, Physics, Psych, Soc

BEMIDJI STATE UNIVERSITY (MN) .... bemidji.msus.edu **1035/22**
Communic, Geog

BENEDICTINE COLLEGE (KS) .... benedictine.edu **1070/23**
Astro, Bus Admin, Soc

BENEDICTINE UNIVERSITY (IL) .... ben.edu **1060/23**
Bio, Bus Admin, Pre-Med/Pre-Dental

BENNETT COLLEGE (NC) .... bennett.edu **1000/21**
Bus Admin, Ed, Pre-Law, Pre-Med/Pre-Dental

BENNINGTON COLLEGE (VT) .... bennington.edu **1175/26**
Drama, English, Pre-Law

BENTLEY COLLEGE (MA) .... bentley.edu **1130/25**
Bus Admin

BEREA COLLEGE (KY) .... berea.edu **1090/24**
Ag, Bio, Bus Admin, Chem, Ed, English, Home Ec, Nurs

BERKLEE COLLEGE OF MUSIC (MA) .... berklee.edu **1100/24**
Music

BERRY COLLEGE (GA) .... berry.edu **1170/26**
Bio, Bus Admin, Ed, Forest, Pre-Med/Pre-Dental, Psych

BETHANY COLLEGE (WV) .... bethany.wvnet.edu **1050/22**
Bio, Communic, Drama, Econ, Ed, English, For Lang, Music, Physics, Pre-Med/Pre-Dental

BETHEL COLLEGE (IN) .... bethel-in.edu **1060/23**
Ed, Nurs, Philo

BETHEL COLLEGE (MN) .... bethel.edu 1120/24
Bus Admin, Ed, Nurs, Psych

BIOLA UNIVERSITY (CA) .... biola.edu 1090/24
Ed, Philo, Psych, Soc

BIRMINGHAM-SOUTHERN COLLEGE (AL) .... bsc.edu 1190/26
Art, Bio, Bus Admin, Chem, Drama, Ed, English, Hist, Math, Music, Pre-Law, Pre-Med/Pre-Dental, Reli Stu

BLACKBURN COLLEGE (IL) .... blackburn.edu 1000/21
Bio, Bus Admin, Ed, Pre-Med/Pre-Dental, Psych

BLOOMSBURG UNIVERSITY (PA) .... bloomu.edu 1050/22
Art, Chem, Ed, Geog, Geol, Nurs

BLUFFTON COLLEGE (OH) .... bluffton.edu 1060/23
Bus Admin, Chem, Ed, Math, Music

BOSTON ARCHITECTURAL CENTER (MA) .... the-bac.edu 1100/24
Arch

BOSTON COLLEGE (MA) .... bc.edu 1300/29
Bio, Bus Admin, Chem, English, For Lang, Hist, Music, Nurs, Philo, Poli Sci, Pre-Law, Pre-Med/Pre-Dental

BOSTON CONSERVATORY OF MUSIC (MA) .... bostonconservatory.edu 1050/22
Music

BOSTON UNIVERSITY (MA) .... bu.edu 1290/29
Anthro, Art, Astro, Bio, Bus Admin, Communic, Drama, Econ, Ed, Engine, Hist, Math, Music, Philo, Physics, Poli Sci, Pre-Law, Psych

BOWDOIN COLLEGE (ME) .... bowdoin.edu 1370/31
Anthro, Art Hist, Biochem, Bio, Chem, Econ, English, For Lang, Geol, Hist, Math, Music, Philo, Pre-Law, Pre-Med/Pre-Dental

BOWLING GREEN STATE UNIVERSITY (OH) .... bgsu.edu 1050/22
Art, Bus Admin, Ed, Geol, Music

BRADLEY UNIVERSITY (IL) .... bradley.edu 1170/26
Art, Bus Admin, Chem, Comp Sci, Ed, Engine, Nurs, Physics

BRANDEIS UNIVERSITY (MA) .... brandeis.edu 1300/29
Anthro, Biochem, Bio, Chem, Comp Sci, Drama, Econ, English, Hist, Math, Music, Physics, Poli Sci, Pre-Law, Pre-Med/Pre-Dental, Psych

BRENAU UNIVERSITY (GA) .... brenau.edu 1040/22
Drama, Music

BRESCIA UNIVERSITY (KY) .... brescia.edu 1030/22
Art, Bus Admin, Ed, English, Reli Stu

BRIDGEWATER COLLEGE (VA) .... bridgewater.edu 1030/22
Bus Admin, Hist, Music, Psych, Soc

BRIDGEWATER STATE COLLEGE (MA) .... bridgew.edu 1000/21
Communic, Ed, Geog, Hist, Poli Sci, Psych, Soc

BRIGHAM YOUNG UNIVERSITY (UT) .... byu.edu **1199/26**
Art, Astro, Bus Admin, Ed, English, For Lang, Geol, Pre-Law, Pre-Med, Reli Stu, Zoo

BROWN UNIVERSITY (RI) .... brown.edu **1390/31**
*Art, Art Hist, Bio, Biochem, Chem, Classics, Comp Sci, Econ, Engine, English,
For Lang, Geol, Hist, Philo, Poli Sci, Pre-Law, Pre-Med/Pre-Dental, Reli Stu*

BRYAN COLLEGE (TN) .... bryan.edu **1100/24**
Ed, Music, Reli Stu

BRYANT COLLEGE (RI) .... bryant.edu **1097/24**
Bus Admin, Comp Sci, Math

BRYN ATHYN COLLEGE OF THE NEW CHURCH (PA) .... newchurch.edu/college **1140/25**
English, Hist, Reli Stu

BRYN MAWR COLLEGE (PA) .... brynmawr.edu **1315/30**
*Art, Art Hist, Astro, Bio, Chem, Classics, Econ, English, For Lang, Geol, Hist, Physics, Pre-Law,
Pre-Med/Pre-Dental, Psych, Soc*

BUCKNELL UNIVERSITY (PA) .... bucknell.edu **1250/28**
*Bio, Bus Admin, Chem, Comp Sci, Econ, Ed, Engine, English, Hist, Math, Music,
Philo, Pre-Law, Pre-Med/Pre-Dental, Psych, Soc*

BUENA VISTA UNIVERSITY (IA) ....bvu.edu **1100/24**
Bus Admin, Communic, Ed

BUTLER UNIVERSITY (IN) .... butler.edu **1180/26**
*Art, Bus Admin, Chem, Communic, Comp Sci, Drama, Ed, Engine, Music, Pharm,
Pre-Law, Pre-Med/Pre-Dental*

CALDWELL COLLEGE (NJ) .... caldwell.edu **1030/22**
Bus Admin, Ed, Psych

CALIFORNIA COLLEGE OF ARTS AND CRAFTS (CA) .... ccac-art.edu **1070/23**
Arch, Art

CALIFORNIA INSTITUTE OF TECHNOLOGY (CA) .... caltech.edu **1530/34**
Astro, Bio, Chem, Engine, Geol, Math, Physics, Pre-Med/Pre-Dental

CALIFORNIA INSTITUTE OF THE ARTS (CA) .... calarts.edu **1100/24**
Art, Drama, Music

CALIFORNIA, UNIVERSITY OF, AT
    BERKELEY .... berkeley.edu **1340/30**
    *Anthro, Arch, Biochem, Bot, Bus Admin, Chem, Comp Sci, Engine, English,
    For Lang, Geog, Geol, Hist, Math, Music, Philo, Poli Sci, Physics, Pre-Law,
    Pre-Med/Pre-Dental, Psych, Reli Stu, Soc, Zoo*
    DAVIS .... ucdavis.edu **1165/26**
    *Ag, Anthro, Art, Bio, Biochem, Bot, Chem, Engine, English, Geol, Hist, Poli Sci,
    Pre-Law, Pre-Med/Pre-Dental, Zoo*
    IRVINE .... uci.edu **1130/25**
    Art, Bio, Chem, Comp Sci, Drama, Engine, Math, Physics, Pre-Law, Pre-Med/Pre-Dental
    LOS ANGELES .... ucla.edu **1280/29**
    *Anthro, Art Hist, Bio, Biochem, Bus Admin, Chem, Communic, Comp Sci, Drama, Econ,
    Engine, English, For Lang, Hist, Math, Music, Philo, Poli Sci, Pre-Law,
    Pre-Med/Pre-Dental, Psych, Soc*

CALIFORNIA, UNIVERSITY OF, AT *(Continued)*

    RIVERSIDE .... ucr.edu **1100/24**
Ag, Art Hist, Biochem, Bio, Bot, Bus Admin, Drama, Engine, Hist, Math, Music, Poli Sci, Pre-Law, Pre-Med/Pre-Dental, Psych

    SAN DIEGO .... ucsd.edu **1300/29**
Amer St, Biochem, Bio, Chem, Communic, Comp Sci, Drama, Econ, Engine, Math, Music, Physics, Poli Sci, Pre-Law, Pre-Med/Pre-Dental, Psych

    SANTA BARBARA .... ucsb.edu **1182/26**
Art, Art Hist, Bio, Bus Admin, Classics, Comp Sci, Ed, Econ, Engine, For Lang, Geog, Geol, Music, Philo, Physics, Poli Sci, Pre-Law, Pre-Med/Pre-Dental, Psych, Reli Stu, Soc, Zoo

    SANTA CRUZ .... ucsc.edu **1145/25**
Amer St, Anthro, Bio, Chem, Comp Sci, English, Math, Music, Physics, Pre-Med/Pre-Dental, Psych

CALIFORNIA LUTHERAN UNIVERSITY (CA) .... clunet.edu **1040/22**
Bus Admin, Communic, Ed, Psych

CALIFORNIA MARITIME ACADEMY (CA) .... csum.edu **1050/22**
Bus Admin, Engine

CALIFORNIA POLYTECHNIC U. AT POMONA (CA) .... csupomona.edu **1000/21**
Ag, Arch, Bio, Bus Admin, Comp Sci, Engine, Physics, Zoo

CALIFORNIA POLYTECHNIC U. AT SAN LUIS OBISPO (CA) .... calpoly.edu **1183/26**
Ag, Arch, Bio, Bio Chem, Bus Admin, Comp Sci, Communic, Engine, English, Physics

CALIFORNIA STATE UNIVERSITY, AT:

    BAKERSFIELD .... csubak.edu **1000/21**
Bus Admin, Ed, English, Geol, Nurs, Psych

    CHANNEL ISLANDS (CAMARILLO)(CA) .... csuci.edu **1000/21**
Anthro, Art, Bio, Biochem, Bus Admin, Chem, Econ, Ed, English, Pre-Med/Pre-Dental

    CHICO .... csuchico.edu **1070/23**
Ag, Anthro, Bio, Chem, Comp Sci, Econ, Geog, Geol, Nurs, Poli Sci, Psych, Reli Stu

    DOMINGUEZ HILLS .... csudh.edu **1000/21**
Bus Admin, Math, Nurs, Philo, Physics, Psych

    FRESNO .... csufresno.edu **1000/21**
Ag, Amer St, Art, Bus Admin, Chem, Ed, Engine, English, Home Ec, Music, Nurs, Philo, Soc

    FULLERTON .... fullerton.edu **1000/21**
Amer St, Anthro, Bus Admin, Communic, Engine, Hist, Music, Nurs, Poli Sci, Pre-Med/Pre-Dental, Soc

    HAYWARD .... csuhayward.edu **1000/21**
Art, Bus Admin, Comp Sci, Hist, Geol, Music, Soc

    LONG BEACH .... csulb.edu **1000/21**
Anthro, Art, Art Hist, Chem, Classics, Communic, Drama, Econ, Hist, Music, Poli Sci, Pre-Law, Psych

    LOS ANGELES .... calstatela.edu **1000/21**
Art, Bus Admin, Ed, Nurs, Psych, Soc

    MONTEREY BAY .... scumb.edu **1000/21**
Art, Bio, Comp Sci, Ed, English, Math, Pre-Law, Pre-Med/Pre-Dental

    NORTHRIDGE .... csun.edu **1000/21**
Art, Art Hist, Communic, Drama, Econ, English, Geog, Music, Philo, Physics, Poli Sci, Pre-Law, Psych, Soc

    SACRAMENTO .... csus.edu **1000/21**
Anthro, Bus Admin, Communic, Drama, Ed, English, For Lang, Geol, Home Ec, Music, Poli Sci, Psych, Soc

CALIFORNIA STATE UNIVERSITY, AT *(Continued)*
    SAN BERNARDINO .... csusb.edu 1000/21
Art, Bus Admin, Communic, Comp Sci, Ed, Psych, Soc
    SAN JOSE .... sjsu.edu 1060/23
Art, Bus Admin, Chem, Communic, Comp Sci, Math, Music, Nurs,
Physics, Pre-Med/Pre-Dental, Zoo
    SAN MARCOS .... csusm.edu 1000/21
Bus Admin, Comp Sci, Ed, Hist, Poli Sci, Psych, Soc
    STANISLAUS .... csustan.edu 1000/21
Bus Admin, Comp Sci, Ed, Poli Sci, Psych

CALIFORNIA UNIVERSITY OF PENNSYLVANIA (PA) .... cup.edu 1000/21
Ed, English

CALVIN COLLEGE (MI) .... calvin.edu 1185/26
Ed, Engine, English, For Lang, Hist, Nurs, Philo, Physics, Pre-Law

CAMPBELL UNIVERSITY (NC) .... campbell.edu 1040/22
Bus Admin, English, Hist, Poli Sci, Pre-Law

CANISIUS COLLEGE (NY) .... canisius.edu 1100/24
Bio, Bus Admin, Communic, Comp Sci, Ed, English, Hist, Pre-Med/Pre-Dental, Psych

CAPITAL UNIVERSITY (OH) .... capital.edu 1090/24
Bus Admin, Comp Sci, Ed, Hist, Music, Nurs

CARLETON COLLEGE (MN) .... carleton.edu 1370/31
Bio, Chem, Drama, Econ, English, For Lang, Geol, Hist, Math, Physics, Poli Sci,
Pre-Law, Pre-Med/Pre-Dental

CARNEGIE MELLON UNIVERSITY (PA) .... cmu.edu 1350/30
Arch, Art, Bus Admin, Chem, Comp Sci, Drama, Engine, Music, Pre-Med/Pre-Dental, Psych

CARROLL COLLEGE (MT) .... carroll.edu 1090/24
Bio, Nurs, Hist, Pre-Med/Pre-Dental

CARROLL COLLEGE (WI) .... cc.edu 1100/24
Chem, Ed, Nurs, Pre-Med/Pre-Dental, Psych

CARSON-NEWMAN COLLEGE (TN) .... cn.edu 1075/23
Chem, Ed, English, Hist, Music, Nurs, Pre-Med/Pre-Dental, Psych

CARTHAGE COLLEGE (WI) .... carthage.edu 1090/24
Bus Admin, For Lang, Geog, Music, Psych, Reli Stu

CASE WESTERN RESERVE UNIVERSITY (OH) .... cwru.edu 1325/30
Anthro, Art Hist, Astro, Biochem, Bus Admin, Chem, Classics, Comp Sci, Drama, Econ,
Engine, Hist, Math, Music, Nurs, Physics, Pre-Med/Pre-Dental, Psych, Reli Stu

CASTLETON STATE COLLEGE (VT) .... castleton.edu 1000/21
Bus Admin, Psych

CATAWBA COLLEGE (NC) .... catawba.edu 1000/21
Bus Admin, Comp Sci, Drama, Ed

CATHOLIC UNIVERSITY OF AMERICA (DC) .... cua.edu 1170/26
Arch, Classics, Drama, Engine, English, For Lang, Music, Nurs, Poli Sci, Pre-Law, Reli Stu

CEDAR CREST COLLEGE (PA) .... cedarcrest.edu 1070/23
Nurs, Psych

CEDARVILLE UNIVERSITY (OH) .... cedarville.edu 1150/25
Bus Admin, Ed, Music, Nurs

CENTENARY COLLEGE OF LOUISIANA (LA) .... centenary.edu 1180/26
Bio, Bus Admin, Chem, Ed, English, Geol, Music

CENTRAL ARKANSAS, UNIVERSITY OF (AR) .... uca.edu 1070/23
Bus Admin, Nurs

CENTRAL COLLEGE (IA) .... central.edu 1140/25
Bio, Chem, Comp Sci, Ed, English, For Lang

CENTRAL CONNECTICUT STATE UNIVERSITY (CT) .... ccsu.edu 1000/21
Bus Admin, Ed, Engine, Geog, Hist, Music, Psych, Soc

CENTRAL FLORIDA, UNIVERSITY OF (FL) .... ucf.edu 1135/25
Bus Admin, Comp Sci, Communic, Drama, Engine, English, Music, Philo, Psych

CENTRAL MICHIGAN UNIVERSITY (MI) .... cmich.edu 1050/22
Bio, Communic, Drama, Ed, English, Home Ec, Geog, Music, Psych

CENTRAL WASHINGTON UNIVERSITY .... cwu.edu 1000/21
Music

CENTRE COLLEGE (KY) .... centre.edu 1210/27
Art, Biochem, Chem, Classics, Econ, Ed, English, For Lang, Hist, Philo, Physics, Poli Sci, Pre-Law, Pre-Med/Pre-Dental, Psych, Reli Stu

CHAMPLAIN COLLEGE (VT) .... champlain.edu 1010/22
Bus Admin

CHAPMAN UNIVERSITY (CA) .... chapman.edu 1170/26
Art Hist, Bus Admin, Communic, Econ, Music, Pre-Law, Pre-Med/Pre-Dental, Psych

CHARLESTON, COLLEGE OF (SC) .... cofc.edu 1150/25
Bio, Bus Admin, Chem, Communic, Ed, Geol, Math, Poli Sci, Pre-Med/Pre-Dental, Soc

CHARLESTON SOUTHERN UNIVERSITY (SC) .... csuniv.edu 1050/22
Comp Sci, Ed, English, Music

CHARLESTON, UNIVERSITY OF (WV) .... uchaswv.edu 1000/21
Hist, Nurs

CHATHAM COLLEGE (PA) .... chatham.edu 1080/23
Art, Bio, Bus Admin, Communic, English, Hist, Poli Sci, Pre-Law

CHESTNUT HILL COLLEGE (PA) .... chc.edu 1050/22
Ed, English, Pre-Law

CHEYNEY UNIVERSITY OF PENNSYLVANIA (PA) .... cheney.edu 1000/21
Ed

CHICAGO, UNIVERSITY OF (IL) .... uchicago.edu 1360/31
Anthro, Art Hist, Bio, Classics, Econ, English, For Lang, Geog, Geol, Hist, Math, Music, Philo, Physics, Poli Sci, Pre-Law, Pre-Med/Pre-Dental, Psych, Reli Stu, Soc

CHOWAN COLLEGE (NC) ....chowan.edu 900/20
Art, Bus Admin, Comp Sci, English

CHRISTIAN BROTHERS UNIVERSITY (TN) .... cbu.edu 1100/24
Bus Admin, Ed, Engine

CHRISTENDOM COLLEGE (VA) .... christendom.edu 1175/26
Hist, Philo, Reli Stu

CHRISTOPHER NEWPORT UNIVERSITY (VA) .... cnu.edu 1070/23
Bus Admin, Comp Sci, English, Math, Music, Philo, Physics, Poli Sci

CINCINNATI, UNIVERSITY OF (OH) .... uc.edu 1060/23
Arch, Classics, Ed, Engine, English, Math, Music, Nurs, Pharm, Psych

CITADEL, THE (SC) .... citadel.edu 1070/23
Bus Admin, Chem, Ed, Engine, English, Pre-Law

CLAREMONT MCKENNA COLLEGE (CA) .... mckenna.edu 1390/31
Bio, Bus Admin, Chem, Econ, English, Hist, Philo, Poli Sci, Pre-Law, Pre-Med/Pre-Dental, Psych, Reli Stu

CLARK ATLANTA UNIVERSITY (GA) .... cau.edu 1000/21
Bus Admin, Comp Sci, Ed, Math, Physics

CLARK UNIVERSITY (MA) .... clarku.edu 1160/25
Bio, Biochem, Bus Admin, Chem, Communic, Econ, English, For Lang, Geog, Music, Poli Sci, Pre-Law, Pre-Med/Pre-Dental, Psych

CLARKE COLLEGE (IA) .... clarke.edu 1110/24
Art, Art Hist, Bio, Chem, Comp Sci, Drama, Ed, Music, Nurs, Philo

CLARKSON UNIVERSITY (NY) .... clarkson.edu 1200/26
Bus Admin, Engine, Soc

CLEMSON UNIVERSITY (SC) .... clemson.edu 1199/26
Ag, Arch, Bio, Bus Admin, Chem, Comp Sci, Econ, Ed, Engine, English, Forest, For Lang, Physics, Poli Sci, Soc, Zoo

CLEVELAND INSTITUTE OF ART (OH) .... cia.edu 1100/24
Art

CLEVELAND INSTITUTE OF MUSIC (OH) .... cim.edu 1200/26
Music

COASTAL CAROLINA (SC) .... coastal.edu 1040/22
Bus Admin, Comp Sci, Philo

COE COLLEGE (IA) .... coe.edu 1160/25
Bio, Bus Admin, Chem, Classics, Ed, English, Hist, Music, Physics

COGSWELL POLYTECHNIC COLLEGE (CA) .... cogswell.edu 1000/21
Comp Sci, Engine

COKER COLLEGE (SC) .... coker.edu 1000/21
Art, Bus Admin, Drama, Ed, Music, Psych, Soc

COLBY COLLEGE (ME) .... colby.edu 1320/29
Bio, Bus Admin, Chem, Econ, English, For Lang, Physics, Poli Sci,
Pre-Law, Pre-Med/Pre-Dental, Psych, Soc, Reli Stu

COLBY-SAWYER COLLEGE (NH) .... colby-sawyer.edu 1010/21
Nurs

COLGATE UNIVERSITY (NY) .... colgate.edu 1335/30
Bio, Chem, English, Geog, Geol, Hist, Math, Philo, Poli Sci, Pre-Law,
Pre-Med/Pre-Dental, Reli Stu

COLORADO COLLEGE (CO) .... coloradocollege.edu 1270/28
Anthro, Art, Art Hist, Bio, Chem, Econ, English, Geol, Hist, Philo, Poli Sci,
Pre-Law, Pre-Med/Pre-Dental, Psych, Soc

COLORADO, UNIVERSITY OF (CO) .... colorado.edu 1180/26
Anthro, Astro, Bio, Biochem, Bus Admin, Chem, Communic, Econ, Engine, English,
Hist, Geog, Geol, Math, Music, Nurs, Physics, Pre-Med/Pre-Dental, Soc

COLORADO, UNIVERSITY OF (COLORADO SPRINGS) .... uccs.edu 1065/23
Bus Admin, Comp Sci, Ed, Engine, Geog, Nurs, Physics, Psych

COLORADO, UNIVERSITY OF (DENVER) .... cudenver.edu 1060/23
Art, Bio, Bus Admin, Comp Sci, Math, Psych

COLORADO SCHOOL OF MINES (CO) .... mines.edu 1230/27
Comp Sci, Econ, Engine, Geol, Math, Physics, Pre-Med/Pre-Dental

COLORADO STATE UNIVERSITY (CO) .... colostate.edu 1100/24
Ag, Anthro, Art, Art Hist, Bot, Bus Admin, Comp Sci, Engine, Forest, Geol, Poli Sci, Psych, Zoo

COLUMBIA COLLEGE (IL) .... colum.edu 1000/21
Communic, Drama

COLUMBIA COLLEGE (SC) .... columbia.college.sc.edu 1040/22
Bio, Bus Admin, Drama, Ed, Pre-Law, Pre-Med/Pre-Dental, Psych

COLUMBIA UNIVERSITY/BARNARD COLLEGE (NY) .... columbia.edu 1350/30; 1320/30
Anthro, Arch, Art Hist, Biochem, Chem, Classics, Drama, Econ, Engine, English, For Lang,
Geol, Hist, Math, Music, Nurs, Philo, Physics, Poli Sci, Pre-Law, Psych, Reli Stu, Soc

CONCORDIA COLLEGE-MOORHEAD (MN) .... cord.edu 1120/24
Bio, Bus Admin, Ed, For Lang, Math, Music, Pre-Med/Pre-Dental, Psych, Reli Stu, Soc

CONCORDIA UNIVERSITY (NE) .... cune.edu 1050/22
Bus Admin, Ed

CONCORDIA UNIVERSITY (CA) .... cui.edu 1050/22
Bus Admin, Music, Reli Stu

CONNECTICUT, UNIVERSITY OF (CT) .... uconn.edu 1135/25
Ag, Art, Bio, Bot, Bus Admin, Econ, Ed, Engine, Hist, Home Ec, Nurs, Poli Sci, Pharm, Pre-Law,
Pre-Med/Pre-Dental, Psych, Zoo

CONNECTICUT COLLEGE (CT) .... conncoll.edu 1280/29
Art, Bot, Drama, Econ, Ed, English, Hist, Music, Philo, Poli Sci, Pre-Law, Psych

CONVERSE COLLEGE (SC) .... converse.edu 1100/24
Art, Chem, Drama, Ed, Music, Poli Sci

THE COOPER UNION (NY) .... cooper.edu 1460/34
Arch, Art, Engine

CORNELL COLLEGE (IA) .... cornell-iowa.edu 1180/26
Bio, Ed, English, Geol, Hist, Philo, Poli Sci, Pre-Law, Pre-Med/Pre-Dental, Psych, Soc

CORNELL UNIVERSITY (NY) .... cornell.edu 1350/30
*Ag, Arch, Art, Astro, Biochem, Bio, Bot, Chem, Comp Sci, Drama, Econ, Engine, English, Hist,
Philo, Physics, Pre-Med/Pre-Dental, Zoo*

CORNISH COLLEGE OF THE ARTS (WA) .... cornish.edu 1100/24
Art, Drama, Music

COVENANT COLLEGE (GA) .... covenant.edu 1185/26
Hist, Music, Soc

CREIGHTON UNIVERSITY (NE) .... creighton.edu 1165/26
*Art, Bio, Chem, Communic, Drama, Ed, Music, Nurs, Pharm, Physics,
Poli Sci, Pre-Law, Pre-Med/Pre-Dental, Psych, Reli Stu*

CUMBERLAND COLLEGE (KY) .... cumber.edu 1040/22
Chem, Ed, Hist, Music, Reli Stu

CURTIS INSTITUTE OF MUSIC (PA) .... curtis.edu 1100/24
Music

DAEMEN COLLEGE (NY) .... daemen.edu 1000/21
Bio, Bus Admin, Ed, English, Nurs

DALLAS, UNIVERSITY OF (TX) .... udallas.edu 1200/26
*Art, Bio, Biochem, Classics, Comp Sci, Econ, Ed, English, For Lang, Hist,
Philo, Poli Sci, Pre-Law, Pre-Med/Pre-Dental*

DANA COLLEGE (NE) .... dana.edu 1020/22
Drama, Ed, English

DARTMOUTH COLLEGE (NH) .... dartmouth.edu 1430/32
*Anthro, Art, Bio, Chem, Classics, Comp Sci, Drama, Econ, Engine, English, For Lang,
Geog, Geol, Hist, Math, Physics, Poli Sci, Pre-Law, Pre-Med/Pre-Dental, Reli Stu, Soc*

DAVIDSON COLLEGE (NC) .... davidson.edu 1325/30
Bio, Chem, Econ, English, Hist, Math, Philo, Poli Sci, Pre-Law, Pre-Med/Pre-Dental, Reli Stu

DAYTON, UNIVERSITY OF (OH) .... udayton.edu 1170/26
Bus Admin, Ed, Engine, Geol, Poli Sci, Pre-Law, Soc

DELAWARE STATE UNIVERSITY .... dsc.edu 1000/21
Hist, Psych

DELAWARE, UNIVERSITY OF (DE) .... udel.edu 1150/25
Art, Art Hist, Bio, Bot, Bus Admin, Chem, Communic, Econ, Ed, Engine, Nurs, Pre-Med/Pre-Dental

DELAWARE VALLEY COLLEGE (PA) .... devalcol.edu 1020/22
Ag, Bio, Bus Admin, Chem, Pre-Med/Pre-Dental

DENISON UNIVERSITY (OH) .... denison.edu 1210/27
*Art, Bio, Biochem, Drama, Econ, English, Geol, Hist, Music, Philo, Poli Sci,
Pre-Law, Pre-Med/Pre-Dental, Psych, Soc*

DENVER, UNIVERSITY OF (CO) .... du.edu 1130/25
*Art, Art Hist, Bio, Bus Admin, Chem, Communic, Comp Sci, Engine, English, Geog, Hist, Music,
Physics, Pre-Law, Pre-Med/Pre-Dental, Psych, Reli Stu*

DePAUL UNIVERSITY (IL) .... depaul.edu 1140/25
*Amer St, Bus Admin, Chem, Communic, Comp Sci, Drama, Ed, English, Math,
Music, Philo, Poli Sci, Pre-Law, Pre-Med/Pre-Dental, Psych, Reli Stu*

DePAUW UNIVERSITY (IN) .... depauw.edu 1240/27
*Bio, Bus Admin, Chem, Communic, Comp Sci, Econ, English, For Lang, Music,
Philo, Physics, Poli Sci, Pre-Law, Pre-Med/Pre-Dental, Psych, Reli Stu*

DeSALES UNIVERSITY (PA) .... desales.edu 1085/24
Bio, Chem, Drama, English, Philo, Reli Stu

DETROIT MERCY, UNIVERSITY OF (MI) .... udmercy.edu 1100/24
Arch, Engine, Nurs, Philo, Reli Stu

DICKINSON COLLEGE (PA) .... dickinson.edu 1210/27
*Bio, Comp Sci, Ed, English, For Lang, Hist, Math, Physics, Poli Sci, Pre-Law,
Pre-Med/Pre-Dental, Psych, Reli Stu*

DILLARD UNIVERSITY (LA) .... dillard.edu 1030/22
Bio, Bus Admin, Nurs, Pre-Med/Pre-Dental

DOANE COLLEGE (NE) .... doane.edu 1075/23
Bus Admin, Philo, Soc, Reli Stu

DOMINICAN UNIVERSITY OF CALIFORNIA (CA) .... dominican.edu 1010/21
Ed, Nurs, Psych

DOMINICAN UNIVERSITY (IL) .... dom.edu 1070/23
Bus Admin, Psych

DORDT COLLEGE (IA) .... dordt.edu 1110/24
Ag, Ed, Engine

DRAKE UNIVERSITY (IA) .... drake.edu 1155/25
Art, Astro, Bio, Bus Admin, Communic, Ed, For Lang, Music, Pharm, Poli Sci, Pre-Law

DREW UNIVERSITY (NJ) .... drew.edu 1240/28
*Art, Chem, Classics, Drama, Econ, English, For Lang, Hist, Poli Sci, Pre-Law,
Pre-Med/Pre-Dental, Psych, Reli Stu*

DREXEL UNIVERSITY (PA) .... drexel.edu 1140/25
Arch, Comp Sci, Engine

DRURY UNIVERSITY (MO) .... drury.edu 1150/25
Ag, Arch, English, Music, Reli Stu

DUBUQUE, UNIVERSITY OF (IA) .... dbq.edu 1080/23
Bus Admin, Communic, English, Ed, Psych

DUKE UNIVERSITY (NC) .... duke.edu 1400/31
Anthro, Bio, Bot, Chem, Classics, Econ, Engine, English, Hist, Math, Nurs, Philo, Poli Sci, Pre-Law, Pre-Med/Pre-Dental, Psych, Reli Stu

DUQUESNE UNIVERSITY (PA) .... duq.edu 1100/24
Bio, Bus Admin, Chem, Classics, Communic, Ed, Music, Nurs, Pharm, Pre-Med/Pre-Dental, Reli Stu

D'YOUVILLE COLLEGE (NY) .... dyc.edu 1020/22
Bio, Ed, English, Nurs, Psych, Soc

EARLHAM COLLEGE (IN) .... earlham.edu 1170/26
Anthro, Astro, Bio, Chem, Ed, English, For Lang, Geol, Math, Philo, Pre-Med/Pre-Dental, Psych, Reli Stu, Soc

EAST CAROLINA UNIVERSITY (NC) .... ecu.edu 1036/22
Art, Art Hist, Econ, Ed, Engine, English, Hist, Math, Music, Nurs, Pre-Med/Pre-Dental, Psych

EAST STROUDSBURG UNIVERSITY (PA) .... esu.edu 1000/21
Bio, Comp Sci

EAST TENNESSEE STATE UNIVERSITY (TN) .... etsu.edu 1030/22
Art, Bus Admin, Econ, Hist, Nurs

EASTERN COLLEGE (PA) .... eastern.edu 1090/24
Bus Admin, Nurs, Soc

EASTERN CONNECTICUT STATE UNIVERSITY (CT) .... easternct.edu 1000/21
Amer St, Art Hist, Bio, Bot, Bus Admin, Communic, Comp Sci, Econ, Ed, Hist, Math, Poli Sci, Psych, Soc

EASTERN ILLINOIS UNIVERSITY (IL) .... eiu.edu 1010/21
Art, Bot, Bus Admin, Ed, English, Home Ec, Psych, Zoo

EASTERN KENTUCKY UNIVERSITY (KY) .... eku.edu 1000/21
Communic, Ed, Nurs, Poli Sci

EASTERN MENNONITE UNIVERSITY (VA) .... emu.edu 1070/23
Ed, Nurs, Reli Stu

EASTERN MICHIGAN UNIVERSITY (MI) .... emich.edu 1000/21
Bus Admin, Chem, Comp Sci, Ed, English, Hist, Music, Nurs, Physics, Poli Sci, Psych

EASTERN NAZARENE COLLEGE (MA) .... enc.edu 1030/22
Bus Admin, English

EASTERN OREGON UNIVERSITY (OR) .... eou.edu 1000/21
Bio, Bus Admin, Ed

ECKERD COLLEGE (FL) .... eckerd.edu 1160/26
Bio, Bus Admin, Comp Sci, English, For Lang, Pre-Med/Pre-Dental, Reli Stu

EDGEWOOD COLLEGE (WI) .... edgewood.edu 1050/22
Art, Ed, Nurs

EDINBORO UNIVERSITY OF PENNSYLVANIA (PA) .... edinboro.edu 1000/21
Art, Art Hist, Ed, English, Geog, Geol, Physics

ELIZABETHTOWN COLLEGE (PA) .... etown.edu 1140/25
Bio, Bus Admin, Ed, English, Pre-Law, Reli Stu

ELMHURST COLLEGE (IL) .... elmhurst.edu 1000/21
Bio

ELMIRA COLLEGE (NY) .... elmira.edu 1140/25
Bus Admin, Ed, Hist, Nurs, Psych

ELMS COLLEGE (MA) .... elms.edu 1020/22
Ed, Nurs

ELON UNIVERSITY (NC) .... elon.edu 1150/26
Bio, Bus Admin, Communic, Drama, Ed, Philo, Poli Sci, Psych

EMBRY-RIDDLE AERONAUTICAL UNIVERSITY (FL) .... emu.edu 1110/24
Comp Sci, Engine

EMERSON COLLEGE (MA) .... emerson.edu 1170/26
Drama, English, Pre-Law

EMMANUEL COLLEGE (MA) .... emmanuel/edu 1040/22
Art, Bio

EMORY & HENRY COLLEGE (VA) .... ehc.edu 1055/22
Bus Admin, For Lang

EMORY UNIVERSITY (GA) .... emory.edu 1325/30
*Anthro, Art Hist, Bio, Bus Admin, Chem, Classics, Econ, English, For Lang, Hist,
Nurs, Poli Sci, Pre-Law, Pre-Med/Pre-Dental, Psych, Reli Stu, Soc*

ERSKINE COLLEGE (SC) .... erskine.edu 1122/24
Bio, Bus Admin, Ed, Hist, Pre-Med/Pre-Dental

EUREKA COLLEGE (IL) .... eureka.edu 1050/22
Bus Admin, Comp Sci, Ed, English

EVANSVILLE, UNIVERSITY OF (IN) .... evansville.edu 1150/25
Comp Sci, Drama, Nurs, Physics, Pre-Med/Pre-Dental

FAIRFIELD UNIVERSITY (CT) .... fairfield.edu 1160/25
Bio, Bus Admin, Communic, Math, Nurs, Physics, Pre-Med/Pre-Dental, Psych

FAIRLEIGH DICKINSON (NJ) .... fdu.edu 1020/22
Art, Bus Admin, English, Pre-Law

FAIRMONT STATE COLLEGE (WV) .... fscwv.edu 1000/21
Bus Admin, Ed, Hist, Nurs, Psych

FAULKNER UNIVERSITY (AL) .... faulkner.edu 1000/21
Bus Admin

FERRIS STATE UNIVERSITY (MI) .... ferris.edu 1000/21
Bus Admin, Comp Sci, Nurs, Pharm

FISK UNIVERSITY (TN) .... fisk.edu 1010/21
Bus Admin, Math, Physics, Pre-Law, Soc

FITCHBURG STATE COLLEGE (MA) .... fsc.edu 1020/22
Bio, Communic, Nurs, Psych

FIVE TOWNS COLLEGE (NY) .... ftc.edu 1000/21
Music

FLAGLER COLLEGE (FL) .... flagler.edu 1100/24
Bus Admin, Communic, Ed, Pre-Law, Psych

FLORIDA, UNIVERSITY OF (FL) .... ufl.edu 1270/27
Ag, Anthro, Arch, Art, Astro, Bot, Bus Admin, Classics, Communic, Drama, Engine, English, Forest, For Lang, Geol, Hist, Math, Music, Nurs, Pharm, Philo, Physics, Poli, Sci, Pre-Law, Pre-Med/Pre-Dental, Soc, Zoo

FLORIDA A&M (FL) .... famu/edu 1000/21
Arch, Bus Admin, Communic, Ed, Engine, English, Pharm, Physics, Pre-Law, Pre-Med/Pre-Dental

FLORIDA ATLANTIC UNIVERSITY (FL) .... fau.edu 1060/23
Bus Admin, Ed, Engine, Hist, Math, Psych

FLORIDA GULF COAST UNIVERSITY (FL) .... fgcu.edu 1015/21
Bus Admin, Comp Sci, Ed, English, Nurs

FLORIDA INSTITUTE OF TECHNOLOGY (FL) .... fit.edu 1160/25
Astro, Bio, Biochem, Bus Admin, Chem, Communic, Comp Sci, Engine, Physics, Psych

FLORIDA INTERNATIONAL UNIVERSITY (FL) .... fiu.edu 1120/24
Arch, Art, Bio, Bus Admin, Ed, Engine, Geog, Nurs, Poli Sci, Psych, Soc

FLORIDA SOUTHERN COLLEGE (FL) .... flsouthern.edu 1050/22
Bio, Chem, Communic, Drama, Ed, Music, Pre-Med/Pre-Dental

FLORIDA STATE UNIVERSITY (FL) .... fsu.edu 1170/26
Amer St, Art, Art Hist, Bus Admin, Chem, Classics, Comp Sci, Drama, Econ, Ed, English, Hist, Home Ec, Music, Philo, Physics, Pre-Med/Pre-Dental, Psych, Reli Stu

FONTBONNE COLLEGE (MO) .... fontbonne.edu 1050/22
Communic, Drama, Ed, Math

FORDHAM UNIVERSITY (NY) .... fordham.edu 1165/26
Classics, Communic, Drama, English, Philo, Pre-Law, Pre-Med/Pre-Dental, Reli Stu

FORT HAYS STATE UNIVERSITY (KS) .... fhsu.edu 1050/22
Art, English, Music

FORT LEWIS COLLEGE (CO) .... fortlewis.edu 1000/21
Anthro, Bio, English, Geol, Physics, Pre-Law

FRAMINGHAM STATE COLLEGE (MA) .... framingham.edu 1040/22
Bio, Biochem, Bus Admin, Chem, Econ, Psych

FRANCISCAN UNIVERSITY OF STEUBENVILLE (OH) .... franuniv.edu 1099/24
English, Nurs, Philo, Psych, Reli Stu

FRANKLIN COLLEGE (IN) .... franklincollege.edu 1050/23
Communic, Drama, Ed, Pre-Med

FRANKLIN & MARSHALL COLLEGE (PA) .... fandm.edu 1255/28
*Amer Stu, Bio, Bus Admin, Chem, English, Geol, Physics, Poli Sci, Pre-Law,
Pre-Med/Pre-Dental, Psych, Soc*

FREED-HARDEMAN UNIVERSITY (TN) .... fhu.edu 1080/23
Bus Admin, Ed, Pre-Med/Pre-Dental, Reli Stu

FROSTBURG STATE UNIVERSITY (MD) .... frostburg.edu 1000/21
Art, Bus Admin, Comp Sci, Ed, Geog, Philo

FURMAN UNIVERSITY (SC) .... furman.edu 1250/28
*Art, Bio, Bus Admin, Chem, Comp Sci, Geol, Hist, Music, Poli Sci, Pre-Law,
Pre-Med/Pre-Dental, Psych, Reli Stu*

GANNON UNIVERSITY (PA) .... gannon.edu 1058/23
Bus Admin, Engine, Nurs

GENEVA COLLEGE (PA) .... geneva.edu 1120/24
Communic, Ed, Engine

GEORGETOWN COLLEGE (KY) .... georgetowncollege.edu 1080/23
Bio, Bus Admin, Chem, Communic, Ed, English, Hist, Pre-Law, Soc

GEORGETOWN UNIVERSITY (DC) .... georgetown.edu 1330/30
*Amer St, Anthro, Bio, Bus Admin, Chem, Classics, Econ, English, For Lang, Hist, Nurs,
Philo, Physics, Poli Sci, Pre-Law, Pre-Med/Pre-Dental, Psych, Reli Stu, Soc*

GEORGE FOX UNIVERSITY (OR) .... georgefox.edu 1080/23
Bus Admin, Ed, Soc

GEORGE MASON UNIVERSITY (VA) .... gmu.edu 1160/25
*Amer St, Anthro, Art Hist, Bus Admin, Comp Sci, Drama, Econ, English, Math,
Nurs, Philo, Physics, Poli Sci, Psych, Pre-Law*

GEORGE WASHINGTON UNIVERSITY (DC) .... gwu.edu 1240/28
Amer St, Anthro, Art Hist, Bus Admin, Chem, Comp Sci, Econ, Geog, Hist, Philo, Poli Sci, Pre-Law, Psych

GEORGIA, UNIVERSITY OF (GA) .... uga.edu 1195/26
*Ag, Art Hist, Astro, Bio, Biochem, Chem, Classics, Communic, Drama, Econ, Ed, English, For Lang,
Forest, Geog, Hist, Home Ec, Music, Pharm, Philo, Poli Sci, Pre-Law, Pre-Med/Pre-Dental, Psych, Zoo*

GEORGIA INSTITUTE OF TECHNOLOGY (GA) .... gatech.edu 1305/29
Arch, Bus Admin, Chem, Comp Sci, Econ, Engine, Hist, Math, Physics, Psych

GEORGIA SOUTHERN UNIVERSITY (GA) .... gasou.edu 1040/22
Art, Bus Admin, Ed, Hist, Home Ec, Nurs

GEORGIA SOUTHWESTERN STATE UNIVERSITY (GA) .... gsw.edu 1000/21
Ed, English, Nurs

GEORGIA STATE UNIVERSITY (GA) .... gsu.edu 1070/23
*Astro, Bio, Bus Admin, Chem, Communic, Comp Sci, Econ, Ed, Math, Music,
Nurs, Philo, Physics, Psych, Soc*

GETTYSBURG COLLEGE (PA) .... gettysburg.edu **1200/26**
Bio, Bus Admin, Communic, Drama, English, Hist, Pre-Law, Pre-Med/Pre-Dental, Psych, Soc

GONZAGA UNIVERSITY (WA) .... gonzaga.edu **1180/26**
Bio, Bus Admin, Communic, Ed, Engine, English, Hist, Philo, Poli Sci, Pre-Law, Pre-Med/Pre-Dental

GORDON COLLEGE (MA) .... gordon.edu **1199/26**
Art, Bio, Ed, English, Music, Reli Stu, Soc

GOSHEN COLLEGE (IN) .... goshen.edu **1140/25**
English, Music, Nurs, Physics

GOUCHER COLLEGE (MD) .... goucher.edu **1174/26**
Bus Admin, Chem, Comp Sci, Drama, Ed, English, Hist, Pre-Law

GRACELAND UNIVERSITY (IA) .... graceland.edu **1001/21**
Bus Admin, Ed, Nurs

GRAMBLING STATE UNIVERSITY (LA) .... gram.edu **1000/21**
Bus Admin, Ed, Nurs, Poli Sci, Soc

GRAND VALLEY STATE UNIVERSITY (MI) .... gvsu.edu **1080/23**
Anthro, Art, Drama, Engine, English, For Lang, Pre-Law, Psych

GREEN MOUNTAIN COLLEGE (VT) .... greenmt.edu **1040/22**
Bus Admin

GREENSBORO COLLEGE (NC) .... gborocollege.edu **1000/21**
Drama

GRINNELL COLLEGE (IA) .... grinnell.edu **1334/30**
*Anthro, Bio, Chem, Comp Sci, Econ, English, For Lang, Hist, Physics,
Poli Sci, Pre-Law, Pre-Med/Pre-Dental, Psych, Soc*

GROVE CITY COLLEGE (PA) .... gcc.edu **1270/28**
Bio, Bus Admin, Econ, Ed, Engine, English, Poli Sci

GUILFORD COLLEGE (NC) .... guilford.edu **1140/25**
*Art, Bio, Bus Admin, Econ, Ed, English, Geol, Hist, Physics, Poli Sci,
Pre-Law, Pre-Med/Pre-Dental, Psych, Reli Stu*

GUSTAVUS ADOLPHUS COLLEGE (MN) .... gustavus.edu **1200/26**
Bio, Bus Admin, Chem, Classics, Ed, English, For Lang, Geol, Music, Nurs, Physics, Psych

GWYNEDD-MERCY COLLEGE (PA) .... gmc.edu **1020/22**
Bio, Communic, English, Nurs, Pre-Law

HAMILTON COLLEGE (NY) .... hamilton.edu **1280/29**
Bio, Chem, Econ, English, Hist, Philo, Poli Sci, Pre-Law, Pre-Med/Pre-Dental, Reli Stu

HAMLINE UNIVERSITY (MN) .... hamline.edu **1120/24**
Anthro, Art, Bio, Chem, English, Physics, Pre-Law, Pre-Med/Pre-Dental, Psych, Soc

HAMPDEN-SYDNEY COLLEGE (VA) .... hsc.edu **1120/24**
Bio, Classics, Econ, English, Hist, Poli Sci, Pre-Law, Pre-Med/Pre-Dental

HAMPTON UNIVERSITY (VA) .... hamptonu.edu 1020/22
Bus Admin, Psych

HANOVER COLLEGE (IN) .... hanover.edu 1150/25
Bus Admin, Communic, Drama, Ed, English, Hist, Philo, Physics, Psych, Soc

HARDIN-SIMMONS UNIVERSITY (TX) .... hsutx.edu 1020/22
Bio, Communic, Ed, Music

HARDING UNIVERSITY (AR) .... harding.edu 1120/24
Bus Admin, Ed, Music, Nurs, Reli Stu

HARTFORD, UNIVERSITY OF (CT) .... hartford.edu 1050/23
Bus Admin, Engine, Music

HARTWICK COLLEGE (NY) .... hartwick.edu 1130/25
Bus Admin, Geol, Music, Nurs, Poli Sci, Pre-Law, Soc

HARVARD UNIVERSITY (MA) .... harvard.edu 1435/32
Amer St, Anthro, Art, Art Hist, Astro, Biochem, Bio, Chem, Classics, Comp Sci, Econ, English, For Lang, Geol, Hist, Math, Music, Philo, Physics, Poli Sci, Pre-Law, Pre-Med/Pre-Dental, Psych, Soc

HARVEY MUDD COLLEGE (CA) .... hmc.edu 1450/32
Bio, Chem, Comp Sci, Engine, Math, Physics, Pre-Med/Pre-Dental

HASTINGS COLLEGE (NE) .... hastings.edu 1090/24
Bus Admin, Communic, Ed, Music, Physics

HAVERFORD COLLEGE (PA) .... haverford.edu 1400/31
Astro, Bio, Chem, Econ, English, For Lang, Hist, Philo, Physics, Pre-Law, Pre-Med/Pre-Dental, Psych, Reli Stu

HAWAII, UNIVERSITY OF (HI) .... uhm.hawaii.edu 1085/24
Ag, Amer St, Anthro, Art, Astro, Bot, Drama, For Lang, Poli Sci, Pre-Law, Zoo

HAWAII PACIFIC UNIVERSITY (HI) .... hpu.edu 1080/23
Bus Admin, Communic, Comp Sci, Econ, Nurs, Pre-Med/Pre-Dental

HEIDELBERG COLLEGE (OH) .... heidelberg.edu 1035/22
Bio, Bus Admin, Econ, Ed, Hist, Music, Poli Sci, Pre-Law, Pre-Med/Pre-Dental

HENDERSON STATE UNIVERSITY (AR) .... hsu.edu 1020/22
Bus Admin, Ed, Nurs

HENDRIX COLLEGE (AR) .... hendrix.edu 1235/27
Bio, Bus Admin, Chem, Comp Sci, Econ, English, Math, Physics, Pre-Law, Pre-Med/Pre-Dental, Psych, Reli Stu, Soc

HIGH POINT UNIVERSITY (NC) .... highpoint.edu 1020/22
Comp Sci

HILLSDALE COLLEGE (MI) .... hillsdale.edu 1170/26
Amer St, Bus Admin, Ed, Hist, Poli Sci

HIRAM COLLEGE (OH) .... hiram.edu 1150/25
Bio, Chem, Comp Sci, Ed, English, Hist, Math, Music, Pre-Law, Pre-Med/Pre-Dental, Reli Stu

HOBART & WILLIAM SMITH COLLEGE (NY) .... hws.edu **1190/26**
Amer Stu, Bio, Chem, Econ, English, Hist, Poli Sci, Pre-Law, Pre-Med/Pre-Dental, Psych

HOFSTRA UNIVERSITY (NY) .... hofstra.edu **1100/24**
Anthro, Art, Bus Admin, Communic, Drama, Music, Poli Sci, Pre-Law, Pre-Med/Pre-Dental, Soc

HOLLINS UNIVERSITY (VA) .... hollins.edu **1140/25**
Amer St, Art, Art Hist, English, For Lang, Hist, Pre-Law, Psych

HOLY CROSS, COLLEGE OF THE (MA) .... holycross.edu **1250/28**
Bio, Chem, Classics, Econ, English, Hist, Math, Philo, Poli Sci, Pre-Law, Pre-Med/Pre-Dental

HOLY NAMES COLLEGE (CA) .... hnc.edu **1000/21**
Ed, Psych

HOOD COLLEGE (MD) .... hood.edu **1130/25**
Bio, Bus Admin, Ed, Hist, Philo, Pre-Med/Pre-Dental, Psych

HOPE COLLEGE (MI) .... hope.edu **1185/26**
Bio, Chem, Geol, Music, Poli Sci, Pre-Law, Pre-Med/Pre-Dental, Psych

HOUGHTON COLLEGE (NY) .... houghton.edu **1160/25**
Art, Bio, Chem, Ed, Music, Pre-Med/Pre-Dental, Psych, Reli Stu

HOUSTON BAPTIST UNIVERSITY (TX) .... hbu.edu **1060/23**
Bio, Chem, Pre-Med/Pre-Dental

HOUSTON, UNIVERSITY OF (TX) .... uh.edu **1040/23**
Arch, Art, Bus Admin, Communic, Engine, Music, Psych

HOWARD UNIVERSITY (DC) .... howard.edu **1060/23**
*Arch, Bus Admin, Communic, Engine, English, Nurs, Poli Sci, Pre-Law,
Pre-Med/Pre-Dental, Soc, Zoo*

HUMBOLDT STATE UNIVERSITY (CA) .... humboldt.edu **1050/22**
Anthro, Art, Bot, Forest, Geog, Geol, Zoo

HUNTINGDON COLLEGE (AL) .... huntingdon.edu **1120/24**
Chem, Ed, Music, Pre-Med/Pre-Dental

HUNTINGTON COLLEGE (IN) .... huntcol.edu **1060/23**
Ed

HUSSON COLLEGE (ME) .... husson.edu **1000/21**
Bus Admin, Comp Sci, Ed, Nurs

IDAHO, UNIVERSITY OF (ID) .... uidaho.edu **1105/24**
Ag, Arch, Bus Admin, Communic, Engine, Forest, Geol

ILLINOIS, UNIVERSITY OF, AT:
    URBANA-CHAMPAIGN .... uiuc.edu **1220/27**
      *Ag, Anthro, Arch, Astro, Bus Admin, Chem, Communic, Comp Sci, Drama, Ed, Engine,
      English, Forest, For Lang, Hist, Math, Music, Nurs, Pharm, Physics, Poli Sci, Pre-Law,
      Pre-Med/Pre-Dental, Psych, Soc*
    CHICAGO .... uic.edu **1080/23**
      *Arch, Art, Art Hist, Bio, Bus Admin, Classics, Econ, Engine, English, For Lang, Hist,
      Math, Music, Nurs, Pharm, Philo, Poli Sci, Pre-law, Pre-Med/Pre-Dental, Psych*

ILLINOIS COLLEGE (IL) .... ic.edu 1130/25
Bio, Bus Admin, Communic, Comp Sci, Econ, Ed, English, For Lang, Hist, Math,
Poli Sci, Pre-Law, Soc

ILLINOIS INSTITUTE OF TECHNOLOGY (IL) .... iit.edu 1240/28
Arch, Engine, Math

ILLINOIS STATE UNIVERSITY (IL) .... ilstu.edu 1040/22
Drama, Ed, Poli Sci, Pre-Law

ILLINOIS WESLEYAN UNIVERSITY (IL) .... iwu.edu 1245/28
Bio, Chem, Drama, English, Music, Nurs, Physics, Pre-Law, Pre-Med/Pre-Dental, Psych

IMMACULATA UNIVERSITY (PA) .... immaculata.edu 1035/22
Bus Admin, Nurs

INDIANA STATE UNIVERSITY (IN) .... indstate.edu 1000/21
Art, Bus Admin, Communic, Drama, Ed, Geog, Music, Physics

INDIANA UNIVERSITY (IN) .... indiana.edu 1110/24
Bio, Bus Admin, Chem, Communic, Drama, Ed, For Lang, Geog, Geol, Hist, Music,
Nurs, Pre-Med/Pre-Dental, Psych, Soc, Zoo

INDIANA UNIVERSITY OF PENNSYLVANIA .... iup.edu 1150/25
Anthro, Art, Art Hist, Bio, Bus Admin, Communic, Ed, Geog, Hist, Nurs, Philo, Soc

INDIANA U./PURDUE U./INDIANAPOLIS (IN) .... iupui.edu 1000/21
Econ, Ed, Nurs, Soc

INDIANA INSTITUTE OF TECHNOLOGY (IN) .... indtech.edu 1100/24
Bus Admin

IONA COLLEGE (NY) .... iona.edu 1000/21
Bus Admin

IOWA, UNIVERSITY OF .... uiowa.edu 1160/25
Art, Astro, Biochem, Bus Admin, Communic, Drama, Ed, Engine, English, For Lang,
Music, Nurs, Pharm, Physics, Poli Sci, Pre-Law, Pre-Med/Pre-Dental, Psych, Reli Stu

IOWA STATE UNIVERSITY (IA) .... iastate.edu 1160/25
Ag, Bio, Bus Admin, Chem, Comp Sci, Ed, Engine, Forest, Home Ec, Physics, Pre-Med/Pre-Dental, Soc, Zoo

ITHACA COLLEGE (NY) .... ithaca.edu 1183/26
Biochem, Bus Admin, Chem, Communic, Music, Pre-Med/Pre-Dental

JACKSONVILLE STATE (AL) .... jsu.edu 1000/21
Comp Sci, Ed, Nurs

JACKSONVILLE UNIVERSITY (FL) .... ju.edu 1070/23
Art, Bio, Bus Admin, Communic, Drama, Music, Nurs, Physics, Pre-Med/Pre-Dental

JAMES MADISON UNIVERSITY (VA) .... jmu.edu 1165/26
Art, Bus Admin, Ed, Communic, Comp Sci, Drama, For Lang, Music, Poli Sci, Pre-law, Pre-Med/
Pre-Dental, Psych, Soc

JAMESTOWN COLLEGE (ND) .... jc.edu 1050/22
Comp Sci, Ed, English, Nurs

JOHN BROWN UNIVERSITY (AR) .... jbu.edu 1120/24
Music, Reli Stu

JOHN CARROLL UNIVERSITY (OH) .... jcu.edu 1140/25
Bus Admin, Communic, English, Poli Sci, Psych, Reli Stu

JOHNS HOPKINS UNIVERSITY (MD) ....jhu.edu 1385/31
Art Hist, Bio, Chem, Classics, Engine, Geog, Music, Nurs, Philo, Poli Sci, Pre-Law, Pre-Med/Pre-Dental

JOHNSON C. SMITH (NC) .... jcsu.edu 1000/21
Communic, Soc

JOHNSON STATE COLLEGE (VT) .... jsc.vsc.edu 1000/21
Drama, Ed, English, Music

JUDSON COLLEGE (AL) .... judson.edu 1045/22
Art, Bus Admin, Communic, Ed, English, Music, Psych

JUILLIARD SCHOOL(NY) .... juilliard.edu 1120/24
Drama, Music

JUNIATA COLLEGE (PA) .... juniata.edu 1170/26
Art, Bio, Bus Admin, Chem, Communic, Ed, English, Geol, Hist, Pre-Law, Pre-Med/Pre-Dental

KALAMAZOO COLLEGE (MI) .... kzoo.edu 1300/28
Amer St, Bio, Chem, Classics, Econ, English, For Lang, Hist, Physics, Pre-Law, Pre-Med/Pre-Dental, Soc

KANSAS, UNIVERSITY OF (KS) .... ukans.edu 1100/24
Anthro, Arch, Art, Art Hist, Astro, Chem, Communic, Drama, Engine, For Lang, Geog, Hist, Pharm, Pre-Med/Pre-Dental, Zoo

KANSAS STATE UNIVERSITY (KS) .... ksu.edu 1100/24
Ag, Arch, Bio, Biochem, Bus Admin, Communic, Ed, Engine, English, Home Ec, Math, Physics, Pre-Law, Pre-Med/Pre-Dental

KEAN UNIVERSITY (NJ) .... kean.edu 1000/21
Ed, Psych, Soc

KEENE STATE COLLEGE (NH) ....keene.edu 1000/21
Art, Communic, Drama, Ed, English, Geog, Music, Psych

KENNESAW STATE UNIVERSITY (GA) .... kennesaw.edu 1045/22
Bus Admin, Chem, English, Hist, Nurs

KENT STATE UNIVERSITY (OH) .... kent.edu 1010/21
Arch, Art, Communic, Comp Sci, Ed, Music, Nurs, Physics

KENTUCKY, UNIVERSITY OF (KY) .... uky.edu 1130/25
Ag, Arch, Bio, Bus Admin, Classics, Communic, Ed, Engine, English, Hist, Music, Pharm, Pre-Med/Pre-Dental, Psych, Zoo

KENTUCKY WESLEYAN COLLEGE (KY) .... kwc.edu 1030/22
Bio, Bus Admin, Chem, Communic, Ed, English, Hist, Pre-Med/Pre-Dental, Psych, Reli Stu

KENYON COLLEGE (OH) .... kenyon.edu **1280/29**
Anthro, Art, Bio, Chem, Classics, Drama, Econ, English, Hist, Math, Music, Philo, Physics, Poli Sci, Pre-Law, Pre-Med/Pre-Dental, Psych, Reli Stu

KETTERING UNIVERSITY (MI) ....kettering.edu **1220/27**
Engine

KING COLLEGE (TN) .... king.edu **1090/24**
Ed, English, Nurs, Reli Stu

KING'S COLLEGE (PA) .... kings.edu **1060/23**
Bio, Bus Admin, Chem

KNOX COLLEGE (IL) .... knox.edu **1220/27**
Anthro, Art, Bio, Biochem, Chem, English, Hist, Math, Physics, Poli Sci, Pre-Law, Pre-Med/Pre-Dental, Soc

KUTZTOWN UNIVERSITY (PA) .... kutztown.edu **1000/21**
Art, Ed, Poli Sci

LAFAYETTE COLLEGE (PA) .... lafayette.edu **1270/28**
Anthro, Art, Bio, Bus Admin, Chem, Comp Sci, Econ, Engine, English, Geol, Hist, Pre-Law, Pre-Med/Pre-Dental, Psych

LAKE FOREST COLLEGE (IL) .... lfc.edu **1140/25**
Art, Art Hist, Bio, Chem, Econ, Ed, English, For Lang, Hist, Music, Poli Sci, Pre-Law, Pre-Med/Pre-Dental, Psych, Soc

LAMAR UNIVERSITY (TX) .... lamar.edu **1000/21**
Ed, Engine, Geol, Soc

LAMBUTH UNIVERSITY (TN) .... lambuth.edu **1035/22**
Art, Bio, Ed, Hist

LA SALLE UNIVERSITY (PA) .... lasalle.edu **1100/24**
Bus Admin, Chem, Comp Sci, English, Math, Pre-Law, Reli Stu, Psych

LASELL COLLEGE (MA) .... lasell.edu **1000/21**
Bus Admin, Ed

LA VERNE, UNIVERSITY OF (CA) .... ulv.edu **1010/21**
Bus Admin, Ed

LAWRENCE UNIVERSITY (WI) .... lawrence.edu **1244/28**
Art, Bio, Chem, Drama, English, For Lang, Hist, Music, Philo, Physics, Pre-Law, Pre-Med/Pre-Dental, Reli Stu

LEBANON VALLEY COLLEGE OF PENNSYLVANIA (PA) .... lvc.edu **1108/24**
Bus Admin, Math, Music, Nurs, Psych

LEHIGH UNIVERSITY (PA) .... lehigh.edu **1281/29**
Arch, Bio, Bus Admin, Chem, Comp Sci, Engine, English, Geol, Hist, Poli Sci

LEMOYNE COLLEGE (NY) .... lemoyne.edu **1100/24**
Bio, Bus Admin, Communic, Drama, English, Psych

LENOIR-RHYNE COLLEGE (NC) .... lrc.edu 1020/22
Bus Admin, Soc

LESLEY UNIVERSITY (MA) .... lesley.edu 1045/22
Bus Admin, Ed

LETOURNEAU COLLEGE (TX) .... letu.edu 1150/25
Bus Admin, Ed, Engine

LEWIS & CLARK COLLEGE (OR) .... lclark.edu 1220/27
*Bio, Biochem, Bus Admin, Communic, Drama, English, For Lang, Physics,
Pre-Med/Pre-Dental, Soc*

LEWIS-CLARK STATE COLLEGE (ID) .... lcsc.edu 1000/21
Art, Bio, Drama, Ed, For Lang, Nurs

LINDENWOOD UNIVERSITY (MO) .... lindenwood.edu 1060/23
Ed, Psych

LINFIELD COLLEGE (OR) .... linfield.edu 1080/23
Bio, Bus Admin, Chem, Econ, Ed, For Lang

LOCK HAVEN UNIVERSITY (PA) ....lhup.edu 1000/21
Art, Bio, Chem, Ed, Music, Poli Sci

LONG ISLAND UNIVERSITY (BROOKLYN) (NY) .... liu.edu 1000/21
Chem, English, Nurs

LONG ISLAND UNIVERSITY (C.W.POST) (NY) .... liu.edu 1070/23
Art, Ed, Psych

LONG ISLAND UNIVERSITY (SOUTHAMPTON) (NY) .... liu.edu 1090/24
Art, Bio, Bus Admin, Chem, Drama, Ed, English, Psych

LONGWOOD UNIVERSITY (VA) .... lwc.edu 1080/23
Bus Admin, Drama, Ed, English, Music, Pre-Law, Psych

LORAS COLLEGE (IA) .... loras.edu 1085/23
Art, Bio, Bus Admin, Chem, Communic, Ed, English, Hist, Physics, Pre-Law, Psych

LOUISIANA COLLEGE (LA) .... lacollege.edu 1050/22
Ed, English, Music, Nurs, Reli Stu

LOUISIANA-LAFAYETTE, UNIVERSITY OF (LA) .... louisiana.edu 1000/21
*Art, Bio, Bus Admin, Chem, Comp Sci, Ed, Engine, English, Geol, Math, Music, Nurs,
Physics, Pre-Med/Pre-Dental, Zoo*

LOUISIANA STATE UNIVERSITY (LA) .... lsu.edu 1095/24
*Ag, Anthro, Arch, Art, Astro, Biochem, Bot, Chem, Communic, Econ, Engine,
English, Geog, Geol, Hist, Math, Music, Philo, Physics, Poli Sci, Pre-Law,
Pre-Med/Pre-Dental, Psych, Reli Stu, Zoo*

LOUISVILLE, UNIVERSITY OF (KY) .... louisville.edu 1020/22
Bus Admin, Chem, Engine, Music, Poli Sci, Soc

LOWELL, UNIVERSITY OF MASSACHUSETTS AT (MA) .... uml.edu 1085/23
Art Hist, Bus Admin, Comp Sci, Engine, Math, Music, Physics

LOYOLA COLLEGE (MD) .... loyola.edu 1190/26
Bio, Bus Admin, Communic, Engine, Pre-Law, Pre-Med/Pre-Dental

LOYOLA MARYMOUNT UNIVERSITY (CA) .... lmu.edu 1140/25
Art, Bus Admin, Communic, Engine

LOYOLA UNIVERSITY OF CHICAGO (IL) .... luc.edu 1140/25
Bio, Communic, Drama, Hist, Music, Nurs, Philo, Physics, Pre-Med/Pre-Dental, Psych

LOYOLA UNIVERSITY OF NEW ORLEANS (LA) .... loyno.edu 1220/27
*Bio, Bus Admin, Chem, Comp Sci, Communic, Econ, English, Hist, Music, Philo,
Pre-Law, Pre-Med/Pre-Dental, Reli Stu*

LUTHER COLLEGE (IA) .... luther.edu 1170/25
Bio, Bus Admin, Ed, Music, Nurs, Psych

LYCOMING COLLEGE (PA) .... lycoming.edu 1100/24
Art, Astro, Bio, Chem, English, Philo, Pre-Med/Pre-Dental, Psych, Reli Stu

LYNCHBURG COLLEGE (VA) .... lynchburg.edu 1045/22
Bio, Communic, Math, Pre-Law, Pre-Med/Pre-Dental, Soc

LYNDON STATE COLLEGE (VT) .... lsc.vsc.edu 1000/21
Bio, Communic, English, Psych

LYON COLLEGE (AR) .... lyon.edu 1150/25
Drama, Ed, English, For Lang, Math, Psych

MACALESTER COLLEGE (MN) .... macalester.edu 1320/30
*Anthro, Art, Bio, Chem, Classics, Communic, Drama, Econ, English, Geog,
Hist, Philo, Physics, Poli Sci, Pre-Law, Pre-Med/Pre-Dental, Psych*

MacMURRAY COLLEGE (IL) .... mac.edu 1010/21
Nurs

MAINE, UNIVERSITY OF (ME) .... umaine.edu 1090/24
Ag, Bot, Bus Admin, Comp Sci, Drama, Econ, Engine, Forest, Music, Philo

MAINE, UNIVERSITY OF (FARMINGTON) (ME) .... umf.maine.edu 1070/23
Bus Admin, Ed, Geog, Psych

MALONE COLLEGE (OH) .... malone.edu 1080/23
Bus Admin, Math, Nurs

MANCHESTER COLLEGE (IN) .... manchester.edu 1000/21
Bus Admin, Ed, Psych, Soc

MANHATTAN COLLEGE (NY) .... manhattan.edu 1100/24
Bus Admin, Ed, Engine, Poli Sci, Pre-Law

MANHATTAN SCHOOL OF MUSIC (NY) .... msmnyc.edu 1100/24
Music

MANHATTANVILLE COLLEGE (NY) .... manhattanville.edu 1100/24
Art, Art Hist, Bus Admin, Drama, Econ, Ed, English, Hist, Music, Poli Sci, Psych, Soc

MANSFIELD UNIVERSITY OF PENNSYLVANIA (PA) .... mnsfld.edu 1000/21
Communic, Ed, English, For Lang, Geog, Philo

MARIETTA COLLEGE (OH) .... marietta.edu 1100/24
Art, Bus Admin, Engine, English, Physics, Pre-Law

MARIST COLLEGE (NY) .... marist.edu 1165/26
Bio, Bus Admin, Comp Sci, Communic, Poli Sci, Psych

MARQUETTE UNIVERSITY (WI) .... marquette.edu 1180/26
*Bio, Bus Admin, Chem, Communic, Comp Sci, English, Engine, Hist,
Nurs, Philo, Poli Sci, Pre-Law, Pre-Med/Pre-Dental, Psych, Reli Stu*

MARSHALL UNIVERSITY (WV) .... marshall.edu 1000/21
Bus Admin, Chem, Communic, Ed, Nurs

MARY BALDWIN COLLEGE (VA) .... mbc.edu 1070/23
Art, Bus Admin, Chem, Communic, Drama, Hist, Physics, Poli Sci, Psych, Soc

MARYGROVE COLLEGE (MI) .... marygrove.edu 1000/21
Comp Sci

MARYLAND INSTITUTE-COLLEGE OF ART (MD) .... mica.edu 1130/25
Art

MARYLAND, UNIVERSITY OF (MD) .... maryland.edu 1195/26
*Ag, Anthro, Arch, Astro, Bot, Bus Admin, Communic, Comp Sci, Econ, Ed, Engine,
Hist, Music, Pharm, Philo, Physics, Poli Sci, Pre-Law, Zoo*

MARYLAND, UNIVERSITY OF (BALTIMORE COUNTY) (MD) .... umbc.edu 1220/27
Amer St, Art, Chem, Classics, Comp Sci, Drama, Econ, Nurs, Physics, Poli Sci, Pre-Law

MARYMOUNT UNIVERSITY (VA) .... marymount.edu 1000/21
Nurs, Psych

MARYVILLE COLLEGE (TN) .... maryvillecollege.edu 1105/24
Bio, Chem, Music, Psych

MARYVILLE UNIVERSITY-ST. LOUIS (MO) .... maryville.edu 1090/24
Art, Ed, Nurs

MARY WASHINGTON COLLEGE (VA) .... mwc.edu 1199/26
Amer St, Bio, Bus Admin, Comp Sci, Econ, Geog, Hist, Pre-Med/Pre-Dental, Psych

MARYWOOD UNIVERSITY (PA) .... marywood.edu 1020/22
Art, Ed, Home Ec, Music Reli Stu

MASSACHUSETTS, UNIVERSITY OF (MA) .... umass.edu 1140/25
*Astro, Bus Admin, Chem, Communic, Comp Sci, Econ, Engine, English,
Hist, Nurs, Poli Sci, Pre-Law, Pre-Med/Pre-Dental, Psych, Zoo*

MASSACHUSETTS, UNIVERSITY OF (BOSTON) (MA) .... umb.edu 1060/23
*Amer St, Bus Admin, Classics, English, Geog, Hist, Music, Nurs, Philo, Physics,
Poli Sci, Pre-Law, Psych, Soc*

MASSACHUSETTS, UNIVERSITY OF (DARTMOUTH) (MA) .... umassd.edu 1070/23
Art, Chem, Engine, Nurs, Psych, Soc

MASSACHUSETTS COLLEGE OF ART (MA) .... massart.edu 1100/24
Art

MASSACHUSETTS COLLEGE OF LIBERAL ARTS (NO. ADAMS)(MA) mcla.mass.edu 1075/23
Bus Admin, Communic, English, Philo, Physics, Soc

MASSACHUSETTS COLLEGE OF PHARMACY (MA) .... mcp.edu 1066/23
Pharm

MASSACHUSETTS INSTITUTE OF TECHNOLOGY (MA) .... mit.edu 1470/33
Arch, Astro, Biochem, Bio, Bus Admin, Chem, Comp Sci, Econ, Engine,
Geol, Math, Physics, Poli Sci, Pre-Law, Pre-Med/Pre-Dental

MASSACHUSETTS MARITIME ACADEMY (MA) .... mma.edu 1040/22
Engine

MASSACHUSETTS STATE COLLEGE SYSTEM (MA) 1005/21
Ed

MASTER'S COLLEGE, THE (CA) .... masters.edu 1100/24
Bus Admin, Communic, English, Reli Stu

McDANIEL COLLEGE (MD) .... mdc.edu 1130/25
Bio, Bio Chem, Bus Admin, Drama, Ed, Music, Pre-Med/Pre-Dental, Soc

McKENDREE COLLEGE (IL) .... mckendree.edu 1140/25
Bio, Chem, Comp Sci, Hist, Nurs

McMURRY UNIVERSITY (TX) .... mcm.edu 1040/22
Bus Admin, Nurs

MEMPHIS COLLEGE OF ART (TN) .... mca.edu 1000/21
Art

MEMPHIS, UNIVERSITY OF (TN) .... memphis.edu 1060/23
Art, Communic, Ed, Engine, English, Music, Nurs

MERCER UNIVERSITY (GA) .... mercer.edu 1190/26
Bus Admin, Econ, Ed, Engine, English, Music, Pharm, Psych

MEREDITH COLLEGE (NC) .... meredith.edu 1070/23
Bio, Bus Admin, English, Music, Psych

MERCY COLLEGE (NY) .... mercynet.edu 1000/21
Nurs, Psych

MERCYHURST COLLEGE (PA) .... mercyhurst.edu 1070/23
Anthro, Art, Bus Admin, English, Poli Sci, Pre-Law, Reli Stu

MERRIMACK COLLEGE (MA) .... merrimack.edu 1100/23
Bus Admin, English, Psych, Soc

MESSIAH COLLEGE (PA) .... messiah.edu 1175/26
Art, Bus Admin, Ed, Engine, English, Philo

MIAMI UNIVERSITY (OH) .... muohio.edu 1199/27
Arch, Bot, Bus Admin, Econ, Ed, English, Hist, Music, Poli Sci, Pre-Law, Pre-Med/Pre-Dental,
Psych, Zoo

MIAMI, UNIVERSITY OF (FL) .... miami.edu 1185/26
Arch, Bio, Biochem, Communic, Drama, Ed, Hist, Music, Pre-Med/Pre-Dental

MICHIGAN, UNIVERSITY OF (MI) .... umich.edu 1275/27
*Amer St, Anthro, Arch, Art, Art Hist, Astro, Bot, Bus Admin, Chem, Classics, Communic,
Comp Sci, Econ, Ed, Engine, English, Forest, For Lang, Geog, Hist, Math, Music, Nurs,
Pharm, Philo, Physics, Poli Sci, Pre-Law, Pre-Med/Pre-Dental, Psych, Soc, Zoo*

MICHIGAN, UNIVERSITY OF (DEARBORN) (MI) .... umd.umich.edu 1090/24
Bus Admin, Chem, Comp Sci, Econ, Engine, Math, Physics, Pre-Law, Pre-Med/Pre-Dental

MICHIGAN STATE UNIVERSITY (MI) .... msu.edu 1100/24
*Ag, Biochem, Bio, Bot, Bus Admin, Chem, Communic, Econ, Ed, Engine, English, Forest,
Geog, Hist, Home Ec, Math, Music, Poli Sci, Pre-Law, Pre-Med/Pre-Dental, Psych, Soc*

MICHIGAN TECHNOLOGICAL UNIVERSITY (MI) .... mtu.edu 1170/26
Bus Admin, Engine, Forest, Geol

MIDDLEBURY COLLEGE (VT) .... middlebury.edu 1420/32
Art, Bio, Classics, Drama, Econ, English, For Lang, Geog, Hist, Physics, Poli Sci, Pre-Law, Pre-Med/Pre-Dental

MIDDLE TENNESSEE STATE UNIVERSITY (TN) .... mtsu.edu 1050/22
Bus Admin, Ed, English, Hist, Psych

MIDWESTERN STATE UNIVERSITY (TX) .... mwsu.edu 1000/21
Nurs

MILLERSVILLE UNIVERSITY OF PENNSYLVANIA (PA) .... millersville.edu 1060/23
Art, Bio, Bus Admin, Chem, Comp Sci, English, Hist, Poli Sci, Pre-Law, Psych

MILLIGAN COLLEGE (TN) .... milligan.edu 1090/24
Bio, Bus Admin, Chem, Communic, Ed, Hist, Nurs, Philo, Psych, Reli Stu

MILLIKIN UNIVERSITY (IL) .... millikin.edu 1080/23
Art, Drama, Ed, Music

MILLS COLLEGE (CA) .... mills.edu 1150/25
Art, Communic, Ed, For Lang, Music, Psych

MILLSAPS COLLEGE (MS) .... millsaps.edu 1180/26
Bio, Bus Admin, Chem, Classics, Comp Sci, English, Geol, Hist, Math, Music, Pre-Law, Pre-Med/Pre-Dental

MILWAUKEE SCHOOL OF ENGINEERING (WI) .... msoe.edu 1185/26
Arch, Engine, Nurs

MINNESOTA STATE UNIVERSITY (MOORHEAD) (MN) .... mstate.edu 1040/22
Art, Music

MINNESOTA, UNIVERSITY OF (MN) .... umn.edu 1150/25
*Ag, Amer St, Art Hist, Biochem, Bus Admin, Communic, Drama, Econ, Ed, Engine,
Forest, Geog, Geol, Hist, Nurs, Pharm, Poli Sci, Pre-Law, Psych, Soc*

MINNESOTA, UNIVERSITY OF (DULUTH) (MN) .... d.umn.edu 1070/23
Bio, Communic, Ed, Engine, Geol, Music, Soc

MINNESOTA, UNIVERSITY OF (MORRIS) (MN) .... mrs.umn.edu 1150/25
Bio, Chem, Comp Sci, Ed, English, For Lang, Geol, Hist, Pre-Law, Pre Med/Pre-Dental, Psych

COLLEGE MISERICORDIA (PA) .... miseri.edu 1000/21
Biochem, Bio, Bus Admin, Chem, Communic, Ed, English, Hist, Nurs

MISSISSIPPI COLLEGE (MS) .... mc.edu 1095/24
Bus Admin, Ed, Music, Nurs, Reli Stu

MISSISSIPPI STATE UNIVERSITY (MS) .... msstate.edu 1090/24
Ag, Arch, Biochem, Bus Admin, Comp Sci, Ed, Engine, Forest, Pre-Med/Pre-Dental, Soc

MISSISSIPPI, UNIVERSITY OF (MS) .... olemiss.edu 1090/24
Bus Admin, Communic, Engine, English, Pharm, Physics, Pre-Law

MISSISSIPPI UNIVERSITY FOR WOMEN (MS) .... muw.edu 1115/24
Bus Admin, Ed, English, Nurs

MISSOURI, UNIVERSITY OF (MO) .... missouri.edu 1170/26
Ag, Art Hist, Bus Admin, Communic, English, Forest, Hist, Psych

MISSOURI, UNIVERSITY OF (KANSAS CITY) (MO) .... umkc.edu 1100/24
Art, Comp Sci, Music, Psych

MISSOURI, UNIVERSITY OF (ROLLA) (MO) .... umr.edu 1260/28
Bio, Chem, Comp Sci, Engine, Hist, Nurs

MISSOURI, UNIVERSITY OF (ST. LOUIS) .... umsl.edu 1080/23
Bus Admin, Communic, Ed, Psych

MOBILE, UNIVERSITY OF (AL) .... umobile.edu 1050/24
Bio, Bus Admin, Comp Sci, Ed, Music, Nurs

MOLLOY COLLEGE (NY) 1010/21
Nurs, Psych

MONMOUTH COLLEGE (IL) .... monmouth.edu 1065/23
Bio, Bus Admin, Chem, Econ, Ed, Pre-Med/Pre-Dental

MONMOUTH UNIVERSITY (NJ) .... monmouth.edu 1040/22
Art, Bus Admin, Communic, Comp Sci, Music

MONTANA COLLEGE OF MINERAL SCIENCE & TECHNOLOGY (MT) ...... mcmst.edu 1111/24
Comp Sci, Engine

MONTANA, UNIVERSITY OF (MT) .... umt.edu 1080/23
Astro, Bot, Bus Admin, Classics, Communic, Comp Sci, Drama, Ed, Forest, Pharm, Zoo

MONTANA STATE UNIVERSITY (BILLINGS) (MT) .... msubillings.edu 1000/21
Art, Ed

MONTANA STATE UNIVERSITY (MT) .... montana.edu 1090/24
Ag, Arch, Art, Engine, For Lang, Forest

MONTCLAIR STATE (NJ) .... montclair.edu 1100/24
Art, Bus Admin, Classics, Ed, English, Home Ec, Psych

MONTEVALLO, UNIVERSITY OF (AL) .... montevallo.edu 1000/21
Art, Communic, Ed, English, Home Ec, Music

MONTSERRAT COLLEGE OF ART (MA) .... montserrat.edu 1000/21
Art

MONTREAT COLLEGE (NC) .... montreat.edu 1010/21
Bus Admin

MOORE COLLEGE OF ART (PA) .... moore.edu 1030/22
Art

MORAVIAN COLLEGE (PA) .... moravian.edu 1125/25
Art, Bus Admin, Communic, Comp Sci, Ed, Music, Nurs, Psych, Soc

MOREHOUSE COLLEGE (GA) .... morehouse.edu 1070/23
Bus Admin, Comp Sci, Hist, Reli Stu, Soc

MORGAN STATE UNIVERSITY (MD) 1000/21
Arch, Bio, Engine

MORNINGSIDE COLLEGE (IA) .... morningside.edu 1060/23
Bio, Communic, Nurs, Pre-Med/Pre-Dental

MOUNT HOLYOKE COLLEGE (MA) .... mtholyoke.edu 1250/28
*Art Hist, Biochem, Bio, Chem, Drama, Econ, English, For Lang, Hist, Math, Poli Sci,
Pre-Law, Pre-Med/Pre-Dental, Psych*

MOUNT MERCY COLLEGE (IA) .... mtmercy.edu 1085/23
Bio, Bus Admin, Ed, English, Nurs, Philo, Soc

MOUNT ST. JOSEPH, COLLEGE OF (OH) .... msj.edu 1020/22
Art, Bio, Bus Admin, Chem, Comp Sci, Ed, English, Math, Music, Nurs, Pre-Law, Pre-Med/Pre-Dental

MOUNT ST. MARY'S COLLEGE (CA) .... msmc.la.edu 1060/23
Bio, Bus Admin, Music, Nurs

MOUNT ST. MARY'S COLLEGE (MD) .... msmary.edu 1080/23
Bus Admin, Ed, Poli Sci, Pre-Law, Pre-Med/Pre-Dental

MOUNT ST. MARY COLLEGE (NY) .... msmc.edu 1040/22
Nurs

MOUNT UNION COLLEGE (OH) .... muc.edu 1075/23
Bus Admin, Comp Sci, Ed

MUHLENBERG COLLEGE (PA) .... muhlenberg.edu 1200/26
*Art, Bio, Biochem, Bus Admin, Communic, Drama, English, Hist, Math, Philo, Pre-Law,
Pre-Med/Pre-Dental, Psych, Reli Stu*

MURRAY STATE UNIVERSITY (KY) .... murraystate.edu 1070/23
Ag, Art, Bio, Chem, Communic, Comp Sci, Ed, English, Hist, Math, Music, Nurs

MUSEUM OF FINE ARTS, SCHOOL OF THE (MA) .... smfa.edu 1070/23
Art

MUSKINGUM COLLEGE (OH) .... muskingum.edu 1070/23
Bus Admin, Chem, Communic, Comp Sci, Ed, Geol, Hist, Music, Physics, Psych, Reli Stu

NAZARETH COLLEGE OF ROCHESTER (NY) .... naz.edu 1135/25
Bio, Bus Admin, Ed, English, For Lang

NEBRASKA, UNIVERSITY OF (NE) .... unl.edu 1125/25
Ag, Arch, Astro, Bus Admin, Communic, Econ, Music, Pre-Law

NEBRASKA WESLEYAN UNIVERSITY (NE) .... nebrwesleyan.edu 1110/24
Bio, Pre-Med/Pre-Dental, Psych

NEVADA, UNIVERSITY OF, AT:
      LAS VEGAS .... unlv.edu 1010/21
      Arch, Art, Bus Admin, Drama, Ed, Engine, Hist, Music, Nurs, Psych
      RENO .... unr.edu 1046/22
      Ag, Biochem, Bus Admin, Communic, Ed, Engine, Music, Nurs,
      Physics, Pre-Med/Pre-Dental, Soc

NEW COLLEGE (FL) .... ncf.edu 1316/29
Anthro, Bio, Chem, English, Math, Philo, Physics, Pre-Med/Pre-Dental, Psych

NEW ENGLAND CONSERVATORY (MA) .... newenglandconservatory.edu 1100/24
Music

NEW HAMPSHIRE, UNIVERSITY OF (NH) .... unh.edu 1113/24
Ag, Bio, Bus Admin, Chem, Communic, Drama, Ed, Engine, English,
Hist, Music, Philo, Physics, Pre-Med/Pre-Dental, Pre-Law, Psych

NEW JERSEY, COLLEGE OF (NJ) .... tcnj.edu 1270/28
Art, Ed, Engine, English, Math, Nurs, Pre-Law, Pre-Med/Pre-Dental, Psych

NEW JERSEY INSTITUTE OF TECHNOLOGY (NJ) .... njit.edu 1145/25
Arch, Comp Sci, Engine

NEWMAN UNIVERSITY (KS) ....newmanu.edu 1160/25
Bus Admin, Math, Psych, Reli Stu

NEW MEXICO INSTITUTE OF MINING (NM) .... nmt.edu 1190/26
Engine, Geol, Physics

NEW MEXICO STATE UNIVERSITY (NM) .... nmstu.edu 1040/22
Ag, Anthro, Bio, Bus Admin, Chem, Comp Sci, Ed, Engine, Math

NEW MEXICO, UNIVERSITY OF (NM) .... unm.edu 1050/22
Amer St, Anthro, Art, Bio, Ed, For Lang, Geol, Hist, Nurs, Pharm, Psych, Soc

NEW ORLEANS, UNIVERSITY OF (LA) .... uno.edu 1010/21
Bus Admin, Ed, English, Engine, Geog, Physics, Soc

NEW SCHOOL UNIVERSITY (EUGENE LANG COLLEGE) (NY) .... newschool.edu 1200/26
Drama, Ed, English

NEW YORK, CITY UNIVERSITY OF, AT
      BARUCH COLLEGE .... baruch.cuny.edu 1080/23
      Bus Admin, Comp Sci, Econ
      BROOKLYN COLLEGE...brooklyn.cuny.edu 1040/22
      Bio, Chem, Comp Sci, Drama, Ed, Geol, Physics, Pre-Med/Pre-Dental

NEW YORK, CITY UNIVERSITY OF, AT *(Continued)*

    CITY COLLEGE .... ccny.cuny.edu **1050/22**
    Anthro, Arch, Art Hist, Chem, Ed, Econ, Engine, English, Hist,
    Physics, Poli Sci, Pre-Law, Pre-Med/Pre-Dental

    HERBERT LEHMAN COLLEGE .... lehmman.cuny.edu **1000/21**
    Ed, For Lang, Psych

    HUNTER COLLEGE .... hunter.cuny.edu **1040/22**
    Anthro, Art, Art Hist, Bio, Chem, Classics, Communic, Comp Sci, Drama, Ed,
    English, Geog, Nurs, Pre-Law, Psych

    JOHN JAY COLLEGE OF CRIMINAL JUSTICE .... jjay.cuny.edu **1000/21**
    Poli Sci, Psych

    QUEENS COLLEGE .... qc.edu **1040/22**
    Anthro, Art Hist, Comp Sci, Econ, Ed, English, Music, Psych, Soc

NEW YORK INSTITUTE OF TECHNOLOGY (NY) .... nyit.edu **1070/23**
Arch, Engine

NEW YORK, STATE UNIVERSITY OF, AT

    ALBANY .... albany.edu **1170/26**
    Anthro, Art, Art Hist, Bio, Bus Admin, Chem, Comp Sci, Econ, For Lang, Geol,
    Math, Philo, Physics, Poli Sci, Pre-Law, Pre-Med/Pre-Dental, Psych, Soc

    BINGHAMTON .... binghamton.edu **1200/26**
    Anthro, Art, Art Hist, Bio, Biochem, Bus Admin, Chem, Comp Sci,
    Drama, English, Engine, For Lang, Geol, Hist, Math, Music, Nurs,
    Philo, Physics, Poli Sci, Pre-Law, Pre-Med/Pre-Dental, Psych, Soc

    BROCKPORT, COLLEGE AT .... brockport.edu **1050/22**
    Bus Admin, Communic, Comp Sci, Drama, Geol, Hist, Nurs, Poli Sci, Psych

    BUFFALO .... buffalo.edu **1150/25**
    Amer St, Anthro, Arch, Art, Bus Admin, Chem, Classics, Ed, Engine, English,
    Geog, Hist, Math, Music, Nurs, Pharm, Pre-Law, Pre-Med/Pre-Dental

    FREDONIA, COLLEGE AT .... fredonia.edu **1110/24**
    Amer St, Bus Admin, Communic, Ed, English, Hist, Music

    GENESEO, COLLEGE AT .... geneseo.edu **1240/28**
    Bio, Biochem, Bus Admin, Ed, Geol, Music, Philo, Physics, Pre-Med/Pre-Dental, Soc

    MARITIME COLLEGE .... sunymaritime.edu **1040/22**
    Engine

    NEW PALTZ, COLLEGE AT .... newpaltz.edu **1150/25**
    Bus Admin, Communic, Ed, Engine, English, For Lang, Geog, Psych

    ONEONTA, COLLEGE AT .... oneonta.edu **1095/24**
    Econ, Ed, English, Geog, Geol, Home Ec, Music, Philo, Pre-Law

    OSWEGO, COLLEGE AT .... oswego.edu **1100/24**
    Bus Admin, Communic, Comp Sci, Ed, Pre-Law, Psych, Zoo

    PLATTSBURGH, COLLEGE AT .... plattsburgh.edu **1070/23**
    Anthro, Bus Admin, Communic, Geol, Nurs

    POTSDAM, COLLEGE AT .... potsdam.edu **1050/22**
    Art, Bus Admin, Comp Sci, Ed, Math, Music, Psych

    PURCHASE, COLLEGE AT .... purchase.edu **1060/23**
    Art, Communic, Drama, English, Music, Poli Sci, Pre-Law, Psych

    STONY BROOK .... sunysb.edu **1150/25**
    Anthro, Art Hist, Astro, Biochem, Bio, Chem, Comp Sci, Engine, English, For Lang,
    Geo,Hist, Music, Philo, Physics, Poli Sci, Pre-Law, Pre-Med/Pre-Dental, Psych, Reli Stu

NEW YORK UNIVERSITY (NY) .... nyu.edu **1340/30**
Art, Art Hist, Bus Admin, Classics, Communic, Drama, Econ, For Lang, Math,
Music, Nurs, Philo, Physics, Pre-Med/Pre-Dental, Psych

NIAGARA UNIVERSITY (NY) .... niagara.edu **1055/23**
Bus Admin, Drama, English, Pre-Law

NICHOLS STATE UNIVERSITY (LA) .... nichols.edu **1000/21**
Bio, Chem, Ed, Nurs

NORTH CAROLINA SCHOOL OF THE ARTS (NC) .... ncarts.edu **1130/25**
Drama, Music

NORTH CAROLINA, UNIVERSITY OF, AT
    ASHEVILLE .... unca.edu **1167/26**
    Art, Classics, Ed, Hist, Psych, Soc
    CHAPEL HILL .... unc.edu **1240/28**
    Amer St, Anthro, Art Hist, Bio, Bot, Bus Admin, Chem, Classics, Communic, Drama, Ed, English, For Lang, Hist, Nurs, Pharm, Poli Sci, Pre-Law, Pre-Med/Pre-Dental, Reli Stu, Soc
    CHARLOTTE .... uncc.edu **1065/23**
    Bus Admin, Chem, For Lang, Geog, Nurs, Poli Sci, Pre-Law, Pre-Med/Pre-Dental, Psych, Reli Stu
    GREENSBORO .... uncg.edu **1050/22**
    Art, Bus Admin, Classics, Communic, Comp Sci, Drama, Ed, Music, Nurs, Psych
    PEMBROKE .... uncp.edu **1000/21**
    Bio, Bus Admin, Communic
    WILMINGTON .... uncwil.edu **1100/24**
    Bio, Bus Admin, Chem, English, Pre-Law, Psych, Soc

NORTH CAROLINA STATE UNIVERSITY (NC) .... ncsu.edu **1140/25**
Ag, Arch, Astro, Bot, Chem, Econ, Engine, Forest, Math, Physics, Pre-Law, Zoo

NORTH CENTRAL COLLEGE (IL) .... noctrl.edu **1110/24**
Bio, Bus Admin, Chem, Communic, Comp Sci, Poli Sci, Pre-Law, Pre-Med/Pre-Dental, Zoo

NORTH DAKOTA STATE UNIVERSITY (ND) .... ndsu.nodak.edu **1100/24**
Ag, Arch, Ed, Engine, Pharm

NORTH DAKOTA, UNIVERSITY OF (ND) .... und.nodak.edu **1070/23**
Art, Bio, Bus Admin, Chem, Communic, Ed, Engine, English, Nurs

NORTH FLORIDA, UNIVERSITY OF (FL) .... unf.edu **1140/25**
Bus Admin, Communic, Comp Sci, Ed, Music, Nurs

NORTH GEORGIA COLLEGE (GA) .... ngcsu.edu **1080/23**
Bus Admin

NORTH TEXAS, UNIVERSITY OF (TX) .... unt.edu **1070/23**
Communic, Music, Soc

NORTHEASTERN ILLINOIS UNIVERSITY (IL) .... neiu.edu **1000/21**
Comp Sci, Ed, English

NORTHEASTERN UNIVERSITY (MA) .... neu.edu **1199/27**
Bus Admin, Comp Sci, Engine, English, Hist, Pharm, Philo

NORTHERN ARIZONA (AZ) .... nau.edu **1050/22**
Astro, Bot, Ed, Forest, Psych

NORTHERN COLORADO, UNIVERSITY OF .... unco.edu **1030/22**
Bus Admin, Econ, Ed, Hist, Music, Nurs, Soc

NORTHERN ILLINOIS UNIVERSITY (IL) .... niu.edu **1045/22**
Art, Bio, Biochem, Bus Admin, Chem, Communic, Ed, Engine, Home Ec, Geol, Nurs, Physics, Philo

NORTHERN IOWA, UNIVERSITY OF (IA) .... uni.edu **1080/23**
Art, Bus Admin, Ed

NORTHERN KENTUCKY UNIVERSITY (KY) .... nku.edu **1000/21**
Bus Admin, Communic, Ed, English

NORTHERN MICHIGAN UNIVERSITY (MI) .... nmu.edu **1086/24**
Art, Bio, Chem, Comp Sci, Ed, English, Math, Nurs, Physics, Soc

NORTHLAND COLLEGE (WI) .... northland.edu **1080/23**
Bio, Geol

NORTHWESTERN COLLEGE (IA) .... nwciowa.edu **1099/24**
Bio, Chem, Drama, Ed, Hist, Music, Physics, Reli Stu

NORTHWESTERN COLLEGE (MN) .... nwc.edu **1080/23**
Ed, Psych, Reli Stu

NORTHWESTERN STATE UNIVERSITY OF LOUISIANA (LA) .... nsula.edu **1000/21**
Bus Admin, Comp Sci, Ed, Hist, Music, Nurs, Pharm

NORTHWESTERN UNIVERSITY (IL) .... northwestern.edu **1380/31**
*Amer Stu, Anthro, Astro, Chem, Classics, Communic, Drama, Econ, Engine, English,
Hist, Math, Music, Poli Sci, Pre-Law, Pre-Med/Pre-Dental, Psych, Reli Stu, Soc*

NORTHWOOD UNIVERSITY (MI) .... northwood.edu **1000/21**
Bus Admin

NOTRE DAME, UNIVERSITY OF (IN) .... nd.edu **1340/30**
*Anthro, Arch, Bus Admin, Chem, Engine, English, Hist, Poli Sci, Philo, Physics,
Pre-Med/Pre-Dental, Pre-Law, Psych, Reli Stu, Soc*

NOVA SOUTHEASTERN UNIVERSITY (FL) .... nova.edu **1090/24**
Bus Admin, Pre-Med/Pre-Dental

NYACK COLLEGE (NY) .... nyackcollege.edu **1000/21**
Bus Admin, Ed, Music, Psych, Reli Stu

OAKLAND UNIVERSITY (MI) .... oakland.edu **1040/22**
Bus Admin, Chem, Communic, Comp Sci, Econ, Engine, Nurs

OBERLIN COLLEGE (OH) .... oberlin.edu **1320/30**
*Art Hist, Bio, Chem, Classics, English, Hist, Math, Music, Philo, Physics, Pre-Law,
Pre-Med/Pre-Dental, Reli Stu, Soc*

OCCIDENTAL COLLEGE (CA) .... oxy.edu **1200/26**
Bio, Chem, Econ, Ed, Math, Physics, Poli Sci, Pre-Law, Pre-Med/Pre-Dental, Reli Stu

OGLETHORPE UNIVERSITY (GA) .... ogelthorpe.edu **1210/27**
Bio, Bus Admin, Econ, English, Poli Sci, Pre-Law

OHIO NORTHERN UNIVERSITY (OH) .... onu.edu **1125/24**
Bio, Biochem, Bus Admin, Chem, Engine, Pharm

OHIO STATE UNIVERSITY (OH) .... osu.edu 1140/25
Ag, Arch, Art, Biochem, Bus Admin, Chem, Drama, Econ, Ed, Engine, English, For Lang, Geog, Hist, Math, Nurs, Pharm, Philo, Physics, Poli Sci, Pre-Law, Pre-Med/Pre-Dental, Psych

OHIO UNIVERSITY (OH) ....ohiou.edu 1100/24
Art, Bot, Bus Admin, Communic, Drama, Ed, Engine, English, Hist, Math, Music, Physics, Pre-Law, Psych, Zoo

OHIO WESLEYAN UNIVERSITY (OH) .... owu.edu 1210/27
Bio, Bot, Chem, Communic, Econ, Poli Sci, Pre-Med/Pre-Dental, Pre-Law, Psych

OKLAHOMA BAPTIST UNIVERSITY (OK) ....okbu.edu 1130/25
Ed, Music, Nurs, Psych, Reli Stu

OKLAHOMA CITY UNIVERSITY (OK) ....okcu.edu 1100/24
Bio, Bus Admin, Communic, Comp Sci, Drama, English, Music, Poli Sci, Pre-Law, Psych

OKLAHOMA, UNIVERSITY OF (OK) ....ou.edu 1155/25
Arch, Astro, Bus Admin, Chem, Classics, Communic, Engine, English, Geog, Geol, Hist, Poli Sci, Pre-Law, Psych, Zoo

OKLAHOMA STATE UNIVERSITY (OK) .... (no www here) osu.okstate.edu 1110/24
Ag, Bio, Bus Admin, Drama, Ed, Engine, Forest, Geog, Geol, Physics, Poli Sci, Soc, Zoo

OLD DOMINION UNIVERSITY (VA) .... odu.edu 1030/22
Art, Bus Admin, Econ, Engine, Soc

OLIN COLLEGE OF ENGINEERING (MA) .... olin.edu 1490/34
Engine

OLIVET NAZARENE UNIVERSITY (IL) .... olivet.edu 1070/23
Ed, Nurs, Reli Stu

OREGON, UNIVERSITY OF (OR) .... uoregon.edu 1120/24
Anthro, Arch, Art, Art Hist, Bus Admin, Chem, Communic, Comp Sci, Ed, Geog, Math, Music, Psych

OREGON INSTITUTE OF TECHNOLOGY (OR) ....oit.edu 1020/22
Bus Admin, Engine

OREGON STATE UNIVERSITY (OR) .... orst.edu 1075/23
Ag, Biochem, Bot, Engine, Forest, Home Ec, Physics, Zoo

OTIS ART INSTITUTE/PARSONS (CA) .... otisart.edu 1000/21
Art

OTTERBEIN COLLEGE (OH) .... otterbein.edu 1075/23
Art, Chem, Drama, English, Music, Psych

OUACHITA BAPTIST UNIVERSITY (AR) .... obu.edu 1075/23
Ed, Music, Reli Stu

OZARKS, COLLEGE OF THE (MO) .... cofo.edu 1055/22
Ag, Bus Admin, Comp Sci, Ed, Math, Philo, Physics, Psych

PACE UNIVERSITY (NY) .... pace.edu 1125/25
Bus Admin, Comp Sci, Nurs, Psych, Soc

PACIFIC LUTHERAN UNIVERSITY (WA) .... plu.edu 1118/24
Bus Admin, Comp Sci, Music, Nurs, Pre-Med/Pre-Dental

PACIFIC UNIVERSITY (OR) .... pacificu.edu 1110/24
Bus Admin, English, For Lang, Physics

PACIFIC, UNIVERSITY OF THE (CA) .... uop.edu 1160/25
Art, Bus Admin, Ed, Engine, Music, Pharm

PALM BEACH ATLANTIC COLLEGE (FL) .... pbac.edu 1100/24
Bus Admin, Ed, Pharm, Psych

PARSONS SCHOOL OF DESIGN (NY) .... parsons.edu 1080/23
Art

PENNSYLVANIA ACADEMY OF THE FINE ARTS (PA) .... pafa.edu 1000/21
Art

PENNSYLVANIA, UNIVERSITY OF (PA) .... upenn.edu 1380/31
Amer St, Anthro, Art, Art Hist, Astro, Biochem, Bus Admin, Classics, Econ, Engine,
English, For Lang, Geol, Hist, Math, Nurs, Philo, Physics, Poli Sci, Pre-Law, Psych, Soc

PENNSYLVANIA STATE UNIVERSITY (ERIE) (PA) .... pserie.psu.edu 1070/23
Bus Admin, English, Math, Physics

PENNSYLVANIA STATE UNIVERSITY (PA) .... psu.edu 1199/26
Ag, Arch, Astro, Biochem, Bot, Bus Admin, Chem, Comp Sci, Ed, Engine, Forest,
Geog, Nurs, Pre-Med/Pre-Dental, Zoo

PEPPERDINE UNIVERSITY (CA) .... pepperdine.edu 1230/27
Bio, Bus Admin, Communic, Comp Sci, For Lang

PERU STATE COLLEGE (NE) .... peru.edu 1000/21
Ed

PHILADELPHIA BIBLICAL UNIVERSITY (PA) .... pbu.edu 1050/22
Ed, Music

PHILADELPHIA UNIVERSITY (PA) .... philau.edu 1050/22
Bus Admin

PINE MANOR COLLEGE (MA) .... pmc.edu 900/19
Amer St, Art Hist, Bio, Bus Admin, Communic, Poli Sci, Psych

PITTSBURGH, UNIVERSITY OF (PA) .... pitt.edu 1170/26
Anthro, Art Hist, Astro, Biochem, Bus Admin, Chem, Classics, Communic, Ed, Engine, English,
For Lang, Hist, Nurs, Pharm, Philo, Pre-Law, Pre-Med/Pre-Dental, Psych, Reli Stu

PITTSBURGH, UNIVERSITY OF (BRADFORD) (PA) .... upb.pitt.edu 1000/21
Bio, Comp Sci, Nurs

PITTSBURGH, UNIVERSITY OF (GREENSBURG) (PA) .... pitt.edu/~upg 1005/21
Anthro, Bus Admin, English

PITTSBURGH, UNIVERSITY OF (JOHNSTOWN) (PA) .... pitt.edu/~upjweb 1100/24
Bus Admin, Comp Sci, Ed, Engine

PITZER COLLEGE (CA) .... pitzer.edu 1220/27
Anthro, Bio, English, Hist, Pre-Med/Pre-Dental, Pre-Law, Psych, Soc

PLYMOUTH STATE COLLEGE (NH) .... plymouth.edu 1000/21
Ed, English

POINT LOMA NAZARENE UNIVERSITY (CA) .... ptloma.edu 1120/24
Bus Admin, Ed, Home Ec, Nurs

POINT PARK COLLEGE (PA) .... ppc.edu 1040/22
Bio, Drama, English, Psych

POLYTECHNIC UNIVERSITY OF NEW YORK (NY) .... poly.edu 1230/27
Engine

POMONA COLLEGE (CA) .... pomona.edu 1420/32
Amer St, Anthro, Art Hist, Bio, Chem, Econ, English, For Lang, Geol, Hist, Math, Music, Philo, Physics, Poli Sci, Pre-Law, Pre-Med/Pre-Dental, Psych, Reli Stu, Soc

PORTLAND STATE UNIVERSITY (OR) .... pdx.edu 1040/22
Art, Bus Admin, Comp Sci, English, Music, Pre-Law, Psych

PORTLAND, UNIVERSITY OF (OR) .... up.edu 1126/25
Bus Admin, Engine, Hist, Nurs, Philo, Poli Sci, Reli Stu

PRATT INSTITUTE (NY) .... pratt.edu 1140/25
Arch

PRESBYTERIAN COLLEGE (SC) .... presby.edu 1150/25
Bio, Bus Admin, English, Poli Sci, Pre-Law, Pre-Med/Pre-Dental

PRINCETON UNIVERSITY (NJ) .... princeton.edu 1440/32
Arch, Art Hist, Bio, Biochem, Chem, Classics, Comp Sci, Drama, Econ, Engine, English, For Lang, Geol, Hist, Math, Music, Philo, Physics, Poli Sci, Pre-Law, Pre-Med/Pre-Dental, Reli Stu

PRINCIPIA COLLEGE (IL) .... prin.edu/college 1120/24
Anthro, Art, Bus Admin, Ed, English, Philo, Pre-Law, Soc

PROVIDENCE COLLEGE (RI) .... providence.edu 1199/26
Bio, Bus Admin, Chem, Ed, English, Hist, Philo, Poli Sci, Pre-Law

PUERTO RICO, UNIVERSITY OF (PR) .... upr.clu.edu 1100/24
Bus Admin, Ed

PUERTO RICO, UNIVERSITY OF (CAYEY) (PR) .... wwwcuc.upr.clu.edu 1000/21
Bio, Bus Admin, Chem, Ed

PUERTO RICO, UNIVERSITY OF (MAYAGUEZ) (PR) .... uprm.edu 1170/26
Chem, Engine, For Lang, Math

PUGET SOUND, UNIVERSITY OF (WA) .... ups.edu 1220/27
Bio, Bus Admin, Chem, English, Music, Pre-Law, Pre-Med/Pre-Dental, Soc

PURDUE UNIVERSITY (IN) .... purdue.edu 1140/25
Ag, Biochem, Bot, Bus Admin, Chem, Engine, Forest, Geol, Nurs, Pharm

QUEENS COLLEGE (NC) .... queens.edu **1140/25**
Bus Admin, English, Hist, Music, Pre-Law

QUINCY UNIVERSITY (IL) .... quincy.edu **1050/22**
Bus Admin, Hist, Soc

QUINNIPIAC UNIVERSITY (CT) .... quinnipiac.edu **1100/24**
Bus Admin, Communic, Comp Sci

RADFORD UNIVERSITY (VA) .... radford.edu **1000/21**
Bus Admin, Ed, Geog, Poli Sci, Pre-Law

RAMAPO COLLEGE OF NEW JERSEY (NJ) .... ramapo.edu **1050/22**
Bus Admin, Comp Sci, Hist

RANDOLPH-MACON COLLEGE (VA) .... rmc.edu **1120/24**
Bio, Bus Admin, Econ, English, Poli Sci, Pre-Law, Pre-Med/Pre-Dental, Psych

RANDOLPH-MACON WOMAN'S COLLEGE (VA) .... rmwc.edu **1185/26**
Art, Bio, Classics, Communic, English, Pre-Law, Pre-Med/Pre-Dental, Psych

REDLANDS, UNIVERSITY OF (CA) .... redlands.edu **1120/24**
Art, Bus Admin, Ed, English, Music, Poli Sci, Pre-Law, Pre-Med/Pre-Dental

REED COLLEGE (OR) .... reed.edu **1370/31**
Art Hist, Bio, Chem, English, Hist, Math, Philo, Physics, Pre-Law, Pre-Med/Pre-Dental, Psych

REGIS COLLEGE (MA) .... regiscollege.edu **1000/21**
Communic, English

REGIS UNIVERSITY (CO) .... regis.edu **1080/23**
*Bus Admin, Communic, Comp Sci, Ed, Hist, Nurs, Philo, Pre-Med/Pre-Dental,
Psych, Reli Stu, Soc*

REINHARDT COLLEGE (GA) .... reinhardt.edu **1000/21**
Bio, Bus Admin, Communic

RENSSELAER POLYTECHNIC INSTITUTE (NY) ....rpi.edu **1300/29**
Arch, Bio, Bus Admin, Chem, Comp Sci, Engine, Geol, Math, Physics

RHODE ISLAND COLLEGE (RI) .... ric.edu **1000/21**
Bio, Econ, Ed, Hist, Music, Philo

RHODE ISLAND SCHOOL OF DESIGN (RI) .... risd.edu **1160/25**
Arch, Art

RHODE ISLAND, UNIVERSITY OF (RI) .... uri.edu **1080/23**
Anthro, Comp Sci, Engine, English, Nurs, Pharm, Poli Sci, Pre-Law

RHODES COLLEGE (TN) .... rhodes.edu **1290/29**
*Art, Bio, Bus Admin, Chem, Classics, Econ, English, For Lang, Hist, Music, Physics,
Poli Sci, Pre-Law, Pre-Med/Pre-Dental, Psych, Reli Stu*

RICE UNIVERSITY (TX) .... rice.edu **1400/31**
*Anthro, Arch, Biochem, Bio, Chem, Comp Sci, Engine, English, Hist,
Math, Music, Physics, Pre-Law, Pre-Med/Pre-Dental*

RICHARD STOCKTON COLLEGE OF NEW JERSEY (NJ) .... stockton.edu 1132/25
Bus Admin, Chem, Econ, Philo, Physics, Poli Sci, Pre-Med/Pre-Dental

RICHMOND, UNIVERSITY OF (VA) .... richmond.edu 1270/28
Bio, Bus Admin, Chem, English, Hist, Poli Sci, Pre-Law, Pre-Med/Pre-Dental, Reli Stu

RIDER UNIVERSITY (NJ) .... rider.edu 1010/21
Amer St, Bio, Bus Admin, Chem, Communic, Comp Sci, Ed, Music, Pre-Med/Pre-Dental

RIPON COLLEGE (WI) .... ripon.edu 1140/25
Bio, Biochem, Bus Admin, Chem, Econ, English, Hist, Poli Sci, Pre-Law, Pre-Med/Pre-Dental

ROANOKE COLLEGE (VA) .... roanoke.edu 1115/24
Art, Bio, Bus Admin, Chem, English, Hist, Music, Poli Sci, Pre-Law, Psych, Reli Stu, Soc

ROBERT MORRIS COLLEGE (PA) .... robert-morris.edu 1003/21
Bus Admin, Comp Sci, Communic, Ed, English

ROCHESTER, UNIVERSITY OF (NY) .... rochester.edu 1320/30
*Art, Art Hist, Biochem, Bio, Chem, Comp Sci, Econ, Engine, English, For Lang,
Geol, Music, Philo, Poli Sci, Pre-Law, Pre-Med/Pre-Dental, Psych*

ROCHESTER INSTITUTE OF TECHNOLOGY (NY) .... rit.edu 1160/25
Bio, Bus Admin, Comp Sci, Engine, Math

ROCKFORD COLLEGE (IL) .... rockford.edu 1040/22
Art, Bio, Bus Admin, Drama, English, Nurs, Pre-Law, Psych

ROCKHURST UNIVERSITY (MO) .... rockhurst.edu 1100/24
Bus Admin, Chem, Math, Psych, Reli Stu

ROGER WILLIAMS UNIVERSITY (RI) .... rwu.edu 1065/23
Arch, Bus Admin, Communic, Ed, Engine, Psych

ROLLINS COLLEGE (FL) .... rollins.edu 1160/25
Chem, Classics, Drama, English, Physics, Psych, Reli Stu

ROOSEVELT UNIVERSITY (IL) .... roosevelt.edu 1000/21
Bus Admin, Music

ROSE-HULMAN INSTITUTE OF TECHNOLOGY (IN) .... rose-hulman.edu 1380/31
Chem, Comp Sci, Econ, Engine, Math, Physics

ROSEMONT COLLEGE (PA) .... rosemont.edu 1100/24
Art, Art Hist, English, For Lang, Hist, Pre-Law, Psych

ROWAN UNIVERSITY (NJ) .... rowan.edu 1130/24
Art, Bus Admin, Communic, Ed, Engine, Hist, Music, Philo, Physics, Reli Stu

RUSSELL SAGE COLLEGE (THE SAGE COLLEGES) (NY) .... sage.edu 1040/22
Nurs

RUTGERS UNIVERSITY (NJ) .... rutgers.edu 1200/26
*Ag, Anthro, Art Hist, Biochem, Bio, Bus Admin, Chem, Drama, Econ, Ed, Engine, English, For Lang,
Hist, Music, Pharm, Philo, Physics, Poli Sci, Pre-Law, Pre-Med/Pre-Dental, Psych, Reli Stu*

RUTGERS UNIVERSITY (CAMDEN) (NJ) .... rutgers.edu 1160/25
Comp Sci, English, Hist, Pre-Law, Soc

SACRED HEART UNIVERSITY (CT) .... sacredheart.edu 1060/23
Biochem, Bus Admin, Psych

SAGINAW VALLEY STATE UNIVERSITY (MI) .... svsu.edu 1000/21
Ed, Nurs

ST. AMBROSE UNIVERSITY (IA) .... sau.edu 1030/22
Communic, Comp Sci

ST. ANDREWS PRESBYTERIAN COLLEGE (NC) .... sapc.edu 1030/22
Biochem, Bus Admin, Ed, Philo

ST. ANSELM COLLEGE (NH) .... anselm.edu 1110/24
Classics, Econ, English, For Lang, Nurs, Pre-Law, Psych, Soc,

ST. BONAVENTURE UNIVERSITY (NY) .... sbu.edu 1070/23
Bus Admin, Communic, Ed, English, Philo, Poli Sci, Pre-Law, Reli Stu

ST. CATHERINE, COLLEGE OF (MN) .... stkate.edu 1100/24
Bus Admin, Ed, Music, Nurs, Reli Stu, Soc

ST. CLOUD STATE UNIVERSITY (MN) .... stcloudstate.edu 1020/22
Communic, Ed

ST. EDWARD'S UNIVERSITY (TX) .... stedwards.edu 1040/22
Art, Bus Admin, Communic, Comp Sci, Drama, Psych

ST. FRANCIS COLLEGE (NY) .... stfranciscollege.edu 1000/21
Bus Admin, Psych

ST. JOHN FISHER COLLEGE (NY) .... sjfc.edu 1065/23
Bus Admin, Communic

ST. JOHN'S UNIVERSITY (NY) .... stjohns.edu 1040/22
Bus Admin, Pharm

SAINT JOHN'S UNIVERSITY/COLLEGE OF SAINT BENEDICT (MN) ...... csbsju.edu 1150/25
Bio, Bus Admin, Chem, Classics, Comp Sci, Econ, Ed, Hist, Nurs, Philo,
Physics, Poli Sci, Pre-Law, Pre-Med/Pre-Dental, Reli Stu

SAINT JOSEPH COLLEGE (CT) .... sjc.edu 1000/21
Ed

ST. JOSEPH'S COLLEGE (IN) .... saintjoe.edu 1010/21
Bus Admin, Ed, Psych

ST. JOSEPH'S COLLEGE (ME) .... sjcme.edu 1050/22
Ed, Nurs

ST. JOSEPH'S COLLEGE (NY) .... sjcny.edu 1050/22
Bus Admin, Comp Sci, Ed, Hist, Math, Psych

SAINT JOSEPH'S UNIVERSITY (PA) .... sju.edu 1210/26
Bus Admin, English, Hist, Poli Sci, Pre-Med/Pre-Dental, Reli Stu

ST. LAWRENCE UNIVERSITY (NY) .... stlawu.edu 1160/25
Econ, English, Geol, Poli Sci, Pre-Law, Psych, Soc

ST. LOUIS COLLEGE OF PHARMACY (MO) .... slcop.edu 1180/26
Pharm, Pre-Med/Pre-Dental

SAINT LOUIS UNIVERSITY (MO) .... slu.edu 1150/25
Bio, Chem, Communic, Ed, Nurs, Philo, Pre-Med/Pre-Dental

SAINT MARTIN'S COLLEGE (WA) .... stmartin.edu 1060/23
Psych

SAINT MARY COLLEGE (KS) .... smcks.edu 1030/22
English

SAINT MARY'S COLLEGE (IN) .... saintmarys.edu 1110/24
Art, Bus Admin, Communic, Ed, English, Nurs, Philo, Pre-Law, Reli Stu

SAINT MARY'S COLLEGE OF CALIFORNIA (CA) .... stmarys-ca.edu 1115/24
Bus Admin, Ed, Psych, Soc

ST. MARY'S COLLEGE OF MARYLAND (MD) .... smcm.edu 1250/28
Anthro, Bio, Econ, English, Hist, Math, Music, Poli Sci, Pre-Med/Pre-Dental, Psych

ST. MARY'S UNIVERSITY OF MINNESOTA (MN) .... smumn.edu 1070/23
Bus Admin, Chem, Communic, Comp Sci, Drama, Ed, Hist, Philo, Reli Stu

ST. MARY'S UNIVERSITY (TX) .... stmarytx.edu 1070/23
Bus Admin, English, Poli Sci, Pre-Law, Pre-Med/Pre-Dental, Soc

SAINT MICHAEL'S COLLEGE (VT) .... smcvt.edu 1115/24
Bio, Bus Admin, Chem, Communic, Ed

ST. NORBERT COLLEGE (WI) .... snc.edu 1140/25
Bio, Bus Admin, Communic, Comp Sci, Ed, English, Hist

ST. OLAF COLLEGE (MN) .... stolaf.edu 1260/28
*Amer St, Art, Bio, Chem, Econ, English, Math, Music, Nurs, Philo, Physics,
Pre-Law, Pre-Med/Pre-Dental, Psych*

SAINT PETER'S COLLEGE (NJ) .... stpeters.edu 1000/21
English, Reli Stu

SAINT ROSE, COLLEGE OF (NY) .... strose.edu 1090/24
Art, Bus Admin, Ed, Soc

SAINT SCHOLASTICA, COLLEGE OF (MN) .... css.edu 1100/24
Bio, Chem, Ed, Nurs, Psych

SAINT THOMAS AQUINAS COLLEGE (NY) .... stac.edu 1060/23
Ed, Psych

SAINT THOMAS, UNIVERSITY OF (MN) .... stthomas.edu 1145/25
Bus Admin, Communic, Geol, Philo

SAINT THOMAS, UNIVERSITY OF (TX) .... stthom.edu 1140/25
Chem, Philo, Pre-Med/Pre-Dental, Psych, Reli Stu

ST. VINCENT COLLEGE (PA) .... stvincent.edu 1080/23
Bio, Bus Admin, Chem, Pre-Med/Pre-Dental, Psych, Reli Stu

SALEM COLLEGE (NC) .... salem.edu 1120/24
Art, Art Hist, Bus Admin, Econ, English, Pre-Law, Soc

SALEM STATE COLLEGE (MA) .... sscmass.edu 1000/21
Art, Art Hist, Chem, Comp Sci, Drama, Geog, Hist

SALISBURY STATE UNIVERSITY (MD) .... ssu.edu 1125/24
Ed, English, Geog, Philo, Pre-Law, Psych

SAMFORD UNIVERSITY (AL) .... samford.edu 1115/24
Bus Admin, Communic, Music, Nurs, Pharm, Reli Stu

SAN DIEGO STATE UNIVERSITY (CA) .... sdsu.edu 1080/23
Art, Art Hist, Astro, Bus Admin, Chem, Communic, Ed, Engine, English, Geog, Geol, Hist, Nurs, Soc

SAN DIEGO, UNIVERSITY OF (CA) .... acusd.edu 1150/25
Bus Admin, Nurs, Pre-Law, Pre-Med/Pre-Dental, Reli Stu

SAN FRANCISCO ART INSTITUTE (CA) .... sfai.edu 1000/21
Art

SAN FRANCISCO CONSERVATORY OF MUSIC (CA) .... sfcm.edu 1150/25
Music

SAN FRANCISCO, UNIVERSITY OF (CA) .... usfca.edu 1094/24
Bus Admin, Econ, Nurs, Pre-Law, Pre-Med/Pre-Dental, Psych

SAN FRANCISCO STATE UNIVERSITY (CA) .... sfsu.edu 1000/21
Anthro, Astro, Communic, Drama, English, Hist, Pre-Law, Soc

SAN JOSE STATE UNIVERSITY (CA) .... sjsu.edu 1060/23
Art, Bus Admin, Chem, Communic, Comp Sci, Math, Music, Nurs, Physics, Pre-Med/Pre-Dental, Zoo

SANTA CLARA UNIVERSITY (CA) .... scu.edu 1225/27
Bus Admin, Communic, Comp Sci, Engine, English, Hist, Music, Philo, Physics, Poli Sci, Pre-Law, Psych, Reli Stu

SANTA FE, COLLEGE OF (NM) .... csf.edu 1110/24
Art, Communic, Drama

SARAH LAWRENCE COLLEGE (NY) .... slc.edu 1230/27
Amer St, Drama, English, Geog, Pre-Law

SCHOOL OF THE ART INSTITUTE OF CHICAGO (IL) .... saic.ed 1120/24
Art

SCHREINER UNIVERSITY (TX) .... schreiner.edu 1000/21
Bus Admin

SCIENCES IN PHILADELPHIA, UNIVERSITY OF THE (PA) ...... usip.edu 1120/24
Bio, Biochem, Bus Admin, Chem, Comp Sci, Pharm

SCRANTON, UNIVERSITY OF (PA) .... scranton.edu 1140/25
Bio, Bus Admin, Communic, Pre-Med/Pre-Dental

SCRIPPS COLLEGE (CA) .... scrippscol.edu 1250/28
Art, Art Hist, Bio, Drama, English, For Lang, Pre-Law, Pre-Med/Pre-Dental

SEATTLE PACIFIC UNIVERSITY (WA) .... spu.edu 1199/26
Bio, Drama, Engine, English, Nurs

SEATTLE UNIVERSITY (WA) .... seattleu.edu 1120/24
Bus Admin, Drama, Engine, English, Nurs, Pre-Law

SETON HALL UNIVERSITY (NJ) .... shu.edu 1060/23
Bus Admin, Communic, Ed, Nurs, Philo, Pre-Law, Pre-Med/Pre-Dental, Psych, Reli Stu

SETON HILL COLLEGE (PA) .... setonhill.edu 1000/21
Art, Drama, Music

SHAW UNIVERSITY (NC) .... shawuniversity.edu 1010/21
Bus Admin, Soc

SHAWNEE STATE UNIVERSITY (OH) .... shawnee.edu 1000/21
Art, Ed

SHENANDOAH UNIVERSITY (VA) .... su.edu 1010/21
Music, Nurs

SHEPHERD COLLEGE (WV) .... shepherd.edu 1080/24
Art, Bus Admin, Chem, Ed, English, Hist, Music, Psych

SHIPPENSBURG UNIVERSITY (PA) .... ship.edu 1070/23
Bio, Bus Admin, Chem, Comp Sci, Ed, Physics, Psych, Soc

SHORTER COLLEGE (GA) .... shorter.edu 1050/22
Chem, Ed, Music

SIENA COLLEGE (NY) .... siena.edu 1115/24
Bio, Biochem, Bus Admin, Chem, Poli Sci, Pre-Law, Pre-Med/Pre-Dental, Psych

SIENA HEIGHTS UNIVERSITY (MI) .... sienaheights.edu 1000/21
Art, Psych

SILVER LAKE COLLEGE (WI) .... sl.edu 1000/21
Bus Admin, Ed, Reli Stu

SIMMONS COLLEGE (MA) .... simmons.edu 1100/24
Bus Admin, Communic, Ed, Math, Nurs, Psych, Soc

SIMPSON COLLEGE (IA) .... simpson.edu 1120/24
Bus Admin, Ed, Math, Music, Psych

SKIDMORE COLLEGE (NY) .... skidmore.edu 1300/29
Amer St, Anthro, Art, Art Hist, Bio, Biochem, Bus Admin, Chem, Classics, Drama, Ed, English, For Lang, Geol, Music, Philo, Poli Sci, Pre-Law, Pre-Med/Pre-Dental, Psych

SLIPPERY ROCK UNIVERSITY (PA) .... sru.edu 1000/21
Communic, Drama, Ed, English, For Lang, Music

SMITH COLLEGE (MA) .... smith.edu **1300/29**
Amer St, Anthro, Art, Art Hist, Bio, Econ, Engine, English, For Lang, Geol, Hist, Music, Philo, Physics, Poli Sci, Pre-Law, Pre-Med/Pre-Dental, Psych

SONOMA STATE UNIVERSITY (CA) .... sonoma.edu **1020/22**
Anthro, Art Hist, Bus Admin, Chem, Geog, Music, Nurs, Physics, Psych, Soc

SOUTH, UNIVERSITY OF THE (TN) .... sewanee.edu **1230/27**
Amer St, Anthro, Bio, Chem, Econ, Drama, English, Forest, For Lang, Hist, Poli Sci, Physics, Pre-Law, Pre-Med/Pre-Dental, Reli Stu

SOUTH ALABAMA, UNIVERSITY OF (AL) .... usouthal.edu **1060/23**
Bio, Bus Admin, Communic, English, For Lang, Nurs, Philo, Soc

SOUTH CAROLINA, UNIVERSITY OF (SC) .... sc.edu **1095/24**
Bus Admin, Communic, Comp Sci, Drama, Ed, Engine, English, For Lang, Geog, Geol, Hist, Nurs, Pharm, Physics, Poli Sci, Pre-Law

SOUTH DAKOTA, UNIVERSITY OF (SD) .... usd.edu **1050/22**
Art, Bio, Bus Admin, Nurs, Pre-Med/Pre-Dental

SOUTH DAKOTA SCHOOL OF MINES AND TECHNOLOGY (SD) .... sdsmt.edu **1135/25**
Engine, Geol, Math, Physics

SOUTH DAKOTA STATE UNIVERSITY (SD) .... sdstate.edu **1060/23**
Engine, Nurs, Soc

SOUTH FLORIDA, UNIVERSITY OF (FL) .... usf.edu **1060/23**
Amer St, Anthro, Bus Admin, Chem, Drama, Ed, Engine, For Lang, Music, Nurs, Philo

SOUTHEASTERN LOUISIANA STATE UNIVERSITY (LA) .... selu.edu **1000/21**
Communic, Comp Sci, Ed, English

SOUTHERN CALIFORNIA, UNIVERSITY OF (CA) .... usc.edu **1250/27**
Astro, Arch, Bus Admin, Communic, Drama, Ed, Engine, Math, Music, Pharm, Psych

SOUTHERN CONNECTICUT STATE UNIVERSITY (CT) .... southernct.edu **1000/21**
Chem, Communic, Comp Sci, Econ, Ed, English, Geog, Physics, Poli Sci, Psych, Soc

SOUTHERN ILLINOIS UNIVERSITY (CARBONDALE) (IL) .... siu.edu/siuc **1010/21**
Bot, Bus Admin, Communic, Engine, Forestry, Geog, Hist, Music, Poli Sci, Psych, Zoo

SOUTHERN ILLINOIS UNIVERSITY (EDWARDSVILLE) (IL) .... siue.edu **1010/21**
Ed, Engine, Nurs, Poli Sci

SOUTHERN MAINE, UNIVERSITY OF (ME) .... usm.maine.edu **1050/22**
Art, Bus Admin, Chem, Communic, Comp Sci, Drama, Engine, Music, Nurs

SOUTHERN METHODIST UNIVERSITY (TX) .... smu.edu **1200/26**
Anthro, Art, Art Hist, Bus Admin, Communic, Drama, Engine, Reli Stu

SOUTHERN MISSISSIPPI, UNIVERSITY OF (MS) .... usms.edu **1010/21**
Bus Admin, Drama Ed, Hist, Music, Nurs

SOUTHERN OREGON UNIVERSITY (OR) .... sou.edu **1040/22**
Bus Admin, Ed, For Lang, Soc

SOUTHERN POLYTECHNIC UNIVERSITY (GA) .... spsu.edu 1050/22
Arch, Comp Sci, Engine, Math

SOUTHERN UTAH UNIVERSITY (UT) .... suu.edu 1015/22
Drama, Ed

SOUTHWEST BAPTIST UNIVERSITY (MO) .... sbuniv.edu 1040/22
Ed, Music, Reli Stu

SOUTHWEST MISSOURI STATE UNIVERSITY (MO) .... smsu.edu 1070/23
Drama, Ed, Math, Poli Sci, Pre-Law

SOUTHWEST TEXAS STATE UNIVERSITY (TX) .... swt.edu 1035/22
Bus Admin, Ed, Math

SOUTHWESTERN OKLAHOMA STATE UNIVERSITY (OK) .... swosu.edu 1000/21
Ed, Pharm

SOUTHWESTERN UNIVERSITY (TX) .... southwestern.edu 1242/26
Art, Bio, Bus Admin, Chem, Communic, Drama, Econ, English, For Lang, Hist, Music, Philo, Poli Sci, Pre-Law, Pre-Med/Pre-Dental, Psych, Reli Stu, Soc

SPELMAN COLLEGE (GA) .... spelman.edu 1080/24
Bio, Chem, Comp Sci, Econ, English, Poli Sci, Pre-Law, Pre-Med/Pre-Dental, Soc

SPRING HILL COLLEGE (AL) .... shc.edu 1080/23
Bio, Bus Admin, Chem, Communic, English, Hist, Poli Sci, Pre-Law, Pre-Med/Pre-Dental

SPRINGFIELD COLLEGE (MA) .... spfldcol.edu 1000/21
Psych

STANFORD UNIVERSITY (CA) .... stanford.edu 1430/32
Amer St, Anthro, Bio, Chem, Classics, Communic, Comp Sci, Econ, Engine, English, Math, Music, Physics, Poli Sci, Pre-Law, Pre-Med/Pre-Dental, Psych, Reli Stu, Soc

STEPHEN F. AUSTIN STATE UNIVERSITY (TX) .... sfasu.edu 1000/21
Forest

STEPHENS (MO) .... stephens.edu 1040/22
Bus Admin, Communic, Drama, Psych

STETSON UNIVERSITY (FL) .... stetson.edu 1136/25
Bus Admin, Chem, Comp Sci, Ed, English, Hist, Math, Music, Pre-Law, Pre-Med/Pre-Dental, Psych, Reli Stu

STEVENS INSTITUTE OF TECHNOLOGY (NJ) .... stevens-tech.edu 1320/30
Comp Sci, Engine

STONEHILL COLLEGE (MA) .... stonehill.edu 1160/25
Bio, Bus Admin, Chem, Comp Sci, Poli Sci, Pre-Law, Psych

SUFFOLK UNIVERSITY (MA) .... suffolk.edu 1000/21
Bus Admin, Communic, Poli Sci, Soc

SUNY COLLEGE OF ENVIRONMENTAL SCIENCE & FORESTRY (NY) .... esf.edu 1130/25
Forest

SUSQUEHANNA UNIVERSITY (PA) .... susqu.edu 1140/25
Bio, Biochem, Bus Admin, Communic, Drama, Music, Pre-Med/Pre-Dental, Psych

SWARTHMORE COLLEGE (PA) .... swarthmore.edu 1430/32
Art Hist, Biochem, Bio, Classics, Econ, Ed, Engine, English, Hist,
Philo, Physics, Poli Sci, Pre-Law, Pre-Med/Pre-Dental, Psych

SWEET BRIAR COLLEGE (VA) .... sbc.edu 1140/25
Art Hist, For Lang, Math, Psych

SYRACUSE UNIVERSITY (NY) .... syracuse.edu 1180/26
Arch, Art, Art Hist, Bus Admin, Communic, Comp Sci, Drama, Engine, Forest,
Music, Poli Sci, Pre-Law, Psych, Reli Stu, Soc

TABOR COLLEGE (KS) .... tabor.edu 1060/23
Ed

TAMPA, UNIVERSITY OF (FL) .... utampa.edu 1095/23
Bus Admin, Communic, Music

TAYLOR UNIVERSITY (IN) .... taylor.edu 1090/26
Bus Admin, Comp Sci, Psych, Reli Stu

TEMPLE UNIVERSITY (PA) .... temple.edu 1100/24
Arch, Art, Biochem, Bio, Bus Admin, Chem, Communic, Comp Sci, Drama, English,
For Lang, Music, Pharm, Pre-Law, Pre-Med/Pre-Dental, Soc

TENNESSEE TECHNOLOGICAL UNIVERSITY (TN) .... tntech.edu 1100/24
Ed, Engine

TENNESSEE, UNIVERSITY OF (TN) .... utk.edu 1110/24
Ag, Anthro, Arch, Art, Bot, Bus Admin, Chem, Classics, Ed, Engine, English, Forest, Hist,
Physics, Poli Sci, Pre-Law, Pre-Med/Pre-Dental, Reli Stu, Zoo

TEXAS, UNIVERSITY OF, AT
      ARLINGTON .... uta.edu 1030/22
      Arch, Bus Admin, Communic, Comp Sci, Engine, Poli Sci
      AUSTIN .... utexas.edu 1220/26
      Amer St, Arch, Astro, Bio, Bot, Bus Admin, Classics, Communic, Comp Sci,
      Drama, Ed, Engine, For Lang, Geog, Geol, Hist, Math, Music, Pharm, Philo,
      Physics, Poli Sci, Pre-Med/Pre-Dental, Psych, Zoo
      DALLAS .... utdallas.edu 1225/29
      Bus Admin, Comp Sci, Engine, Hist, Physics
      SAN ANTONIO .... utsa.edu 1000/21
      Arch, Art, Bio, Bus Admin, Engine, Pre-Med/Pre-Dental
      TYLER .... uttyl.edu 1067/22
      Comp Sci, Engine, Math, Nurs, Psych

TEXAS A&M (TX) .... tamu.edu 1178/26
Ag, Arch, Bus Admin, Chem, Econ, Ed, Engine, Forest, Geol, Poli Sci, Pre-Med/Pre-Dental, Zoo

TEXAS A&M AT GALVESTON (TX) .... tamug.edu 1140/25
Bus Admin

TEXAS CHRISTIAN UNIVERSITY (TX) .... tcu.edu 1130/25
Bio, Bus Admin, Communic, Drama, Ed, Geol, Hist, Nurs, Reli Stu

TEXAS LUTHERAN UNIVERSITY (TX) .... tlu.edu 1080/23
Bio, Bus Admin, Chem, Music

TEXAS TECH UNIVERSITY (TX) .... ttu.edu 1100/25
Ag, Arch, Art, Bus Admin, Ed, Engine, hist, Home Ec, Math

TEXAS WESLEYAN COLLEGE (TX) .... txwesleyan.edu 1010/21
Bus Admin, Communic, Ed, Psych

THOMAS MORE COLLEGE (KY) .... thomasmore.edu 1038/22
Bio, Bus Admin, Chem, Comp Sci, Physics, Pre-Med/Pre-Dental

TOLEDO, UNIVERSITY OF (OH) .... utoledo.edu 1040/22
Bus Admin, Econ, Engine, Hist, Pharm

TOUGALOO COLLEGE (MS) .... tougaloo.edu 1000/21
Bio, Ed

TOWSON UNIVERSITY (MD) .... towson.edu 1080/23
Art, Bus Admin, Chem, Communic, Drama, Music, Nurs

TRANSYLVANIA UNIVERSITY (KY) .... transy.edu 1200/26
Bio, Bus Admin, Chem, Comp Sci, Ed, Philo, Pre-Med/Pre-Dental, Psych

TRINITY COLLEGE (CT) .... trincoll.edu 1300/29
*Amer St, Art Hist, Bio, Bus Admin, Chem, Econ, Engine, English, Hist, Math,
Philo, Pre-Law, Pre-Med/Pre-Dental, Reli Stu*

TRINITY COLLEGE (DC) .... trinitydc.edu 1100/24
Bus Admin, For Lang, Math, Poli Sci, Pre-Law, Soc

TRINITY UNIVERSITY (TX) .... trinity.edu 1298/29
*Art, Art Hist, Bio, Bus Admin, Chem, Classics, Communic, Econ, Ed, English,
For Lang, Hist, Philo, Physics, Poli Sci, Pre-Law, Pre-Med/Pre-Dental, Soc*

TRI-STATE UNIVERSITY (IN) .... tristate.edu 1060/23
Engine

TRUMAN STATE UNIVERSITY (MO) ....truman.edu 1210/27
Bio, Bus Admin, Chem, Ed, English, For Lang, Nurs, Pre-Med/Pre-Dental

TUFTS UNIVERSITY (MA) ....tufts.edu 1300/29
*Bio, Chem, Classics, Drama, Econ, Engine, English, Hist, Philo, Poli Sci,
Pre-Law, Pre-Med/Pre-Dental, Psych*

TULANE UNIVERSITY (LA) ....tulane.edu 1310/29
*Amer St, Anthro, Arch, Art, Bio, Biochem, Bus Admin, Drama, Engine, For Lang, Hist,
Math, Philo, Poli Sci, Pre-Law, Pre-Med/Pre-Dental, Psych*

TULSA, UNIVERSITY OF (OK) ....utulsa.edu 1240/27
Anthro, Art, Bio, Bus Admin, Communic, Comp Sci, Engine, English, Geol, Psych

TUSKEGEE UNIVERSITY (AL) .... tuskegee.edu 1000/21
Ag, Arch, Engine, Nurs, Physics, Pre-Law, Pre-Med/Pre-Dental

UNION COLLEGE (NY) .... union.edu 1230/27
Bio, Chem, Engine, Hist, Math, Poli Sci, Pre-Law, Pre-Med/Pre-Dental, Psych

UNION UNIVERSITY (TN) .... uu.edu 1100/24
Art, Chem, Music, Nurs, Physics, Reli Stu

U. S. AIR FORCE ACADEMY (CO) .... usafa.edu 1270/28
Bus Admin, Comp Sci, Engine, Math, Physics, Poli Sci

U. S. COAST GUARD ACADEMY (CT) .... cga.edu 1260/28
Engine

U. S. MILITARY ACADEMY (NY) .... usma.edu 1265/28
Econ, Engine, Hist, Poli Sci

U. S. NAVAL ACADEMY (MD) .... usna.edu 1300/29
Chem, Engine, Poli Sci

URSINUS COLLEGE (PA) .... ursinus.edu 1199/26
Bio, Bus Admin, Chem, Econ, Ed, Physics, Poli Sci, Pre-Law, Pre-Med/Pre-Dental

UTAH, UNIVERSITY OF (UT) .... utah.edu 1100/24
*Bio, Bus Admin, Chem, Comp Sci, Drama, Engine, English, For Lang, Pharm,
Poli Sci, Pre-Law, Pre-Med/Pre-Dental*

UTAH STATE UNIVERSITY (UT) .... usu.edu 1050/22
Ag, Chem, Drama, Ed, English, Forest, Home Ec, Music

UTICA COLLEGE (NY) .... ucsu.edu 1010/22
Bus Admin

VALPARAISO UNIVERSITY (IN) .... valpo.edu 1180/26
Bio, Bus Admin, Ed, Engine, For Lang, Math, Music, Nurs, Pre-Med/Pre-Dental, Psych, Reli Stu

VANDERBILT UNIVERSITY (TN) .... vanderbilt.edu 1340/30
*Anthro, Art Hist, Bio, Classics, Econ, Ed, Engine, English, Geol, Hist, Music, Nurs, Philo,
Physics, Poli Sci, Pre-Law, Pre-Med/Pre-Dental, Psych*

VASSAR COLLEGE (NY) .... vassar.edu 1375/30
*Art, Art Hist, Astro, Bio, Comp Sci, Drama, Econ, English, Hist, Math, Music, Philo,
Pre-Law, Pre-Med/Pre-Dental, Psych*

VERMONT, UNIVERSITY OF (VT) .... uvm.edu 1160/25
*Ag, Bio, Bot, Bus Admin, Chem, Econ, For Lang, Geog, Geol, Hist, Nurs,
Physics, Poli Sci, Pre-Law, Pre-Med/Pre-Dental, Reli Stu, Psych, Zoo*

VILLA JULIE COLLEGE (MD) .... vjc.edu 1080/23
Nurs

VILLANOVA UNIVERSITY (PA) .... villanova.edu 1230/27
*Astro, Bio, Bus Admin, Communic, Econ, Engine, Math, Nurs, Philo,
Poli Sci, Pre-Law, Pre-Med/Pre-Dental*

VIRGINIA, UNIVERSITY OF (VA) .... virginia.edu 1300/29
*Amer St, Arch, Art, Astro, Bio, Biochem, Bus Admin, Chem, Classics, Econ, Engine, English,
For Lang, Hist, Music, Nurs, Poli Sci, Pre-Law, Pre-Med/Pre-Dental, Psych, Reli Stu, Soc*

VIRGINIA COMMONWEALTH UNIVERSITY (VA) .... vcu.edu 1040/22
*Art, Bus Admin, Drama, Engine, For Lang, Music, Nurs, Pharm, Pre-Med/Pre-Dental,
Pre-Law, Psych, Reli Stu*

VIRGINIA MILITARY INSTITUTE (VA) .... vmi.edu 1120/24
Bus Admin, Chem, Econ, Engine, Hist, Pre-Law

VIRGINIA POLYTECHNIC INSTITUTE (VA) .... vpi.edu 1165/26
Ag, Arch, Biochem, Bus Admin, Chem, Engine, Forest, Hist, Psych

VIRGINIA WESLEYAN UNIVERSITY (VA) .... vwc.edu 1007/20
Bio, Bus Admin, Communic, Poli Sci, Pre-Law, Pre-Med/Pre-Dental, Psych, Reli Stu, Soc

VISUAL ARTS, SCHOOL OF (NY) .... schoolofvisualarts.edu 1064/23
Art, Bus Admin

VITERBO COLLEGE (WI) .... viterbo.edu 1055/23
Chem, Drama, Music, Nurs

WABASH COLLEGE (IN) .... wabash.edu 1180/26
Bio, Chem, Classics, Econ, English, Hist, Math, Philo, Poli Sci, Pre-Law, Pre-Med/Pre-Dental, Psych, Reli Stu

WAGNER COLLEGE (NY) .... wagner.edu 1090/24
Amer St, Bus Admin, Drama, Ed, Soc

WAKE FOREST UNIVERSITY (NC) .... wfu.edu 1310/29
*Bio, Bus Admin, Chem, Econ, English, For Lang, Hist, Math, Physics,
Poli Sci, Pre-Law, Pre-Med/Pre-Dental, Psych, Reli Stu*

WALLA WALLA COLLEGE (WA) .... wwc.edu 1000/21
Engine, Nurs, Pre-Med/Pre-Dental

WALSH UNIVERSITY (OH) .... walsh.edu 1000/21
Ed, English, Nurs

WARREN WILSON COLLEGE (NC) .... warren-wilson.edu 1135/25
English, Hist, Pre-Law

WARTBURG COLLEGE (IA) .... wartburg.edu 1140/25
Bio, Communic, Ed, English, Hist, Music, Pre-Med/Pre-Dental, Reli Stu

WASHINGTON COLLEGE (MD) .... washcoll.edu 1150/25
Amer St, Bio, Bus Admin, Hist, Pre-Med/Pre-Dental, Psych

WASHINGTON & JEFFERSON COLLEGE (PA) .... washjeff.edu 1130/25
Art, Bio, Bus Admin, Chem, Econ, Ed, English, Hist, Poli Sci, Pre-Law, Pre-Med/Pre-Dental, Psych

WASHINGTON & LEE UNIVERSITY (VA) .... wlu.edu 1325/30
*Art, Bio, Bus Admin, Chem, Communic, Econ, English, For Lang, Geol, Hist, Math,
Poli Sci, Pre-Law, Pre-Med/Pre-Dental*

WASHINGTON UNIVERSITY IN ST. LOUIS (MO) .... wustl.edu 1380/31
*Anthro, Arch, Art, Art Hist, Bio, Bus Admin, Chem, Comp Sci, Engine, English,
For Lang, Geol, Math, Philo, Physics, Pre-Law, Pre-Med/Pre-Dental*

WASHINGTON STATE UNIVERSITY (WA) .... wsu.edu 1060/23
Ag, Anthro, Arch, Biochem, Bus Admin, Communic, Econ, Ed, Engine, English, Home Ec, Pharm, Soc, Zoo

WASHINGTON, UNIVERSITY OF (WA) .... washington.edu 1145/25
*Anthro, Arch, Art, Astro, Biochem, Bot, Bus Admin, Chem, Comp Sci, Drama, Econ, Ed, Engine,
Forest, Geol, Hist, Math, Nurs, Philo, Physics, Pre-Law, Pre-Med/Pre-Dental, Psych, Zoo*

WAYNE STATE UNIVERSITY (MI) .... wayne.edu 1000/21
Engine, For Lang, Nurs, Pharm, Pre-Med/Pre-Dental

WAYNESBURG COLLEGE (PA) .... waynesburg.edu 1000/21
Communic, Nurs

WEBER STATE UNIVERSITY (UT) .... weber.edu 1030/22
Art, Communic, Comp Sci, Drama, Ed, Math, Music, Physics, Zoo

WEBSTER UNIVERSITY (MO) .... webster.edu 1110/24
Drama, Nurs, Psych

WELLESLEY COLLEGE (MA) .... wellesley.edu 1350/30
Art, Art Hist, Bio, Chem, Econ, Ed, English, For Lang, Hist, Math, Physics,
Poli Sci, Pre-Law, Pre-Med/Pre-Dental, Reli Stu

WELLS COLLEGE (NY) .... wells. edu 1110/24
Amer St, Bio, Bus Admin, Chem, Drama, Ed, English, For Lang, Hist, Music,
Pre-Law, Pre-Med/Pre-Dental, Psych, Soc

WESLEYAN COLLEGE (GA) .... wesleyan-college.edu 1100/24
Amer St, Art, Bus Admin

WESLEYAN UNIVERSITY (CT) .... wesleyan.edu 1380/31
Amer St, Art, Astro, Bio, Chem, Drama, Econ, English, Hist, Math, Poli Sci,
Pre-Law, Pre-Med/Pre-Dental, Psych, Reli Stu

WEST CHESTER UNIVERSITY (PA) .... wcupa.edu 1040/22
Art, Bio, Bus Admin, Chem, Communic, Comp Sci, For Lang, Music, Poli Sci, Pre-Law, Soc

WEST FLORIDA, UNIVERSITY OF (FL) .... uwf.edu 1090/24
Bus Admin, Comp Sci, Ed, Psych

WEST VIRGINIA UNIVERSITY (WV) .... wvu.edu 1040/22
Art, Bus Admin, Communic, Drama, Engine, Forest, Music

WEST VIRGINIA WESLEYAN COLLEGE (WV) .... wvwc.edu 1040/22
Art, Bio, Comp Sci, Drama, Ed, English, Hist, Physics

WESTERN CONNECTICUT STATE UNIVERSITY (CT) .... wcsu.ctstateu.edu 1000/21
Amer St, Anthro, Art, Astro, Bus Admin, Ed, English, Music, Nurs, Soc

WESTERN ILLINOIS UNIVERSITY (IL) .... wiu.edu 1010/21
Ag, Chem, Communic, Ed, English, Geog, Music, Soc

WESTERN KENTUCKY UNIVERSITY (KY) .... wku.edu 1000/21
Ag, Bio, Comp Sci, Ed, Hist, Nurs, Physics, Psych, Soc

WESTERN MICHIGAN UNIVERSITY (MI) .... wmich.edu 1100/24
Art, Bus Admin, Communic, Comp Sci, Drama, Ed, English, Engine, For Lang, Hist,
Home Ec, Music, Nurs, Physics, Psych

WESTERN NEW ENGLAND COLLEGE (MA) .... wnec.edu 1060/23
Bus Admin, Comp Sci, Ed, Engine, Psych

WESTERN STATE COLLEGE OF COLORADO .... western.edu 1000/21
Bio, Bus Admin, Drama, English, Hist, Geol, Music

WESTERN WASHINGTON UNIVERSITY (WA) .... wwu.edu 1120/24
Art, Communic, Ed, English, Geog, Pre-Law, Soc

WESTFIELD STATE COLLEGE (MA) .... wsc.mass.edu 1050/23
Ed, English, Music, Poli Sci, Psych

WESTMINSTER COLLEGE (MO) .... wcmo.edu 1140/25
Bio, Econ, English, Hist, Pre-Law, Pre-Med/Pre-Dental, Psych

WESTMINSTER COLLEGE (PA) .... westminster.edu 1080/24
Bio, Comp Sci, Pre-Med/Pre-Dental, Soc

WESTMINSTER COLLEGE OF SALT LAKE CITY (UT) .... wcslc.edu 1120/24
Art, Bio, Bus Admin, Communic, Comp Sci, Engine, English, Hist, Nurs,
Philo, Physics, Poli Sci, Psych

WESTMONT COLLEGE (CA) .... westmont.edu 1220/27
Bio, Chem, Econ, Hist, Pre-Law, Pre-Med/Pre-Dental, Psych, Reli Stu

WHEATON COLLEGE (IL) .... wheaton.edu 1327/29
Art, Bio, Chem, Communic, Ed, English, Hist, Math, Music, Philo, Physics,
Pre-Law, Pre-Med/Pre-Dental, Psych, Reli Stu, Soc

WHEATON COLLEGE (MA) .... wheatonma.edu 1195/26
Art, Art Hist, Astro, Bio, Drama, Econ, English, For Lang, Hist, Math,
Poli Sci, Pre-Law, Pre-Med/Pre-Dental, Psych, Soc

WHEELING JESUIT (WV) .... wju.edu 1031/22
Bio, Bus Admin, Chem, English, Hist, Math, Nurs, Philo, Psych, Reli Stu

WHEELOCK COLLEGE (MA) .... wheelock.edu 1000/21
Ed

WHITMAN COLLEGE (WA) .... whitman.edu 1340/30
Astro, Bio, Chem, Classics, Drama, Econ, English, For Lang, Geol, Hist, Math, Music,
Philo, Physics, Poli Sci, Pre-Law, Pre-Med/Pre-Dental, Psych, Soc

WHITTIER COLLEGE (CA) .... whittier.edu 1090/24
Bus Admin, Chem, Econ, Ed, English, Poli Sci, Pre-Law

WHITWORTH COLLEGE (WA) .... whitworth.edu 1160/26
Art, Chem, Communic, Ed, English, Music, Physics, Psych, Reli Stu

WICHITA STATE UNIVERSITY (KS) .... wichita.edu 1000/21
Bus Admin, Communic, English

WIDENER UNIVERSITY (PA) .... widener.edu 1060/23
Bus Admin, Ed, Engine, Nurs

WILBERFORCE UNIVERSITY (OH) .... wilberforce.edu 1000/21
Bus Admin, Poli Sci, Pre-Law

WILKES UNIVERSITY (PA) .... wilkes.edu 1037/22
Bio, Comp Sci, Engine, English, Hist, Math, Nurs, Pre-Med/Pre-Dental, Psych

WILLAMETTE UNIVERSITY (OR) .... willamette.edu 1230/27
Art Hist, Bio, Chem, Econ, English, Hist, Math, Music, Poli Sci, Pre-Law,
Pre-Med/Pre-Dental, Psych, Soc

WILLIAM JEWELL COLLEGE (MO) .... jewell.edu 1130/25
Bio, Bus Admin, Ed, English, Music, Nurs

WILLIAM & MARY, COLLEGE OF (VA) .... wm.edu 1335/30
Amer St, Bio, Bus Admin, Comp Sci, Drama, Ed, For Lang, Geol, Hist, Physics,
Poli Sci, Pre-Med/Pre-Dental, Reli Stu

WILLIAM PATERSON UNIVERSITY (NJ) .... wpunj.edu 1070/23
Anthro, Communic, Comp Sci, English, Hist, Music, Psych, Soc

WILLIAMS COLLEGE (MA) .... williams.edu 1400/32
Amer St, Art, Art Hist, Astro, Bio, Chem, Classics, Comp Sci, Econ, English, Hist,
Poli Sci, Pre-Law, Pre-Med/Pre-Dental, Psych

WILMINGTON COLLEGE (OH) .... wilmington.edu 1000/21
Ag, Ed, English, Hist

WILSON COLLEGE (PA) .... wilson.edu 1050/23
Econ, Pre-Law, Psych, Soc

WINGATE UNIVERSITY (NC) .... wingate.edu 1050/22
Art, Communic, Hist, Music

WINONA STATE UNIVERSITY (MN) .... winona.msus.edu 1050/22
Bio, Communic, English, Pre-Med/Pre-Dental, Soc

WINTHROP UNIVERSITY (SC) .... winthrop.edu 1055/22
Art, Bio, Bus Admin, Chem, Drama, Ed, English, Hist, Math, Poli Sci, Psych

WISCONSIN LUTHERAN COLLEGE (WI) .... wlc.edu 1100/24
Art, Chem, Communic, Ed, Math, Music, Reli Stu

WISCONSIN, UNIVERSITY OF, AT
        EAU CLAIRE .... uwec.edu 1099/24
        Bio, Bus Admin, Chem, English, Math, Nurs
        GREEN BAY .... uwgb.edu 1030/22
        Art, Bus Admin, Hist, Psych
        LA CROSSE .... uwlax.edu 1080/23
        Astro, Bus Admin, Chem, Communic, Comp Sci, Geog, Soc
        MADISON .... wisc.edu 1220/27
        Ag, Anthro, Art, Art Hist, Astro, Biochem, Bot, Bus Admin, Chem, Classics, Communic,
        Comp Sci, Drama, Ed, Engine, English, For Lang, Forest, Geog, Geol, Hist, Home Ec, Math,
        Music, Nurs, Pharm, Philo, Physics, Poli Sci, Pre-Law, Pre-Med/Pre-Dental, Psych, Soc, Zoo
        MILWAUKEE .... uwm.edu 1080/23
        Anthro, Arch, Bio, Bus Admin, Chem, Drama, Econ, Ed, English, For Lang,
        Hist, Nurs, Physics, Poli Sci, Pre-Law
        PLATTEVILLE .... uwplatt.edu 1050/23
        Ag, Bio, Chem, Ed, Engine, English
        STEVENS POINT .... uwsp.edu 1080/23
        Art, Bio, Bus Admin, Chem, Communic, Drama, Ed, Home Ec, Math, Music, Soc
        STOUT .... uwstout.edu 1000/21
        Bus Admin, Home Ec, Psych

WITTENBERG UNIVERSITY (OH) .... wittenberg.edu 1162/26
Art, Bio, Bus Admin, Chem, Ed, English, Geog, Hist, Music, Poli Sci,
Pre-Law, Pre-Med/Pre-Dental, Psych, Reli Stu

WOFFORD COLLEGE (SC) .... wofford.edu 1195/26
Bio, Chem, Comp Sci, Econ, Ed, English, For Lang, Hist, Math, Philo,
Pre-Law, Pre-Med/Pre-Dental, Psych, Soc

WOODBURY UNIVERSITY (CA) .... woodburyu.edu 1000/21
Arch, Bus Admin

WOOSTER, COLLEGE OF (OH) .... wooster.edu 1200/26
Art Hist, Bio, Chem, Classics, Drama, Econ, English, Geol, Hist, Math, Music,
Poli Sci, Pre-Law, Pre-Med/Pre-Dental, Reli Stu, Soc

WORCESTER POLYTECHNIC INSTITUTE (MA) .... wpi.edu 1285/29
Bio, Biochem, Bus Admin, Comp Sci, Econ, Engine, Math, Physics, Pre-Law

WORCESTER STATE COLLEGE (MA) .... worcester.edu 1000/21
Bus Admin, Chem, Communic, Ed, Nurs, Philo, Psych

WRIGHT STATE UNIVERSITY (OH) .... wright.edu 1050/22
Econ, Engine, Geol, Nurs

WYOMING, UNIVERSITY OF (WY) .... uwyo.edu 1066/23
Ag, Amer St, Astro, Bio, Bot, Bus Admin, Chem, Econ, Ed, Engine, Geog, Geol,
Pharm, Pre-Law, Pre-Med/Pre-Dental, Psych, Zoo

XAVIER UNIVERSITY (OH) .... xu.edu 1160/25
Bio, Bus Admin, Chem, Classics, Communic, Econ, Hist, Philo, Physics, Psych, Reli Stu

XAVIER UNIVERSITY OF LOUISIANA (LA) .... xula.edu 1080/23
Bio, Bus Admin, Chem, Ed, Music, Pharm, Pre-Med/Pre-Dental, Psych

YALE UNIVERSITY (CT) .... yale.edu 1450/32
Amer St, Anthro, Arch, Art, Art Hist, Bio, Biochem, Classics, Drama, Econ, English, For Lang,
Hist, Math, Music, Philo, Poli Sci, Pre-Law, Pre-Med/Pre-Dental, Psych, Reli Stu, Soc

YESHIVA UNIVERSITY (NY) .... yu.edu 1220/27
Bio, Bus Admin, Comp Sci, Hist, Physics, Poli Sci, Pre-Med/Pre-Dental, Psych

YORK COLLEGE OF PENNSYLVANIA (PA) .... ycp.edu 1100/24
Bus Admin, Communic, Ed, Nurs

YOUNGSTOWN STATE UNIVERSITY (OH) .... ysu.edu 1000/21
Art, Bus Admin

SECTION FOUR

APPENDICES

APPENDIX A
The 1000 Colleges Used In This Study

Abilene Christian University
Abilene, Texas 79699

Adelphi University
Garden City, NY 11530

Adrian College
Adrian, Michigan 49221

◆ **Agnes Scott College**
Decatur, Georgia 30030

Akron, University of
Akron, Ohio 44325

◆ **Alabama, University of**
Tuscaloosa, Alabama 35487

Alaska Pacific University
Anchorage, Alaska 99508

Alaska, University of
Anchorage, Alaska 99508

Alaska, University of
Fairbanks, Alaska 99775

Albany College of Pharmacy
Albany, New York 12208

Albertson College of Idaho
Caldwell, Idaho 83605

◆ **Albion College**
Albion, Michigan 49224

Albright College
Reading, Pennsylvania 19612

Alderson-Broaddus College
Phillipi, West Virginia 26416

◆ **Alfred University**
Alfred, New York 14802

◆ **Allegheny College**
Meadville, Pennsylvania 16335

◆ **Alma College**
Alma, Michigan 48801

Alverno College
Milwaukee, Wisconsin 53234

American Academy of Dramatic Arts
New York, New York 10016

American International College
Springfield, Massachusetts 01109

◆ **American University**
Washington, DC 20016

◆ **Amherst College**
Amherst, Massachusetts 01002

Anderson University
Anderson, Indiana 46012

Andrews University
Berrien Springs, Michigan 49104

Anna Maria College
Paxton, Massachusetts 01612

Appalachian State University
Boone, North Carolina 28608

Aquinas College
Grand Rapids, Michigan 49506

Arcadia University
Glenside, Pennsylvania 19038

◆ **Arizona, University of**
Tucson, Arizona 85721

◆ **Arizona State University**
Tempe, Arizona 85287

◆ **Arkansas, University of**
Fayetteville, Arkansas 72701

Art Center College of Design
Pasadena, California 91103

Art Institute of Chicago, School of the
Chicago, Illinois 60603

Arts, University of the
Philadelphia, Pennsylvania 19102

Asbury College
Wilmore, Kentucky 40390

Ashland University
Ashland, Ohio 44805

Assumption College
Worcester, Massachusetts 01609

◆ **Auburn University**
Auburn University, Alabama 36849

Augsburg College
Minneapolis, Minnesota 55454

Augusta State University
Augusta, Georgia 30964

◆ **Augustana College**
Rock Island, Illinois 61201

Augustana College
Sioux Falls, South Dakota 57197

◆ **Austin College**
Sherman, Texas 75091

Averett College
Danville, Virginia 24541

Avila University
Kansas City, Missouri 64145

◆ Phi Beta Kappa Schools ▮ Predominantly African-American Institutions

Azusa Pacific University
Azusa, California 91702

B

Babson College
Wellesley, Massachusetts 02157

Baker University
Baldwin City, Kansas 66006

Baldwin-Wallace College
Berea, Ohio 44017

Ball State University
Muncie, Indiana 47306

Bard College,
Annandale-on-Hudson, New York 12504

Barry University
Miami Shores, Florida 33161

◆ **Bates College**
Lewiston, Maine 04240

◆ **Baylor University**
Waco, Texas 76798

Belhaven College
Jackson, Mississippi 39202

Bellarmine University
Louisville, Kentucky 40205

Belmont Abbey College
Belmont, North Carolina 28012

Belmont University
Nashville, Tennessee 37212

◆ **Beloit College**
Beloit, Wisconsin 53511

Bemidji State University
Bemidji, Minnesota 56601

Benedictine College
Atchison, Kansas 66002

Benedictine University
Lisle, Illinois 60532

◆ **Bennett College**
Greensboro, North Carolina 27401

Bennington College
Bennington, Vermont 05201

Bentley College
Waltham, Massachusetts 02154

Berea College
Berea, Kentucky 40404

Berklee College of Music
Boston, Massachusetts 02215

Berry College
Rome, Georgia 30149

Bethany College
Bethany, West Virginia 26032

Bethel College
Mishawaka, Indiana 46545

Bethel College
St. Paul, Minnesota 55112

Biola University
La Mirada, California 90639

◆ **Birmingham-Southern College**
Birmingham, Alabama 35254

Blackburn College
Carlinville, Illinois 62626

Bloomsburg University
Bloomsburg, Pennsylvania 17815

Bluffton College
Bluffton, Ohio 45817

Boston Architectural Center
Boston, Massachusetts 02115

◆ **Boston College**
Chestnut Hill, Massachusetts 02167

Boston Conservatory
Boston, Massachusetts 02215

◆ **Boston University**
Boston, Massachusetts 02215

◆ **Bowdoin College**
Brunswick, Maine 04011

◆ **Bowling Green State University**
Bowling Green, Ohio 43403

Bradley University
Peoria, Illinois 61625

◆ **Brandeis University**
Waltham, Massachusetts 02254

Brescia University
Owensboro, Kentucky 42301

Bridgewater College
Bridgewater, Virginia 22812

Bridgewater State College
Bridgewater, Massachusetts 02325

Brigham Young University
Provo, Utah 84602

◆ **Brown University**
Providence, Rhode Island 02912

Bryan College
Dayton, Tennessee 37321

Bryant College
Smithfield, Rhode Island 02917

Bryn Athyn College of the New Church
Bryn Athyn, Pennsylvania 19009

◆ Phi Beta Kappa Schools ■ Predominantly African-American Institutions

Bryn Mawr College
Bryn Mawr, Pennsylvania 19010

◆ **Bucknell University**
Lewisburg, Pennsylvania 17837

Buena Vista University
Storm Lake, Iowa 50588

Butler University
Indianapolis, Indiana 46208

C

Caldwell College
Caldwell, New Jersey 07006

California College of Arts and Crafts
San Francisco, California 94107

California Institute of the Arts
Valencia, California 91355

California Institute of Technology
Pasadena, California 91125

California, University of, at
◆ **Berkeley,** California 94720
◆ **Davis,** California 95616
◆ **Irvine,** California 92717
◆ **Los Angeles,** California 90024
◆ **Riverside,** California 92521
◆ **San Diego,** California 92093
◆ **Santa Barbara,** California 93106
◆ **Santa Cruz,** California 95064

California Lutheran University
Thousand Oaks, California 91360

California Maritime Academy
Vallejo, California 94590

California Polytechnic State University
Pomona, California 91768

California Polytechnic State University
San Luis Obispo, California 93407

California, State University of, at
Bakersfield, California 93311
Camarillo, California 93012
◆ **Chico,** California 95929
Dominguez Hills, Carson, California 90747
Fresno, California 93740
Fullerton, California 92834
Hayward, California 94542
Long Beach, California 90840
Los Angeles, California 90032
Monterey Bay, California 93955
Northridge, California 91330
Sacramento, California 95819
San Bernardino, California 92407
San Jose, California 95192
San Marcos, California 92096
Stanislaus, California 95382

Calvin College
Grand Rapids, Michigan 49456

Campbell University
Buies Creek, North Carolina 27506

Capital University
Columbus, Ohio 43209

◆ **Carleton College**
Northfield, Minnesota 55057

◆ **Carnegie Mellon University**
Pittsburgh, Pennsylvania 15213

Carroll College
Helena, Montana 59625

Carroll College
Waukesha, Wisconsin 53186

Carson-Newman College
Jefferson City, Tennessee 37760

Carthage College
Kenosha, Wisconsin 53140

◆ **Case Western Reserve University**
Cleveland, Ohio 44106

Catawba College
Salisbury, North Carolina 28144

Catholic University of America
Washington, DC 20064

Cedar Crest College
Allentown, Pennsylvania 18104

Cedarville University
Cedarville, Ohio 45314

Centenary College of Louisiana
Shreveport, Louisiana 71104

Central Arkansas, University of
Conway, Arkansas 72035

Central College
Pella, Iowa 50219

Central Connecticut State University
New Britain, Connecticut 06050

Central Florida, University of
Orlando, Florida 32816

Central Michigan University
Mount Pleasant, Michigan 48859

Centre College
Danville, Kentucky 40422

Champlain College
Burlington, Vermont 05402

Chapman College
Orange, California 92866

Coastal Carolina University
Conway, South Carolina 29528

◆ Phi Beta Kappa Schools   ■ Predominantly African-American Institutions

College of Charleston
Charleston, South Carolina 29424

Charleston Southern University
Charleston, South Carolina 29423

Charleston, University of
Charleston, West Virginia 25304

◆ Chatham College
Pittsburgh, Pennsylvania 15232

Chestnut Hill College
Philadelphia, Pennsylvania 19118

Cheyney University of Pennsylvania
Cheyney, Pennsylvania 19319

◆ Chicago, University of
Chicago, Illinois 60637

Chowan College
Murfreesboro, North Carolina 27855

Christian Brothers University
Memphis, Tennessee 38104

Christopher Newport University
Newport News, Virginia 23606

Christendom College
Front Royal, Virginia 22630

◆ Cincinnati, University of
Cincinnati, Ohio 45221

Citadel, The
Charleston, South Carolina 29409

◆ Claremont McKenna College
Claremont, California 91711

∎ Clark Atlanta University
Atlanta, Georgia 30314

◆ Clark University
Worcester, Massachusetts 01610

Clarke College
Dubuque, Iowa 52001

Clarkson University
Potsdam, New York 13676

Clemson University
Clemson, South Carolina 29634

Cleveland Institute of Art
Cleveland, Ohio 44106

Cleveland Institute of Music
Cleveland, Ohio 44106

◆ Coe College
Cedar Rapids, Iowa 52402

Cogswell Polytechnic College
Sunnyvale, California 94089

Coker College
Hartsdale, South Carolina 29550

◆ Colby College
Waterville, Maine 04901

Colby-Sawyer College
New London, New Hampshire 03257

◆ Colgate University
Hamilton, New York 13346

◆ Colorado College
Colorado Springs, Colorado 80903

◆ Colorado, University of
Boulder, Colorado 80309

Colorado, University of
Colorado Springs, Colorado 80933

Colorado, University of
Denver, Colorado 80217

Colorado School of Mines
Golden, Colorado 80401

◆ Colorado State University
Fort Collins, Colorado 80523

Columbia College
Chicago, Illinois 60605

Columbia College
Columbia, South Carolina 29203

◆ Columbia University
New York, New York 10027
  ◆ Barnard College, New York, NY 10027

Concordia University
Irvine, California 92612

Concordia College
Moorhead, Minnesota 56560

Concordia University
Seward, Nebraska 68434

◆ Connecticut, University of
Storrs, Connecticut 06269

◆ Connecticut College
New London, Connecticut 06320

Converse College
Spartanburg, South Carolina 29302

Cooper Union College, The
New York, New York 10003

◆ Cornell College
Mount Vernon, Iowa 52314

◆ Cornell University
Ithaca, New York 14853

Cornish College of the Arts
Seattle, Washington 98102

Covenant College
Lookout Mountain, Georgia 30750

◆ Phi Beta Kappa Schools ∎ Predominantly African-American Institutions

Creighton University
Omaha, Nebraska 68178

Cumberland College
Williamsburg, Kentucky 40769

Curtis Institute of Music
Philadelphia, Pennsylvania 19103

D **Daemen College**
Amherst, New York 14226

◆ **Dallas, University of**
Irving, Texas 75062

Dana College
Blair, Nebraska 68008

◆ **Dartmouth College**
Hanover, New Hampshire 03755

◆ **Davidson College**
Davidson, North Carolina 28036

Dayton, University of
Dayton, Ohio 45469

Delaware State University
Dover, Delaware 19901

◆ **Delaware, University of**
Newark, Delaware 19716

Delaware Valley College of Pennsylvania
Doylestown, Pennsylvania 18901

◆ **Denison University**
Granville, Ohio 43023

◆ **Denver, University of**
Denver, Colorado 80208

DePaul University
Chicago, Illinois 60604

◆ **DePauw University**
Greencastle, Indiana 46135

DeSales University
Center Valley, Pennsylvania 18034

Detroit Mercy, University of
Detroit, Michigan 48221

◆ **Dickinson College**
Carlisle, Pennsylvania 17013

■ **Dillard University**
New Orleans, Louisiana 70122

Doane College
Crete, Nebraska 68333

Dominican University
River Forest, Illinois 60305

Dominican University of California
San Rafael, California 94901

Dordt College
Sioux Center, Iowa 51250

◆ **Drake University**
Des Moines, Iowa 50311

◆ **Drew University**
Madison, New Jersey 07940

Drexel University
Philadelphia, Pennsylvania 19104

Drury University
Springfield, Missouri 65802

Dubuque, University of
Dubuque, Iowa 52001

◆ **Duke University**
Durham, North Carolina 27706

Duquesne University
Pittsburgh, Pennsylvania 15282

D'Youville College
Buffalo, New York 14201

E ◆ **Earlham College**
Richmond, Indiana 47374

East Carolina University
Greenville, North Carolina 27858

East Stroudsburg University
East Stroudsburg, Pennsylvania 18301

Eastern College
St. Davids, Pennsylvania 19087

Eastern Connecticut State University
Willimantic, Connecticut 06226

Eastern Kentucky University
Richmond, Kentucky 40475

Eastern Illinois University
Charleston, Illinois 61920

Eastern Mennonite University
Harrisonburg, Virginia 22802

Eastern Michigan University
Ypsilanti, Michigan 48197

Eastern Nazarene College
Quincy, Massachusetts 02170

Eastern Oregon University
La Grande, Oregon 97850

◆ **Eckerd College**
St. Petersburg, Florida 33733

Edgewood College
Madison, Wisconsin 53711

Edinboro University of Pennsylvania
Edinboro, Pennsylvania 16444

Elizabethtown College
Elizabethtown, Pennsylvania 17022

◆ Phi Beta Kappa Schools   ■ Predominantly African-American Institutions

Elon University
Elon University, North Carolina 27244

Elmhurst College
Elmhurst, Illinois 60126

◆ **Elmira College**
Elmira, New York 14901

Elms College
Chicopee, Massachusetts 01013

Embry-Riddle Aeronautical University
Daytona Beach, Florida 32114

Emerson College
Boston, Massachusetts 02116

Emmanuel College
Boston, Massachusetts 02115

Emory and Henry College
Emory, Virginia 24327

◆ **Emory University**
Atlanta, Georgia 30322

Erskine College
Due West, South Carolina 29639

Eureka College
Eureka, Illinois 61530

Evansville, University of
Evansville, Indiana 47722

◆ **Fairfield University**
Fairfield, Connecticut 06430

Fairleigh Dickinson University
Teaneck, New Jersey 07666

Fairmont State University
Fairmont, West Virginia 26554

Faulkner University
Montgomery, Alabama 36109

Ferris State University
Big Rapids, Michigan 49307

◆▮ **Fisk University**
Nashville, Tennessee 37208

Fitchburg State College
Fitchburg, Massachusetts 01420

Five Towns College
Dix Hills, New York 11746

Flagler College
St. Augustine, Florida 32085

◆ **Florida, University of**
Gainesville, Florida 32611

◆ **Florida A&M University**
Tallahassee, FL 32307

Florida Atlantic University
Boca Raton, Florida 33431

Florida Gulf Coast University
Fort Myers, Georgia 33965

Florida Institute of Technology
Melbourne, Florida 32901

◆ **Florida International University**
Miami, Florida 33199

Florida Southern College
Lakeland, Florida 33801

◆ **Florida State University**
Tallahassee, Florida 32306

Fontbonne College
St. Louis, Missouri 63105

◆ **Fordham University**
Bronx, New York 10458

Fort Hays State University
Hays, Kansas 67601

Fort Lewis College
Durango, Colorado 81301

Framingham State College
Framingham, Massachusetts 01701

Franciscan University of Steubenville
Steubenville, Ohio 43952

Franklin College
Franklin, Indiana 46131

◆ **Franklin & Marshall College**
Lancaster, Pennsylvania 17604

Freed-Hardeman University
Henderson, Tennessee 38340

Frostburg State University
Frostburg, Maryland 21532

◆ **Furman University**
Greenville, South Carolina 29613

Gannon University
Erie, Pennsylvania 16541

Geneva College
Beaver Falls, Pennsylvania 15010

Georgetown College
Georgetown, Kentucky 40324

◆ **Georgetown University**
Washington, DC 20057

George Fox University
Newberg, Oregon 97132

George Mason University
Fairfax, Virginia 22030

◆ **George Washington University**
Washington, DC 20052

◆ Phi Beta Kappa Schools ▮ Predominantly African-American Institutions

◆ **Georgia, University of**
Athens, Georgia 30602

Georgia Institute of Technology
Atlanta, Georgia 30332

Georgia Southern University
Statesboro, Georgia 30460

Georgia Southwestern University
Americus, Georgia 31704

Georgia State University
Atlanta, Georgia 30303

◆ **Gettysburg College**
Gettysburg, Pennsylvania 17325

Gonzaga University
Spokane, Washington 99258

Gordon College
Wenham, Massachusetts 01984

Goshen College
Goshen, Indiana 46526

◆ **Goucher College**
Towson, Maryland 21204

Graceland University
Lamoni, Iowa 50140

Grambling State University
Grambling, Louisiana 71245

Grand Valley State University
Allendale, Michigan 49401

Greensboro College
Greensboro, North Carolina 27401

◆ **Grinnell College**
Grinnell, Iowa 50112

Grove City College
Grove City, Pennsylvania 16127

Guilford College
Greensboro, North Carolina 27410

◆ **Gustavus Adolphus College**
St. Peter, Minnesota 56082

Gwynedd-Mercy College
Gwnedd Valley, Pennsylvania 19437

◆ **Hamilton College**
Clinton, New York 13323

◆ **Hamline University**
St. Paul, Minnesota 55104

◆ **Hampden-Sydney College**
Hampden-Sydney, Virginia 23943

◆ **Hampton University**
Hampton, Virginia 23668

Hanover College
Hanover, Indiana 47243

Harding University
Searcy, Arkansas 72149

Hardin-Simmons University
Abilene, Texas 79698

Hartford, University of
Hartford, Connecticut 06117

Hartwick College
Oneonta, New York 13820

◆ **Harvard University**
Cambridge, Massachusetts 02138

Harvey Mudd College
Claremont, California 91711

Hastings College
Hastings, Nebraska 68901

◆ **Haverford College**
Haverford, Pennsylvania 19041

Hawaii Pacific University
Honolulu, Hawaii 96813

◆ **Hawaii, University of**
Manoa, Honolulu, Hawaii 96822

Heidelberg College
Tiffin, Ohio 44883

Henderson State University
Arkadelphia, Arkansas 71999

◆ **Hendrix College**
Conway, Arkansas 72032

High Point University
High Point, North Carolina 27262

Hillsdale College
Hillsdale, Michigan 49242

◆ **Hiram College**
Hiram, Ohio 44234

◆ **Hobart & William Smith Colleges**
Geneva, New York 14456

◆ **Hofstra University**
Hempstead, New York 11550

◆ **Hollins University**
Roanoke, Virginia 24020

◆ **Holy Cross, College of the**
Worcester, Massachusetts 01610

Holy Names College
Oakland, California 94619

Hood College
Frederick, Maryland 21701

◆ **Hope College**
Holland, Michigan 49423

◆ Phi Beta Kappa Schools ■ Predominantly African-American Institutions

Houghton College
Houghton, New York 14744

Houston Baptist University
Houston, Texas 77074

Houston, University of
Houston, Texas 77004

◆■ Howard University
Washington, DC 20059

Humboldt State University
Arcata, California 95521

Huntingdon College
Montgomery, Alabama 36106

Huntington College
Huntington, Indiana 46750

Husson College
Bangor, Maine 04401

◆ Idaho, University of
Moscow, Idaho 83844

Illinois, University of, at
◆ Urbana-Champaign, Illinois 61801
◆ Chicago, Illinois 60680

◆ Illinois College
Jacksonville, Illinois 62650

Illinois Institute of Technology
Chicago, Illinois 60616

Illinois State University
Normal, Illinois 61761

◆ Illinois Wesleyan University
Bloomington, Illinois 61702

Immaculata University
Immaculata, Pennsylvania 19345

Indiana State University
Terre Haute, Indiana 47809

◆ Indiana University
Bloomington, Indiana 47405

Indiana University of Pennsylvania
Indiana, Pennsylvania 15705

I.U. - P.U. - Indianapolis University
Indianapolis, Indiana 46202

Indiana University of Technology
Fort Wayne, Indiana 46803

Iona College
New Rochelle, New York 10801

◆ Iowa, University of
Iowa City, Iowa 52242

◆ Iowa State University of Science
& Technology
Ames, Iowa 50011

Ithaca College
Ithaca, New York 14850

Jacksonville State University
Jacksonville, Alabama 36265

Jacksonville University
Jacksonville, Florida 32211

James Madison University
Harrisonburg, Virginia 22807

Jamestown College
Jamestown, North Dakota 58405

John Brown University
Siloam Springs, Arkansas 72761

John Carroll University
Cleveland, Ohio 44118

◆ Johns Hopkins University
Baltimore, Maryland 21218

Johnson State College
Johnson, Vermont 05656

Johnson C. Smith University
Charlotte, North Carolina 28216

Judson College
Marion, Alabama 36756

Juilliard School
New York, New York 10023

Juniata College
Huntingdon, Pennsylvania 16652

◆ Kalamazoo College
Kalamazoo, Michigan 49006

◆ Kansas, University of
Lawrence, Kansas 66045

◆ Kansas State University
Manhattan, Kansas 66506

Kean University of New Jersey
Union, New Jersey 07083

Keene State College
Keene, New Hampshire 03435

Kennesaw State College
Marietta, Georgia 30144

◆ Kent State University
Kent, Ohio 44242

◆ Kentucky, University of
Lexington, Kentucky 40506

Kentucky Wesleyan College
Owensboro, Kentucky 42301

◆ Kenyon College
Gambier, Ohio 43022

Kettering University
Flint, Michigan 48504

King College
Bristol, Tennessee 37620

King's College
Wilkes-Barre, Pennsylvania 18711

◆ **Knox College**
Galesburg, Illinois 61401

Kutztown University
Kutztown, Pennsylvania 19530

L ◆ **Lafayette College**
Easton, Pennsylvania 18042

◆ **Lake Forest College**
Lake Forest, Illinois 60045

Lamar University
Beaumont, Texas 77710

Lambuth University
Jackson, Tennessee 38301

LaSalle University
Philadelphia, Pennsylvania 19141

Lasell College
Newton, Massachusetts 02466

La Verne, University of
La Verne, California 91750

◆ **Lawrence University**
Appleton, Wisconsin 54912

Lebanon Valley College
Annville, Pennsylvania 17003

◆ **Lehigh University**
Bethlehem, Pennsylvania 18015

LeMoyne College
Syracuse, New York 13214

Lenoir Rhyne College
Hickory, North Carolina 28603

Lesley University
Cambridge, Massachusetts 02138

Letourneau College
Longview, Texas 75607

◆ **Lewis & Clark College**
Portland, Oregon 97219

Lewis-Clark State College
Lewiston, Idaho 83501

Lindenwood University
St. Charles, Missouri 63301

Linfield College
McMinnville, Oregon 97128

Lock Haven University of Pennsylvania
Lock Haven, Pennsylvania 17745

Long Island University-Brooklyn
Brooklyn, New York 11201

Long Island University-C.W. Post
Brookville, New York 11548

Long Island University-Southampton College
Southampton, New York 11968

Longwood University
Farmville, Virginia 23909

Loras College
Dubuque, Iowa 52001

Louisiana College
Pineville, Louisiana 71360

Louisiana-Lafayette, University of
Lafayette, Louisiana 70504

◆ **Louisiana State University**
Baton Rouge, Louisiana 70803

Louisville, University of
Louisville, Kentucky 40292

Lowell, University of
Lowell, Massachusetts 01854

◆ **Loyola College**
Baltimore, Maryland 21210

◆ **Loyola Marymount University**
Los Angeles, California 90045

◆ **Loyola University of Chicago**
Chicago, Illinois 60611

Loyola University
New Orleans, Louisiana 70118

◆ **Luther College**
Decorah, Iowa 52101

Lycoming College
Williamsport, Pennsylvania 17701

Lynchburg College
Lynchburg, Virginia 24501

Lyndon State College
Lyndonville, Vermont 05851

Lyon College
Batesville, Arkansas 72503

M ◆ **Macalester College**
St. Paul, Minnesota 55105

MacMurray College
Jacksonville, Illinois 62650

Maine, University of
Farmington, Maine 04938

◆ **Maine, University of**
Orono, Maine 04469

◆ Phi Beta Kappa Schools ■ Predominantly African-American Institutions

Malone College
Canton, Ohio 44709

Manchester College
North Manchester, Indiana 46962

◆ Manhattan College
Riverdale, New York 10471

Manhattan School of Music
New York, New York 10027

Manhattanville College
Purchase, New York 10577

Mansfield University of Pennsylvania
Mansfield, Pennsylvania 16933

◆ Marietta College
Marietta, Ohio 45750

Marist College
Poughkeepsie, NY 12601

◆ Marquette University
Milwaukee, Wisconsin 53201

Marshall University
Huntington, West Virginia 25755

◆ Mary Baldwin College
Staunton, Virginia 24401

▌ Marygrove College
Detroit, Michigan 48221

Maryland Institute-College of Art
Baltimore, Maryland 21217

◆ Maryland, University of Baltimore County
Baltimore, Maryland 21250

◆ Maryland, University of
College Park, Maryland 20742

Marymount University
Arlington, Virginia 22207

Maryville College
Maryville, Tennessee 37804

Maryville University-Saint Louis
St. Louis, Missouri 63141

◆ Mary Washington College
Fredericksburg, Virginia 22401

Marywood University
Scranton, Pennsylvania 18509

Massachusetts College of Art
Boston Massachusetts 02215

Massachusetts College of Liberal Arts
North Adams, Massachusetts 01247

Massachusetts College of Pharmacy
Boston, Massachusetts 02115

◆ Massachusetts, University of
Amherst, Massachusetts 01003

Massachusetts, University of
Boston, Massachusetts 02125

Massachusetts, University of
Lowell, Massachusetts 01854

Massachusetts, University of
North Dartmouth, Massachusetts 02747

◆ Massachusetts Institute of Technology
Cambridge, Massachusetts 02139

Massachusetts Maritime Academy
Buzzards Bay, Massachusetts 02532

Master's College, The
Santa Clarita, California 91321

McDaniel College
Westminster, Maryland 21157

◆ McKendree College
LeBaron, Illinois 62254

McMurry University
Abilene, Texas 79697

Memphis College of Art
Memphis, Tennessee 38112

Memphis, University of
Memphis, Tennessee 38152

Mercer University
Macon, Georgia 31207

Mercy College
Dobbs Ferry, New York 10522

Mercyhurst College
Erie, Pennsylvania 16546

Meredith College
Raleigh, North Carolina 27607

Merrimack College
No. Andover, Massachusetts 01845

Messiah College
Grantham, Pennsylvania 17027

◆ Miami University
Oxford, Ohio 45056

◆ Miami, University of
Coral Gables, Florida 33124

◆ Michigan, University of
Ann Arbor, Michigan 48109

Michigan, University of
Dearborn, Michigan 48128

◆ Michigan State University
East Lansing, Michigan 48824

Michigan Technological University
Houghton, Michigan 49931

◆ Phi Beta Kappa Schools ▌ Predominantly African-American Institutions

◆ **Middlebury College**
Middlebury, Vermont 05753

Middle Tennessee State University
Murfreesboro, Tennessee 37132

Midwestern State University
Wichita Falls, Texas 76308

Millersville University of Pennsylvania
Millersville, Pennsylvania 17551

Milligan College
Milligan College, Tennessee 37682

Millikin University
Decatur, Illinois 62522

◆ **Mills College**
Oakland, California 94613

◆ **Millsaps College**
Jackson, Mississippi 39210

Milwaukee School of Engineering
Milwaukee, Wisconsin 53201

Minnesota State University - Moorhead
Moorhead, Minnesota 56563

Minnesota, University of
Duluth, Minnesota 55812

◆ **Minnesota, University of**
Minneapolis, Minnesota 55455

Minnesota, University of
Morris, Minnesota 56267

Misericordia, College
Dallas, Pennsylvania 18612

Mississippi College
Clinton, Mississippi 39058

Mississippi State University
Mississippi State, Mississippi 39762

◆ **Mississippi, University of**
University, Mississippi 38677

Mississippi University for Women
Columbus, Mississippi 39701

◆ **Missouri, University of**
Columbia, Missouri 65211

Missouri, University of
Kansas City, Missouri 64110

Missouri, University of
Rolla, Missouri 65401

Missouri, University of
St. Louis, Missouri 63121

Mobile, University of
Mobile, Alabama 36663

Molloy College
Rockville Centre, New York 11571

Monmouth College
Monmouth, Illinois 61462

Monmouth University
West Long Branch, New Jersey 07764

Montana College of Mineral Science & Technology
Butte, Montana 59701

Montana, University of
Missoula, Montana 59812

Montana State University
Billings, Montana 59101

Montana State University
Bozeman, Montana 59717

Montevallo, University of
Montevallo, Alabama 35115

Montclair State College
Upper Montclair, New Jersey 07043

Montreat College
Montreat, North Carolina 28757

Montserrat College of Art
Beverly, Massachusetts 01915

Moore College of Art
Philadelphia, Pennsylvania 19103

Moravian College
Bethlehem, Pennsylvania 18018

◆■ **Morehouse College**
Atlanta, Georgia 30314

■ **Morgan State University**
Baltimore, Maryland 21257

Morningside College
Sioux City, Iowa 51106

◆ **Mount Holyoke College**
South Hadley, Massachusetts 01075

Mount Mercy College
Cedar Rapids, Iowa 52402

Mount St. Joseph, College of
Cincinnati, Ohio 45233

Mount St. Mary's College
Emmitsburg, Maryland 21727

Mount St. Mary's College
Los Angeles, California 90049

Mount St. Mary College
Newburgh, New York, 12550

Mount Union College
Alliance, Ohio 44601

◆ **Muhlenberg College**
Allentown, Pennsylvania 18104

◆ Phi Beta Kappa Schools   ■ Predominantly African-American Institutions

Murray State University
Murray, Kentucky 42071

Museum of Fine Arts, School of the
Boston, Massachusetts 02115

Muskingum College
New Concord, Ohio 43762

N

Nazareth College of Rochester
Rochester, New York 14618

◆ **Nebraska, University of**
Lincoln, Nebraska 68588

Nebraska Wesleyan University
Lincoln, Nebraska 68504

Nevada, University of, at
Las Vegas, Nevada 89154
Reno, Nevada 89557

New College
Sarasota, Florida 34243

New England Conservatory of Music
Boston, Massachusetts 02115

◆ **New Hampshire, University of**
Durham, New Hampshire 03824

New Jersey, College of
Ewing, New Jersey 08628

New Jersey Institute of Technology
Newark, New Jersey 07102

Newman Univeristy
Wichita, Kansas 67213

**New Mexico Institute of Mining
and Technology**
Socorro, New Mexico 87801

New Mexico State University
Las Cruces, New Mexico 88003

◆ **New Mexico, University of**
Albuquerque, New Mexico 87131

New Orleans, University of
New Orleans, Louisiana 70148

**New School University - Eugene Lang
College**
New York, New York 10011

New York, City University of, at
◆ **Baruch College,** New York, NY 10010
◆ **Brooklyn College,** Brooklyn, NY 11210
◆ **City College,** New York, New York 10031
◆ **Herbert H. Lehman Coll.,** Bronx, NY 10468
◆ **Hunter College,** New York, NY 10021
  John Jay College, New York, NY 10019
◆ **Queens College,** Flushing, NY 11367

New York Institute of Techology
Old Westbury, New York 11568

New York, State University of, at
◆ **Albany,** New York 12222
◆ **Binghamton,** New York 13902
  Brockport, New York 14420
◆ **Buffalo,** New York 14214
  Fredonia, New York 14063
◆ **Geneseo,** New York 14454
  Maritime College (TNS), New York 10465
  New Paltz, New York 12561
  Oneonta, New York 13820
  Oswego, New York 13126
  Plattsburgh, New York 12901
  Potsdam, New York 13676
  Purchase, New York 10577
◆ **Stony Brook,** New York 11794

◆ **New York University**
New York, New York 10011

Niagara University
Niagara Falls, New York, 14109

Nichols State University
Thibodaux, Louisiana 70310

North Carolina School of the Arts
Winston-Salem, North Carolina 27117

North Carolina, University of, at
  Asheville, North Carolina 28804
◆ **Chapel Hill,** North Carolina 27599
  Charlotte, North Carolina 28223
◆ **Greensboro,** North Carolina 27412
  Pembroke, North Carolina 28372
  Wilmington, North Carolina 28403

◆ **North Carolina State University**
Raleigh, North Carolina 27695

North Central College
Naperville, Illinois 60566

North Dakota State University
Fargo, North Dakota 58105

◆ **North Dakota, University of**
Grand Forks, North Dakota 58202

North Florida, University of
Jacksonville, Florida 32216

North Georgia College
Dahlonega, Georgia 30597

North Texas, University of
Denton, Texas 76203

Northeastern Illinois University
Chicago, Illinois 60625

Northeastern University
Boston, Massachusetts 02115

Northern Arizona University
Flagstaff, Arizona 86011

Northern Colorado University
Greeley, Colorado 80639

Northern Illinois University
DeKalb, Illinois 60115

Northern Iowa, University of
Cedar Falls, Iowa 50614

Northern Kentucky University
Highland Heights, Kentucky 41099

Northern Michigan University
Marquette, Michigan 49855

Northwestern College
Orange City, Iowa 51041

Northwestern College
St. Paul, Minnesota 55113

◆ **Northwestern University**
Evanston, Illinois 60204

Northwestern University of Louisiana
Natchitoches, Louisiana 71497

Northwood University
Midland, Michigan 48640

◆ **Notre Dame, University of**
Notre Dame, Indiana 46556

Nova Southeastern University
Ft. Lauderdale, Florida 33314

Nyack College
Nyack, New York 10960

O **Oakland University**
Rochester, Michigan 48309

◆ **Oberlin College**
Oberlin, Ohio 44074

◆ **Occidental College**
Los Angeles, California 90041

Oglethorpe University
Atlanta, Georgia 30319

Ohio Northern University
Ada, Ohio 45810

◆ **Ohio State University**
Columbus, Ohio 43210

◆ **Ohio University**
Athens, Ohio 45701

◆ **Ohio Wesleyan University**
Delaware, Ohio 43015

Oklahoma Baptist University
Shawnee, Oklahoma 74801

Oklahoma City University
Oklahoma City, Oklahoma 73106

◆ **Oklahoma, University of**
Norman, Oklahoma 73069

Oklahoma State University
Stillwater, Oklahoma 74078

Old Dominion University
Norfolk, Virginia 23529

Olivet Nazarene University
Bourbonnais, Illinois 60914

Olin College of Engineering
Needham, Massachusetts 02492

Oregon Institute of Technology
Klamath Falls, Oregon 97601

◆ **Oregon, University of**
Eugene, Oregon 97403

Oregon State University
Corvallis, Oregon 97331

Otis College of Art and Design
Los Angeles, California 90057

Otterbein College
Westerville, Ohio 43081

Ouachita Baptist University
Arkadelphia, Arkansas 71998

Ozarks, College of the
Point Lookout, Missouri 65726

P **Pace University**
New York, New York 10038

Pacific Lutheran University
Tacoma, Washington 98447

Pacific, U. of the
Stockton, California 95211

Pacific University
Forest Grove, Oregon 97116

Palm Beach Atlantic College
West Palm Beach, Florida 33416

Parsons School of Design
New York, New York 10011

Pennsylvania Academy of the Fine Arts
Philadelphia, Pennsylvania 19102

Pennsylvania State University at Erie
Erie, Pennsylvania 16563

◆ **Pennsylvania State University**
University Park, Pennsylvania 16802

◆ **Pennsylvania, University of**
Philadelphia, Pennsylvania 19104

Pepperdine University
Malibu, California 90263

Philadelphia Biblical University
Langhorne, Pennsylvania 19047

Philadelphia University
Philadelphia, Pennsylvania 19144

Pine Manor College
Chestnut Hill, Massachusetts 02167

Pittsburg State University
Pittsburg, Kansas 66762

Pittsburgh, University of
Bradford, Pennsylvania 16701

Pittsburgh, University of
Greensburg, Pennsylvania 15601

Pittsburgh, University of
Johnstown, Pennsylvania 15904

◆ **Pittsburgh, University of**
Pittsburgh, Pennsylvania 15260

Pitzer College
Claremont, California 91711

Plymouth State College
Plymouth, New Hampshire 03264

Point Loma Nazarene University
San Diego, California 92106

Point Park College
Pittsburgh, Pennsylvania 15222

Polytechnic Institute of New York
Brooklyn, New York 11201

◆ **Pomona College**
Claremont, California 91711

Portland State University
Portland, Oregon 97200

Portland, University of
Portland, Oregon 97203

Pratt Institute
Brooklyn, New York 11205

Presbyterian College
Clinton, South Carolina 29325

◆ **Princeton University**
Princeton, New Jersey 08544

Principia College
Elsah, Illinois 62028

Providence College
Providence, Rhode Island 02918

Puerto Rico, University of
Cayey, Puerto Rico 00736

Puerto Rico, University of
Mayaguez, Puerto Rico 00680

Puerto Rico, University of
Rio Piedras, Puerto Rico 00931

◆ **Puget Sound, University of**
Tacoma, Washington 98416

◆ **Purdue University**
W. Lafayette, Indiana 47907

Q **Queens College**
Charlotte, North Carolina 28274

Quincy University
Quincy, Illinois 62301

Quinnipiac University
Hamden, Connecticut 06518

R **Radford University**
Radford, Virginia 24142

Ramapo College
Mahwah, New Jersey 07430

◆ **Randolph-Macon College**
Ashland, Virginia 23005

◆ **Randolph-Macon Woman's College**
Lynchburg, Virginia 24503

◆ **Redlands, University of**
Redlands, California 92373

◆ **Reed College**
Portland, Oregon 97202

Regis College
Weston, Massachusetts 02193

Regis University
Denver, Colorado 80221

Reinhardt College
Waleska, Georgia 30183

Rensselaer Polytechnic Institute
Troy, New York 12180

Rhode Island College
Providence, Rhode Island 02908

Rhode Island School of Design
Providence, Rhode Island 02903

◆ **Rhode Island, University of**
Kingston, Rhode Island 02881

◆ **Rhodes College**
Memphis, Tennessee 38112

◆ **Rice University**
Houston, Texas 77251

Richard Stockton College of New Jersey
Pomona, New Jersey 08240

◆ **Richmond, University of**
Richmond, Virginia 23173

Rider University
Lawrenceville, New Jersey 08648

◆ **Ripon College**
Ripon, Wisconsin 54971

◆ **Roanoke College**
Salem, Virginia 24153

Robert Morris College
Moon Township, Pennsylvania 15108

◆ **Rochester, University of**
Rochester, New York 14627

Rochester Institute of Technology
Rochester, New York 14623

◆ **Rockford College**
Rockford, Illinois 61108

Rockhurst University
Kansas City, Missouri 64110

Roger Williams University
Bristol, Rhode Island 02809

Rollins College
Winter Park, Florida 32789

Roosevelt University
Chicago, Illinois 60605

Rose-Hulman Institute of Technology
Terre Haute, Indiana 47803

Rosemont College
Rosemont, Pennsylvania 19010

Rowan University
Mahwah, New Jersey 08028

◆ **Rutgers University**
New Brunswick, New Jersey 08854

Rutgers University
Camden, New Jersey 08101

S **Sacred Heart University**
Fairfield, Connecticut 06432

Sage Colleges
Troy, New York 12180

Saginaw Valley State University
University Center, Michigan 48710

St. Ambrose University
Davenport, Iowa 52803

St. Andrews Presbyterian College
Laurinburg, North Carolina 28352

St. Anselm College
Manchester, New Hampshire 03102

St. Bonaventure University
St. Bonaventure, New York 14778

◆ **St. Catherine, College of**
St. Paul, Minnesota 55105

St. Cloud University
St. Cloud, Minnesota 56301

St. Edward's University
Austin, Texas 78704

St. Francis College
Brooklyn, New York 11201

St. John Fisher College
Rochester, New, York 14618

St. John's University
Jamaica, New York 11439

Saint John's University/College of Saint Benedict
Collegeville, Minnesota 56321

Saint Joseph College
W. Hartford, Connecticut 06117

St. Joseph's College
Rensselaer, Indiana 47978

St. Joseph's College
Standish, Maine 04084

St. Joseph's College
Patchogue, New York 11772

◆ **Saint Joseph's University**
Philadelphia, Pennsylvania 19131

◆ **St. Lawrence University**
Canton, New York 13617

St. Louis College of Pharmacy
St. Louis, Missouri 63110

◆ **Saint Louis University**
St. Louis, Missouri 63103

Saint Martin's College
Lacey, Washington 98503

Saint Mary's College
Notre Dame, Indiana 46556

Saint Mary's College of California
Moraga, California 94575

Saint Mary College
Leavenworth, Kansas 66048

◆ **St. Mary's College of Maryland**
St. Mary's City, Maryland 20686

St. Mary's University of Minnesota
Winona, Minnesota 55987

St. Mary's University
San Antonio, Texas 78228

◆ **Saint Michael's College**
Colchester, Vermont 05439

St. Norbert College
DePere, Wisconsin 54115

◆ **St. Olaf College**
Northfield, Minnesota 55057

St. Peter's College
Jersey City, New Jersey 07306

◆ Phi Beta Kappa Schools ■ Predominantly African-American Institutions

Saint Rose, College of
Albany, New York 12203

Saint Scholastica, College of
Duluth, Minnesota 55811

St. Thomas Aquinas College
Sparkhill, New York 10976

Saint Thomas, University of
St. Paul, Minnesota 55105

St. Thomas, University of
Houston, Texas 77006

St. Vincent College
Latrobe, Pennsylvania 15650

Salem College
Winston-Salem, North Carolina 27108

Salem State College
Salem, Massachusetts 01970

Salisbury State University
Salisbury, Maryland 21801

Samford University
Birmingham, Alabama 35229

◆ San Diego State University
San Diego, California 92182

◆ San Diego, University of
San Diego, California 92110

San Francisco Art Institute
San Francisco, California 94133

San Francisco Conservatory of Music
San Francisco, California 94122

San Francisco, University of
San Francisco, California 94117

◆ San Francisco State University
San Francisco, California 94132

San Jose State University
San Jose, California 95192

◆ Santa Clara University
Santa Clara, California 95053

Santa Fe, College of
Santa Fe, New Mexico 87501

Sarah Lawrence College
Bronxville, New York 10708

School of the Art Institute of Chicago
Chicago, Illinois 60603

Schreiner University
Kerrville, Texas 78028

Sciences in Philadelphia, University of the
Philadelphia, Pennsylvania 19104

Scranton, University of
Scranton, Pennsylvania 18510

◆ Scripps College
Claremont, California 91711

Seattle Pacific University
Seattle, Washington 98119

Seattle University
Seattle, Washington 98122

Seton Hall University
South Orange, New Jersey 07079

Seton Hill College
Greensburg, Pennsylvania 15601

▌ Shaw University
Raleigh, North Carolina 27601

Shawnee State University
Portsmouth, Ohio 45662

Shenandoah University
Winchester, Virginia 22601

Shepherd College
Shepherdstown, West Virginia 25443

Shippensburg University
Shippensburg, Pennsylvania 17257

Shorter College
Rome, Georgia 30165

Siena College
Loudonville, New York 12211

Siena Heights University
Adrian, Michigan 49221

Silver Lake College
Mantiowoc, Wisconsin 54220

Simmons College
Boston, Massachusetts 02115

Simpson College
Indianola, Iowa 50125

◆ Skidmore College
Saratoga Springs, New York 12866

Slippery Rock University
Slippery Rock, Pennsylvania 16057

◆ Smith College
Northampton, Massachusetts 01063

◆ South, University of the
Sewanee, Tennessee 37383

South Alabama, University of
Mobile, Alabama 36688

◆ South Carolina, University of
Columbia, South Carolina 29208

◆ South Dakota, University of
Vermillion, South Dakota 57069

South Dakota School of Mines and Technology
Rapid City, South Dakota 57701

South Dakota State University
Brookings, South Dakota 57006

South Florida, University of
Tampa, Florida 33620

Southeastern Louisiana State
Hammond, Louisiana 70402

◆ **Southern California, University of**
Los Angeles, California 90089

Southern Connecticut State University
New Haven, Connecticut 06515

Southern Illinois University
Carbondale, Illinois 62901

Southern Illinois University
Edwardsville, Illinois 62026

Southern Maine, University of
Portland, Maine 04103

◆ **Southern Methodist University**
Dallas, Texas 75275

Southern Mississippi, University of
Hattiesburg, Mississippi 39406

Southern Oregon University
Ashland, Oregon 97520

Southern Polytechnic University
Marietta, Georgia 30060

Southern Utah University
Cedar City, Utah 84720

Southwest Baptist University
Bolivar, Missouri 65613

Southwest Missouri State University
Springfield, Missouri 65804

Southwest Texas State University
San Marcos, Texas 78666

◆ **Southwestern University**
Georgetown, Texas 78627

◆∎ **Spelman College**
Atlanta, Georgia 30314

Spring Hill College
Mobile, Alabama 36608

◆ **Stanford University**
Stanford, California 94305

Stephen F. Austin State University
Nagogdoches, Texas 75962

◆ **Stetson University**
Deland, Florida 32720

Stevens Institute of Technology
Hoboken, New Jersey 07030

Stonehill College
North Easton, Massachusetts 02357

Suffolk University
Boston, Massachusetts 02108

Susquehanna University
Selinsgrove, Pennsylvania 17870

◆ **Swarthmore College**
Swarthmore, Pennsylvania 19081

◆ **Sweet Briar College**
Sweet Briar, Virginia 24595

◆ **Syracuse University**
Syracuse, New York 13210

T

Tabor College
Hillsboro, Kansas 67063

Tampa, University of
Tampa, Florida 33606

Taylor University
Upland, Indiana 46989

◆ **Temple University**
Philadelphia, Pennsylvania 19122

Tennessee Tech University
Cookeville, Tennessee 38505

◆ **Tennessee, University of**
Knoxville, Tennessee 37996

Texas, University of, at
  Arlington, Texas 76019
◆ **Austin,** Texas 78712
  Dallas, Richardson, Texas 75083
  San Antonio, Texas 78249
  Tyler, Texas 75799

◆ **Texas A & M**
College Station, Texas 77843

Texas A & M at Galveston
Galveston, Texas 77553

◆ **Texas Christian University**
Fort Worth, Texas 76129

Texas Lutheran University
Seguin, Texas 78155

Texas Tech University
Lubbock, Texas 79409

Texas Wesleyan College
Fort Worth, Texas 76105

Thomas College
Waterville, Maine 04901

Thomas More College
Crestview Hills, Kentucky 41017

◆ Phi Beta Kappa Schools   ∎ Predominantly African-American Institutions

Toledo, University of
Toledo, Ohio 43606

■ **Tougaloo College**
Tougaloo, Mississippi 39174

Towson University
Towson, Maryland 21204

Transylvania University
Lexington, Kentucky 40508

◆ **Trinity College**
Hartford, Connecticut 06106

◆ **Trinity College**
Washington, DC 20017

◆ **Trinity University**
San Antonio, Texas 78212

Tri-State University
Angola, Indiana 46703

◆ **Truman State University**
Kirksville, Missouri 63501

◆ **Tufts University**
Medford, Massachusetts 02155

◆ **Tulane University**
New Orleans, Louisiana 70118

◆ **Tulsa, University of**
Tulsa, Oklahoma 74104

■ **Tuskegee University**
Tuskegee, Alabama 36088

U ◆ **Union College**
Schenectady, New York 12308

Union University
Jackson, Tennessee 38305

U.S. Air Force Academy
Colorado Springs, Colorado 80840

U.S. Coast Guard Academy
New London, Connecticut 06320

U.S. Military Academy
West Point, New York 10996

U.S. Naval Academy
Annapolis, Maryland 21402

◆ **Ursinus College**
Collegeville, Pennsylvania 19426

◆ **Utah, University of**
Salt Lake City, Utah 84112

Utah State University
Logan, Utah 84322

Utica College
Utica, New York 13502

V ◆ **Valparaiso University**
Valparaiso, Indiana 46383

◆ **Vanderbilt University**
Nashville, Tennessee 37240

◆ **Vassar College**
Poughkeepsie, New York 12601

◆ **Vermont, University of**
Burlington, Vermont 05401

Villa Julie College
Stevenson, Maryland 21153

◆ **Villanova University**
Villanova, Pennsylvania 19085

◆ **Virginia, University of**
Charlottesville, Virginia 22904

Virginia Commonwealth University
Richmond, Virginia 23284

Virginia Military Institute
Lexington, Virginia 24450

◆ **Virginia Polytechnic Institute**
Blacksburg, Virginia 24061

Virginia Wesleyan College
Norfolk, Virginia 23502

Visual Arts, School of
New York, New York 10010

Viterbo College
La Crosse, Wisconsin 54601

W ◆ **Wabash College**
Crawfordsville, Indiana 47933

Wagner College
Staten Island, New York 10301

◆ **Wake Forest University**
Winston-Salem, North Carolina 27109

Walla Walla College
College Place, Washington 99324

Walsh University
North Canton, Ohio, 44720

Warren Wilson College
Asheville, North Carolina 28815

Wartburg College
Waverly, Iowa 50677

Washington College
Chestertown, Maryland 21620

◆ **Washington & Jefferson College**
Washington, Pennsylvania 15301

◆ **Washington & Lee University**
Lexington, Virginia 24450

◆ **Washington University in St. Louis**
St. Louis, Missouri 63130

◆ Phi Beta Kappa Schools ■ Predominantly African-American Institutions

◆ **Washington, University of**
Seattle, Washington 98195

◆ **Washington State University**
Pullman, Washington 99164

◆ **Wayne State University**
Detroit, Michigan 48202

Waynesburg College
Waynesburg, Pennsylvania 15370

Weber State University
Ogden, Utah 84408

Webster University
St. Louis, Missouri 63119

◆ **Wellesley College**
Wellesley, Massachusetts 02481

◆ **Wells College**
Aurora, New York 13026

Wesleyan College
Macon, Georgia 31210

◆ **Wesleyan University**
Middletown, Connecticut 06457

West Chester University
West Chester, Pennsylvania 19383

West Florida, University of
Pensacola, FL 32514

◆ **West Virginia University**
Morgantown, West Virginia 26506

West Virginia Wesleyan College
Buckhannon, West Virginia 26201

Western Connecticut State University
Danbury, Connecticut 06810

Western Illinois University
Marcomb, Illinois 61455

Western Kentucky University
Bowling Green, Kentucky 42101

◆ **Western Michigan University**
Kalamazoo, Michigan 49008

Western New England College
Springfield, Massachusetts 01119

Western State College of Colorado
Gunnison, Colorado 81231

Western Washington University
Bellingham, Washington 98225

Westfield State College
Westfield, Massachusetts 01086

Westminster College
Fulton, Missouri 65251

Westminster College
Wilmington, Pennsylvania 16172

Westminster College of Salt Lake City
Salt Lake City, Utah 84105

Westmont College
Santa Barbara, California 93108

Wheaton College
Wheaton, Illinois 60187

◆ **Wheaton College**
Norton, Massachusetts 02766

Wheeling Jesuit University
Wheeling, West Virginia 26003

Wheelock College
Boston, Massachusetts 02215

◆ **Whitman College**
Walla Walla, Washington 99362

Whittier College
Whittier, California 90608

Whitworth College
Spokane, Washington 99251

Wichita State University
Wichita, Kansas 67260

Widener University
Chester, Pennsylvania 19013

■ **Wilberforce University**
Wilberforce, Ohio 45384

Wilkes University
Wilkes-Barre, Pennsylvania 18766

◆ **Willamette University**
Salem, Oregon 97301

William Jewell College
Liberty, Missouri 64068

◆ **William & Mary, College of**
Williamsburg, Virginia 23187

William Paterson University
Wayne, New Jersey 07470

◆ **Williams College**
Williamstown, Massachusetts 01267

Wilmington College
Wilmington, Ohio 45177

◆ **Wilson College**
Chambersburg, Pennsylvania 17201

Wingate University
Wingate, North Carolina 28174

Winona State University
Winona, Minnesota 55987

Winthrop University
Rock Hill, South Carolina 29733

◆ Phi Beta Kappa Schools   ■ Predominantly African-American Institutions

Wisconsin Lutheran College
Milwaukee, Wisconsin 53226

◆ **Wisconsin, University of, at**
Eau Claire, Wisconsin 54701
Green Bay, Wisconsin 54311
LaCrosse, Wisconsin 54601
◆ **Madison,** Wisconsin 53706
◆ **Milwaukee,** Wisconsin 53201
Platteville, Wisconsin 53818
Stevens Point, Wisconsin 54481
Stout, Menomonie, Wisconsin 54751

◆ **Wittenberg University**
Springfield, Ohio 45501

◆ **Wofford College**
Spartanburg, South Carolina 29303

Woodbury University
Burbank, California 91510

◆ **Wooster, College of**
Wooster, Ohio 44691

Worcester Polytechnic Institute
Worcester, Massachusetts 01609

Worcester State College
Worcester, Massachusetts 01602

Wright State University
Dayton, Ohio 45435

◆ **Wyoming, University of**
Laramie, Wyoming 82071

 Xavier University
Cincinnati, Ohio 45207

▮ **Xavier University of Louisiana**
New Orleans, Louisiana 70125

 ◆ **Yale University**
New Haven, Connecticut 06520

✡ **Yeshiva University**
New York, New York 10033

York College of Pennsylvania
York, Pennsylvania 17403

Youngstown State University
Youngstown, Ohio 44555

◆ Phi Beta Kappa Schools   ▮ Predominantly African-American Institutions   ✡ Predominantly Jewish Institutions

APPENDIX B

The Miscellaneous Majors Colleges Used In This Study

Aeronautics, College of
Flushing, NY 11369

Andrews University
Berrien Springs, MI 49104

Antioch College
Yellow Springs, OH 45387

Atlantic, College of the
Bar Harbor, ME 04609

Aurora University
Aurora, Il 60506

Bay Path College
Longmeadow, MA 01106

Bellevue University
Bellevue, NE 68005

Black Hills State University
Spearfish, SD 57799

Boise State University
Boise, ID 83725

Bradford College
Haverhill, MA 01835

Brooks Institute of Photography
Santa Barbara, CA 93108

Cabrini College
Radnor, PA 19087

Carlow College
Pittsburgh, PA 15213

Central Oklahoma University
Edmond, OK 73034

■ **Central State University**
Wilberforce, OH 45384

Centenary College
Hackettstown, NJ 07840

Cincinnati College of Mortuary Science
Cincinnati, OH 45224

Clarion University of Pennsylvania
Clarion, PA 16214

Cleveland State University
Cleveland, OH 44115

Columbia College - Hollywood
Tarzana, CA 91356

Columbus College of Art & Design
Columbus, OH 43215

Cortland State College
Cortland, NY 13045

Curry College
Milton, MA 02186

Daniel Webster College
Nashua, NH 03063

David Lipscomb University
Nashville TN 37204

Davis & Elkins College
Elkins, WV 26241

Deep Springs College
Deep Springs Via Dyer, NV 89010

Defiance College, The
Defiance, OH 43512

Eastern Montana College
Billings, MT 59101

Eastern New Mexico University
Portales, NM 88130

**Eugene Lang College
(New School Social Research)**
New York, NY 11743

Fashion Institute of Technology
New York, NY 10001

Findlay, University of
Findlay, OH 45840

Hampshire College
Amherst, MA 01002

Holy Family College
Philadelphia, PA 19114

Kansas City Art Institute
Kansas City, MO 64111

Kendall College of Art and Design
Grand Rapids, MI 49503

Lake Erie College
Painesville, OH 44077

Landmark College
Putney, VT 05346

Langston University
Langston, OK 73050

Lees-McRae College
Banner Elk, NC 28604

Loma Linda University
Loma Linda, CA 92350

Lourdes College
Sylvania, OH 43560

Madonna University
Livonia, MI 48150

Marian College of Fond du Lac
Fond du Lac, WI 54935

APPENDIX B *(Continued)*

The Miscellaneous Majors Colleges Used In This Study

Mesa State College
Grand Junction, CO 81502

Metropolitan State College
Denver, CO 80204

Minnesota State University - Mankato
Mankato, MN 56001

Minnesota State University - Moorhead
Moorhead, MN 56563

Mitchell College
New London, CT 06320

Mt. St. Claire
Clinton, IA 52732

University of New England
Biddeford, ME 04005

New Haven, University of
New Haven, CT 06516

University of New England
Biddeford, ME 04005

New Haven, University of
New Haven, CT 06516

New School for Social Research
New York, NY 11743

North Carolina Wesleyan College
Rocky Mount, NC 27804

Northeastern Louisiana University
Monroe, LA 71209

Northwestern Oklahoma State University
Alva, OK 73717

Norwich University
Northfield, VT 05663

Park University
Cahokia, IL 62206

Pfeiffer College
Misenheimer, NC 28109

Prescott College
Prescott, AZ 86301

Ramapo College of New Jersey
Mahwah, NJ 07430

Ringling School of Art & Design
Sarasota, FL 34234

Rowan University
Glassboro, NJ 08028

St. Elizabeth, College of
Convent Station, NJ 07960

Saint John's College
Annapolis, MD 21404

Saint Leo College
Saint Leo, FL 33574

Saint Peter's College
Jersey City, NJ 07306

Saint Thomas University
Miami, FL 33054

Salem International University
Salem, WV 26426

Salve Regina-The Newport College
Newport, RI 02840

Sam Houston State University
Huntsville, TX 77341

Simon's Rock College of Bard
Great Barrington, MA 01230

Southern Illinois, U. of
Edwardsville, IL 62026

Southern New Hampshire, University of
Manchester, NH 03106

Spring Arbor College
Spring Arbor, MI 49283

SUNY-Farmingdale
Farmingdale, NY 11735

Texas Woman's University
Denton, TX 76204

Thomas Aquinas College
Santa Paula, CA 93060

Tusculum College
Greenville, TN 37743

United States Merchant Marine Academy
Kings Point, NY 11024

Unity College
Unity, ME 04988

Virginia Intermont College
Bristol, VA 24201

Webb Institute
Glen Cove, NY 11542

William Woods University
Fulton, MO 65251

Wisconsin, University of
Oshkosh, WI 54901

APPENDIX C
Single Sex Colleges Included In This Study

WOMEN'S COLLEGES

Agnes Scott College (GA)
Alverno (WI)
Bay Path College (MA)
Bennett College (NC)
Alverno Collee (WI)
Bryn Mawr College (PA)
Cedar Crest College (PA)
Chatham College (PA)
Converse College(SC)
Hollins College (VA)
Immaculata (PA)
Judson College (AL)
Lesley (MA)
Mary Baldwin College (VA)

Meredith College (NC)
Mills College (CA)
Mount Holyoke College (MA)
Randolph-Macon Woman's Coll. (VA)
Regis (MA)
Rosemont College (PA)
St. Catherine, College of (MN)
Saint Joseph's (CT)
Saint Mary's College (IN)
Salem College (NC)
Scripps College (CA)
Seton Hill (PA)
Simmons College (MA)
Smith College (MA)

Spelman College (GA)
Sweet Briar College (VA)
Texas Woman's College
Trinity College (DC)
Wellesley College (MA)
Wesleyan College (GA)

MEN'S COLLEGES

Hampden-Sydney College (VA)
Morehouse College (GA)
Wabash College (IN)

APPENDIX D

Anyone who has been touched by the problem of alcohol or substance abuse, or who has worked with those struggling in recovery, knows that higher education will increasingly have to meet the needs of these persons. Several colleges are trying to address the needs of these students, and The Wellness Institute at Ball State has published a list of wellness dorms. Unfortunately, the grant for this no longer exists, but Ball State in Muncie, Indiana has done a fine job with young people in this area. You might call them at 765-285-8259.

Respectfully submitted,
Joseph W. Streit
Long-time Secondary School Counselor in New Jersey

APPENDIX E

A Simplified Timetable and Checklist for Seniors Planning on College*

SEPTEMBER - OCTOBER	Write for college catalogs, applications, financial aid information and pick up a financial aid booklet, continuing from your junior year.
SEPTEMBER - OCTOBER	Inquire at your high school Guidance Office about upcoming college nights.
SEPTEMBER - NOVEMBER	Continue campus visits as senior year academic commitments permit.
SEPTEMBER	Deadline for mailing in the late October or early November National College Exam Forms.
OCTOBER	Think about which two teachers you will ask to write college recommendations for you.
LATE OCTOBER	Deadline for mailing in the December National College Exam Forms.
NOVEMBER	Prepare a final list of colleges. Talk to your counselor about need-based funds. And look into merit-based money awarded by the colleges themselves.
	Talk to your counselor and/or a favorite teacher - show them your completed college essay, if your colleges require one.
NOVEMBER 1-15	Many early applications due.
NOVEMBER OR DECEMBER	Attend, with your parents, a local financial aid night given by an area high school.
NOVEMBER - DECEMBER	Apply to colleges. But always check deadlines. Some may be earlier.
DECEMBER 1	ROTC Scholarship applications to be in.
EARLY DECEMBER	Last call for mailing in the National College Exam Forms (SAT/ACT).
DECEMBER 15	Profile of Financial Aid Form (Step 1) due to College Scholarship Service (CSS).
JANUARY	Fill out the Financial Aid Form (FAF/FAFSA/PROFILE) or Family Financial Statement. Your counselor has it. This form will probably help you get a good deal of your total scholarships, jobs, and loans. It is the big one.
JANUARY - FEBRUARY	Send mid-year reports to colleges.
FEBRUARY 1	Profile application (Step 2) to College Scholarship Service (CSS).
MARCH	Local scholarship forms available in the guidance office.
EARLY APRIL	All colleges will notify you by this time if they will accept you or not. The more competitive colleges usually deliberate longer and many of these top schools wait until the first week of April to notify you.
MID-APRIL	If unhappy with the financial aid package at any of the colleges where you have been accepted, call that office and discuss it.
LATE APRIL	Send deposit to selected college.
MAY 1	Inform all colleges which accepted you whether or not you plan to attend.
MAY 1	Notify Guidance Office of your choice of college.
MAY - JUNE	Apply for summer jobs so that you can meet summer earnings expectations.
	Don't forget to graduate from high school!
SUMMER	Attend college orientation.

NOTE: Before your senior year, prepare preliminary list of colleges you're interested in and those you would like to visit. Spring visits in the junior year are advised.

APPENDIX F
The Get-Going Form

A simple, useful form to use with the college-bound to get them started applying to colleges. The student and/or counselor and/or parent should fill in four colleges below, complete with address and zip codes.

Dear Student:

Within the next two weeks, please write to the Director of Admissions at the schools listed below, requesting information. A sample letter is included at the bottom of the page.

1. _____
   _____
   _____

2. _____
   _____
   _____

3. _____
   _____
   _____

4. _____
   _____
   _____

SAMPLE LETTER

Date

Director of Admissions
Name of College
Address of College and Zip Code

Dear Director:

I am a student of Easthampton High School in Easthampton, Massachusetts and expect to graduate in June, 2005.

I am interested in your school and would appreciate your sending me an application for admission and information concerning your financial aid program, and your _____ program of studies. Thank you.

Very truly yours,

Your signature
Your Name
Your Address and Zip Code

ABOUT THE AUTHOR

Fred E. Rugg

Raised by an older sister, **FRED E. RUGG** was one of a handful of "Huckleberry Finn" cases that the top universities accepted in the 1960's. He is a writer, speaker, workshop presenter, and author. Unlike virtually all other college guidebook people, Rugg is one of the *true* professionals, having directed secondary college counseling programs for 20 years in all types of communities. A 1967 Applied Math graduate from Brown, Rugg is the holder of advanced degrees in secondary school guidance and administration. Early in his career he was employed as a statistician for two New England companies and worked his way through Ivy League Brown - the only member of his class to enter public school teaching. Offering dozens of workshops yearly from coast to coast, Fred is an often animated, charismatic and humorous speaker, and is the only one giving monthly seminars who draws a crowd. In addition, he is a consultant to dozens of secondary schools and his evening speaking engagements for parents and students are popular and fun. He has lived and worked just about everywhere in America, has been married for over 35 years, and has two daughters. Beginning with his first volunteer assignment (Brown Youth Guidance), Rugg has been a perennial volunteer, and he's taught courses at four colleges. A native of New England, he has been based in Colorado and Florida, and now resides in California. As always, he is totally independent of the colleges.

PARENTS

Do you have a few questions on the colleges that you'd like to pose to Fred Rugg?
For $100.^{00}, you can quiz him for 30 minutes. Master and Visa Cards accepted.

✂ **PLEASE CLIP AND MAIL TO:** ✂

Rugg's Recommendations • P.O. Box 417 • Fallbrook, CA 92088

Please send me _____ copies of *Rugg's Recommendations on the Colleges* at $23.95 (plus shipping/see page 220) each.

I have enclosed my check in the amount of $_____

VISA **MasterCard**

Name _____

Address _____

City _____ State _____ Zip _____

For additional information call 760-728-4467 or 760-728-4558.
Other products and resources from Rugg's appear on pages 218-219.

FROM RUGG'S RECOMMENDATIONS...

INFORMATION THAT IS TO THE POINT, THAT YOU CAN USE IMMEDIATELY

Saving the college counselor enormous time with lists and answers found nowhere else - presented from the secondary school point of view!
FROM RUGG, YOU ALWAYS GET A NEW SLANT ON THE COLLEGES

---

1. THE NEW BOOK: *RUGG'S RECOMMENDATIONS ON THE COLLEGES 21st Ed.*

Locating Quality Undergraduate Colleges For Counselors, Parents & Students.
ISBN #1-883062-53-5 • LC89-062896 • $23.95 • © 2004 by Frederick E. Rugg
★ Over 1200 Entry Changes in the New BURGUNDY Book★

Rugg's Recommendations on the Colleges enters its 3rd decade recommending quality departments at quality colleges. It is the primary brainstorming source for secondary public school counselors in creating a student's initial college list. Two new majors have been added and there are wholesale changes on over 30 others. Rugg's 21st edition is available listing 10,000 quality departments at 1000 quality colleges. The guidebook has been designated nationally as "a revered staple, the book parents and students must start with" in the search for a college to attend. The 21st edition is the accumulation of 35 years of work in the undergraduate college admissions process, and as always, *Rugg's* is independent of the colleges. There are over 1200 entry changes since the 20th edition, 102 majors, 150 recommended departments per major.

"A Revered Staple."
—West Coast Library Reviewer

"Thank you for delivering such an incredibly useful tool for our students."
—Mrs. Lynn Reed
Niagara-Wheatfield H.S. (NY)

"A gem."
—College Bound, Evanston, Illinois

"As always, your wise advice is priceless!"
—Pat Foster, parent
Tempe, AZ

---

2. THE SPECIAL REPORT: *TWENTY MORE TIPS ON THE COLLEGES, Revised*

Twenty new behind the scenes tips. Ideal for counselors, parents, and students. 10th Edition.
ISBN #1-883062-54-3 • $8.95 • © 2004

Brutally honest information about colleges and the application process. This Special Report, *Twenty More Tips on the Colleges,* offers insights into assessing a college or university from the first "hello." Author Rugg succinctly presents 20 key tips to assist counselors, parents and students in selecting the best college for a student. Rugg honestly assesses the value of several college rating and reference books. Tips include colleges with high success rates for medical school acceptance, and what to consider before deciding to attend a military school. Overlooked state institutions, as well as other important and helpful comments, are included. The college search and selection process is incomplete without reading the valuable information contained within this Special Report.

"I have known Fred Rugg for over thirty years, since we were on the staff together at Bristol (RI) High School. Fred has developed an uncanny insight and he is able to ask the right questions of both student and admission officer. Always up-to-date; never disappointing. Read his material; attend the seminars. They are great!"
—Robert Jeffrey, Independent Consultant
Orlando, FL

"I have used your information for years. It is a wonderful resource."
—Harriet Gershman, Academic
Counseling Services, Evanston, IL

---

3. *FORTY TIPS ON THE COLLEGES :* THE REVISED SPECIAL REPORT *10th edition*

For all college bound students, parents, and their counselors. 19 pages. Over 30 college entry changes for 2004.
ISBN # 1-883062-55-1 • $9.95 (money back guarantee) • Revised 2004

Get the "insider's" advice on college admissions. In *Forty Tips on the Colleges*, author Rugg shares with the reader 40 key tips on the college admissions process. Rugg spent in excess of 2000 hours visiting with over 7000 secondary school counselors in 45 states, to compile the information contained in this transcript. These insightful suggestions provide the reader with some of the unwritten do's and don'ts in the college admissions process. Rugg presents his 40 tips, accompanied by his personal observations of the campuses, with honesty and a sense of humor. *Forty Tips on the Colleges* offers straight talk about selecting a college and gaining admission. The special report contains helpful advice for the student, parent and school counselor alike. Topics include previously unpublished tips on which colleges really care about their students; colleges with good learning disabilities programs; and how to choose a college where the student "fits in." The tips also contain helpful information concerning financial aid, college applications and SAT/ACT scores. Throughout this transcript, Rugg cites several helpful reference books. This ***must read*** is our most popular special report.

"I think Rugg's materials are great, and he was wonderful when my son went to school. Rugg is the best."
—Linda Endler, SAT Prep
Naples, FL

---

4. THE SPECIAL REPORT: *THIRTY QUESTIONS ON THE COLLEGES, Revised 10th Edition*

For all college bound students, parents and their counselors. 21 pages.
ISBN # 1-883062-56-X• $9.95 • Revised 2004 • Over 40 college entry changes

Thirty frequently asked questions with some answers even Deans of Admissions can't give you. This Special Report includes: The state university all others should visit and copy • 140 recommended colleges where black youngsters will maximize their education • What makes individuals happy at college? • Community college graduates – how do top colleges really view them at transfer time? • The best of the best journalism schools • Understanding student body make-up • Engineering schools – how to choose them and the best bets around the USA. And 22 other topics based on over 250 counselor meetings across the country. Counselors and parents find this transcript form extremely useful (yes, it's O.K. to copy it with appropriate acknowledgement).

""When I attended the college admissions institute this past summer, all of the private H.S. counselors and Ivy School directors of admission said that Rugg's work was the best."
—Colorado Public Secondary School
Counselor

5. SPECIAL REPORT: *FINANCIAL AID IN LESS THAN 3000 WORDS, REVISED*
ISBN #1-883062-57-8 • $6.95 • Completely Revised 2004 • 10th Edition

From his 30 years studying the college admissions process, Rugg has boiled down the financial aid game in this special 6-page report. Find out why several U.S. publishers offered big money to buy this report outright. Takes the counselor and parent step-by-step through the aid process, with authentic examples of awards and family situations of present college frosh. This special report closes with 14 revised tips on financial aid for counselors, parents, and students that Rugg has put together from hundreds of meetings with counselors and parents around the country.

Especially for parents and counselors—gets Financial Aid off the Counselor's back.

"Rugg is the only critic who has been in the trenches, worked the cities, lived all over, and has the network and the contacts in place."
—Vern Vargas, College Counselor, Moreau H.S., Hayward, CA.

6. *THIRTY SEMINAR SHEETS* $25

Our most popular lists are now available separately. Includes all of the rankings in #7 below, plus colleges where the following youngsters maximize their education: Jewish (130), Hispanic (130), Asian (85), and Black (135). *Call us for a sample—5 sheets for $5.*

"Helpful and enjoyable, too."
—Barbara Castille
Greensburg, PA

7. *THE COLLEGE SEMINAR SUBSTITUTE*
For Secondary School Counselors, public and private • *$55 (lists updated monthly)*

Can't make it to a college seminar? Do the next best thing: Order this special package. *The College Seminar Substitute* provides you with 96% of the 60 items covered in our seminar agenda. In this package you receive Rugg's four Special Reports, *Twenty More Tips on the Colleges, Forty Tips on the Colleges, Thirty Questions and Answers, Financial Aid In Less Than 3000 Words*, plus 30 seminar handouts. These handouts contain over 1800 entries—a wealth of information. Topics covered include: a listing of safe campuses, college guidebook ratings, up-and-coming colleges; snob schools; prestigious school rankings; underrated schools, the top 200 schools for the learning disabled, the most generous schools, new information on financial aid; advice on school recommendations; a listing of intense (rigorous) schools; big colleges that play small; rated Catholic colleges; and four minority lists. This package gives the counselor a foundation in understanding and navigating the admission game. See why over 7500 secondary school counselors have attended Rugg's College Admission Seminars.

"It is the best single source of information that we have. It answers the questions most frequently asked by parents. Your college materials help both the beginning and experienced counselor. The various ratings and lists inspire both students and their parents to further research the college scene. When parents and students are clueless, your information provides direction and humor in beginning the college selection process."
—Ira Lipton, Counselor, East Hampton (NY) High School

8. SPECIAL! *SEND IT ALL!* $70

Includes 1 book, 4 special reports, 30 seminar sheets—all our products.

"I love your book!."
—Carol Gill, Educational Consultant
Dobbs Ferry, NY

➡ **ORDER FORM ON REVERSE**

THE 2004 RUGG COLLEGE ADMISSION SEMINAR SCHEDULE	La Jolla, CA February 27, 2004	Boston, MA May 14, 2004	Columbus, OH October 1, 2004
	Philadelphia, PA April 30, 2004	Seattle, WA August 6, 2004	E. Hanover, N.J. October 29, 2004

For more information: Call or write for a brochure; e-mail us at frugg@thegrid.net; or visit our Website at http://www.ruggsrecs.com

2004 PRODUCT ORDER FORM

ITEM #	TITLE OR DESCRIPTION	PRICE	QTY	AMOUNT
1	*Rugg's Recommendations on the Colleges:* The Book (21st ed.)	$23.95		
2	*20 More Tips on the Colleges:* Revised Special Report (10th ed.)	$ 8.95		
3	*Forty Tips on the Colleges:* Revised Special Report (10th ed.)	$ 9.95		
4	*Thirty Questions & Answers:* Revised Special Report (10th ed.)	$ 9.95		
5	*Financial Aid in Less Than 3000 Words:* Revised Special Report (10th ed.)	$ 6.95		
6	*Thirty Seminar Sheets: Colleges*	$25.00		
7	*College Seminar Substitute:* Includes 2 thru 6	$55.00		
8	SEND IT ALL!!! Send one of each (Items 1-6)	$70.00		

Order 5 or more books:	Only $20.00 each! Discount price available *only* on the *book*.	SUBTOTAL	
Prepaid Orders over $89:	Subtract $4 from total.	Less $4 for prepaid orders over $89	
International Orders:	Shipping and handling cost: Actual Cost.	Sales Tax (CA only) 7.75%	
California Residents:	Please add 7.75% sales tax.	Shipping	
SHIPPING CHARGES: (all orders mailed first class)	$ 0-15 Postage $2 $16-35 Postage $5 $36+ Postage $6	TOTAL ENCLOSED	

Name _____

Address _____

City _____ State _____ Zip _____

Send to:
RUGG'S RECOMMENDATIONS
P.O. Box 417 • Fallbrook, CA 92088

**For information on our 2004 COLLEGE ADMISSIONS SEMINARS,
call us at 760-728-4558 or Fax 760-728-4467 OR visit our Website at http://www.ruggsrecs.com**